The Justice Motive in Everyday Life

The Justice Motive in Everyday Life contains new essays in honor of Melvin J. Lerner, a pioneer in the psychological study of justice. The contributors to this volume are internationally renowned scholars in the fields of psychology, business, and law. They examine the role of justice motivation in a wide variety of contexts, including workplace violence, affirmative action programs, helping or harming innocent victims (for example, Jews in Nazi-occupied Europe), and how people react to their own fate (for example, sexual harassment and police brutality). Contributors explore fundamental issues such as whether people's interest in justice is motivated by self-interest or a genuine concern for the welfare of others, when and why people feel a need to punish transgressors, how a concern for justice emerges during the development of societies and individuals, and the relation of justice motivation to moral motivation. How an understanding of justice motivation can contribute to the amelioration of major social problems is also examined.

Michael Ross is Professor of Psychology at the University of Waterloo. He has been an associate editor of the *Journal of Personality* and consulting editor for the *Journal of Personality and Social Psychology, Social Cognition,* the *British Journal of Social Psychology*, the *Canadian Journal of Behavioral Science, Personality and Social Psychology Bulletin*, and *Memory*.

Dale T. Miller is Professor of Psychology at Princeton University. He is coeditor of *Social Stigma* (1984) and *Cultural Divides: Understanding and Overcoming Group Conflict* (1999) and has been a consulting editor for the *Journal of Personality and Social Psychology* and the *Canadian Journal of Behavioral Science.*

Melvin J. Lerner

The Justice Motive in Everyday Life

Edited by

MICHAEL ROSS

University of Waterloo

DALE T. MILLER

Princeton University

CAMBRIDGE
UNIVERSITY PRESS

CAMBRIDGE UNIVERSITY PRESS
Cambridge, New York, Melbourne, Madrid, Cape Town, Singapore, São Paulo, Delhi

Cambridge University Press
The Edinburgh Building, Cambridge CB2 8RU, UK

Published in the United States of America by Cambridge University Press, New York

www.cambridge.org
Information on this title: www.cambridge.org/9780521802154

First published 2002
This digitally printed version 2008

A catalogue record for this publication is available from the British Library

Library of Congress Cataloguing in Publication data

The justice motive in everyday life / edited by Michael Ross, Dale T. Miller.
p. cm.
Includes bibliographical references and index.
ISBN 0-521-80215-6
1. Justice. 2. Motivation (Psychology) I. Lerner, Melvin J., 1929– II. Ross, Michael, 1944– III. Miller, Dale T.
JC578 .J886 2001
172′.2 – dc21 2001035036

ISBN 978-0-521-80215-4 hardback
ISBN 978-0-521-08793-3 paperback

To Melvin J. Lerner,
extraordinary psychologist, colleague, mentor, and friend

Contents

List of Contributors *page* xi

Introduction

1 Overview of the Volume 3
MICHAEL ROSS AND DALE T. MILLER

2 Pursuing the Justice Motive 10
MELVIN LERNER

Theoretical Perspectives on the Justice Motive

3 Doing Justice to the Justice Motive 41
LEO MONTADA

4 The Justice Motive in Perspective 63
RIËL VERMUNT

5 Perverse Justice and Perverse Norms: Another Turn of the Screw 79
JOSÉ-MIGUEL FERNÁNDEZ-DOLS

6 Justice Motivation and Moral Motivation 91
C. DANIEL BATSON

Victim Derogation and the Belief in a Just World

7 Why We Reject Innocent Victims 109
CAROLYN L. HAFER

8 Helping and Rationalization as Alternative Strategies for Restoring the Belief in a Just World: Evidence from Longitudinal Change Analyses 127
BARBARA REICHLE AND MANFRED SCHMITT

9 Violence in the Workplace: The Explanatory Strength of Social (In)Justice Theories 149
HERMAN STEENSMA

10 The Just World and Winston Churchill: An Approach/ Avoidance Conflict about Psychological Distance When Harming Victims 168
ROBERT FOLGER AND S. DOUGLAS PUGH

The Justice Motive and Prosocial Behavior

11 Just World, Social Responsibility, and Helping Behavior 189
HANS W. BIERHOFF

12 Policies to Redress Social Injustice: Is the Concern for Justice a Cause Both of Support and of Opposition? 204
D. RAMONA BOBOCEL, LEANNE S. SON HING, CAMILLA M. HOLMVALL, AND MARK P. ZANNA

13 Justice and Empathy: What Motivates People to Help Others? 226
STEVEN L. BLADER AND TOM R. TYLER

14 The Justice Motive and Altruistic Helping: Rescuers of Jews in Nazi-Occupied Europe 251
JANUSZ REYKOWSKI

15 Acting Righteously: The Influence of Attitude, Moral Responsibility, and Emotional Involvement 271
JOSEPH DE RIVERA, ELENA GERSTMANN, AND LISA MAISELS

Justice-based Reactions to Transgressors

16 Redistributive Justice: Its Social Context 291
NEIL VIDMAR

17 Just Punishments: Research on Retributional Justice 314
JOHN DARLEY

18 Deservingness, Entitlement, and Reactions to Outcomes 334
N. T. FEATHER

19 Just World Processes in Demonizing 350
JOHN H. ELLARD, CHRISTINA D. MILLER, TERRI-LYNNE BAUMLE, AND JAMES M. OLSON

Justice and Reaction to One's Own Fate

20 Belief in a Just World as a Personal Resource in School 365
CLAUDIA DALBERT AND JÜRGEN MAES

21 Awakening to Discrimination 382
FAYE J. CROSBY AND STACY A. ROPP

22 Deservingness and Perceptions of Procedural Justice in Citizen Encounters with the Police 397
JASON SUNSHINE AND LARRY HEUER

23 Fairness Judgments as Cognitions 416
E. ALLAN LIND

Name Index 433

Subject Index 441

Contributors

C. Daniel Batson, *University of Kansas*

Terri-Lynne Baumle, *University of Calgary*

Hans-Werner Bierhoff, *University of Bochum, Germany*

Steven L. Blader, *New York University*

D. Ramona Bobocel, *University of Waterloo, Canada*

Faye J. Crosby, *University of California, Santa Cruz*

Claudia Dalbert, *Martin Luther University, Halle-Wittenberg, Germany*

John Darley, *Princeton University*

Joseph de Rivera, *Clark University*

John H. Ellard, *University of Calgary*

N. T. Feather, *Flinders University of South Australia*

José-Miguel Fernández-Dols, *Universidad Autonoma de Madrid, Spain*

Robert Folger, *Tulane University*

Elena Gerstmann, *Clark University*

Carolyn L. Hafer, *Brock University, Canada*

Larry Heuer, *Barnard College, Columbia University*

Leanne S. Son Hing, *University of Waterloo, Canada*

Camilla M. Holmvall, *University of Waterloo, Canada*

Melvin J. Lerner, *Distinguished Professor Emeritus, University of Waterloo, Canada*

E. Allan Lind, *Duke University*

Jürgen Maes, *University of Trier, Germany*

Lisa Maisels, *Clark University*

Christina D. Miller, *University of Western Ontario*

Dale T. Miller, *Princeton University*

Leo Montada, *University of Trier, Germany*

James M. Olson, *University of Western Ontario*

S. Douglas Pugh, *San Diego State University*

Barbara Reichle, *University of Trier, Germany*

Janusz Reykowski, *Warsaw School of Advanced Social Psychology*

Stacy A. Ropp, *University of California, Santa Cruz*

Michael Ross, *University of Waterloo, Canada*

Manfred Schmitt, *University of Trier, Germany*

Herman Steensma, *University of Leiden, The Netherlands*

Jason Sunshine, *New York University*

Tom R. Tyler, *New York University*

Neil Vidmar, *Duke University School of Law*

Riël Vermunt, *University of Leiden, The Netherlands*

Mark P. Zanna, *University of Waterloo, Canada*

INTRODUCTION

1. Overview of the Volume

MICHAEL ROSS AND DALE T. MILLER

This volume begins with an intellectual history written by Mel Lerner, to whom the book is dedicated. Mel is a major founder of the study of justice in psychology. In addition to his many theoretical and empirical contributions, Mel has done more than anyone to promote the psychological study of justice. He founded the International Society for Justice Research and has organized countless international conferences on justice. He also was founding editor of both *Social Justice Research* and Plenum Press's series on Critical Issues in Justice. It is sometimes claimed that the research interests of psychologists reflect their personalities and values. This is certainly true of Mel. His work is fueled by his own abhorrence of injustice and compassion for the unfortunate.

As a social psychologist, Mel has much in common with Kurt Lewin. Like Lewin, Mel believes that psychologists can and should conduct research on issues of critical social significance. Like Lewin, Mel also believes that capturing socially and personally meaningful phenomena in the laboratory requires high-impact experiments. Mel's conviction that experiments can illuminate important psychological processes, while strong, is no stronger than his conviction that this goal can be realized only if the experimental setting engages participants. The fact that he has the sensibilities of an experimentalist and is a consummate experimental craftsman has not kept Mel from leaving the laboratory when he has found himself interested in the role of justice processes in real-world contexts. His research on people's reactions to unemployment and corporate downsizing and on people's reactions to the competing demands of family caregiving are cases in point.

His work on the antecedents and consequences of the justice motive has powerfully influenced the contributors to this volume. The geographical distribution, scholarly backgrounds, and seniority of the contributors evince the scope of Mel's impact. The contributors hail from Europe, the United States, Canada, and Australia. Their research disciplines include psychology, business, and law. Some of the contributors are leading senior scholars in their fields; others are quite early in their careers. To a person, they share Mel's passionate interest in justice and his belief that psychology can contribute to the understanding and solution of major social problems.

The chapters in the volume are organized into five sections. The chapters in the first section concern theoretical perspectives on the justice motive. Although their approaches and emphases vary, collectively the authors address four fundamental questions. Does the justice motive reflect a genuine concern for justice or a concern with protecting one's own interests? How does the justice motive emerge during the development of societies or of individuals? What is the relation between justice motivation and other important motivations (e.g., moral motivation)? When does the justice motive promote prosocial or harmful behaviors? These are big questions, but Mel has always inspired others to tackle big issues, as he has consistently done so himself. In addressing these questions, the authors expand on themes that Lerner originally expounded in his theoretical analyses of the justice motive.

Leo Montada asks why people apply standards of justice. Although Montada acknowledges that individuals sometimes refer to justice only for tactical reasons, he notes that justice concerns are paramount in many situations. Justice has a prescriptive function, and people are often obliged to observe the norms of justice, regardless of their self-interest. He finds evidence for this prescriptive function of justice in his studies of the responses of privileged individuals to less fortunate others, such as poor people in the Third World. He also describes some of the important psychological phenomena that result from trade-offs between justice concerns and self-interest, including victim blame and "free riding."

Riël Vermunt adopts a historical approach to show how justice concerns emerge from struggles among groups in a society over the allocation of resources. He argues that although the emergence of Protestantism had a major impact on the development of the justice motive, this motive can be traced to even earlier social movements and historical occurrences.

José-Miguel Fernández-Dols focuses on a paradox that renders the study of the justice motive fascinating to many researchers and theorists. As Lerner has observed, the justice motive is a double-edged sword. It can promote heinous as well as virtuous actions. Fernandez-Dols examines the dark side of good moral intentions. He details how a concern for the welfare of native North Americans led the Spanish crown to draft laws that had horrendous consequences for the intended beneficiaries. Fernández-Dols concludes his discussion of the unfortunate consequences of good moral intentions with an analysis of the behavioral and psychological consequences of "perverse norms." Perverse norms are formal standards that are widely perceived to be legitimate but that are transgressed, for various reasons, by many members of a social group (e.g., speeding laws).

In the final chapter in this section, Daniel Batson argues that justice and moral motivation should be kept theoretically distinct. After carefully defining the different forms of each motivation, Batson examines their developmental origins and psychological implications. He presents an analysis of moral hypocrisy, a motivational state in which people strive to appear moral while circumventing the costs to self of actually being moral. Batson also clarifies the difference between moral motivation and the motivation *not* to be immoral.

The chapters in the second section relate the justice motive to approach and avoidance reactions to victims. Approach responses include apology and restitution; avoidance responses include derogation and mistreatment of victims. Hafer describes experiments that extend previous research by Lerner and test fundamental aspects of his theory. Lerner demonstrated that observers who could not or would not help innocent victims disparaged the victims. He suggested that the injustice of undeserved victimization threatened observers' belief in a just world; they maintained their belief by inferring that the sufferers deserved their fate. Lerner did not provide *direct* evidence, however, that injustice per se is threatening or motivates the derogation of innocent victims. In a series of experiments, Carolyn Hafer offers evidence of these missing links. Her findings provide strong confirmation for Lerner's analysis. She also empirically examines the function of the need to believe in a just world. Hafer links this belief to people's desire to invest in long-term goals and to achieve these objectives through just means. Hafer's functional analysis supports Lerner's linkage of belief in a just world to a "personal contract."

In their chapter, Barbara Reichle and Manfred Schmitt examine how observers attempt to restore justice when confronted with long-standing social equalities that challenge their belief in a just world.

Reichle and Schmitt report the results of two large-scale longitudinal surveys conducted on representative samples of German respondents. Respondents are asked to react to injustices suffered by members of their own social group and by members of more distant groups. Although the findings are complex, Reichle and Schmitt identify some intriguing and theoretically important patterns.

The authors of the final two chapters in this section examine reactions to victimization in the workplace. As Hermann Steensma documents in his chapter, violence in the workplace is all too common. Even relatively mild forms of workplace aggression, such as bullying, can have detrimental effects on the psychological and physical health of the victims, as well as serious financial costs for organizations. Steensma presents studies that examine the causes and effects of physical violence and bullying in the workplace. He relates his findings to a variety of justice-related issues, including the differing reactions of victims of, and onlookers to, transgressions.

Robert Folger and S. Douglas Pugh study harmdoers' reactions to their victims. Their harmdoers are managers who lay off capable employees for financial reasons. Folger and Pugh discuss how justice-related motivations lead many managers to avoid, disparage, and psychologically abuse employees whom they have unfairly dismissed. Folger and Pugh describe the costs of such unmerited treatment to the individuals and organizations involved.

The authors of chapters in the third section examine variables that influence whether or not observers will offer help to people in need. Hans-Werner Bierhoff studies individual differences in belief in a just world and feelings of social responsibility. He identifies two components of social responsibility – moral fulfillment (e.g., being a dependable friend) and adherence to social rules (e.g., obeying the law). He proposes that adherence to social rules predicts prosocial behavior and that high believers in a just world tend to follow social prescriptions.

Ramona Bobocel and her coauthors examine people's reactions to policies designed to remedy social injustice in the workplace. They probe why such policies inevitably encounter strong backing from some observers and strong antagonism from others. Their research demonstrates the importance of people's justice judgments. Both opposition to, and support for, social policies aimed at ameliorating injustice may reflect people's concern for justice.

Steve Blader and Tom Tyler focus on empathic emotion and justice judgments. They note that empathy and justice concerns can independently affect prosocial behavior. They also describe the reciprocal influence of empathy and justice concerns. Empathic emotion can affect justice judgments, and justice judgments sometimes influence the experience of empathic emotion.

Janusz Reykowski uses interview data to assess the motives of rescuers of Jews in Nazi-occupied Europe. He asks the question: What makes some people voluntarily carry out risky altruistic actions on behalf of members of an out-group? Among other factors, he identifies the importance of empathy and judgments of deserving. He notes that the perception of injustice, by itself, is not a sufficient condition for remedial action. To engage in risky altruistic action, people must conclude that the injustice occurs in their own world and to people who are similar to themselves.

In the final chapter in this section, Joseph de Rivera and his colleagues also examine the factors that lead some people to act when they perceive injustice, although in this instance the personal costs of helping are low. Students who favor a nuclear test ban are given an opportunity to argue for their beliefs by writing a letter to their congressperson. De Rivera and his colleagues conclude that moral outrage motivates such protest actions.

The authors of the chapters in the fourth section study people's reactions to transgressors. The chapters by Neil Vidmar and John Darley concern retributive justice. When a transgression occurs, how do people decide whether and how much to punish the harmdoer? Vidmar addresses this question by exploring the functions of retribution. On the basis of field studies of criminal cases, he offers the counterintuitive proposal that individuals punish transgressions committed by members of their own group more severely than they would penalize offenses by people belonging to an out-group. Vidmar suggests that transgressions by in-group members are particularly likely to threaten community values; punitive reactions serve to reaffirm those values.

Darley explores such fundamental questions as what constitutes a crime and why people feel a need to punish transgressors. He proposes various answers derived from philosophical and legal sources. He then uses field and laboratory experiments to examine the merits of these answers. Darley concludes, for example, that we punish in order to inflict a penalty proportional to the magnitude of the crime, rather than to rehabilitate the offender or to deter others.

Norman Feather contrasts the concepts of entitlement and deservingness. He uses deservingness to refer to judgments about the appropriateness of outcomes. He relates entitlement to a framework of formal (e.g., legal requirements) or informal rules. He presents a model that outlines consistencies and conflicts between deservingness and entitlement. The model can help explain people's judgments about how much to punish a harmdoer.

John Ellard and his colleagues experimentally examine situations and personal dispositions that lead onlookers to characterize harmdoers as evil. They note that judgments of evilness depend, in part, on the motivations and cognitions of the beholder. The authors suggest that by demonizing harmdoers, perceivers may fail to attain a more comprehensive understanding of the factors that lead people to inflict terrible injury on others.

The authors of the chapters in the final section discuss people's justice-based reactions to their own fates. Claudia Dalbert and Jürgen Maes correlate individual differences in belief in a just world with students' reactions to school. Dalbert and Maes predict and find an interesting set of associations. For example, students with a high belief in a just world feel more fairly treated by their teachers and are more likely to attribute their achievements internally. Internal attributions may serve the function of causing students to view themselves as deserving their outcomes.

Faye Crosby and Stacy Ropp begin by describing a well-replicated finding first reported some years ago by Crosby: Employed women who are objectively the victims of sex discrimination with respect to salary tend to report no awareness that they are personally disadvantaged. By contrast, these same women readily acknowledge that employed women, in general, do suffer from sex discrimination. Crosby and Ropp discuss the motivational and cognitive factors that lead individuals to deny that they are victimized (including belief in a just world). They also describe recent interviews with female faculty members at Stanford University who brought complaints against the university for sex discrimination. On the basis of information gleaned from the interviews, Crosby and Ropp speculate about the conditions that lead women to recognize and fight injustice in the workplace.

Jason Sunshine and Larry Heuer report a field test of the justice theory prediction that feelings of deservingness strongly affect people's satisfaction with their outcomes. A survey of individuals who had experienced a recent encounter with a New York City police officer revealed support for justice theory. Not surprisingly, most people prefer to be treated respectfully by the police. As predicted, however, the impact of favorable treatment on judgments of procedural fairness is greater when respondents' notions of entitlement are high rather than low.

In the final chapter, Allan Lind argues that theorists have devoted insufficient attention to the functions and cognitive bases of fairness judgments. He suggests that people use their assessment of the overall fairness of their treatment to decide how much of their time and resources to invest in a relationship. Lind proposes that people construct such overall fairness judgments rapidly; they then use these judgments without much reevaluation to guide their decisions and behavior. He describes research that supports his theory, as well as the practical implications of thinking about fairness judgments in this manner.

2. Pursuing the Justice Motive

MELVIN J. LERNER

I have spent the greater part of my life as a psychologist trying to understand why people care about justice. Where does the justice motive come from, and how does it appear in people's lives during the normal course of events as well as during critical periods? From the outset I thought these were the most fascinating, important questions one could imagine. And I was convinced that the commonly available answers, based on the internalization and implementation of the "social contract," were, at best, only partially true, and if taken as the complete gospel terribly misleading.

It seemed obvious to me that people learn many social rules and that societies have numerous norms and regulations, but that the ones associated with justice have a special status at both the individual and societal levels. It is easy enough to demonstrate, as ethno-methodologists have, that people walk around with an acute, but often tacit, sensitivity to their own and other's entitlements – what they deserve, what they are entitled to from x or y. The relative deprivation literature suggests that no amount of "desired resources" can bring satisfaction to people who believe they deserve more, and that no amount of deprivation can lead to outrage and resentment if people believe they are entitled to no more than they have. At the macro-level of analysis, at least in Western societies, justice has a special status superseding all other norms and values. The requirements of justice have the power to legitimize and, at times, to demand the sacrifice of liberty, lives, and happiness. No other secular norm or value has comparable power.

Obviously, then, there is something fundamentally important about the theme of justice in personal lives and interpersonal relations. Assuming this to be so, any satisfactory psychosocial theory of the origins and manifestations of justice, must, at a minimum, provide a compelling explanation for this pervasive and unique power. Such a theory would need to contemplate psychological processes to explain why most people become committed to deserving what they want and why they become upset if other people's outcomes do not correspond to what they perceive them to deserve.

I have had two hunches about this, and both remain sufficiently compelling to me that I will try here, once again, to persuade you of their plausibility, if not of their validity.

The Personal Contract: Giving Up the Pleasure Principle for the Reality Principle

The first I have termed the "personal contract," not only to contrast it with the more familiar "social contract," but also because this term implies the operative psychological structure and dynamics.

My best guess was based on the work of Freud and others who had observed that children typically learn to delay indulging the immediate gratification of their desires and instead engage in time and tension binding so that they can ultimately obtain more desirable outcomes. In order to do that, I thought, the child would have to participate in the more or less conscious self-dialogue of making a promise to him- or herself that the anticipated delayed outcomes would, in fact, occur, and that they would be worth the costs of both the sacrifice of immediate pleasures and the necessary additional efforts. In order to adopt this "reality principle," the rational part of the child controls the impulses to seek immediate gratification by adopting what I termed the "personal contract." Most children will eventually utilize this personal contract as the organizing principle for much of their lives. However, even as adults, while most people are strongly invested in maintaining and living by their personal contracts, the desire for immediate gratification does not disappear. It remains in the background, ready to reassert itself, especially when the person is confronted with evidence that foregoing the immediate gratification and engaging in additional efforts may not lead to the desired outcome. If the "contract" is not viable, then why not just do what feels good at the time?

As a consequence, as long as the rational self is committed to long-term gains, the person must avoid any events that reduce the ability to control and channel such impulses toward the more beneficial courses of action. Clearly, evidence that an individual or another person is deprived, or will be deprived, of what he or she deserves threatens the viability of the personal contract. When confronted with such an instance of appropriate investments not leading to just deserts, the individual will be motivated to restore justice for the sake of maintaining his or her own personal contract. Research with Jannine Braband (Braband & Lerner, 1975) and Gary Long (Long & Lerner, 1974) confirmed the important hypothesis that children's previously assessed general willingness to delay gratification was predictive of their later following rules of deserving in allocating desired resources, as opposed to maximizing their personal shares.

Justice Takes More Forms than "Equity"

Even if I have convinced you, as I have myself, that there is considerable validity to the idea of the "personal contract" as the basis for our concern with deserving and justice, that still leaves unexplained many of the major issues associated with how justice appears in our lives. For example, the terms of the "personal contract" imply an "equity" rule of justice, where outcomes are expected to correspond to the prior investments and costs, that is, greater investments are followed by greater outcomes, and the motivational glue holding the personal contract together as a guide for behavior is easily reduced to a form of rational, or enlightened, self-interest: Presumably, people construct and maintain their personal contracts because that appears to be the most profitable way to behave. It was obvious, however, from what I could see happening around me that justice often takes other forms, and that the experience of injustice and the requirements of justice often have virtually nothing to do with, and are distinctly different from, self-interest, rational or otherwise.

I noticed that in my own family life, what I thought was just or deserving took several forms. There were many times when I allocated resources to family members according to their needs without regard to who had earned those resources. At other times, equality in the form of equal treatment, equal shares, equal respect appeared to be what was required. There were still other times when it seemed natural and right for the older child to have "more" – more freedom, more privileges, and, at times, more money – than the younger siblings, or for the parents to have more than the children. And then, of course, there were those times when someone deserved punishment, even me. It was not all that unusual for me to punish myself for being negligent or careless. Therefore, it was quite easy to demonstrate, at least to my own satisfaction, that various forms of justice, reflecting such considerations as merit, need, equality, and relative status, appeared even in the family context.

So, the next questions became, which form of justice becomes operative, and what are the organizing principles, the eliciting cues? The obvious answers had no appeal to me. Fathers act the way they do toward their spouses and children because of the social norms extant in their culture, playing out their socially determined roles, or the equally common explanations based on the various forms of the self-interest model. For example, people adopt the rule or norm that promises them the most desirable outcomes (Walster and others); people adopt the rule that will facilitate their gaining other desired goals; people adopt equity rules when they want to promote productivity, and the equality rule when their goal is to promote harmonious relationships (Deutsch and others); people adopt those rules that provide the best blend and coordination of various goals (Leventhal and others). I was and am still convinced that these attempts at explanation miss the point! They fail to recognize that people may use a distribution rule as an instrumental device at times, but that on most occasions the justice rule appears as a moral imperative, a personal expressive act intended to do the "right thing." If this is true, one is still left with questions of "when?" and "why?" a particular expressive act occurs.

Creating a Meaningful Stable World Generates Three Basic Cognitive-Affective Templates: Identity, Unit, Non-Unit

The answer that I came up with and still have faith in seems, in retrospect, to be an amalgamation of early theories of emotional and moral development I had used to generate lectures for medical students, the symbolic interaction material I had learned from Leonard Cottrell's seminar, and the discussions in Mitzi Jahoda's seminar of Asch's persuasive use of Gestalt insights to understand social behavior.

Basically, it came down to this. Exchange theories, including equity theory, begin with the proposition that people will try to maximize their outcomes. Supposedly, everything a person does is shaped by, and happens in the service of, maximizing outcomes. Although this notion is consistent with many first principles in biology and economics, it seemed to me that it failed to appreciate the importance of the human mind and its connections to the emotions. Obviously, people do try to get what they want, but it seemed equally, if not more, plausible that the first principle of the human psyche, both throughout development and in terms of its relative centrality to human functioning, is that infants, children, and adults create and seek to maintain a stable representation of their world. In the process, they populate it with people and with stable ways of moving from one place to another, all the time attaching more or less positive or negative feelings, emotions, and evaluations to the various aspects of their world.

But even if this is true, what does it have to do with justice? This is where the assumptions from "symbolic interaction" (Herbert Mead, out of Cottrell) come into play. The borrowed assumption is that repeated sequences of experiences acquire the status of structures in a person's mind and, as such, act as templates that assimilate and organize subsequent experiences and actions. Based upon what I recalled from various developmental theories, I thought that one could identify three sequences of early experiences that serve as organizing mental templates. The earliest consists of the infant's experiences of being fed and cared for. Out of the blooming, buzzing confusion that is infancy first emerges the repeated experience of having one's desires gratified by, and of empathic attachment to, other people. As developmental theorists have described, initially there is no real separation of egos, so that others' experiences occur to one's self. Cues of pain and pleasure from others automatically, empathically, elicit similar reactions in the infant. My hunch, then, was that the experiences of empathic arousal from merged identities and the meeting of needs forms the earliest template.

The next critical sequences appear as the child's increasing ability to act upon the environment and lessening dependence upon others to influence his or her own experiences lead to a sense of being a distinct "self." Along with the development of a separate ego, the child realizes that how one is treated and the important experiences one has are organized around principles of "similarity" and "difference." For example, the critical factor in how a child is treated by others, both adults and children, is explicitly contingent upon certain identifiable attributes of similarity and difference. Also, children from the same family or neighborhood, of the same age or gender, play together, are expected to share equally, and are treated similarly by others. While those of a different age or gender, from a different family or neighborhood, are not only treated differently and given more or less by adults, but are typically less cooperative and friendly and often antagonistic.

As a result, the cognitive-affective residues of these two repeated early experiences form the next two basic templates: one consisting of the perception of similarity, cooperative and friendly interactions, and similar outcomes, and the other involving the perception of difference, interfering or antagonistic interactions, and different outcomes.

Certainly other templates appear later, but these three that I have labeled, "identity," "unit," and "non-unit" are the earliest to develop and therefore, I assumed, have the greatest continuing influence on the organization of subsequent experiences, including and especially the sense of what is just and fair and who is entitled to what. The elements of these templates, derived from those early repeated experiences, include the perception of others, ways of interacting, and typical outcomes.

The earliest "identity" template consists of the perception of being psychologically merged with another person (the same person). The acquisition of desired resources occurs vicariously, for example, her pleasure is experienced as my pleasure, and the outcomes involve meeting the other's needs. The "unit" template consists of the perception of "similarity" to the other, cooperative facilitating interaction, and similar outcomes, while the "non-unit" begins with the perception of "difference" from the other, impeding or antagonistic interactions, and different outcomes.

The Effects of Later Experiences: Separating and Reintegrating "Person" and "Process"

Identifying and describing these earliest and therefore most influential templates is only the beginning. There is more. In the normal course of events at least two things occur to shape how these templates appear in a person's life. To begin with, through maturation and experience, people early on distinguish between behaviors that are attributed to impersonal processes, courses of action that anyone can engage in, and those that follow from the attributes of the particular person. For example, someone failing a course may attribute the failure to the kind of person he or she is, as opposed to his or her not having put in the required hours of study. Construing the other person as an occupant of a particular position in a causal process changes the person's reactions to a "similar" other (unit relation) from trying to maintain equal outcomes to a state of relative equality based upon a consideration of past events, that is, an equitable relation based upon relative investments and costs. Similarly, the person's empathic reaction to someone (identity relation) will be changed from trying to meet that person's immediate needs to considering the antecedent events that created the need and possible courses of action most beneficial to the person (Lerner, 1975; Lerner, 1977; Lerner, Miller, & Holmes, 1976).

Also, early on, people find themselves in situations where elements from more than one template are salient, for example, having to cooperate with one of "them" or to compete with a "similar" other. What happens then? The answer I came up with is that the person focuses on one aspect as the primary defining feature of the encounter, either maintaining the particular relation to the other, similar or different, or maintaining the kind of activity, cooperative or antagonistic. Meanwhile, the elements of the other template set the limiting conditions. Then, typically preconsciously and rather quickly, the person constructs a coherent, culturally familiar definition of the situation, including a conception of how to act and how to allocate resources. For example, finding that one is in a zero-sum or antagonistic situation with a "similar" other elicits actions in accordance with the rules of either justified self-interest or some kind of formal contest, depending upon whether the outcome or the relation to the other becomes the primary focus. Consider the situation where many students want the same highly desired fellowship. They are all similar, not only in their salient statuses but also in terms of their prior claim to the highly desired resource, but since it is indivisible they stand in a competitive relation to it. If gaining the fellowship is the focus, then they would be expected to do whatever they can, without violating any appropriate rules, to gain the desired resource for themselves. They would participate as parallel competitors with similar opportunities. However, if maintaining their unit-relation to one another is the dominant concern, then the importance of the scarce resource will be minimized and the "losers" will be compensated by alternative, often symbolic, payoffs. When one must cooperate with a "different" other to reach one's goals, and the outcomes are most important, then some form of contract ensuring the coordination of efforts and appropriate distribution of outcomes intuitively seems appropriate for dealing with "that kind of" person. But if maintaining the "difference" is the focus, then the recognition of superior/inferior statuses in the activities and outcomes will seem more appropriate.

If these descriptions of how people deal with potentially conflicting entitlements of person and process are not compelling to you, I hope you can take the time to read one of the more complete descriptions of these important events (Lerner, 1981). Then try to imagine, relying on your intuitive reaction, what would feel right, be intuitively compelling, in a situation where, for example, you have to compete with someone who is similar to you in important ways, or cooperate with one of "them" to get what you want or need. What thoughts, images, come to mind?

Some Hunches about How "Is" Becomes "Ought"

Although I had convinced myself of the validity and value of these descriptions of the psychological underpinnings of interpersonal relations, it was only much later that I confronted the question of why these events are imbued with the experiences of "ought," justice, and fairness. It is one thing to describe how people act or want to act, or the expectations they have, for example, because of repeated past experiences – I have come to expect that similar people will have similar outcomes – but another to explain how one gets from those events to judgments of what ought to occur as well as to the contingent strong emotions, such as "similar people 'ought' to have the same outcomes," and "I will be upset and angry if that does not happen." My best hunch is that those initial repeated earlier experiences become fundamental templates of the construction of people's worlds and that people are enormously invested in maintaining the integrity of their cognitive structure, the way they perceive and organize their experiences. I think there is evidence that damaging, even chipping away, at those organizing templates can have strong aversive emotional consequences, including physiological reactions of nausea or disgust, or, at the extreme, terrors of chaos and helplessness.

That may be the case, but where does the "ought" component experience come from? The answer is simply that regularities, in time, create the experience of "ought" in relation to subsequent comparable events. Sociologists have noted that common ways of behaving eventually become imbued with normative requirements. The "familiar" becomes the "desirable," and one "ought" to do that which is preferable. More generally, the human mind seems to distinguish between contingent events that are probable and those that are assumed to be certain. People may feel surprised or frustrated by improbable events, but their reactions, when an assumed certainty does not happen, include the experiences of "ought" and "should."

Consider for a moment what would happen if you got up from your chair and, with thoughts about getting something from the kitchen, rather mindlessly walked toward the door. If, after the assumed requisite amount of time and effort, you realized that you were not at the door but rather somewhere else, this violation of implicit certainty about the outcomes of your actions would elicit not only surprise, but your more or less conscious thought that I "should be" or "ought to be" at the door. This thought will direct your search for a satisfactory explanation of why the "ought" did not occur. Now, is this kind of "should" or "ought" experience psychologically different from the "ought" associated with moral judgments? Probably, in some important respects, but I think not in psychological origins. This, however, needs much more discussion.

In Summary: Basic Outline of the Justice Motive

So I am suggesting that, for example, children's repeated experiences of equal treatment and outcomes for similar others become a fundamental part of their cognitive structure, their way of organizing their experiences in creating a stable world. As a consequence, a child assumes that it is only natural and right for similar people to be treated in the same way. Any instance where that does not occur automatically elicits the judgment of unfairness. If the violation, and hence the threat to the integrity of the person's cognitive system, is sufficiently flagrant, the awareness of the injustice will elicit emotions of anger or sadness. Of course, changes in the person's specific beliefs about what is true and right can occur in response to later shifts in fundamental assumptions. According to some developmental theorists, however, what the person intuitively recognizes as fundamental truths about worthiness and justice is much less amenable to change. When such change does occur, possibly as in some religious conversions, it seems to be preceded by painful extended periods of personal confusion and chaos, that is, by persistent threats to, and then a breakdown of, the person's fundamental assumptions about the world.

What all this comes down to is that I had developed a theory of how justice appears in our lives that stands in stark contrast to the commonly held views. According to the most familiar and widely accepted theories, people are driven by the dominant and omnipresent desire to maximize outcomes. As a result, they naturally select and promote rules of fairness that they believe will facilitate their acquisition of the maximal share of the desired outcomes, and if, after due consideration of alternative courses of action and their relative payoffs, ignoring the rules of justice appears to be in their best interests, they will of course do so. The operative terms pertaining to this portrayal of justice are instrumental, conditional, and maximizing outcomes. By contrast, almost from the outset it seemed obvious to me that justice judgments and reactions appear automatically in people's lives and that they emerge out of the perceptions of persons relations to the others: "who" the other(s) are, psychologically the "same," "similar," or "different," and the nature of the encounter, whether it consists of vicariously acquiring, or facilitating, or hindering the acquisition of desired outcomes. People's reactions, based on "who" is entitled to "what" from "whom," follow naturally and inevitably from this construction of the situation. The operative terms in Lerner's theory of the justice motive are: Justice judgments are "automatic" and "compelling" and "emerge" from basic cognitions (Lerner, 1977, 1981, 1982).

Rediscovering Social Norms: Status Roles and Self-Interest

From early on, one could, with little effort, find evidence in the research literature consistent with the ideas presented here, including publications reporting that most people find it is more natural and appropriate to have cooperative and friendly relations with others who are similar, "like us," rather than with one of "them," and that people believe that similar people should have similar or shared outcomes, but more than "them." There are also several studies documenting empathic reactions to others, even prior strangers, when efforts are made to meet a person's needs without concern for relative merit or equal outcomes. Also, one could point to evidence from the laboratory confirming the everyday observation that people are often willing to do that which is just and fair, even at the cost of commonly desired resources.

More recently, especially within the last ten years, research published in the most prestigious journals has provided considerable evidence of people often sacrificing or ignoring justice considerations in favor of more directly self-serving goals. For example, research participants asked to role-play being a supervisor or manager recommended ignoring workers' relative productivity and paying them equally, or even paying less productive workers more, in order to facilitate the group's productivity. Fairness was ignored in order to do that which was good for the company. Similarly, in another set of studies students role-playing supervisors and managers recommended ignoring relative contributions and paying desired employees more if they were likely to leave the company. Conversely, they recommended paying considerably less to similarly productive employees who were not likely to leave the company. There are many more similar examples in the literature, but the important point here is that these publications not only document a willingness to sacrifice justice to serve other desired goals, but also make it apparent that self-serving behavior also rings "true" in terms of what we have all come to expect of what happens in our society. We believe that this is how contemporary managers, supervisors, and even we ourselves, commonly act.

Trying to make sense out of this literature made me realize that I had been so focused on looking for psychological origins and the fundamental principles of the organization and functioning of the justice motive that I had forgotten the most obvious and publicly prevalent rules of justice – societal norms. Having once taught Introduction to Sociology, using Homans's *The Human Group*, and Newcomb's early texts to teach introductory social psychology, I should have been ashamed of myself. But then it all became clear. Everyone "knows" the appropriate norms: Managers are supposed to have a moral obligation to promote the welfare of the company, including that of the employees and corporate investors. These stakeholders deserve managers who will act in ways that will benefit the company's market share and security. For managers to do otherwise would be a violation of their status-role-based obligations. Obviously, the research participants realized that in our society, managers' obligations to the stakeholders to maintain the profitability and, thus, the viability of the company take moral precedence over temporary and rather minor violations of equity norms for a few employees.

Clearly, societal norms prescribe and proscribe ways of treating one another – how one is supposed to behave. These include general norms that apply to everyone in the society and tell us what rights and obligations people have with respect to one another. More specifically, norms are associated with the formal and informal statuses assigned by society, for example, manager, mother or daughter, woman, lazy person. People, virtually everyone, are familiar with these norms. Also, as we all know, the failure to meet one's normative obligations implies greater or lesser social and self-administered sanctions, depending upon the seriousness of the consequences and the sacredness of the normative violation.

How Do Social Norms and Psychological Processes Appear in Peoples Reactions?

As any sociologist could tell you, this system of interrelated norms, supported by sanctions, enables people to organize and coordinate their activities. Most of us, at some level of awareness, recognize this important function and, rather mindlessly, go about the daily routine of doing what we are supposed to do to get what we want by following our various role requirements. And there is good evidence that, when faced with contradictory or confusing expectations or new opportunities, most of us will elect the course of action that we think will provide the greatest benefit to us. We believe that it is not only sensible, but appropriate, to use our rational faculties, whenever possible, to get the best deal for ourselves. Failure to do so would leave us open to others' questioning our motives. Obviously, it is considered normatively appropriate, desirable, to promote one's own interests.

This is where it gets interesting: Although most people assume that people will promote their own interests, research findings support the common observation that, in fact, people often, on the contrary, act in ways that reflect the various, often counternormative, aspects of the justice motive. Their reactions are often automatic and compelling and can sometimes lead to costly, normatively "irrational" efforts to see that other people's entitlements, as defined by their immediate intuitive reactions, are met.

I am arguing that, in effect, people walk around with two moralities (Lerner, 1998a, 1998b). In the consciously available system that we can all talk about and "point to," considerations of what one ought to do, the "right thing," appear as norm-based obligations, employed in the service of enlightened, "rational" self-interest. But we also have moral intuitions that can automatically elicit compelling judgments of right and wrong. What appears to determine whether people will react according to societal norms of rational self-interest or express their automatic justice motive–based reaction without regard to a cost/benefit analysis, are such factors as whether the precipitating event is important enough to elicit injustice-based emotions such as anger and/or sadness, and whether there are normative constraints requiring the person to engage in thoughtful decisions. So the more general theory of the justice motive includes an allegiance to being a good citizen, father, manager, when and if that is the most personally profitable way to act. Furthermore, we believe that everyone knows that this is the sensible way to behave, but that when individuals become aroused by the actual or potential violation of their moral intuitions, their behavior will reflect the demands of their constructions of the world they inhabit. These demands, predictable from the residues of our early experiences, arise from what is immediately, intuitively "known" to be right and wrong, just and unjust (Lerner, 1987).

Equating Justice Motivation with Role-Playing Societal Norms: Errors in Contemporary Research

Even I can detect many loose ends and theoretical ambiguities, in this theory of how moral requirements and the sense of justice appear in people's lives. It almost certainly must be more complex than this. But even with these rudimentary, semiarticulated hunches, several very important things seem to fall in place. For example, it now seems quite obvious that the vast majority of the justice-related articles that have appeared in the major research journals are best understood as exercises in norm enactments. That is, the participants are asked for their reactions to particular past or hypothetical events, or are asked to role-play a part in a simulation of a real-world encounter involving minimal, if any, actual incentives. Of course, most participants play their parts faithfully, and, as a result, the investigators come up with descriptions of the participants' beliefs, best bets as to how they would respond if the event were all really happening to them, now. To generate their reactions, the participants must typically rely upon their best understandings, the normative views, of what they and others care about and how they would behave.

If normative expectations were the sole determinant of people's actions, that would be fine. But they clearly are not. Typically missing from this research are the non-normatively based automatic reactions of people who are completely engaged in, and aroused by, important events in their lives. People, if sufficiently aroused, often react to instances of injustice and undeserved fates, their own as well as others', to unfair allocations of important resources, to the exploitation of those who are vulnerable and blameless, without regard for the predominant norms or for rational self-interest. But nonaroused participants, role-playing their parts in simulations or responding to hypothetical events, will not be able to manifest or even to recall such "irrational," personally costly acts. Without engaging their research participants' justice-based motives and emotions, investigators inevitably produce evidence that people comply with the requirements of societal norms. Of course, this may include their acting according to norms of fairness and justice, but only in ways that serve rational self-interest.

It seems evident that as most social psychologists turned from doing rather costly, difficult, "high-impact" experiments to doing basically top-of-the-head methods-simulations, vignettes, and surveys to study justice, their results reflected their participants' understandings of how the justice-related norms appeared in their own lives. However, they publish their findings not as descriptions of people's understandings of social norms, but rather as how much and in what ways people care about justice. In so doing, they arrive at and propagate the misleading conclusion that the justice motive appears in people's lives as a form of rational self-interest (1998b).

Fortunately, very recently, some young investigators have emotionally aroused their participants by a vivid, compelling portrayal of an injustice. Their findings have revealed a remarkable degree of subsequent concern with justice that has manifested itself in clearly counternormative, irrational subsequent efforts to restore justice, by enhanced blaming of either the victims or the perpetrators. Their results revealed that those irrational blaming reactions were clearly justice-motivated and were unlikely to appear among participants who were not emotionally aroused by the injustice or who, if aroused, believed that justice had already been done. Hopefully, other investigators will reconsider the importance of using high-impact research settings to study the forms and importance of the justice motive.

In the meantime, since the early 1980s important events in my personal life led me to move my work out of the laboratory and into the real world. What laboratory research I have undertaken has considered additional motives and psychological processes that might explain people harming or helping one another. Much to my surprise, and quite contrary to any talents I might have, I found myself becoming involved in the activities of an entrepreneur in the service of justice research.

The Family Crisis of Alzheimer's-Generated Dependency

A grave family crisis, created by my mother's increasing debilitation by Alzheimer's disease, led to my turning most of my efforts to issues of aging in our society.

I would never have imagined, in advance, the devastating effects that Alzheimer's has on so many people. Of course, my mother, who, in the initial stages, suffered terribly from episodes of complete craziness interspersed with periods of complete lucidity with no memory of the former, was the most victimized. My father, who lived with my mother in a small condominium in Miami, became the caretaker, guardian, and, eventually, "keeper" of my increasingly tormented and delusional mother. Such efforts consumed his entire life and energy, as is typical with Alzheimer's caregivers.

From early on, my father refused to institutionalize my mother, especially because of her aperiodic, unpredictable in both onset and duration, periods of lucidity. Obviously, it would have been unbearably cruel for her to "wake up" and find herself in an institution, surrounded only by strangers. He also refused to have "strangers" living with them to help with his all-consuming duties. He wanted and continually asked his two daughters, whose husbands were retired and whose children were off on their own, to leave their homes and come to Miami to share in the care of their mother. For various reasons, which are well studied, they resisted; but then all four of the children, in constant communication with each other, struggled to find some solution. After much consultation with professionals, so to speak, it came down to trying to get both parents to enter an assisted living facility near my sisters' homes in Ohio. In spite of our entreaties, my father insisted on going back to the warm weather and taking care of my mother in their Miami condo, still asking my sisters to help him there. Not long after ward, he died of a massive heart attack. Then, a year or so later, my mother died in an institution.

Obviously, I was involved from the very outset, although not nearly as directly implicated as my two sisters, since I was not retired, nor were we empty-nested. I could not, however, help suffering along with everyone and struggling to find an acceptable solution. Rather early in the process, I realized that one indirect effect on all of us could be a breakdown in our relations with one another. After all, there was a great deal of pressure on my sisters to get directly involved in ways that would clearly consume much, if not all, of their time and energies, and in so doing they might resent their male siblings, whom they may have viewed as being relatively exempt because of the societal norms and my father's expectations. Also, they were placed in an obvious zero-sum relation to one another for a scarce, highly valued resource time for themselves and their immediate families: Any help given by one of them would obviously lessen the pressure on the others for caregiving.

My subsequent reading of the literature confirmed the obvious: Under such circumstances, relations among the siblings often deteriorate. But why? My initial thoughts about what was happening among us did not correspond with the image of siblings dominated by self-interest, all of them maneuvering, trying to negotiate the best arrangement for themselves and so engendering the increasing distrust and dislike of the others. In fact, in the earliest stages of the crisis we were consumed with empathic concern for one another's welfare. I spent much more time worrying about my sisters' awful conflicts than about my own welfare. And I have every reason to believe such concerns were reciprocated. We were looking for solutions that met everyone's genuine needs. Once we realized that, then it all seemed to fall into place.

Extending Justice Motive Theory to Family Dynamics in a Continuing Crisis of Parental Dependency

My, and my brother's and sisters', reactions at the outset of the crisis are clearly described by what happens in what I have termed an "identity relation": empathic reaction to cues of suffering and efforts to meet the person's needs. If the typical description of the crisis of deteriorated families was accurate, then we were destined to end up in a typical "non-unit" relation with one another, viewing each other as "different," one of "them," and competitively bargaining for the best deal for ourselves. But then how could that happen? How would it be possible to change from being in an "identity relation," looking out for each other's welfare, to distrusting, disliking, and competing with one another?

The answer I came up with was implied by the initial theory. What were the salient, relevant cues in the situation? Initially they were our own, our parents', and our siblings' suffering, leading to a focus on the common good. But what if eventually it became apparent that our siblings were more concerned about their own welfare and less about ours? How might that happen? Well, it could happen because that was actually the case; but, on the other hand, it could also happen because, as cognitive theorists would suggest, we each had more explicit and compelling information about our own grief and the demands for our time than was available to the other siblings. In other words, even with no motivationally biased processing of information, an "objective" assessment could lead each person to reliably underestimate the other siblings' needs and the costs that they were incurring.

Thus, when each of us assessed how much help to give or receive from the others, we arrived at the judgment that we were getting less and expected to give more than would appear justified if we all cared about one another's welfare. Each of us, then, was highly vulnerable to the judgment that the others did not care as much for, were not as identified with, "us" as they were with "them." If these thoughts were communicated directly, or even indirectly by altering one's behavior toward the sister or brother, who was holding mirror-image views, then the identity relation could be eroded, if not entirely replaced. But with what?

My hunch was that, eventually, we all would realize that, even if we would not, or could not, be constantly concerned with one another's welfare, we nonetheless had a great deal in common, were members of the same family, were all parents with children, and so forth. As a result, with these similarity cues most salient, we would try to establish equality in outcomes – relatively equal contributions and costs. But then, as noted in the marriage literature, that "equality" stuff does not tend to work very well. If for no other reason than the systematically biased availability of information about one's own costs and contributions, it becomes apparent to all participants that the others are not living up to their end of the bargain. And certainly the mirror-image-based reactions of the others would lead to distrust, dislike, and cues of being very "different" from them in important ways. There is no way, however, to remove oneself from the common dependent parents. Thus, the siblings may feel constrained to defensively bargain and compete with each other. In this manner, the family members' reactions, primarily influenced by the systematically biased information available to them, may change from the initial empathic concern for one another's welfare (identity relation), to a preoccupation with equality in costs (unit relation), and then, eventually, to a distrust of one another's motives (non-unit relation). By the way, it is also possible to predict from this theory what events are capable of reinstituting an identity relation among the family members. Can you guess what they are?

Well, in essence, that was the theory, It seemed to me to be a valid extension of my earlier work on the forms of justice, and I was sufficiently persuaded of its validity to persuade others to join me in getting funding to do the research. These included David Reid at York University and David Chiriboga, then in human development and aging at the University of California, San Francisco. Eventually, two separate projects, populations, and funding agencies enabled us to test various aspects of this model. The initial findings were sufficiently promising to merit publication as an article in a major journal (Lerner et al., 1991) and as a chapter in an edited volume on aging (Lerner, Somers, & Reid, 1982). Although the follow-up analyses, for various reasons, were never completed, I believe the data from a second and, in one case, a third wave are still available.

The Puzzle of the Contented Elderly: Understanding the Difference Between Pain and Suffering

While all this was going on, I succeeded in getting funding to spend a year, in addition to my sabbatical year, reorienting myself to the problems of aging. This included time to pick the brains of experts in gerontology at Simon Fraser University and in the human development and aging program at the University of California, San Francisco, and to immerse myself in some of the literature. Very early in this process, even before I left Waterloo, I read a well-known article by a psychiatrist describing how some of the elderly, upon reaching a certain age, go through an extended process of reminiscence and review of their lives that, if completed successfully, leads to their becoming profoundly contented and untroubled souls. What a challenge to comprehend, to make sense of this! These "old-old" (vs. "young-old") people are faced with the increasing imminence of death, and increasingly inflicted with physical ailments and the loss of people they care about. Their lives are increasingly lonely and painful, with no hope of getting better, just worse, and then death. How is it possible that, in spite of all that pain, loss, and suffering, and completely in touch with this reality, they are able to be contented, at peace with themselves, and to take full pleasure in the simple things of life? Of course, my more cynical friends would find rather easy ways to explain all this, in rather mundane, even at times obscene, terms (just plain b.s.). But I wanted to take it at face value and to treat it as if it were all true. So, together with trying to develop a theoretically appealing and psychologically credible explanation, I spent considerable time interviewing "old-old" people whom friends and experts claimed had aged successfully and had reached this stage of semi-nirvana. As a result, I did find some people who seemed to fit this literally incredible description.

How could this happen? The key seemed to me to be in the difference, psychologically, between pain and suffering, or between loss and feeling deprived or cheated. Pain, it seemed to me, is a rather direct experience with no extra meaning. If it hurts, it hurts, and that's that. But suffering involves an additional form of anguish that implies the judgment "this is bad, this is dangerous, and it should not be happening to me." It requires a perspective-based evaluation of the pain as inappropriate, unfair. This assumption, obviously derived from my work on justice and entitlement, led to various questions about the nature and origins of people's various perspectives and about what would lead people to adopt one or another perspective vis-a-vis a particular event. Also, there was a growing literature that claimed to demonstrate that people feel much better about terrible things that happen to them if they compare their fates to someone much worse off.

This all raised questions of how people can shift perspective, what the developmental theorists might describe as "decentering." I thought of the work of Mike Chandler on decentering and recentering and the various levels of abstraction in people's reactions to events – concrete, symbolic, and metarepresentational. These thoughts enabled me to arrive at a model of how people might react to a "painful" event by changing perspectives and then having the critical experience of feeling better, and then changing perspectives and feeling much worse, eventually arriving at the realization that they had a choice as to how to feel about their painful experience – better or worse, depending upon what perspective they choose to adopt.

The key event, however, is recognizing and fully appreciating that one does not need to be at the mercy of any particular perspective and, thus, that one does not need to suffer. Pain cannot be avoided, but whether or not to suffer can be a choice. The net result is the liberating realization that one is free and in control of, not the pain, but the suffering. Even with pain, freed from the fear and anguish of suffering, people can achieve contentment without resorting to psychological defense mechanisms that require denial and defending themselves against the painful parts of their lives. It is sort of like achieving "enlightenment" in the Asian sense. Monique Gignac did some fascinating research related to this theory for her Ph.D. thesis, and we published a theoretical paper in a volume devoted to the psychology of coping with life crises and losses (Lerner & Gignac, 1992).

The Heroic Motive: Or, How I Almost Got My Nose Broken

But possibly the "wildest" idea I had came from trying to explain how sane adults, "terrorists," could thoughtfully plan and commit acts intended to kill and maim innocent women and children. Given the obvious innocence of young children, that was not possible according to my justice motive theory, and did not follow from "de-individuation" notions, either. The answer I came up with probably stemmed directly from my accidentally teasing a very sophisticated and competent clinical psychologist about his tennis game. It all started out quite innocently, as a kind of joke, or at least so I thought, but I was sure he was getting angry with me, and I mean *really* upset. Then I wondered how he would react if I started insulting his wife or kids. He later confirmed my suspicion that he would have taken me outside and kicked my ass around the corner and back.

But why? Why would someone that familiar with pathology allow himself to become so emotionally involved and willing to become violent: to do *what*? Protect his and his family's honor? From whom? And from what? The obviously dumb comments of some neurotic colleague? Why would protecting one self and one's loved ones' "honor" be so important that a normal, sane person would hurt another and risk being hurt himself? I came up with some notions about people coming to believe they could do anything to, or for, others as a warrior serving a "sacred" cause (Lerner, 1991). Conversely, the failure to protect that which is "sacred" would doom one to a shameful, unhappy life as one of the "bad guys." Jim Meindl and I eventually did some very interesting research on what we termed the "heroic motive" for his master's thesis (Meindl & Lerner, 1983) and Ph.D. dissertation (Meindl & Lerner, 1984).

Justice and Victims in the New Economy

My most recent and continuing concerns as both a citizen and a social psychologist arose from my awareness of the terrible systemically generated injustices in our society. Ever since the Reagan administration, with the sanctification of greed and competition by the free enterprise economists, I have been aware of the hardening of people's hearts to the suffering of society's economic and racial victims. It seemed to me that my students, even in relatively "nice" Ontario, were increasingly focused on their own economic well-being and essentially uninterested in issues of victimization, discrimination, and social justice. Of course, the received wisdom was that the "trickle-down" effect would eventually take care of them, the victims; and in the meantime everyone was supposed to do whatever they could on their own behalf. Presumably, if everyone did their best, individuals and corporations, to compete with one another for the largest share of the pie, productivity would increase, profits would grow, and everyone would share in the increased wealth as the profits were reinvested to create new jobs. Although the post-Reagan years have shown that, for various reasons, there has been considerable economic growth, there has been very little "trickling down." In fact, economic disparities have increased, with the most wealthy gaining the most, even proportionally, and those with the lowest-paying jobs, and the deprived minorities, gaining very little, if anything, from the increased general wealth.

What happened, according to some economists, was that the increased profits were not reinvested in ways that would create new and better jobs, but rather were used to acquire other assets. Companies invested in advanced technology deemed to be much more productive and efficient than employees and, where employees were needed, looked to the cheapest labor markets around the world. Plants were closed or downsized, as jobs were farmed out to hungrier workers in some more deprived location or simply replaced by more efficient technology. All that was simply good business practice, serving the best interests of the corporations and their stakeholders and, therefore, the entire economy. But what about those people in the United States and Canada who needed decent jobs to keep themselves and their families off welfare?

As it happened, a friend of mine was responsible for creating and implementing programs to help the unemployed in the province of Ontario find work. Consequently, on almost a daily basis I was aware of the dimensions and the growing seriousness of what was happening in the Canadian version of the post-Reagan economy. New plant closures and downsizing swamped my friend and her staff as they searched for more effective ways to help the victims of the "new economy' get back on their feet. From what I could tell, the main impediment they faced was that there were simply not enough jobs available that paid decent wages, certainly not wages comparable to the salaries that had been lost. What would happen then to these victims and their families when their compensation ended? And what kind of future could the generation entering this kind of job market expect?

Coping with Undeserved Job Loss and Downward Mobility

I agree with those political economists on the left, that is, the non-Friedman types, who argue that our present economic policies will create increasing numbers of innocent victims before anything like a trickle-down effect is noticeable. To be sure, productivity and profits will increase, and those who have the intellectual skills needed to generate and manage the advanced technology will be well paid, but larger segments of those without those particularly valued skills will become redundant, unnecessary in the productive sector of the economy. For the most part, they will simply have nothing to sell that is not cheaper to buy elsewhere, and there will be increasing numbers of people competing for even the poorly paying remaining jobs. Also, the typical vocational careers of those with salable skills will consist of a series of time-limited contracts, probably with several employers. After all, that is the most efficient way for most employers to function – hire employees "as needed" and "just in time," with minimal remaining inventory. But what happened to job security and the ability to plan for one's future?

Two research projects came out of these observations and concerns: One has been completed, for the most part, but the other, the more important, has not. The former was intended to help my friend generate more effective ways to help victims of job loss as well as to examine some current ideas about coping with crises. In a research project funded by the province of Ontario, Darryl Somers and I gave questionnaires to employees who had recently been notified that they were to lose their jobs in several weeks; just before the actual closing took place, similar and additional measures were taken.

We were particularly interested in looking at the relations between employees' purportedly "functional illusions" of relatively high optimism, self-esteem, and sense of control, and various measures of their sense of well-being and efforts to gain reemployment. Using this panel design, the regression analyses of the cross-lag disclosed several theoretically interesting and potentially useful findings. These included fairly clear evidence that the "functional illusions" were primarily functional in maintaining the employees' sense of well-being, but otherwise were clearly dysfunctional, especially for those employees whose qualifications placed them at most risk of not finding another job. For those people, remaining relatively upset and angry was most likely to elicit the efforts required to find employment. This was especially evident as the actual closure date approached. By the way, the belief in a just world had the same relation to active efforts at job seeking – the less-qualified employees who were less confident that they lived in a just world were most likely to be trying to find another job. (For those interested, these findings and many others can be found in the chapter Darryl Somers and I contributed to the volume I edited with Leo Montada and Siggy Filipp, published by Erlbaum (Lerner & Somers, 1992b), and in a report to the Province of Ontario Ministry of Labour (Lerner & Somers, 1992a)).

Although I have not begun the second project, I have published an article (Lerner, 1997) and a chapter (Lerner, 1996) describing what I believe to be the central crisis that contemporary economic policies have created for our society (Lerner, 1997). Basically, what it comes down to is that rather large numbers of people, by virtue of their lack of marketable skills and limited intellectual abilities, are literally not needed to create the wealth. No amount of retraining can help them to find a valuable place in the productive sectors of the economy, and as the means of production and of providing services become more technologically advanced, larger numbers of otherwise good employees will be rendered redundant. It also appears that even larger sectors of the generation now entering the job market, essentially those with average or inferior intellectual abilities, will have to compete with people from economically deprived areas for the remaining unskilled jobs.

If this is true, then the majority of job entrants who grew up in nice middle-class homes will be unable to achieve that kind of lifestyle for themselves. As they come to recognize the economic realities facing them, will they experience hopeless downward mobility? What will they do then? How will they deal with the loss of self-esteem? What kind of lifestyle will they adopt? How will these experiences shape their political attitudes and relations with other people and other kinds of people? All of these questions, and more, suggest panel studies with relatively straightforward designs that could provide extremely valuable information for psychology and for society as a whole. I am sure, or at least I hope, that someone will do them.

The Peripatetic Entrepreneur: Creating the International Journal and the Society Devoted to Justice Research

Between times when all this was going on, I was fortunate enough to be invited to Europe, on some occasions for extended stays. In the early 1980s, I made such a journey at the invitation of Robert Pagès, director of one of the two active centers of social psychology in Paris. One of his doctoral students had published a review of the just world literature in a major French journal, and they were interested in my coming to their laboratory to give several lectures and to engage in discussions with the students and faculty. For me, those were most memorable of times, and I was absolutely and totally charmed by both Paris and the people I met. Some of them remain good friends to this day. But, for the most part, nothing came of those meetings by way of relevant research. In general, "collective representation" seems to pervade everything done by anyone I know there. But I also discovered, later, that at least two well-known social psychologists, Willem Doise (now in Geneva) and Gabriel Moser, have used my theory of the justice motive and its various forms in their French-language texts. Also, apparently I made an impression on one of the members of Pagès's group who has published extensively on the psychology of religion, Pierre DeConchy. I think he was instrumental in the belief in a just world monograph being awarded a prize by the International Society for the Scientific Study of Religion (a prize he had previously won).

Soon after my first visit to Paris, Kjell Tornblom invited me to Goteborg, Sweden, promising good times and companionship in exchange for lectures. Then, psychologists at the University of Leiden arranged for me to spend a year as the Cleveringa Professor in the Faculties of Law and Social Sciences. They informed me that the rotating professorship was created to honor someone who had been appointed dean of their faculty of law during the Nazi occupation. When he had given his acceptance speech in the sixteenth-century building, as required by tradition, he had praised the Jewish faculty that had been dismissed and exhorted the members of the audience to resist the Nazi occupation. Prior to speaking, he had packed his bags and deposited them in the anteroom, because he expected to be arrested and interned. He was, but fortunately he survived. How could I turn down the honor, the privilege, the opportunity to honor him and to give my own acceptance speech in the exact same place (Lerner, 1986)? Going to Leiden on that occasion signaled the beginning of many great adventures.

Shortly before going to Leiden, I had agreed to create and edit a multidisciplinary international journal devoted to justice research. At Leiden we put on international conferences and workshops, the main purpose of which, for me, was to generate manuscripts for the journal. But those meetings were so stimulating and enjoyable for one and all that we created an International Center for Social Justice Research, with a newsletter, and reduced subscriptions for the journal. As many of you know, the meetings over the past fifteen years have continued to be great experiences, and there are now active efforts to transform the "center" into a scientific society.

All through the period of working with the people in the Netherlands, I also stayed in close contact with the group in Trier, Germany, led by Leo Montada. His group consisted of several very bright, industrious young people working on various aspects of the belief in a just world and reactions to victims for their doctorates. It became immediately apparent to me that Leo's group at Trier was the most active and productive center of justice research in Europe and North America. Under Leo's leadership, they first carefully and systematically refined the measure of BJW, and then constructed a better, new one. Or, I should say, new ones. Then they set about using them and other equally empirically refined measures in surveys of various kinds of people's reactions to various kinds of victims.

The vast array of data they collected over the years is very impressive, and their ability to find meaningful theoretical inferences in their complex sophisticated analyses is almost incredible. However, their findings come across as truly credible and interesting, especially when presented by Leo Montada, Barbara Reichle, Claudia Dalbert, Jurgen Maes, and Manfred Schmitt. In 1993, Leo and I were awarded a *Forschungspreis* by the Max Planck Foundation that included a substantial stipend. A portion of those funds enabled us to hold a workshop on research related to belief in a just world, the proceeds of which were eventually published in a volume we edited for Plenum Press (Montada & Lerner, 1998).

More recently, in addition to the wonderful experiences and continuing contacts in France, Germany, and the Netherlands, I have been invited to Lisbon to give talks and to consult with Jorge DaGloria and Jorge Jesuinho at ISCTE and with Isabel Correia and George Valla, who have a substantial grant to do just world research. Jose Miguel Fernandez Dols and his students in Madrid are involved in research on various aspects of the justice motive and what he calls "perverse norms," norms that have destructive effects on the social fabric because they are effectively unfulfillable. And I have been in contact with Adrian Furnham, Nick Emler, and others in the U.K. who have published papers related to my work on justice.

And Now . . .

With no commitment to travel again until late spring 2001, I can now complete the coediting of the chapters submitted to the volume on personality and social psychology for the twelve-volume *Comprehensive Handbook* being published by Wylie Press. Also, there are two large manuscripts, close to my heart, that are under review and will almost certainly require revision before publication. I can also handle the recent submissions to the book series I edit, Critical Issues in Social Justice, and maintain my contacts for teaching and research at the nearby university. And finally, I may agree to coedit a handbook of justice research and theory. All of this, of course, needs to be fit in around daily swimming in my pool, brisk walks, and leisurely wine-accompanied meals on our patio overlooking the pool and lake at the end of the garden. Needless to say, you are all invited to visit this lovely part of the world.

REFERENCES

Braband, J., & Lerner, M. J. (1975). "A little time and effort" . . . Who deserves what from whom? *Personality and Social Psychology Bulletin, 1,* 177–180.

Lerner, M. J. (1975). The justice motive in social behavior: Introduction. *Journal of Social Issues, 31,* 1–20.

(1977). The justice motive: Some hypotheses as to its origins and forms. *Journal of Personality, 45,* 1–52.

(1981). Justice motive in human relations: Some thoughts on what we know and need to know about justice. In M. J. Lerner & S. C. Lerner (Eds.), *Justice motive in social behavior: Adapting to times of scarcity and change.* New York: Plenum.

(1982). Justice motive in human relations and the economic model of man. In V. Derlega & J. Grzelak (Eds.), *Cooperation and helping behavior.* New York: Academic Press.

(1986). *Justice motive in social relations: adapting to times of scarcity and change* (Cleveringa Memorial Lecture). Leiden, Netherlands: E. J. Brill.

(1987). Integrating societal and psychological rules of entitlement: The basic task of each social actor and fundamental problem for the social sciences. *Social Justice Research, 1*, 107–125.

(1991). The belief in a just world and the "heroic motive": Searching for "constants" in the psychology of religious ideology. *International Journal for the Psychology of Religion, 1*, 27–32.

(1996). Victims without harm doers: Human casualties in the pursuit of corporate efficiency. In L. Montada & M. J. Lerner (Eds.), *Current societal concerns about justice*. New York: Plenum.

(1997). Preventing the societal crises of failed expectations and threatened self-esteem in the new economies: A proposal for helping the "generation at risk." *Social Justice Research, 10*, 241–252.

(1998a). The "intuitive" and "normative" senses of justice: A social psychological theory of their origins, structures and dynamics. In Joao Lopes Alvez (Ed.), *Etica e o Futuro da Democria* [Ethics and the future of democracy] (pp. 475–484). Lisboa: Edicoes-Colibri.

(1998b). The two forms of the "belief in a just world": Some thoughts on why and how people care about victims. In L. Montada & M. J. Lerner (Eds.), *Responses to victimization and belief in a just world*. New York: Plenum.

Lerner, M. J., & Gignac, A. M. (1992). Is it coping or is it growth? A cognitive affective model of contentment among the elderly. In L. Montada, S-A. Filipp, & M. J. Lerner (Eds.), *Life crises and experiences of loss in adulthood*. Hillsdale, NJ: Erlbaum.

Lerner, M. J., & Goldberg, J. H. (1999). When do people blame victims? In S. Chaiken & Y. Trope (Eds.), *Dual-process theories in social psychology*, New York: Guilford.

Lerner, M. J., Miller, D. T., & Holmes, J. G. (1976). Deserving and the emergence of forms of justice. In L. Berkowitz (Ed.), *Advances in experimental social psychology* (Vol. 9). New York: Academic Press.

Lerner, M. J., & Somers, D. (1992a). What do displaced workers need from counselors? Unrealistic optimism or harsh reality. In *National Consultation on Vocational Counseling* (pp. 160–167). Toronto: Career Center, University of Toronto.

(1992b). Coping with job-loss through plant closure: The benefits and costs of positive illusions. In L. Montada, S-A. Filipp, & M. J. Lerner (Eds.), *Life Crises and Experiences of Loss in Adulthood*. Hillsdale, New Jersey: Erlbaum.

Lerner, M. J., Somers, D. G., Reid, D. G., Chiriboga, D., & Tierney, M. (1991). Adult children as caregivers: Egocentric biases in judgments of sibling contributions. *The Gerontologist, 31*, 746–755.

Lerner, M. J., Somers, D., Reid, D., & Tierney, M. (1989). Sibling conflicts induced by dependent elderly parents: The social psychology of individual and social dilemmas. In S. Spacapan & S. Oskamp (Eds.), *The Social Psychology of Aging: Claremont Symposium on Applied Social Psychology*. Newbury Park, CA: Sage.

Long, G. T., & Lerner, M. J. (1974). Deserving, the "personal contract," and altruistic behavior by children. *Journal of Personality and Social Psychology, 29*, 551–556.

Meindl, J., & Lerner, M. J. (1983). The Heroic Motive in interpersonal relations. *Journal of Experimental Social Psychology, 19,* 1–20.

(1984). Exacerbation of extreme responses to an out-group. *Journal of Personality and Social Psychology, 47,* 71–84.

Montada, L., & Lerner, M. J. (Eds.) (1998). *Reactions to victimization and belief in a just world.* New York: Plenum.

THEORETICAL PERSPECTIVES ON THE JUSTICE MOTIVE

3. Doing Justice to the Justice Motive

LEO MONTADA

In 1977, Melvin Lerner's article "The Justice Motive: Some Hypotheses as to Its Origins and Forms" was published in the *Journal of Personality*. In my view this is the best piece about justice ever written by a psychologist. The article outlined all essential features of a meaningful psychological construction of a justice motive: the "categorical" normative quality of justice; the justice motive as a primary or "primordial" motive rather than a derivative of other motives, such as self-interest or social responsibility; the important role that deservingness plays in the perception of entitlements and in appraisals of distributions and social exchanges as just or unjust; and the diversity of manifestations that this motive can take. Later on, this line of conceptualization was further elaborated and enriched by new empirical evidence and theoretical arguments (cf. Lerner, 1980, 1987, 1996, 1998).

Yet Melvin Lerner's conception of the justice motive was not embraced by all justice scholars. In this chapter, I will address and support one of the most controversial claims of Lerner's justice conception, namely, that justice is a primary and not a secondary or derived motive.

Justice as a Normative Standard

Justice is "a" normative standard for evaluation. The normative, prescriptive nature of justice has to be taken into account in every analysis as well as in empirical research. The objects of evaluation are:

- distributions within populations, distributions of goods, rights, duties, positions, loads, opportunities, fates, health risks, and so forth;

- social exchanges of goods, love, trust, acknowledgment, loyalty, help, but also of harm, criticism, hostility, mistrust, and so forth;
- retributions for good and bad deeds;
- procedures for making decisions, for example, in lawsuits, in the allocation or withdrawal of scarce goods, in dismissals, and so forth.
- Inasmuch as distributions, social exchanges, retributions, and decision-making procedures are influenced, if not prescribed, by the constitution, laws, and institutional rules of society, the laws and institutions, politics, and constitution of any given society are also the objects of justice appraisals. These include, for instance, the economic system, labor law, the welfare system, the educational system, criminal law, environmental protection law, the code of criminal procedure, and so on.

Although the singular is most commonly used when talking about the "standard of justice," the plural form would in fact be more appropriate in view of the multitude of heterogeneous standards (principles or rules) of justice that exist.

For instance, distributions of resources, duties, and charges can be appraised as just either if all members of a specified group or population have (received) equal shares, or if individual differences in needs, performances, abilities, gender, social status, seniority, and so forth are taken into account when the distribution is made.

Social exchanges can be appraised as just if they correspond to rules of objective or subjective equity (e.g., ensuring an equal ratio of investments and benefits for all exchange partners), to direct objective or subjective reciprocity (e.g., reciprocity of positive and negative acts), to chained reciprocity (e.g., the generational contract, in which supportive exchanges across at least three generations are balanced), or to rules of subjective reciprocity (e.g., when parents who do their best to care for their children and invest large amounts of money in their education feel compensated for their efforts by the love of their children). When different standards are applied to a situation, appraisals of justice or injustice vary according to the rules or principles involved. When different rules and principles are applied by different people or different groups or social systems, conflicts about justice result.

Yet in spite of the variety and heterogeneity of justice principles, justice generally seems to be viewed as a "singular" standard. When people claim justice for observed or experienced injustice, they typically do not reflect on the whole spectrum of rules and principles which could be applied in that specific case. Quite often, people act or react on the basis of a single, spontaneously selected rule or principle.

The Justice Motive

As an empirical science, psychology does not have to provide reasons for the validity of justice principles, in either general or specific cases. Among the questions to be answered empirically are: Which principles are applied by whom in which cases? What is the impact of justice appraisals on people's emotions and actions? And above all: Why do people apply standards of justice? In this chapter I will deal only with the last question.

One answer to this question is that people have a justice motive. An alternative answer is that they believe that it is to their own advantage to apply or to respect standards of justice. These two answers are radically different. The first answer implies that people want justice. The second answer implies that people observe rules of justice or use justice arguments to attain their own goals. In the first answer justice is an element of the goal state, in the second it is a means to achieving the goal state.

Looking at the social psychological literature we find that the second answer is propounded in prominent publications about justice (a review is given by Tyler et al., 1997). For example, in their equity theory of social exchange, Walster, Berscheid, and Walster (1978) – in accordance with Homans (1961) and Adams (1963) – seem to consider equity to be a strategic choice intended to maximize individual gains within a group, community, or society in which the rules of justice have normative status. By individual gains they mean gains in resources.

Walster and colleagues (1978) answer the question of why people care about justice by referring to self-interest. Specifically, they argue that social systems have established norms of fairness that regulate social exchanges and the allocation of resources. People expect others to follow these norms, and they observe the norms themselves because they believe that this is the best rational choice, that is, the best way of reaping long-term benefits.

This rational choice hypothesis mirrors social contract theory in political philosophy. Philosophers from Hobbes (1648, 1968) to Rawls (1971) have tackled the question of why humans found states. Their answer is that people living in a fictitious original prestate situation consented to establish a state with powerful institutions, laws, and rules of justice because they believed that this would best serve their own interests. What the state founders expected was mutual advantage (Hardin, 1996).

Versions of rational choice theory are found throughout the social sciences. One such version is found in Thibaut and Walker's (1975) theory of procedural justice. In conflicts with the law, defendants are brought to court. In social conflicts, people often turn to third parties to help them resolve their problems – to friends, parents, and other authorities, including judges, arbitrators, and mediators. For the most part, when third parties are involved in the settlement of conflicts or sentencing, they more or less have control over the outcome. Inasmuch as people attempt to maximize their own outcomes, they care about the procedures followed. In situations where they have only limited control over the outcome because the authorities have decisional power, they seek procedural control and attempt to influence the outcome by having voice, by presenting arguments, their own views, and evidence. Therefore, people view those procedures in which they have voice and influence as fair. Most importantly, according to Thibaut and Walker, they care about procedural justice (voice and influence) because they want to maximize their own outcomes.

Lind and Tyler (1988), in their group value theory of procedural justice, emphasize the way people are treated by authorities. According to their theory, people care about their valuation and status in their group, community, company, or society and infer this status from the way they are treated by authorities. Because the way one is treated by authorities has an impact on one's self-esteem – as is assumed by political theorists such as Lane (1988) and Rawls (1971) as well as by psychologists (cf. Tyler, Degouey, & Smith, 1996; Van den Bos et al., 1997) – the concern for decent treatment in conflict resolution procedures would appear to be motivated by the striving to gain or to maintain high self-esteem and a positive self-concept.

What I find missing in these theoretical accounts is the normative, prescriptive core of justice. Justice is an ought, a moral imperative for social life. It is not a means for attaining personal aims, but an end in itself (Montada, 1998). People are obliged to observe the norms of justice, whether or not this is in their self-interest. Moreover, they are entitled to claim justice from other actors, organizations, state institutions, and so forth, not only for themselves but also for others.

Is the Prescriptive Nature of Justice Represented in Rational Choice Analyses?

I do not mean to devaluate the rational choice approach when I deny that the justice motive can be reduced to self-interest, whatever the concrete meaning of self-interest may be. The core of the justice motive, namely the concern for justice, would be lost if justice were primarily observed for the sake of some other concern, such as self-interest. In every rational choice explanation of the justice motive, it is not the concern for justice that is the primary motivational factor, but concerns for the subjects' self-interest, group value, etc. If justice matters at all, then it matters only insofar as it serves these other concerns. And in my view, this implies that justice as a prescriptive normative standard is overlooked.

When actors choose to pursue equity, for instance, do they do so in their own interest, or do they view equity as a prescriptive standard to be respected per se in social exchanges? What does equity mean as a justice standard in social exchange? It means that exchange relationships are unjust when the partners to the interaction have unequal ratios of individual investments and benefits. When the equity principle is applied, inequity is unjust and demands to be rectified. The disadvantaged are entitled to claim equity, and anybody observing inequity is entitled or even obliged to claim equity for the disadvantaged. Those who are overbenefited within an exchange relation are morally obliged to establish equity. The prescriptive nature of justice norms is not dependent on the actors' self-interest or on observers' sympathy with the advantaged or disadvantaged party in a social exchange relationship. Of course, self-interest may motivate actors to interpret and to balance the investments and benefits to their own advantage, and observers' sympathy with advantaged actors, for instance, may motivate them to discount the investments or overestimate the benefits of the disadvantaged in order to avoid or cope with feelings of injustice. But such distortions of objective justice motivated by the justice motive (Lerner, 1977) are not what Walster and colleagues (1978) wanted to explain by referring to self-interest. What they wanted to explain was why people care about justice.

Thibaut and Walker (1975), too, wanted to explain why people care about justice, namely procedural justice. Their answer was that people want to be able to influence the authorities' decisions by having voice.

Indeed, it would be grossly unjust if, in a dispute, voice were to be withheld from a party.

Concern for justice may mean that people claim justice for themselves – equitable shares in their social exchanges, voice in disputes, and so forth. It is incontestable that this serves self-interest. Concern for justice may also mean that people claim justice for all parties involved, equitable shares for all actors, and equal voice for all parties. Equal justice for all involved in a case does not and must not result in maximum benefit for the subject who raises these claims. Equitable shares are usually less than the maximum share, and voice may benefit the other party if he or she has the better arguments. There is consent among philosophers of justice that justice is claimed not only for oneself, but also for others.

It is conceivable that Walster and her colleagues, as well as Thibaut and Walker, had this latter meaning of justice concerns in mind, and not the selfish first meaning. If this were true, what explanatory function could be attributed to self-interest? The answer is the same as that given in social contract theories in political philosophy: The advantages of justice are not reaped in individual situations, but in the long run, where it protects against exploitation by more powerful others, arbitrary victimization, and arbitrary unfavorable decisions against anyone and, by implication, against oneself. Thus, for most people (perhaps not for the most powerful, who would be able to push through their self-interest regardless), claiming justice for all is, in the long run, a rational choice serving their self-interest, whereas claiming justice only for oneself (and those close to oneself) undermines justice in the long run: The rules of justice are valid for all within a social system.

Lind and Tyler's (1988) group value theory of procedural justice has inspired a wide range of research activities and generated an impressive body of knowledge about the favorable impact of perceived decent treatment by authorities (Tyler et al., 1997; Vermunt & Törnblom, 1996). The question as to the justice component of group value theory remains open, however: Is everyone entitled to claim decent, respectful treatment by authorities? Respectful treatment by benevolent authorities may enhance self-esteem and have further beneficial effects, including the willingness to accept their decisions, but that alone does not imply that justice is involved. Only if authorities were obliged to treat everyone in a respectful or even friendly manner would people be entitled to claim this kind of treatment. But is everyone truly entitled to decent treatment? Or is this kind of treatment deserved and claimable only by certain people?

Brockner and associates (1998) and Heuer and associates (1999) have approached this question empirically. Their investigations identify self-esteem as a moderator variable: Specifically, having "voice" and influential informational input into an ongoing dispute is more closely correlated with perceived procedural fairness in high self-esteem populations than in low self-esteem populations. Subjects with high self-esteem seem to assume that they deserve respectful treatment. Consequently, they and only they tend to associate respectful treatment with fairness and tend to resent unfairness if they do not get what they expect.

Assuming that justice is a normative standard in procedures, it is the duty of the authorities involved to act justly (and not a matter of benevolence). Moreover, the parties involved are entitled to demand that the authorities observe their duties and should not have to beg for benevolent, respectful treatment.

From a normative perspective, the question of which procedures are just is a crucial one. Although Thibaut and Walker's (1975) book is entitled *Procedural Justice,* the authors deal more with control than with justice. Preferences for procedures that give the parties involved more control over the outcome may well be motivated by self-interest. Therefore, it is crucial to ask whether the parties involved feel entitled to have been granted control. Leventhal (1980) outlined some further rules of justice, such as impartiality of the third party, consistent use of arguments, consideration of relevant information, representation of the interests of all concerned, and justification of a decision by making reference to ethical principles. These are criteria that have emerged in Western cultures as procedural oughts that can be claimed by any party. However, a higher level of education is probably required for individuals to be able to understand what exactly these criteria mean, and to determine whether authorities observe these rules or violate them.

Empirically, we need indicators of perceived entitlements. The global question of the "fairness of the procedure" may not be as sensitive to perceived justice as other concepts, such as perceived politeness or felt satisfaction. We need evidence of the discriminant validity of the assessment measures used, of their predictive validity, construct validity, and other facets of validity. The whole arsenal of methods to prove the validity of measures should be considered.

Justice as an End or Justice as a Means?

Of course, the rules of justice may be applied for reasons other than establishing justice. Other concerns, such as self-interest, may provide the motivation.

- Politicians may fight for more justice merely in order to win the votes of those whose claims they are voicing.
- In business exchanges, equity rules may be observed because the actors expect that this will pay off in the long run.
- Companies may expect just wages to increase efficiency by stabilizing the motivation and performance of their employees.
- Retaliation may be used for the rational reason that it will stop continued defection by another party.
- Applying the rule of parity in allocations within a group may be a rational choice aimed at furthering the social cohesion of the group.

In these cases, justice is not the primary concern – if it is a concern at all – but comes into play as a means of pursuing the actors' other concerns. This is a tactical use of justice, which does not require that the actors have internalized the relevant justice principles, that they believe in the validity of the principles, or that they are convinced that these principles should be applied by everyone in similar cases. It can be assumed that concerns for justice – if they exist at all – will be trumped by the actors' primary concerns if there is a conflict between the two.

This is not the case when justice is the actors' primary concern, or at least one of the main concerns. In these cases, actors are committed to establishing, reestablishing, or maintaining justice or whatever they hold to be just. In such cases, concerns for justice will not easily be trumped by other concerns.

It is well known in psychology that actors usually have more than one concern in a given situation and that different concerns may come into conflict. We need to develop indicators to show that justice was one of the concerns taken into consideration in a given situation, even if it was ultimately trumped by other concerns. If justice was considered only for tactical reasons, actors who neglected justice in order to achieve the desired outcomes should not be expected to show signs of moral disquiet.

In cases in which justice is a concern in itself, its neglect causes feelings of guilt and/or efforts to correct one's actions, to compensate for the resulting injustice, to beg for pardon, to excuse or justify one's actions, to minimize the unjust consequences mentally, to deny the injustice by blaming the victims or the disadvantaged, and so forth. These are possible indicators of the neglect of justice concerns by acting subjects.

In social interactions, the rules of justice may be neglected or violated by others. In this case, subjects' concern for justice may be indicated by explicit claims for justice, resentment of others' behavior, criticism of this behavior, punishment or retaliation, and also by mental reconstructions aimed at minimizing or denying the perceived injustices, as shown in the literature on belief in a just world (cf. Lerner, 1977, 1980; Montada & Lerner, 1998, for overviews). Both victims of injustices and observers who are not directly affected may have concerns for justice and be forced to cope with experienced or perceived injustice in one way or another.

The Justice Motive as a Primary or "Primordial" Motive

What does it mean to conceive of the justice motive as a primordial one? And why does this matter? As stated above, it means that the concern for justice is *not* conceived of as a means to achieve other goals, for example, self-interest. Moreover, it means that the justice motive cannot be reduced or derived from any other motive. From this perspective, the question, "Why do people care about justice?" cannot be read meaningfully as pertaining to other concerns (e.g., self-interest) that motivate justice concerns. The question can only be read as pertaining to the ontogenetic sources of justice motives. This approach has been taken by Lerner in several of his writings (Lerner, 1977, 1980, 1998).

It is probably true that the justice motive is built up by socializing agents and experiences. The internalization of social norms, including justice rules, is effected by reward and punishment, identification, self-concept formation in social interactions, and further fostering conditions. In this respect, socialization processes are related to motives such as self-interest and self-esteem: We all prefer rewards to punishment, we all aspire to a personal and social identity that is positively valued by the authorities and our peers. Let us assume that we have all built up a justice motive by means of socializing processes that rely on self-related motives. Would that mean that the justice motive is reducible to self-related motives? Not at all. The justice motive – once built up or "internalized" – is no longer dependent on the motivational conditions that contributed to its development. It has a quality of its own that is not reducible to these conditions.

The same is true of the social contract theory of establishing justice rules within a society or state. It is assumed that in the fictitious original situations, the state founders consented to introduce justice rules for the rational reason that this would, in the long run, serve their own interests. This was presumably the rational decision of those who had to decide "under the veil of ignorance" whether they personally would have a powerful position or a weak position in the newly founded state (Rawls, 1971). However, once established, the rules of justice have normative validity, whether or not a citizen believes that their application or observance is in his or her own interest. As with moral rules, justice imperatives are valid categorically, not just conditionally (e.g., under the condition that they promote a person's self-interest).

Traps of Reductionism

Reducing the number of human motives seems to correspond to the ideal of parsimony in theory construction. Of two theories, the one with fewer postulates is more parsimonious. Such a comparison presupposes that both theories explain the same empirical phenomena and allow the same predictions. A motivation theory that posits only a small number of motives – or even a single one – would seem to be more parsimonious than one that offers a larger number of motives.

The parsimony argument may have contributed to the reductionistic stance that the justice motive (as well as other motives, such as altruism, social responsibility, love, etc.) can in fact be reduced to, or "unmasked" as, self-interest. The economic analysis of behavior (Ramb & Tietzel, 1993) suggests that a great variety of (if not all) behavior can be explained by assuming some degree of self-interest as the basic motivation. This is illustrated in the following examples (cf. Montada, 1998):

- Hypothetically, caring for disabled parents can easily be traced back to selfish motivations, such as the desire to cultivate a favorable public image, or to ensure that the parents' love or financial support are not lost.
- Hypothetically, improvements in community or state care for the poor can be interpreted as enhancing political leaders' chances of being elected by these less-privileged voters.

- As mentioned earlier, the avoidance of opportunistic and selfish behavior can reasonably be interpreted as self-serving in the context of continued social exchanges.

The economic theory of behavior allows an elegant "explanation" of every action by tracing a path to basic self-interest (e.g., Baurmann & Kliemt, 1995). With some ingenuity it is always possible to generate hypotheses that reduce every "surface" motive to an underlying self-interest or to "unmask" it as ultimately serving self-interest. This kind of hypothesizing may be creative, but it clearly does not constitute valid scientific proof of the hypotheses proposed. Instead of asking the scientific question, "What explains X?," rational choice theorists ask, "How might a rational choice theory explain X?" (Green & Shapiro, 1994, p. 203). Bunge has therefore criticized the fact that rational choice modeling has "inhibited the search for alternatives" (Bunge, 1989, p. 210).

Approaching the scientific task of explaining the interindividual and intraindividual variance in human behavior with a single-motive model is counterproductive, because this single-motive (maximizing one's self-interest) does not contribute to the explanation of the variance. The statement that a person's behavior is motivated by self-interest has no informational value as long as alternative motives such as altruism, social responsibility, the justice motive, and moral obligation are not excluded. Furthermore, the statement has no scientific validity as long as alternative motivational hypotheses are not empirically tested and excluded. The apparent parsimony of a single-motive model is offset by the necessary increase in the number of corollary hypotheses needed to predict and explain the variance and diversity of behaviors. By analogy, when libido was portrayed as the single omnipresent motivating force in psychoanalysis, it lost predictive and explanatory power: The prediction and explanation of obvious inter- and intraindividual differences in behavior called for other explanatory constructs. Single-motive conceptions may best be understood as anthropological predecisions without scientific validation or utility. They are part of a belief system, not of a scientific knowledge system.

Rational choice modeling – as I understand it – does not predict or explain individual preferences. Instead, rational choice modeling requires knowledge about individual preferences. The "explanation" is reduced to a standard: Each player tries to maximize his or her own utility functions (i.e., to realize his or her own preferences) under the assumption that all other players will do the same. An external observer does not need to know any more than the actors' preferences and this logic of rationality in order to predict individual decisions. As Kliemt (1996) has stated, it is more an explication of a decision in a specific language than an explanation or prediction in the sense of identifying behavioral laws in order to explain and predict individual preferences.

Empirical Evidence of a Primordial Justice Motive

In many cases, self-interest and concerns for justice are confounded, in the sense that claiming justice and pursuing one's own interests have the same tangible goal. For those scholars who believe that maximizing one's own benefit is the dominant motive, it seems reasonable to assume that justice arguments are rationally chosen and merely have a tactical function. The following examples show that this is not always the case:

- Protests against one's own relative deprivation aim at improving one's resources (salary, rights, position, etc.). This is in one's own interest. It is hard for observers to determine whether these protests ultimately express justice concerns, self-interest, or both. However, there is much evidence to show that perceived social inequalities do not elicit dissatisfaction and protest as long as the inequalities are not considered to be undeserved or are considered to be under the control and responsibility of persons, groups, or institutions expected to observe the rules of justice (Folger, 1986; Major, 1994).
- Aggression in response to frustration may be motivated by self-interest (this is the conception of Dollard et al., 1939) or by justice concerns (when aggression is interpreted as punishment for frustration). However, it seems clear that if Dollard and colleagues' definition of frustration as the blocking of goal-directed behavior is applied, frustration does not regularly elicit aggression. Only arbitrary frustration, that is, illegitimate, unjustified frustration, elicits aggression, as Pastore (1952) has shown.
- In civil wars, one party may aim to preserve its advantages while the other attempts to overcome its disadvantages (with respect to resources, opportunities, power, etc.). Such conflicts may be con-

strued as conflicts between parties pursuing their self-interest (see the highly sophisticated analysis of recent civil wars in Hardin, 1996) or as conflicts about justice, in which each party believes it is fighting for its legitimate entitlements. For example, Lieberson and Silverman (1965) have shown that minority-group riots are most frequently triggered by a gross injustice inflicted by representatives of the majority against a member of the minority group.
- In all civil suits, the plaintiffs pursue their self-interest, but they also believe they have a legal entitlement to their requests.

In some cases, reference to justice and entitlements is made only for tactical reasons – to justify one's selfish, egoistical position by means of normative arguments. In other cases, justice concerns are the dominant motivation. This seems to be true in all escalating conflicts. As long as every actor is convinced that all parties are pursuing their legitimate self-interest, peaceful bargaining can be expected. Conflicts escalate when at least one party perceives and resents unjust behavior on the part of another. Perceived injustice warrants claims for compensation, punishment, or retaliation. It provokes moral outrage, heavy reproaches, or retributive actions, thus contributing to an escalation of the conflict. There is much evidence that in escalated conflicts, rational decision making is suspended. Traditional self-interest, even interest in health and life, no longer matter. Retaliation is the dominant motive, and appears to be a necessary condition for the restoration of justice (Glasl, 1999).

There are cases in which justice concerns and self-interest do seem to be unconfounded, in the sense that a commitment to justice does not seem to be in the self-interest of the actors. This may be the case in experiments in which groups of individuals earn money for performing specific tasks, and one member of the group is then given the task of distributing the earnings among the members at his or her own discretion. When the members of the group are not acquainted with one another, do not expect to meet again, and nobody is informed about the distribution of the earnings, it would be in the self-interest of the distributor to keep a much larger share for him- or herself than would be justified by any justice principle.

In our search for cases in which the concern for justice and self-interest are not confounded, we have studied the ways in which relatively privileged people respond to the life conditions of less fortunate others: poor people in the Third World, unemployed individuals in their own country, physically handicapped people, and foreign guest workers with unfavorable working and living conditions (Montada, Schmitt, & Dalbert, 1986; Montada & Schneider, 1989, 1991; Montada, Schneider, & Reichle, 1988).

How do people in relatively privileged life situations respond emotionally when confronted with the hardships and misery of the disadvantaged? With sympathy or angry reproaches, pride in their own achievements, satisfaction about their higher standard of living, feelings of guilt about their relatively privileged situation (which they may not consider to be entirely deserved), or resentment about the unjust treatment of the disadvantaged? We found large interindividual differences in these emotional responses. With respect to their intensity, guilt – which in this case we called *existential guilt* – and *resentment* were normally distributed emotions in large heterogeneous samples, rather than being rare or "exotic" abnormalities. Guilt and resentment have meaningful correlates; for example, perception of the existing inequalities as unjust, cognitions that one's own higher standard of living and the lower standard of living of others are causally related, or at least related in the sense that the inequalities could be reduced by means of redistribution, and preference for a need-based principle of justice (over a performance-based one). It has been shown that both guilt and resentment dispose people to engage in prosocial activities in favor of the disadvantaged. Guilt is more closely associated with personal "sacrifice," resentment with political protest.

Are guilt and resentment reducible to self-interest? Self-interest was also evaluated in these studies. One possibility is that the privileged fear revenge by the disadvantaged or loss of personal resources through forced redistribution. We therefore assessed fear of loss as a first indicator of self-interest. Fear was found to be moderately correlated with the perception that one's own advantages are causally related to the disadvantages of others, but uncorrelated with the perception that this inequality is unjust. As a second indicator of self-interest, we assessed anger toward the disadvantaged. This proved to be correlated with blaming the disadvantaged for inflicting their fate upon themselves, denying the injustice of the inequalities, perceiving one's own advantages as being deserved, and rejecting activities intended to reduce the inequalities. It would appear, not surprisingly, that guilt and resentment are not reducible to fear of loss or to anger at the disadvantaged.

In these studies, we tried to disentangle justice and self-interest by looking more closely at people who are better off than others, who consider their views and standards of justice to have been violated to their own advantage, and who feel morally uneasy about this. They feel responsible for helping to correct the injustice. Other researchers with similar data sets (de Rivera, Gerstman, & Maisels, 1994; Edelstein and Krettenauer, 1996) have come to similar conclusions.

While justice claims arising from a position of relative deprivation can easily be interpreted to be self-interested, this is not the case when justice is claimed for the disadvantaged by those in a more privileged position. From the perspective of rational choice theory, one could ask: "Isn't it a rational choice, serving self-interest in the long run, to correct the gross inequalities existing all over the world?" The counterquestion to this would be: "Why guilt and resentment instead of fear of violent efforts to restore equality, or cool, strategic deliberation?"

Evidence for the prescriptive nature of justice is provided by all observations of resentment at the violation of a personal or socially shared justice standard. In discussing the rational choice approach, instances of resentment in which the resenting subjects do not have any vested interests of their own, but nonetheless commit themselves to costly and potentially risky attempts to restore justice, are especially important. It is not unusual for social movements to be initiated and supported by people without any vested interests of their own. Think of Keniston's (1970) study of young radicals involved in the anti-Vietnam War movement, and the studies that Haan, Smith, and Block (1968) and Fishkin, Keniston, and McKinnon (1973) conducted into activists in the civil rights movement of the 1960s. Moral orientations and social responsibility were the motivational bases identified there.

It should be noted that the rational choice model was developed to describe decisions in situations of competition for scarce resources. Thus, we need to assess who conceives of a situation as competitive and who does not. It is not the situation per se, but the subjective perception of the situation that induces competition. Social responsibility, justice, love, sympathy, solidarity, harmony, and so forth are features of relationships that restrict competitive orientations or are incompatible with them. Consequently, one might question whether the data on (existential) guilt and resentment are at all relevant to rational choice theory if the people involved do not regard these situations as competitive. We need to be able to distinguish between those who perceive such a situation as competitive and those who perceive it as eliciting solidarity, social justice, social responsibility, and so on.

Phenomena such as the survivor guilt described for Holocaust survivors (Baron, 1987), Hiroshima survivors (Lifton, 1967), and released prisoners of war (Lifton, 1954) demonstrate that not all of those who have been favorably advantaged are able to enjoy their good fortune. They perceive the disadvantaged victims as belonging to their own community of solidarity (Deutsch, 1985). Equality and need are postulated to be the justice principles preferred in close relationships (Deutsch, 1975) and unit relationships (Lerner & Whitehead, 1981). Some empirical tests have corroborated this assumption (cf. Schmitt & Montada, 1981). Managers' feelings of guilt after layoff decisions (Lerner, 1996) indicate that members of management feel more solidarity with the staff than expected. The guilt felt by survivors of layoffs (Brockner, 1994) is another example.

As Ron Cohen (1986) has pointed out, the application of standards of justice depends on the psychological boundaries of the community one has in mind. Susan Opotow (1996) uses the term "scope of justice."

The Construction of Justice

There is no one simple, objective truth about justice. All that I have observed in our own studies and casually in everyday life, and all that I have read in the psychological literature, leads me to the conclusion that the justice motive is omnipresent, that it is what is called an "anthropological constant" in philosophical anthropology. But there is great variety in the actual contents of the motive.

What is considered to be just or unjust varies across individual subjects, cultures, historical periods, situations, and social contexts. It is shaped by personal and/or social constructions. The ingredients for these constructions include the following:

1. the variety of principles of justice available – in the domain of distributive justice, for instance, the need principle, the equality principle, and the merit principle;
2. the evaluation of relevant facts – for instance, the severity of harm in cases of victimization, the equivalence of services in social exchanges;

3. the attributions made (attributions of traits, causality, and responsibility), which impact on, for instance, the perception of entitlements;
4. social comparisons and comparisons of cases – in the case of hardships, for instance, downward or upward comparisons that have different effects on the perceived injustice of the hardships.

The construction of justice and injustice can be observed in processes of emotional coping with experienced injustices (Montada, 1994), in the emergence of perceived entitlements (Major, 1994), in political protest and violence (Martin & Murray, 1986), and in many trade-offs between justice concerns and self-interest. Some of these trade-offs result in psychologically fascinating phenomena. I would like to draw particular attention to three such phenomena.

Blaming innocent victims was observed in many of the experiments conducted by Melvin Lerner and his students (cf. Lerner, 1980) and in many subsequent studies (cf. Montada & Lerner, 1998). Blaming innocent victims is plausibly interpreted as an injustice done by subjects in an attempt to preserve their belief in a just world, which is, or would be, threatened by the fact that innocent people are victimized. Belief in a just and controllable world can be assumed to be a mental resource. It is possible to defend this resource by attributing responsibility and blame to the victims themselves. This is what qualifies the injustice of victimization.

Another exciting phenomenon is the *exchange fiction*, studied and described by Holmes, Miller, and Lerner (1974) and by Lerner (1977, 1980). The basic observation is that people tend to prefer to buy an overpriced article, when they know that the profits will go to help needy people, than to donate directly an amount of money corresponding to the difference. The explanation for this is that helping a needy person establishes a commitment and personal responsibility for this and other needy persons. Therefore, any act of helping is dangerous in several respects: (1) It implies an acknowledgment of injustice (of undeserved neediness), thus threatening one's belief in a just world. (2) It creates a continuing and generalized responsibility that may interfere with self-interest and other personal concerns. (3) It creates further injustices. First, it is unfair to all other similarly needy people who have not been helped. Second, a generalized commitment to help needy people would result in the subjects themselves ending up with less than they deserve. Nevertheless, needy people who are not to blame for having inflicted their fate upon themselves deserve help. This conflict is best solved by an exchange fiction, which allows the donation to be masked as a purchase.

The third phenomenon is the *free-riding dilemma*. Everyone agrees that free riding – profiting without investing – serves self-interest. Those who *do* invest resent free riders for their selfishness. Now for the observation: Opinion polls conducted in Europe in the 1990s found that two-thirds of employees were in principle willing to reduce their working hours and income (on average by 10% to 20%) if this sacrifice would result in the creation of new jobs for the unemployed. However, this generosity has very rarely been translated into action. Why not? As yet, this question cannot be answered by reference to valid empirical data, but at least two hypotheses can be proposed to explain the discrepancy: (1) Self-interest (preserving one's income level) ultimately outweighs the justice motive. (2) Moving the targets of social comparison changes the object and content of the justice motive: From the perspective of undeserved mass unemployment, it would be appropriate for the relatively privileged to share their working time and income. Yet from the perspective of free riders (other full-time employees who are not willing to share their privileges), subjects who do choose to share would be relatively deprived. Because this would be unjust, they finally decide not to share their privileges either.

Discussing the construction of justice may suggest that the construction process is assumed to be rational in the sense of conscious, reflexive, deliberate, planful, goal-oriented decision making. But this need not be the case. Most people probably do not have full decisional control over this construction process, at least not in every situation. What they consider to be just or unjust is not usually a conscious decision but a preconscious, spontaneous intuition; and the trade-offs result from a preconscious dynamic. Referring to Shweder and Haidt (1993) and to Epstein and colleagues (1992), and after reviewing many of the phenomena expressing concern for justice, Melvin Lerner contrasted two processes: rational reflective thinking, with a logical integration of the best knowledge available, and an emotion-driven, "experiential," intuitional process (Lerner, 1998). Lerner argues that belief in a just world and its motivational dynamics represent the latter process.

Conclusion

I am convinced that the justice motive is an anthropological universal, but one with many different faces. At the core of the justice motive is the concern for justice as a set of prescriptive standards for the allocation and withdrawal of goods and rights, loads, duties, and so forth and for the evaluation of social exchanges, retributions, and decision-making procedures. Justice is also a standard for the evaluation of laws, institutions, and constitutional principles, as well as of policies impacting on distributions, exchanges, retributions, and procedures.

It is undisputed that claims for justice are often raised by people who feel unjustly disadvantaged or unjustly treated in some other way. But the standards of justice are generally valid – not only for oneself, but for others. It is this general validity of justice standards that prevents people's concern for justice from being reduced to the ulterior motive of pursuing or defending their self-interest. To equate justice with self-interest would be to misapprehend its very meaning.

Justice means a set of social rules aimed at balancing the self-interests of different people or social units (groups, companies, sub-populations, states, etc.). Justice serves every individual and every social unit because it protects against the selfishness of others. True concern for justice – as opposed to strategic or tactical concern – is to be considered as conflicting with selfishness. Of course, not every pursuit or defense of self-interest is selfish. On some occasions, pursuing or defending one's own interests may be justified by referring to the standards of justice; on other occasions it is selfish. Whether self-interest is considered to be justified or selfish is of central importance. For instance, resentment is to be expected only when the pursuit of justified self-interest is blocked by others, or when claims for justified self-interest are rejected or ignored.

It is clear that not every subjective view of justice is shared by the other parties concerned. If feelings of injustice are to be avoided, it is necessary to do more than simply reject an actor's claims. Instead, some kind of discourse is necessary about what would be a just outcome in the given situation – a discourse aimed at a shared understanding. Otherwise, the frustrated concern for justice will remain virulent.

REFERENCES

Adams, J. S. (1963). Toward an understanding of inequity. *Journal of Abnormal and Social Psychology, 67*, 421–436.

Baron, L. (1987). The holocaust and human decency: A review of research on the rescue of Jews in Nazi-occupied Europe. *Humboldt Journal of Social Relations, 13*, 237–251.

Bauerman, M., & Kliemt, H. (1995). Zur Ökonomie der Tugend. *Ökonomie und Gesellschaft, 11*, 13–44.

Brockner, J. (1994). Perceived fairness and survivors' reactions to layoffs, or how downsizing organizations can do well by doing good. *Social Justice Research, 7,* 345–363.

Brockner, J., Siegel, P. A., Martin, C., Reed, T., Heuer, L., Wiesenfeld, B., Grover, S., & Bjorgvinsson, S. (1998). The moderating effect of self-esteem in reaction to voice: Converging evidence from five studies. *Journal of Personality and Social Psychology, 75,* 394–487.

Bunge, M. (1989). Game theory is not a useful tool for the political scientist. *Epistemologia, 12,* 195–212.

Cohen, R. L. (1986). Membership, intergroup relations, and justice. In M. J. Lerner & R. Vermunt (Eds.), *Social justice in human relations I* (pp. 239–258). New York: Plenum.

deRivera, J., Gerstman, E., & Maisels, L. (1994). The emotional motivation of righteous behavior. *Social Justice Research, 7,* 91–106.

Deutsch, M. (1975). Equity, equality, and need: What determines which value will be used as the basis for distributive justice? *Journal of Social Issues, 31,* 137–149.

(1985). *Distributive justice: A social psychological perspective.* New Haven, CT: Yale University Press.

Dollard, J., Doob, L. W., Miller, N., Mowrer, O. H., & Sears, R. R. (1939). Frustration and aggression. *Journal of Abnormal and Social Psychology, 34,* 289–313.

Edelstein, W., & Krettenauer, T. (1996). Justice as solidarity: A study of political socialization of adolescents from East and West Germany within the theoretical framework of Durkheim's sociology of morality. *Social Justice Research, 9,* 281–304.

Epstein, S., Lipson, A., Hostein, C., & Hus, E. (1992). Irrational reactions to negative outcomes: Evidence for two conceptual systems. *Journal of Personality and Social Psychology, 62,* 328–339.

Fishkin, J., Keniston, K., & McKinnon, C. (1973). Moral reasoning and political ideology. *Journal of Personality and Social Psychology, 27,* 109–119.

Folger, R. (1986). A referent-cognitions theory of relative deprivation. In J. M. Olson, C. P. Herman, & M. P. Zanna (Eds.), *Relative deprivation and social comparison* (pp. 33–55). Hillsdale, NJ: Erlbaum.

Glasl, F. (1990). *Konfliktmanagement.* Bern, Haupt, and Stuttgart: Verlag Freies Geistesleben.

Green, D. P., & Shapiro, I. (1994). *Pathologies of rational choice theory: A critique of applications in political science.* New Haven, CT: Yale University Press.

Haan, N., Smith, M. B., & Block, J. (1968). Moral reasoning of young adults: Political-social behavior, family background, and personality correlates. *Journal of Personality and Social Psychology, 10,* 183–201.

Hardin, R. (1996). Distributive justice in a real world. In L. Montada & M. J. Lerner (Eds.), *Current societal problems about justice* (pp. 9–24). New York: Plenum.

Heuer, L., Blumenthal, E., Douglas, A., & Weinblatt, T. (1999). A deservingness approach to respect as a relationally based fairness judgement. *Personality and Social Psychology Bulletin, 25,* 1279–1292.

Hobbes, T. (1648, 1970). *Leviathan.* London: Dent.

Holmes, J. G., Miller, D. T., & Lerner, M. J. (1974). *Symbolic threat in helping situations: The "exchange fiction."* Unpublished manuscript, University of Waterloo. (Cited from Lerner, 1977.)

Homans, G. C. (1961). *Social behaviour: Its elementary forms.* New York: Harcourt, Brace & World.

Keniston, K. (1970). Student activism, moral development, and morality. *American Journal of Orthopsychiatry, 40,* 577–592.

Kliemt, H. (1996). Rational choice – Erklärungen? In U. Druwe & V. Kunz (Eds.), *Handlungs- und Entscheidungstheorie in der Politikwissenschaft: Eine Einführung in Konzepte und Forschungsgegenstand* (pp. 83–105). Opladen: Leske + Budrich.

Lane, R. E. (1988). Procedural goods in a democracy: How one is treated versus what one gets. *Social Justice Research, 2,* 177–192.

Lerner, M. J. (1977). The justice motive. Some hypotheses as to its origins and forms. *Journal of Personality, 45,* 1–32.

(1980). *The belief in a just world: A fundamental delusion.* New York: Plenum.

(1987). Integrating societal and psychological rules of entitlement: The basic tasks of each social actor and for the social sciences. *Social Justice Research, 1,* 107–125.

(1996). Doing justice to the justice motive. In L. Montada & M. J. Lerner (Eds.), *Current societal concerns about justice* (pp. 1–8). New York: Plenum.

(1998). The two forms of Belief in a Just World: Some thoughts on why and how people care about justice. In L. Montada & M. J. Lerner (Eds.), *Responses to victimizations and Belief in a Just World* (pp. 247–269). New York: Plenum.

Lerner, M. J., & Whitehead, L. A. (1981). Procedural justice viewed in the context of justice motive theory. In G. Mikula (Ed.), *Justice and social interaction* (pp. 219–256). Bern: Hans Huber Publishers.

Leventhal, G. S. (1980). What should be done with equity theory? New approaches to the study of fairness in social relationships. In K. J. Gergen, M. S. Greenberg, & R. H. Willis (Eds.), *Social exchange: Advances in theory and research.* New York: Plenum.

Lieberson, S., & Silverman, R. A. (1965). The precipitants and underlying conditions of race riots. *American Sociological Review, 30,* 887–898.

Lifton, R. J. (1954). "Home by Ship": Reaction patterns of American prisoners of war repatriated from North Korea. *American Journal of Psychiatry, 110,* 733–751.

(1967). *Death in life: Survivors of Hiroshima.* New York: Random House.

Lind, E. A., & Tyler, T. R. (1988). *The social psychology of procedural justice.* New York: Plenum.

Major, B. (1994). From social inequality to personal entitlement: The role of social comparisons, legitimacy appraisals, and group membership. In M. Zanna (Ed.), *Advances in experimental social psychology* (Vol. 26, pp. 293–355). New York: Academic Press.

Martin, J., & Murray, A. (1986). Catalysts for collective violence. In R. Folger (Ed.), *The sense of injustice: Social psychological perspectives.* New York: Plenum.

Montada, L. (1994). Injustice in harm and loss. *Social Justice Research, 7,* 5–28.

(1998). Justice: Just a rational choice? *Social Justice Research, 12,* 81–101.

Montada, L., & Lerner, M. J. (1998). *Responses to victimization and belief in a just world.* New York: Plenum.

Montada, L., Schmitt, M., & Dalbert, C. (1986). Thinking about justice and dealing with one's own privileges: A study of existential guilt. In H. W. Bierhoff, R. Cohen, & J. Greenberg (Eds.), *Justice in social relations* (pp. 125–143). New York: Plenum.

Montada, L., & Schneider, A. (1989). Justice and emotional reactions to the disadvantaged. *Social Justice Research, 3,* 313–344.

(1991). Justice and prosocial commitments. In L. Montada & H. W. Bierhoff (Eds.), *Altruism in social systems* (pp. 58–81). Toronto: Hogrefe & Huber.

Montada, L., Schneider, A., & Reichle, B. (1988). Emotionen und Hilfsbereitschaft. In H. W. Bierhoff & L. Montada (Eds.), *Altruismus: Bedingungen der Hilfsbereitschaft* (pp. 130–153). Göttingen: Hogrefe.

Opotow, S. (1996) Is justice finite? The case of environmental inclusion. In L. Montada & M. J. Lerner (Eds.), *Current societal concerns about justice* (pp. 213–230). New York: Plenum.

Pastore, N. (1952). The role of arbitrariness in the frustration-aggression hypothesis. *Journal of Abnormal and Social Psychology, 47,* 728–731.

Ramb, B.-T., & Tietzel, M. (Eds.). (1993). *Ökonomische Verhaltenstheorie.* München: Franz Vahlen.

Rawls, J. (1971). *A theory of justice.* Cambridge, MA: Belknap.

Schmitt, M., & Montada, L. (1981). Determinanten der Gerechtigkeit. *Zeitschrift für Sozialpsychologie, 13,* 32–44.

Shweder, R. A., & Haidt, J. (1993). The future of moral psychology: Truth, intuition, and the pluralist way. *Psychological Science, 4,* 360–365.

Thibaut, J. W., & Walker, L. (1975). *Procedural justice: A psychological analysis.* Hillsdale, NJ: Erlbaum.

Tyler, T. R., Boeckman, R. J., Smith, H. J., & Huo, Y. Z. (1997). *Social justice in a diverse society.* Boulder, CO: Westview Press.

Tyler, T. R., Degouey, P., & Smith, H. J. (1996). Understanding why the justice of group procedures matters. *Journal of Personality and Social Psychology, 70,* 913–930.

Van den Bos, K., Lind, E. A., Vermunt, R., & Wilke, H. A. M. (1997). How do I judge my outcome when I do not know the outcome of others? The psychology of the fair process effect. *Journal of Personality and Social Psychology, 72,* 1034–1046.

Vermunt, R., & Törnblom, K. (Eds.) (1996). Distributive and procedural justice [special issue]. *Social Justice Research, 9* (4).

Walster, E., Berscheid, E., & Walster, G. W. (1978). *Equity: Theory and research.* Boston: Allyn & Bacon.

4. The Justice Motive in Perspective

RIËL VERMUNT

Introduction

A major topic in the study of social justice is the description and explanation of why people behave justly. In many discussions, the justice motive is conceived of as the opposite of the egoistic motive. Economists believe that individuals strive to maximize their own profit and that social behavior is driven by an egoistic motive. Some sociologists and psychologists are convinced that individuals strive to maximize their own profit but, realizing that unrestricted egoism leads to a war of all against all, behave more altruistically (Walster, Walster, & Berscheid, 1978). Other social scientists have tried successfully to show not only that social behavior is governed by self-interest (Montada, 1998), but that individuals are motivated as well by rules of fairness and justice. But despite the overwhelming evidence to the contrary, the myth of individuals as profit maximizers still exists in the minds of broad categories of individuals, including scientists, in Western societies (Miller & Ratner, 1996). To unravel the intricate threads that create the complexities of the justice motive, Mel Lerner has made a major contribution. His definition of the justice motive in terms of deservingness and entitlement has received much attention in the literature. Moreover, the operations of the justice motive have made visible phenomena, such as blaming innocent victims, that were poorly understood before. It turns out that the justice motive offers a good explanation of people's justice beliefs and behavior, and that empirical evidence supports this explanation.

I thank Dale Miller for his valuable comments on a previous version of this paper.

In this chapter I would like to go into the individual and societal backgrounds of the justice motive. First, I will describe Lerner's view of the justice motive and some of the critical analyses, of which Furby's (1986) is perhaps the sharpest. Then I will outline the main shortcomings of Furby's critique, and describe another way of thinking about the relationship between the justice motive and societal developments.

Lerner's View on the Justice Motive and Some of the Critiques

According to Lerner (1980), adult Americans have a need to see the world as a just place where people get what they deserve. Lerner is convinced that this "belief in a just world" has its roots in the common experience of children that it is often better to give up an immediate reward in order to obtain a larger one later. Children learn to anticipate alternative actions and their consequences; they learn to expect certain outcomes when circumstances are appropriate. These expectations form the basis of concepts like "entitlement" and "deservingness." The process of creating expectations requires a stable environment with relatively constant conditions, so that outcomes can be realized.

The definition of the justice concept and the underlying mechanisms of the justice motive have been challenged by economists and psychologists. Economists believe that human beings are driven by egoistic motives and are not interested in what others deserve or are entitled to. Game theorists, for example, predict that in a dictator game, where an allocator has to divide a good between himself and another player who can only accept the offer of the allocator, the allocator will take all for him- or herself. Also, psychologists challenge some of the fundamental ideas regarding the justice motive. According to Furby (1986), the fact that unfulfilled expectations can lead to a sense of injustice is not restricted to the beliefs and behavior of citizens of the United States. Several results show that feelings of injustice of people in many countries can be explained in terms of unfulfilled promises. Research on quality of life in many countries has shown that the best predictors of life satisfaction are perceived discrepancies between the present situation and situations one can easily imagine. Because of the close relationship between satisfaction and justice (Vermunt, 1989; Vermunt, Spaans, & Zorge, 1989; Brockner and Wiesenfeld, 1996), it is plausible to assume that unfulfilled expectations play an important role in evaluating situations as just or unjust.

Furby (1986) mentions two explanations for the universal link between unfulfilled expectations and feelings of injustice. First, she cites Lerner's learned expectations view, as exemplified by the personal contract that the child develops with the world. According to this formulation, the agreement to give up immediate gratification, in favor of a larger reward later, has the psychological status of a personal contract with the world. But, according to Furby, Lerner's emphasis on delay of gratification "may reflect Lerner's sociohistorical setting rather than something fundamental about the nature of justice" (p. 180). Indeed, Lerner relates principles of the Protestant ethic – with its emphasis on asceticism, strict control of impulses, hard work to obtain the better life – with the emergence of capitalism in Western industrialized countries. Furby, second, states that the fundamental building block for the concept of justice is the relationship between the actions people take and the consequences of those actions. The action-outcome relationships form, according to Furby, the basic elements of justice.

In summary, the most severe critique of Furby on Lerner's delay-of-gratification explanation of justice focuses on the fact that this explanation is based on the basic principles of the Protestant ethic. Because this ethic has developed mainly in Western industrialised countries, the idea that delay of gratification is based on this ethic is not an adequate explanation of the generality of justice phenomena. "If so, it may be unwise to propose delay of gratification as the basic building block for a universal concept of justice" (Furby, 1986, p. 180).

Three comments can be made on Furby's critique on the Protestant ethic explanation of learned expectations. One is that delay of gratification is not the prerogative of the Protestant ethic alone. Roman Catholic doctrine also emphasizes the principle of delayed gratification. In the Middle Ages, people were taught that in the afterlife a large reward was awaiting those who had lived in poverty and had themselves devoted to the works of God and to a life filled with prayer. Those who were prepared to live according to these principles or those who had to live according to these principles passed up small rewards like wealth and a happy life to await the heavenly reward later on. People learned to wait and to be patient, because the reward would come later, after death. The Protestant religion taught that one need not wait until the hereafter to receive the reward. Furthermore, according to the belief of predestination, one could discern in the present indications that showed whether God had a benificial eye on one's life. These indications were an enterprising mind, good health, and wealth. The Calvinistic belief in predestination and the related earthly reflection of the divine reward had as its consequence the belief that the period after which the reward was received could be shortened dramatically, which made the fulfillment of expectations more concrete. Furby's critique on the Protestant ethic explanation of learned expectations is weakened further by the fact that the Catholic and Protestant religions have been spread around the world due to passionate missionary work. More than three hundred years of conversions have brought both religions to most people in the world. Conversion brings along with it the commitment to be patient and to delay gratification. So with the spread of both religions, beliefs about learned expectations and beliefs about justice may have been spread as well. It is therefore safe to say that the ubiquity-of-justice phenomenon is compatible with the delay-of-gratification hypothesis. Based on the foregoing remarks, Furby's critique of Lerner's explanation of justice phenomena seems to be inappropriate so far.

Moreover, Furby states that the most important explanation for the ubiquity of justice is that "the fundamental fact about our world is the correlation between the actions we take and the events we experience" (p. 180): the action-outcome model of learned expectations. She states that children are taught that certain actions will lead to certain outcomes. By trial and error and by principles of social learning, such as positive and negative reinforcement (reward and punishment), the growing child learns that valued outcomes can be obtained by performing specific actions. From early childhood on children are instructed to pay attention to the things they are doing. By attending to the consequences of their actions, children learn to pay attention to the efficiency of their actions. The important question, of course, is why do parents teach their children to be attentive to their actions and to take care of the consequences of their actions? The answer to this question may be fundamental for the definition of justice.

The answer to the question could be that parents believe that it is a social requirement to raise their children in this way. Apparently, parents find it necessary to teach their children to behave in such a way that their actions will lead to predictable outcomes as much as possible. The social environment must have given parents reasons to teach their children to be attentive to the consequences of their actions. One may safely assume, therefore, that the changes in how parents raise their children have a social origin and that parents have perceived these changes, have anticipated them, and have modeled and acted accordingly.

The Societal Context

One can imagine that the way societal arrangements develop or are designed affect the subsequent behavior of members of the society. The allowance, relief, and naturalization of increasing numbers of asylum seekers in many countries have changed our conception of what is a fair distribution of rights and fair treatment. In the Netherlands, for example, asylum seekers have easily received allowance, and all have received a stipend whether they worked or not. The increasing number of asylum seekers has brought about a nationwide discussion on the appropriateness of more restricted rules of allowance, relief, and naturalization. What was judged to be fair in the beginning has changed as the stream of asylum seekers has increased.

The aforementioned example can be complemented by many other examples describing the interaction between individuals and society at large. The description and explanation of these phenomena is the task of sociologists and social psychologists. But it took a long time in the history of both disciplines before a theoretical framework was developed that could do justice to the complex interplay between individual and society, and its development. I will show that the introduction of the concept of social figurations is very well suited to explaining phenomena at the individual level as well as at the societal level, and to explaining how these phenomena and their interactions change over time. Moreover, we will see that this conceptualization gives us more insight into the justice motive.

The Social Figuration

According to Elias (1969), people participate in social figurations. Goudsblom (1987) defines a social figuration as "a make-up of individuals who are mutually dependent on each other" (p. 19). The main characteristic of the concept social figuration is the presence of two parties – the established and the outsiders – who struggle for dominance (Elias & Scotson, 1994). The outsiders challenge the power position of the established party. The established party tries to maintain its position by counterforce, and by distinguishing itself culturally (by cultivating new manners) or psychologically (by developing stereotypes about and prejudice toward the outsiders [Tajfel & Turner, 1986]) from the other party. Social figurations may exist for only a short period of time, such as the social figuration of the established and the outsiders in an English town (Elias & Scotson, 1994), or they may exist for a long time, such as the social figuration of the nobility and the bourgeoisie in France (Elias, 1969), or that of the nobility and peasantry in France and England (Moore Jr., 1965).

By introducing the concept of figuration, Elias wanted to be able to describe the dynamics of social processes. Elias states that constellations of individuals change over time, and that these changes are crucial to understanding social life, both individually and collectively. The most important aspect of this analysis is that the behavior of individuals may lead to changes in the social makeup of a group or society, and that these changes in turn affect the beliefs and behaviors of these individuals and their aftermath. The changes are unplanned, and as such are unpredictable, but the consequences point, according to Elias, in the direction of an increasing control of individual behavior and thus shape personality.

In investigating changes in the social makeup of society, Elias studied changes in cultural beliefs in several domains of social life in different parts of historical Europe. The most important in his study were the changes that could be seen in the use of the term "civilized." What "civilized" means has changed dramatically over time, from medieval Europe to modern times. The changes in the definition of the word "civilized" mark changes in beliefs about what it is appropriate to do in interaction with others. With many examples extracted from books on manners, Elias shows how beliefs and opinions about what it is appropriate to do at dinner, in the public bathroom, when dating, have changed over time. In the last part of his monumental book, Elias describes the changes in society's makeup and specifically in the relationship between the two dominant categories in society that coincide with the changes in cultural beliefs and individual behavior: the nobility and the bourgeoisie.

The feudal period had split up most of the land in Europe into small territories where noblemen reigned. The nobleman was master of his territory, fought his wars, and could do with his serfs as he wished; they were completely dependent on him. The serfs worked the soil and produced what they and their master needed. Life was not easy, but quiet, and people were satisfied with their existence, knowing that the reward of living in poverty and sincerity would come in the hereafter.

During the ninth century, dramatic changes took place in Europe. The increase in population meant that the land around the castle no longer produced enough food. People could not live quietly in the vicinity of the castle, work on the soil, and worship God. They had to seek new venues of farming and raising cattle. The noblemen's sons could no longer be offered pieces of land, as the land had already been subdivided too much. Instead, noblemen were forced to try to enlarge their territories in order to keep their power and to support their serfs. The continous succession of wars that followed resulted in territories' growing larger and larger, until eventually the total area was in the hands of a couple of families. Serfs began to work for themselves and, with the help of cloisters, developed new agricultural methods (Braudel, 1989; Landes, 1998). Many of the serfs went into handcrafts, and gradually a new category of people arose: the bourgeoisie, citizens living in towns. The use of coins for the exchange of goods signified the advent of the bourgeosie, and made this category of people, the citizens, economically more and more powerful. To protect themselves from attacks from the outside, the citizens linked themselves with the noblemen, who were now devoid of income. They became more and more dependent on each other, with the nobility sinking and the bourgeiosie rising in the balance.

The noblemen looked down on the up-and-coming bourgeoisie, but their own fate and that of the bourgeoisie were intertwined. To differentiate themselves from the bourgeoisie, the noblemen cultivated their manners and considered themselves civilized compared to bourgeoisie. Their manners were copied by the bourgeoisie, forcing the nobility to develop ever-new etiquette. According to Elias, the new manners were taught to the children, who internalized the underlying norms and values. In this way, people learned to behave more in line with what etiquette prescribed. In the long run, however, the appropriateness of behavior was internalized.

In short, Elias proposed a theory of civilization in which culture, structure, and personality develop and are neatly interwoven. Before discussing the importance of social figurations for the justice motive, I will discuss Elias's thinking in more detail.

With the term "social figurations," Elias emphasizes the dynamic aspects of social life. In contrast to famous sociologists like Talcott Parsons (1956), Elias was more interested in changes in society than in the status quo. As Elias wrote in his Foreword to the second edition of his work (in 1969), sociology has for too long been interested in continuity, viewing change only as an anomaly of the system, as a disequilibrium. Elias conceived of change as an inherent part of life in society. Under the pressure of new economic, technical, or demographic conditions, individuals change their behavior, causing social institutions to change as well, resulting in changes in behavior and in the personality makeup of individuals. With the idea of cycles of action and reaction, Elias circumvents the pitfall of determinism and reification, and at the same time is able to accomodate the relativism of symbolic interactionism (Berger & Berger, 1972).

Social Figuration Revisited

Despite the advantages of Elias's approach to societal and individual changes, his theory has some serious disadvantages when it comes to illuminating the origins and development of behavior in general and of just behavior in particularly. One major disadvantage is its strong reliance on Freud's theory of psychodynamics. In line with Freud, Elias assumes that human beings are endowded with drives, of which one of the most important is the libido or sexual drive. In the course of the civilization process, the uncontrolled expression of the libido is restricted by the requirements and rules of society. Elias's main idea is that the more civilization progresses, the more restricted people's behavior will become. The mechanism that is responsible for the suppression of the drives is the superego. The do's and don'ts that are enforced by adults as representatives of society (*Fremdzwang*) are incorporated into the self, the superego (*Selbstzwang*). The superego is the gatekeeper that guards the drive-driven thoughts and actions.

A critical revision of Elias's ideas is necessary in order to deal with some of the weak parts of his theory. Three issues I will mention here briefly.

Elias describes personality as consisting of drives and mechanisms to restrict drive-driven behavior – specifically, the id, ego, and superego – and predicts that the development of society and personality inevitably reflect Freud's psychodynamic theory. That seems like circular reasoning.

Moreover, according to Elias, history can be described as an unplanned process that reflects an ever-increasing restraint of drive-driven behavior. This reasoning seems to be logically inconsistent. It is hard to believe that unplanned processes that start and end randomly can produce linearly increasing restraints on individuals. In addition,

Duerr (1988) offers convincing evidence that a linear process of increasing restraint of sexual habits is very unlikely. Duerr's historical overview of the sexual preferences and behaviors of individuals in Europe during the last seven hundred years shows clearly that the do's and don'ts with regard to sexual behavior vary from time period to time period and from class to class. In some periods sexual restraints are less severe than they were in earlier periods, while these restrictions should be more severe, according to Elias. A third issue of the theory has to do with Elias's emphasis on the struggle between nobility and bourgeoisie in France. The continual struggle for dominance between nobility and bourgeoisie was, according to Elias, most visible in what is now the country of France. The theory of civilization that Elias develops is based mainly on what happened between the nobility and bourgeoisie in that country. And although the histories of other countries in Europe are in many respects different from that of France, Elias is justified in restricting his analysis to the developments in France. What happened in other countries may be different from what happened in France, but that does not invalidate his theoretical premise. However, even in France, the growing interdependence between nobility and bourgeoisie was not the only social figuration that occurred, and maybe not even the most important one. From time to time other figurations became visible that had a noticeable influence on societal processes as well as on the beliefs and actions of individuals.

One such important social figuration is that between the gentry and the peasantry, which, Moore (1968) describes as operating during the period analyzed by Elias. Moore describes the struggle between the two classes in society and shows that the way the struggle proceeded resulted in revolutions both from above (Germany and Japan) and from below (Russia and China) and in democratic regimes (England, the United States, and France). Another important struggle in Europe during the last millenium was the one between the clergy and dissidents. During many periods in European history, clashes between clergy and dissidents erupted, with the Inquisition being the most famous instance of the dominant group acting to repress the deviants (Eco, 1984).

It seems to me that a refinement of Elias's ideas on continuity and change in human society and human life is necessary to accomodate recent findings and analyses. One refinement is the recognition of the transient character of social figurations. Social figurations may always exist, in the sense that categories of individuals strive against each other, but in certain times this struggle is more virulent than in other times. Moreover, several social figurations may coexist at the same time, although they may differ in their virulence. The working class and the capitalist class still form a figuration, but nowedays the strivings for power are less virulent, and certainly far less virulent than they were during the 1960s and 1970s. The working class and capitalist class figuration is nowadays less virulent than the figuration that exists between settled Dutch citizens and political and economic refugees from other countries: the so-called asylum seekers. In conclusion, the intensity of conflict between parties in a social figuration can vary across time, and can vary from figuration to figuration within a given period of time.

Montaillou: An Historical Account

It is safe to state that the struggle between groups in society is mainly one regarding the allocation of scarce resources, specifically economically defined, or defined in terms of territory or power. My statement is that such struggles will affect individuals' ideas of what are appropriate actions. By conceiving of justice as meeting expectations based on action-outcome chains, one can assume that expectations about rewards, and about procedures, will change over time depending on the kind of struggle. The struggle for power and domination among groups in society has never been absent, but the groups involved in the struggle have changed, as have the critical action-outcome sequences and hence the conceptions of justice. Support for this claim can be found by investigating beliefs and attitudes about justice held by people in previous historical periods. Many philosophers have written about justice, but however insightful their thoughts are, the beliefs and attitudes of ordinary citizens are known only through indirect sources of information. From these latter sources we know, for example, that Aristotle distinguished three types of justice: the just behavior of the state toward the citizens, the just behavior of citizens toward the state, and the justice done by citizens toward each other. One may assume that these types of justice reflect in some way the prevalent thoughts of the citizens of Athens, either because they were present in everyday life or because they were conspicuously absent. The historical writings give us insight into the intellectual climate of that time as reflected in the philosophers' thoughts, but they give us no insight into the common man's thoughts and feelings about the subject matter.

Although history often uncharitably leaves us with no insight into the thoughts and feelings of common people, it occasionally provides us with useful material, although often gathered for totally different purposes. One such lucky occasion – lucky for the researcher, not for the people involved – was the Inquisition during the Middle Ages in Europe, with its endless interrogations of people as part of a religious purge. In one case, the questions of the interrogators and the answers of people who were imprisoned were recorded. The volumes were preserved in the dusty archives of the Vatican, where they still are available for researchers. Le Roy Ladurie (1985) has translated the Latin text into French and edited the volumes into a readable single volume that has been translated into Dutch. The Dutch translation was the source that I used to try to find out what people's beliefs and attitudes were with regard to the topic of justice. But before I will discuss my findings, let me first give some background information about the time and place and reasons for the inquisitorial investigation.

The Inquisition took place in a southern area of France, in the eastern part of the Pyrenees, between France and Spain. At the beginning of the fourteenth century the dissident group known as the *Waldenzen* (Kathars) settled in this area after being persecuted and driven out of other parts of southern France. A growing number of Catholics in that part of France became followers of the *Waldenzen*, which threatened the canons of the church and prompted them to react. The Inquisition lasted from 1318 to 1325 and resulted in the imprisonment of a great many people. One focus of the Inquisition were the villagers of Montaillou (Le Roy Ladurie, 1985). The clergy was convinced that these villagers had had contact with the *Waldenzen*, who had seduced them into accepting their religious beliefs.

The inquisition court was initiated and carried out by Jacques Fournier, the bishop of Pamiers, the later Pope Benedictus XII, who not only was interested in matters of religious belief and heredicy, but also was very curious about the style of living, daily routine, and opinions of the villagers. The bishop was present during most of the interrogations and very often directed the interrogations himself. Clerics were present to write down all that was revealed. After the interrogations concluded at the end of the day, the clerics compared their writings and produced a final text. The meticulousness of these recordings of the interrogations as well as the fact that they cover a broad range of opinions and behaviors of the villagers gives us an excellent view of the daily life of that time in that part of France.

About 1300, the parish Montaillou counted between 200 and 250 inhabitants. The village of Montaillou provided twenty-five suspects and a couple of witnesses, who gave very detailed information and accounts of the events in that period. Montaillou was situated high up in the mountains and overlooked beautiful scenery that unfolded into the plains in front of the village. The castle was at the highest point of the slope, with the village at its foot. The area around the village was partly cultivated and divided into lots of land of about twenty to thirty acres, which were used for agriculture and stock breeding by their owners. The land was cultivated by a wooden slide plough, a sort of wooden beam pulled by an ox, donkey, or cow. There was some division of labor, especially between men and women. The men ploughed, reaped, and harvested the crop; they also hunted and caught fish. The women worked hard in the fields and in and around the farm; they also cared for water, fires, the vegetable gardens, and the cooking. They bound grain into sheaves and weeded the land. When the children were old enough, they tended the herd. There was no further division of labor. For specialized work, the inhabitants of Montaillou went to the nearest town to visit craftsmen. Carts were not used in the village, nor was iron equipment. The village had no blacksmith.

In the woods around Montaillou, the Kathars hid themselves from the clergy and their accomplices. They earned a living by repairing clothes for the villagers and by making gloves. The feudal power in the area lay in the hands of the count of Foix, who was represented in Montaillou by the *chatelaine* and the bailiff. The *chatelaine* maintained the public order, and the bailiff controled and collected the taxes (tenths). The clergy in the area was represented by the Black Friars, whose armed forces terrorized the community. A third power was formed by the bishop of Parmiers, and a fourth power was the king of France, whose control extended over all of France except Burgundy and the south of France.

The social distance between the nobility and the peasants in Montaillou was small. The most important gap was the one between the clergy and the peasants. The inhabitants of Montaillou had a deep resentment of the clergy's wealth. This belief about wealth was related to beliefs about the allocation of resources and to their own religious beliefs. Wealth was viewed as a source of sin. One of the suspects at the Inquisition court explained it as follows:" You have lived in richness. You have lived in splendor. You have known so many worldly pleasures. How could you be without sins" (Le Roy Ladurie, 1985, p. 433).

The villagers were well aware of the poor people in their village, as they constituted about 25% of the villagers. Beggars, those who had been driven from homes, and those who had suffered from the Inquisition were one large portion of the poor. These people were given alms. In offering alms, no distinction was made between villagers and strangers. The alms were, according to Le Roy Ladurie, not given solely out of goodness and justice. The generosity was explained in terms of selfishness as well, because giving alms was considered a good means of saving one's own soul.

Labor was not respected by the villagers, despite the fact that people worked long days and the system of taxation was exploitative. People in Montaillou took the time to rest, to eat, to exchange news and views. People liked the *dolce far niente*, to sit in the sun or at the fire and to be deloused (Le Roy Ladurie, 1985, p. 443). Labor was not valued by the villagers. Labor was performed mainly for their own salvation, and not for becoming rich.

Social Figuration and Justice

I was able to examine only part of the records of the interrogations. And this part was not selected explicitly to shed light on opinions about justice. So, studying the original records will be necessary to get a clear picture of the justice-related opinions and behaviors of the villagers. But until that time, we will have to do with the present material, of which I present only a small but relevant part in this chapter. I have relied on the exact text of the villagers during the interrogations. What does this material say about the justice beliefs of the villagers?

There was a growing resistance to two decisions taken by the officials of the Catholic Church – decisions that according to many people, among them the villagers, were not in agreement with the life of poverty of Jesus as they knew it from the New Testament. The first decision was the selling of indulgences by the Catholic clergy, and the second was the collection of taxes by the same clergy. During this time it had become common practice among members of the Catholic Church to strive to live in wealth and in material abundance, which they did by selling indulgences to wealthy nobles and town dwellers.

For many people these practices were not acceptable, because they disrespected the vows of poverty espoused by Jesus Christ. Most of the dissident movements of the time focused on the growing wealth of the church. These dissident movements grew, were suppressed during the persecution, and reappeared after the Inquisition. The inevitable reaction from the clergy, each time protest erupted, was the installation of an Inquisition court. The Catholic Church was afraid of the power of the dissident movements and reacted violently each time protest erupted. The dissidents were accused of having commited the most devilish acts, were banned from religious life, and were often tortured. The documents of the Fournier inquisition show clearly the presence of the two main characteristics of a social figuration of clergy and dissidents: maintenance of power by the dominant group and their derogation and stereotyping of the less powerful party, the dissidents.

The peasants did not believe that working hard would do them any good. Becoming rich by working hard was not an aspiration of the peasants. Their life was in the hands of God, and they did not believe that they could do anything about it. In other words, they believed that they had hardly any control over either their present or their future life. They relied on the life in the hereafter. Action-outcome beliefs of the peasants were rather simple and had no impact on their daily lives. Equality for all was the logical consequence of their religious beliefs.

Conclusions

The virulence of the social figuration of clergy and dissidents waxed and waned, and conflicts between the parties were sometimes visible in different parts of Europe during the following centuries. What remained unchanged was the dissidents' rejection of the clergy's wealth obtained by selling indulgences. As a consequence of the conflict, peasants became more susceptible to the advantages of a better life. Gradually, the opinions of the peasants with regard to work changed. Working on the fields became more and more valued. Moreover, new inventions, such as the iron plough, made the labor less harsh. The use of horses made the ploughing faster and less strenuous (Landes, 1998). The peasants obtained knowledge and expertise from the cloisters with regard to improving seeds and maintaining and harvesting the crops. The crops became more and more abundant and could profitably be sold to the wealthy town dwellers and others.

The action-outcome chains changed. Peasants learned that good preparation, knowledge, and hard work rendered more. The farmers taught their children to behave accordingly. The more these actions were rewarded by the parents, the more likely such actions were to become valued by the children for their own sake. The equality and need principles were gradually complemented by the application of the equity principle to evaluate the justice of one's own and others' actions.

Relating the justice motive to principles of the Protestant ethic is surely defensible. What I have tried to show in this chapter is that, although the emergence of Protestantism had a major impact on the development of the justice motive, the roots of these developments lay in an even earlier past and are related to important other developments in society and personality.

REFERENCES

Aristotle (1987). *The Nicomachean ethics.* Translated by David Ross. Oxford: Oxford University Press.

Berger, P. L., & Berger, B. (1972). *Sociology.* New York: Basic Books.

Braudel, F. (1989). *Beschaving, economie en kapitalisme (15de-18de eeuw). Deel 2. Het Spel van de Handel* [Civilization, economy and capitalism, 15th–18th century. Part 2. The game of trade]. Amsterdam: Uitgeverij Contact.

Brockner, J., & Wiesenfeld, B. M. (1994). The interactive impact of procedural and outcome fairness on reactions to a decision: The effects of what you do depend on how you do it. *Psychological Bulletin, 120,* 189–208.

Duerr, H. P. (1988). *Nacktheit und Scham. Der Mythos vom Zivilisationsprozess* [Nudity and shame. The myth of the process of civilization]. Frankfurt am Main: Suhrkamp Verlag.

Eco, U. (1983). *De naam van de roos* [The name of the rose]. Amsterdam: Bert Bakker.

Elias, N. (1969). *Über den Prozess der Zivilisation. Soziogenetische und Psychogenetische Untersuchungen* [About the civilization process. A psychological and sociological investigation]. Bern: Francke Verlag.

Elias, N., & Scotson, J. L. (1994). *The established and the outsiders.* London: SAGE.

Furby, L. (1986). Psychology and justice. In R. Cohen (Ed.), *Justice: Views from the social sciences* (pp. 153–204). New York: Plenum.

Goudsblom, J. (1992). *Vuur en beschaving* [Fire and civilization]. Amsterdam: Meulenhoff.

Landes, D. S. (1998). *The wealth and poverty of nations: Why some are so rich and some so poor.* New York: Norton.

Lerner, M. J. (1977). The justice motive: Some hypotheses as to its origins and forms. *Journal of Personality, 45,* 1–52.

(1980). *The belief in a just world.* New York: Plenum.

Le Roy Ladurie, E. (1985). *Montaillou: A dissident village in the Pyrenees, 1294–1324.* Amsterdam: Bert Bakker.

Mikula, G., & Lerner, M. J. (1994). Justice in close relationships: An introduction. In M. J. Lerner & G. Mikula (Eds.), *Entitlement and the affectional bond* (pp. 1–10). New York: Plenum.

Miller, D. T., & Ratner, R. K. (1996). The power of the myth of self-interest. In L. Montada & M. L. Lerner (Eds.), *Current societal concerns about justice* (pp. 25–48). New York: Plenum.

Montada, L. (1998). Belief in a just world: A hybrid of justice motive and self-interest? In L. Montada & M. J. Lerner (Eds.), *Responses to victimization and belief in a just world* (pp. 217–246). New York: Plenum.

Moore, B., Jr. (1968). *Social origins of dictatorship and democracy. Lord and peasant in the making of the modern world.* Harmondsworth: Penquin.

Parsons, P. (1951). *The social system.* Glencoe, IL.: The Free Press.

Tajfel, H., & Turner, J. (1986). The social identity theory of intergroup behavior. In S. Worchel (Ed.), *Psychology of intergroup relations* (pp. 7–24). Chicago: Nelson Hall.

Vermunt, R. (1989). Happiness and justice: A social psychological view on Ultimate Reality and Meaning. *Ultimate Reality and Meaning, Interdisciplinary Studies in the Philosophy of Understanding, 12* (4), 272–282.

Vermunt, R., Spaans, E., & Zorge, F. (1989). Satisfaction and well-being of Dutch students. *Social Indicators Research, 21* (1), 1–27.

Walster, E., Walster, G. W., & Berscheid, E. (1978). *Equity: Theory and research.* Boston: Allyn and Bacon.

5. Perverse Justice and Perverse Norms: Another Turn of the Screw

JOSÉ-MIGUEL FERNÁNDEZ-DOLS

Introduction

What kind of ethical impact can be claimed for social psychology? For a European, this question is important. The ancestors of European social scientists were nineteenth-century thinkers such as Comte, Marx, Spencer, St. Simon, and Fourier – those brilliant and creative scholars who proposed new models of society designed to overcome human suffering and injustice. Following this first generation came a second wave that included men such as Emile Durkheim and Max Weber, theorists who were more skeptical, even pessimistic, with respect to the founders' schemes for changing the fate of humankind. Max Weber's *Wissenschaft* as *Beruf* is, from this point of view, more than an argument for social scientists' political neutrality: It is a manifesto about the end of an era replete with promises of scientific redemption for humankind. Subsequently, academic social science migrated to America, where the emphasis on scientific respectability came to predominate over concerns about ethical accountability.

But Europeans have always felt a certain nostalgia for that golden age in which social scientists were – sometimes literally – the high priests of a new doctrine, capable of increasing the ethical intelligence of the common people and providing a historical direction for their fellow citizens.

This nostalgia is probably less intense among social psychologists than among other European scholars. For decades, European social psychologists have focused on acquiring the scientific respectability of their American colleagues, either by imitating them or by criticizing them. Nevertheless, some scholars have begun to question the lack of societal impact of social psychologists (e.g., Moscovici, 1989), and a few have even dared to advocate a new discipline, societal psychology (Himmelweit & Gaskell, 1990).

Societal psychology is still undefined, but some of the recent discussions of this topic suggest a longing for the good old days of Europeans such as Lewin, Wertheimer (see Luchins & Luchins, 1978), and others who, once in America, began to "cook up" a new social psychology in everyday American settings, with informal gatherings in crowded bars, heated debates in kitchens, and brown-bag informal seminars around the master's table. In other words, societal psychology appears to consist in nothing more than a demand for a new infusion of courage and ethical responsiveness into social psychology.

Lerner's Psychology of Suffering

I met Melvin Lerner in a social psychologist's – Joe de Rivera's – kitchen. Usually, when social psychologists first meet, their conversation is a hodgepodge of academic gossip, monologues about their own work, and vague promises of future collaboration. With Mel – in Joe's old kitchen – the conversation turned immediately and comfortably to an abstract discussion of issues such as peace, justice, human suffering, and the role of contemporary nations and state bureaucracies, intermingled with allusions to specific empirical studies of his own or others. This first meeting epitomizes the distinctive character of Melvin Lerner's contribution to social psychology: an abstract, empirically based reflection with a moral punch. A prototypical example of that good old "societal social psychology" many European psychologists yearn for. A perfect balance between ethical accountability and scientific respectability.

The most obvious key word for summarizing Lerner's work is "justice," but I prefer another one: "suffering." Lerner's approach to justice consists, in many ways, in an inquiry into the doubly disgraceful fate of those innocents who not only suffer injustice but, to make matters worse, are blamed for their own misery (Lerner, 1980).

What makes this predicament particularly tragic is the chilling discovery that it is caused by the existence of a basic, primitive ethical motive. The justice motive and human suffering are linked, in Lerner's model, in a paradoxical way: The more a person is motivated to look for justice in everyday encounters, the more that person will be willing to blame innocent victims for their uncontrollable fate. In other words, a strong justice motive in combination with low power to eliminate injustice can increase, rather than alleviate, human suffering. As Lerner describes it (Lerner, 1980, 1981), the justice motive has another interesting and rather perverse feature: It does not lead people to actively fight for justice, but rather to passively believe that justice will prevail over injustice sooner or later.

In societal terms, Lerner's psychology is a discourse about how part of the daily dose of cruelty in the world is – paradoxically – based on beliefs and motives that any well-intentioned educator would be happy to instill in his or her own pupils. In fact, I feel that an important, and still not completely explored, application of the belief in a just world concept is the study of political cruelty. The most frightening feature of all past and current cruel regimes is how often they are based on a sincere and ethically inspired commitment to a just world. The regimes of Hitler, Stalin, Mao Zedong, the Khmer Rouge, and other contemporary tyrannies were *originally* the work of rulers driven by a utopian, well-minded vision of a just world and an extreme sense of certitude about how to create this just world (see Chirot, 1994). This certitude led to the killing of millions of people and, unfortunately, to a worldwide culture of cruelty that has infused many political regimes of the twentieth century. For example, the Nazi diaspora has taught the art of persecution and torture to the ruling elites of a dozen distant and apparently unconnected regimes (see Glover, 2000).

Ethical Motives and their Paradoxes: An Example

Spaniards, and Europeans in general, should be particularly concerned about this tragic loop that links ethical concerns and political cruelty. European (current and past) history is, for example, plagued by religious wars that combine the most vicious brutality with the most delicate ethical concerns. In the same vein, most of the European colonial enterprises were infused with sincere religious and ethical concerns that had unexpected, perverse effects. Among these cases, there is one that is particularly worth recalling for Spaniards. It concerns the heated intellectual debate between Las Casas and Sepulveda during the sixteenth century. Although unfamiliar to many people, this debate can be considered, given its political consequences, one of the most important scholarly confrontations in world history. Let me describe it briefly, following Parry's (1981) classic work.

The subject of the debate was the social, political, and ethical status of Native Americans and, as a consequence, the social and political organization of America. Las Casas, a Dominican friar, was the more famous of the two antagonists, largely because of his book *Brevisima relación de la destrucción de las Indias*, a denouncement of the atrocities of Spaniards in the New World. Sepulveda was a reputable humanist and academic, and a friend of Erasmus.

Las Casas defended a progressive view of natives' human rights and the role of Europeans in America. Indians were subjects of the crown, and no European settler was entitled to rule over them; the Spanish Empire should be based, said Las Casas, on the freedom of the Indians and respect for their culture. Europeans had no particular privilege in America – they were just private citizens among other private citizens.

Sepulveda defended a slightly improved version of the status quo existing in American society at that time. He defended the *encomiendas*, a system that, technically, did not enslave natives, but that did accord Europeans a privileged, powerful, and paternalistic position vis-à-vis the natives. The European settlers were responsible for the Indians in their *encomiendas*, a responsibility they shared with individual representatives of the Spanish crown.

The clash between Las Casas and Sepulveda reached such levels of intensity that, in 1550, the Spanish emperor convened a formal debate between them before a panel of eminent jurists. The winner had an important influence on Spanish law during the next hundred years, particularly with regard to the *Ordenanzas sobre Descubrimientos*, a law promulgated in 1573 and intended to be the fundamental framework for the regulation of discoveries and colonial policies. Indeed, the president of the *Consejo* of the Indies ordered that the winner's manuscripts be brought to the site of the institution during the drafting of the law. The loser, on the other hand, was dismissed, and was denied permission even to publish his main book.

Who was the winner and who the loser of the debate? Interestingly enough, the decisive winner was Las Casas. The conception of America that Sepulveda advocated was too stark and harsh for the religious and ethical sensitivity of the crown and its representatives. Las Casas's ideas promoted a body of laws whose ethical goals were extraordinary in their progressiveness, particularly compared to the rather pragmatic ones of other countries, which were generally concerned with the economic exploitation of new lands. The ethical prescriptions of these laws did not please everyone, however. The Spaniards already established in America resented the fact that the laws did not recognize their discoveries and conquests. Moreover, the everyday defense of natives by public officials, remarkable for the time, required such bureaucratic control that a slow and gigantic bureaucracy emerged that paralyzed both American and Spanish society.

The debate between Las Casas and Sepulveda is a good example of how focusing on ethics can have unexpected consequences. The Spanish leaders were confronted with a historically unavoidable combination of events, the discovery of America and the migration of Europeans from an overpopulated continent. The circumstances were so extraordinary that there were no accepted standards for judging who was responsible for the natives' suffering. In fact, the Spaniards had to invent a new discipline, international law, in order to deal with all the new and puzzling moral, political, and administrative problems posed by the new territories. Were the natives human beings? Were the natives citizens of any state? What were the relationships between citizens' rights and religious beliefs? What were the rights of those who founded the "new" territories?

Lerner's (1996) justice motive analysis of "human casualties in the pursuit of corporate efficiency" has a clear parallel to this story – in which "casualties" has a frighteningly more literal meaning. In this vein, just as contemporary managers cannot be considered personally responsible for the market forces that lead to a restructuring process, Spanish leaders should not be held responsible for the series of calamities (and particularly of epidemics) that decimated the American natives. Nevertheless, as managers feel considerable guilt and demoralization, we can assume that Spanish leaders' moral sensibilities were engaged, leading them to sponsor the just-mentioned debate and to agree with the arguments of Las Casas.

Within the justice motive framework, it is not surprising to see that Las Casas's position was much more attractive than that of Sepulveda, since it was inspired by his emotional and compassionate reaction to harmful actions and victims, that is, to the outcome of the discovery process. In other words, we can assume that Spanish leaders, in an obscure, nonrational way, felt guilt (Lerner & Golberg, 1999), which Las Casas eloquently addressed, giving rise to one of the large-scale examples of justice motive consequences in the history of humankind. Laws were slowly deprived of their original spirit, and the decimated Indians were replaced by African slaves. Europeans circumvented Las Casas's doctrine: Africans were considered not as subjects of the crown but as mere objects of trade.

Beyond the Justice Motive

Unfortunately, Las Casas's triumph, or the triumph of a courageous pioneer of the defense of human rights, is not just a case of paradoxical justice motive consequences. In fact, the justice motive framework allows us to understand the first act of this drama – the moral intuition that leads to the recognition of the natives' rights by the Spanish crown – but not the second one, the immediate drafting of a law according to the official moral doctrine.

This "second act" of the drama, and its tragic consequences (the drafting of idealistic rules that undermined the moral and administrative fabric of the Spanish Empire), has provided a focus for my research over the last decade. My own findings and those of my collaborators suggest that, apart from the justice motive, people feel a need for regulation and for the imposition on the world of a normative framework that is capable of guaranteeing some kind of moral order (or at least of ensuring progress toward it).

In other words, our enlarged version of the justice motive framework would include a two-stage process: a justice motive followed by a normative imperative. The normative imperative strengthens and enlarges the consequences of the justice motive, because it institutionalizes them. It makes explicit and coercive what was originally implicit and emotional.

The psychological need for norms, and the deleterious consequences of a society in which this need is not satisfied, has been described, interestingly, not by psychologists but by Emile Durkheim, one of the founders of academic sociology. According to Durkheim (1897), a lack of norms causes collective psychological distress, and ultimately suicide. Interestingly, Durkheim's distress is an emotional phenomenon: Norms are like a "splint" for human "passions," a way of regulating individuals' emotional lives.

What kind of emotions might be regulated by norms? As Max Weber pointed out, there is one particular kind of norm that is especially linked to emotion: Legitimate norms are those perceived as morally right. Their transgression triggers intense guilt in the transgressor, and, for this reason, they are the only ones that guarantee long-term effective social order. Durkheim's scenario (people committing suicide because of a lack of effective norms in their society) is particularly convincing in those cases where legitimate norms are lacking.

The Normative Imperative

If Durkheim and Weber were right, human beings' need for norms would parallel their need for justice. We could say that there is a normative imperative: People need a world in which justice is imposed by a body of legitimate, rightful rules.

Oceja and Rodriguez-Mosquera (1993) and Oceja and Fernandez-Dols (1998) tested the existence of this normative imperative – namely, the extent to which people perceive legitimate norms as necessary in themselves, independent of their efficacy for achieving a particular goal or any other formal consideration.

Subjects were requested to position three important features of any formal norm (e.g., a law) on a ten-step ladder (Cantril, 1965). The features were legitimacy, efficacy, and validity. Subjects were asked to put these features in the order of importance they gave them – the more important the feature, the closer it should placed to the tenth step, while less important features should be put on lower steps. Legitimacy was defined as ethical rightfulness, and efficacy as the capacity for achieving the objectives set by those who establish the norm. Validity was the degree to which a formal norm is supported by an institution.

Different versions of this questionnaire were filled out by subjects from the United States, Canada, Chile, Guatemala, Holland, Hong Kong, and Spain. In all of them, legitimacy was perceived as the most necessary feature of any formal norm, over and above both efficacy and validity. Even though we found interesting relative differences across samples, there was a striking consensus with respect to the primacy of legitimacy. For example, Oceja and Rodriguez-Mosquera (1993) reported that the average rating of legitimacy was 8.84 in Spain, 8.9 in Holland, 8.31 in the United States, and 9.10 in Guatemala, where the corresponding ratings for efficacy were 6.54, 6.29, 7.71, and 7.21. Validity obtained systematically lower ratings in all samples (5.57, 5.83, 5.70, and 6.43). In short, consistent with the normative imperative hypothesis, there was a widespread strong need for moral norms, irrespective of their efficacy or formal features.

The Normative Imperative and Human Suffering: Another Turn of the Screw

Assuming that people need and expect legitimate rules, and that some cultures are probably more demanding than others in this respect,

Fernandez-Dols (1992, 1993) proposed a mechanism that may put innocent victims of the normative imperative in jeopardy. I called this mechanism *"normas perversas."*

Normas perversas (perverse norms) is a dramatic but perhaps misleading designation. The label does *not* allude to formal norms that are intrinsically perverse or ethically incorrect: In fact, it alludes to the opposite case. *"Normas perversas"* are those formal norms that are seen as legitimate, and whose transgression involves sanctions, but which, for some reason, are transgressed by most of the members of the social group. In other words, perverse norms are "openly accepted" as correct or even necessary by the group, but are not observed.

The combination of a normative imperative and coercive power seems to be one of the basic recipes for human suffering. For example, the Prohibition of 1920 in the United States was a well-intentioned law that, according to its main promoter, Senator Volstead, would remove crime and vice from American society. Unfortunately, Prohibition provoked generalized transgression, new and rampant forms of crime, corruption among policemen and politicians, and a general disenchantment that led to its abolition in 1933. In fact, the current debate on the feasibility of the prohibition of drugs (e.g., MacCoun, 1993) might be seen as a debate about the extent to which drug prohibition is another instance of the perverse effects of an ill-directed normative imperative.

The main perverse consequence of generally transgressed coercive norms is not merely societal dysfunction. According to the normative imperative hypothesis, the main consequences of a frustrated normative imperative are similar to those of a frustrated justice motive as described by Lerner.

The first of these consequences is blaming those persons in positions of authority who try to enforce these generally transgressed norms. Enforcers in this situation are perceived as arbitrary and unfair. This effect is particularly insidious because people in this situation are often unable to make a distinction between unfair enforcers and those who try to enforce a generally transgressed but ethically correct norm.

The second consequence of having a social situation ruled by a generally transgressed coercive norm is that transgressions of other norms become more acceptable. People begin to sympathize with irregularities aimed at evading the requirements not just of perverse norms, but of all other norms as well.

Empirical Support

Oceja and Fernandez-Dols (1992; Oceja, 1997) conducted a series of experiments designed to study people's reactions to the effects of a transgressed coercive norm by assessing their judgments about the characters in a case story.

For example, in one of the experiments subjects read one of three slightly different versions of a case story that described a game in which players tried to guess the meanings of a set of words, and a judge decided who was the winner. The best performance obviously consisted of guessing the highest number of correct answers. All three versions of the case story told of how the judge named a winner among the players, and how one of the players (who did not win the prize) stole an ashtray as everybody was leaving the room. The only difference between the three case stories consisted in the players' fulfillment of the norm principle of the game and the behavior of the judge. In the "perverse-norm situation," no player was capable of fulfilling the norms of the game (i.e., no player correctly guessed the meanings of the words). In the "fair situation," the judge chose as winner the best player. In the "unfair situation," the judge chose as winner a player who did not deserve to win (i.e., not the player with the highest number of hits). The subjects' affective judgments of the key characters (the judge, the winner, and the player who stole the ashtray at the end of the session) were measured by semantic differential scales. Comparison across the conditions revealed support for the hypotheses. First, whereas the fair-situation judge was evaluated positively, the judge in the perverse-norm condition was evaluated as negatively as the judge in the openly unfair situation, even though the subjects did not have any proof of the perverse-norm judge's unfair behavior. Second, the perverse-norm situation appeared to make people more tolerant of transgressions generally: In the perverse-norm condition subjects did not show a negative affective evaluation of the character who stole the ashtray.

The generalizability of these findings was supported in the experimental debriefing that followed. Over 90% of the subjects in the perverse-norm situation believed that the features of the case story were similar to real-life situations they had experienced. Furthermore, the debriefing revealed that people perceived a basic equivalence between the unfair and the perverse-norm judges. In these two cases, attributions about the causes of the judge's decision focused on the judge's arbitrariness and previous personal relationship with the winner (51% in the perverse-norm condition and 44% in the unfair condition). In contrast, the behavior of the judge in the fair condition was attributed primarily to the validity of the winner's answers (76%).

These findings are particularly striking if we consider that the subjects were very young undergraduate students with no experience in professional or political settings. The emotional reaction we created in this experiment may be a small-scale representation of a frustrated normative imperative that leads people to blame other victims of the situation and to build up a cynical attitude with respect to any kind of transgression.

This hypothesis was confirmed in a more ecologically valid study (Fernandez-Dols and Oceja, 1994) about a "real" everyday event: the general transgression of speed limits in Spain. Spanish drivers and nondrivers were presented with two case stories in which someone, presumably a policeman or civil servant, allowed a driver to escape a fine. Subjects had to judge the morality of the conduct described in the case on a seven-point scale from 0 (very bad in all cases) to 7 (very good in all cases). In one case the fine was for exceeding the speed limit (universally exceeded in Spain), while in the other case the fine was for driving with more than the legally permitted level of alcohol in the blood. Both cases were described in a neutral, impersonal way that did not suggest any particular negative consequence of these behaviors, nor any circumstances that would make one offence more serious than the other. As we predicted, drivers and nondrivers were significantly more tolerant when the fine concerned the speed limit (the average judgment was 3.13, i.e., close to the central, neutral point of the scale) than when the fine concerned drinking (M = 1.60). These findings suggest that people may tolerate irregularities concerning those norms that are generally transgressed.

Conclusions

In our view, a frustrated normative imperative can lead to negative emotional reactions with respect to social institutions, with long-lasting and negative societal consequences.

A final example, taken from Robert Putnam (1993), may serve to summarize the pattern of distrust and passive cynicism we have found in our experiments. Analyzing the differences in modern Italy's civic and uncivic communities, Putnam vividly describes how mutual distrust is tightly intertwined with the impossibility of accomplishing a normative imperative:

> These remarkably consistent differences go to the heart of the distinction between civic and uncivic communities. Collective life in the civic regions is eased by the expectation that others will probably follow the rules. Knowing that others will, *you* are more likely to go along, too, thus fulfilling *their* expectations. In the less civic regions nearly everyone expects everyone else to violate the rules. It seems foolish to obey the traffic laws or the tax code or the welfare rules, if you expect everyone else to cheat. (The Italian term for such naive behavior is *fesso,* which also means "cuckolded.") So you cheat, too, and in the end everyone's dolorous, cynical expectations are confirmed. (Putnam, 1993, pp. 111–112)

I think Putnam's quotation describes, like the earlier example of the ill-fated policy of the Spanish Empire, a combination of a frustrated justice motive and a normative imperative that is equally frustrated. I also believe that these phenomena are prevalent in our social life, and should be seriously addressed from a theoretical and a practical point of view.

Finally, I hope I have done "justice" to Melvin Lerner's ideas and not strayed from my well-intentioned (and therefore potentially dangerous!) quest for the moral punch that social psychology has never completely lost.

REFERENCES

Cantril, H. (1965). *The pattern of human concerns.* New Brunswick, NJ: Rutgers University Press.

Chirot, D. (1994). *Modern tyrants: The power and prevalence of evil in our age.* New York: The Free Press.

Durkheim, E. (1897). *Le Suicide.* Paris: Alkan.

Fernandez-Dols, J. M. (1992). Procesos escabrosos en Psicología Social: el concepto de norma perversa [Thorny processes in social psychology: The concept of perverse norm]. *Revista de Psicología Social, 7,* 243–255.

Fernández-Dols, J. M. (1993). Norma perversa: Hipótesis teóricas [Perverse norms: Theoretical hypotheses]. *Psicothema, 5* (suplemento), 91–101.

Fernández-Dols, J. M., & Oceja, L. V. (1994). Efectos cotidianos de las normas perversas en la tolerancia a la corrupción [Everyday effects of perverse norms and acceptance of corruption]. *Revista de Psicología Social, 9,* 3–12.

Glover, J. (2000). *Humanity: A moral history of the twentieth century.* New Haven: Yale University Press.

Himmelweit, H. T., & Gaskell, G. (Eds.) (1990). *Societal psychology.* Newbury Park, CA: Sage.

Lerner, M. J. (1980). *The belief in a just world: A fundamental delusion.* New York: Plenum.

(1981). The justice motive in human relations: Some thoughts of what we know and need to know about justice. In M. J. Lerner & S. C. Lerner (Eds.), *The justice motive in social behavior* (pp. 11–35). New York: Plenum.

(1996). Victims without harmdoers: Human casualties in the pursuit of corporate efficiency. In L. Montada & M. J. Lerner (Eds.), *Current societal concerns about justice* (pp. 155–170). New York: Plenum.

Lerner, M. J., & Goldberg, J. H. (1999). When do decent people blame victims? The differing effects of the explicit/rational and implicit/experiential cognitive systems. In S. Chaiken & Y. Trope (Eds.), *Dual-process theories in social psychology* (pp. 627–640). New York: Guilford.

Luchins, A. S., & Luchins, E. H. (1978). *Revisiting Wertheimer's seminars. Volume II: Problems in social psychology.* Cranbury, NJ: Associated University Presses.

MacCoun, R. J. (1993). Drugs and the law: A psychological analysis of drug prohibition. *Psychological Bulletin, 113,* 497–512.

Moscovici, S. (1989). Preconditions for explanation in social psychology. *European Journal of Social Psychology, 19,* 407–430.

Oceja, L. V. (1997). Efectos perversos de las normas incumplidas. Aspectos teóricos y experimentales [Perverse effects of unfulfilled norms: Theoretical and experimental aspects]. Unpublished doctoral dissertation, Universidad Autónoma de Madrid.

Oceja, L. V., & y Fernández-Dols, J. M. (1992). El reconocimiento de la norma perversa y sus consecuencias en los juicios de las personas [The recognition of perverse norm and its consequences in people's judgements]. *Revista de Psicología Social, 7,* 227–240.

Oceja, L. V., & Fernandez-Dols, J. M. (1998). ¿Por qué obedecemos las leyes? Una exploracion de los fundamentos valorativos del comportamiento normativo [Why do we comply with the law? An exploration of the appraisal foundations of normative behavior]. *Anuario de Psicología Juridica, 1998,* 193–205.

Oceja, L. V., & Rodriguez-Mosquera, P. (1993). Legitimistic vs. pragmatical societies. A study on the cultural roots of perverse norms. In J. M. Fernandez-Dols (Convenor), *Perverse norms: Theoretical assumptions and empirical approaches.* Symposium conducted at the Tenth General Meeting of the European Association of Experimental Social Psychology, Lisbon.

Parry, J. H. (1981). *The age of reconnaissance: Discovery, exploration and settlement 1450 to 1650.* Berkeley: University of California Press.

Putnam, R. D. (1993). *Making democracy work: Civic traditions in modern Italy.* Princeton, NJ: Princeton University Press.

6. Justice Motivation and Moral Motivation

C. DANIEL BATSON

What is the relationship between the justice motive, so brilliantly described by Lerner, and moral motivation? Does one subsume the other? Dominant views within moral psychology (e.g., Kohlberg, 1969, 1976) and moral philosophy (Rawls, 1971) might lead one to think that the concept of justice has replaced the concept of morality – or should. I wish to argue that the concepts of justice and morality should be kept distinct and that, specifically, justice motivation and moral motivation should be kept distinct. I think that doing so is necessary lest the theoretical and practical importance of these two forms of motivation be compromised. The first step in my argument is a brief review of the insights into the justice motive provided by Lerner.

The Justice Motive

Need to Believe in a Just World: The Just World Hypothesis

As presented by Lerner (1970, 1980, 1981, 1982; Lerner, Miller, & Holmes, 1976), the core of the justice motive is the need to believe in a just world, a world in which people get what they deserve and deserve what they get – or at least a world in which terrible things do not happen to good people (Lerner & Goldberg, 1999). Early classic experiments by Lerner and Simmons (1966), among others, demonstrated that this motive could be aroused by witnessing innocent suffering, which threatens the belief in a just world. If a low-cost opportunity to remove the apparent injustice is at hand, the justice motive can lead one to act on this opportunity as a means of eliminating the threat – and of garnering the social rewards and self-rewards for doing a good deed. If no such opportunity is at hand, the justice motive can lead one to eliminate the threat by blaming or derogating the sufferer. After all, people who are careless or "not nice" deserve to suffer.

The justice motive identified by Lerner is thus a two-edged sword. Depending on the options available, and the costs associated with each, the motive can lead one to redress injustice or to perpetuate it, even to exacerbate it. This is because the ultimate goal of the justice motive is not to be just. The ultimate goal is to see the world as just, so that one can maintain belief in "the fundamental delusion" that the world is just (Lerner, 1980). Acting justly is but one way to reach this goal.

The scope of Lerner's just world hypothesis is extremely broad. For example, it led to the prediction that young men in the United States who learned that they had "lost" in the Vietnam War draft lottery (by having their birth date drawn early, meaning that they were certain to be drafted) would see themselves as less deserving people, which would be reflected in lower ratings of self-esteem. A dramatic prediction, but one supported by the data (Rubin & Peplau, 1973). Reduction of self-esteem following the innocent misfortune of being selected for the draft suggests a desperate attempt to make sense of a tragic twist of fate: My losing wasn't just chance; I deserved it.

Emergence of the Justice Motive from the Personal Contract

Why would anyone reason thus? Surely any rational adult knows that the world is not just. To feel the need to maintain a belief that it is a just world seems bizarre. How could such a motive arise? How could it survive?

Lerner's answer to these questions was as insightful as his identification, articulation, and demonstration of the existence of the justice motive. Lerner (1981; Lerner, Miller, & Holmes, 1976) argued that the justice motive emerges from the *personal contract*, a contract that we must make with ourselves very early in life if we are to pursue anything more than immediate pleasure. The personal contract is of the form: If I do this now, then I will get that later. Without faith that we will get what we deserve, why pursue long-term goals? Why engage in any future-oriented action at all? The personal contract underlies virtually everything we do. To void it would send one tumbling into an abyss of helplessness and depression. For most of us, this contract is non-negotiable.

It is only a short developmental step from the personal contract to the need to believe in a just world. This step is taken when, as children, we recognize that other people also have goals toward which they work, and that they live in the same world we do. Were we to believe that they do not get what they deserve, our confidence that we will get what we deserve would be shaken. The justice motive is born. It is not taught; it emerges inevitably, necessarily, from our experience of life.

Grounding the justice motive in the personal contract provides a plausible account of the motive's power. Still, maintaining belief in a just world is not easy. This belief is continually challenged by examples of injustice and innocent suffering. The challenges may lead to a probabilistic view: Yes, undeserved suffering occurs ("shit happens"), but even if we do not always get what we deserve, we usually do; it is still worth investing in the future. Or these challenges may lead to a them–us distinction – *their* world is not just, but *ours* is. Such compromises with harsh reality produce individual differences in the degree to which people adhere to a simple, straightforward belief in a just world. These compromises may complicate the expression of the justice motive, but they do not eliminate it. Only surrender of the personal contract would do that (Lerner, 1998; Lerner & Goldberg, 1999).

A Second Form of Justice Motivation

Lerner's justice motive is directed toward the ultimate goal of seeing the world as just, not toward the goal of being just. Is there also a motive actually to be just, to uphold principles of justice as an ultimate goal? Research conducted during the 1980s and 1990s suggested an affirmative answer. It was found that participants presented with scenarios involving injustice, and explicitly reminded of norms of justice, made judgments and resource-allocation recommendations that indicated a concern for justice per se, not simply for the perception of deservingness predicted by the justice motive. This research led Lerner (1998) to propose a second form of justice motivation. Drawing on the conceptual analyses of Epstein (Epstein et al., 1992) and Shweder and Haidt (1993), Lerner proposed that, in addition to the previously described experience- or intuition-based justice motive emergent from the personal contract, there is a reason- or judgment-based motive to adhere to and apply norms of justice that we have been taught. We are taught these norms by parents, teachers, religious leaders, peers, and the culture at large. We learn that they are not to be ignored, and we render judgments about fairness and justice accordingly.

Implicit in Lerner's (1998) description of these two forms of justice motivation is a crucial difference in the mode of their acquisition. This difference, in turn, has profound implications for the way each motive operates. The motive to believe in a just world – Lerner's justice motive – is *emergent*. It is not taught; it is learned naturally and inevitably as a product of the experience of living in a less-than-perfect world with a complex brain that can project the future consequences of present actions. As a result, this justice motive lies deep and is a response to threats to the very foundation of the psyche. Lerner (1998; Lerner & Goldberg, 1999) describes this motive as preconscious, automatic, and closely linked to emotion. It is not likely to be codified in language, and so is not readily accessible to cognitive awareness or analysis. But it is there, exerting a powerful influence.

By contrast, the motive to adhere to justice principles is *received*. It is not learned from direct experience of the world; it is learned didactically from others. As a result, it addresses concerns at higher levels of psychic organization. This motive is codified in language and is readily accessible to cognitive awareness and analysis. When primed, it too can exert a powerful influence, especially when one's judgments or actions are under social scrutiny. But failure to adhere to its dictates is not likely to shake the foundations of one's reality.

Instead, the received norms of justice have much the same status as other learned social norms. They are features of the social terrain to be negotiated if one is to get where one wants to go. Depending on the lay of the land, these received norms may be attended to with care, may be selectively applied, or may be blatantly ignored. Ready cognitive accessibility means that one can easily reframe or rationalize when it is in one's interest to do so.

Lerner (1998) developed his distinction between the implicit/experiential and the explicit/rational origins of these two forms of justice motivation – what I am calling their emergent and received origins – by attending to features of the research paradigms in which evidence of each has been found. Evidence of motivation to believe in a just world, including derogation of innocent victims, is found when (a) research participants are confronted with real (or what they take to be real) situations of clear and powerful injustice, (b) dependent measures are not explicitly and obviously about justice, and (c) one's responses are relatively spontaneous and not under obvious social scrutiny. Evidence of motivation to adhere to norms of justice is found when (a) participants are confronted with hypothetical cases of injustice, (b) dependent measures are explicitly and obviously about justice, and (c) responses are deliberate and under social scrutiny (Lerner, 1998).

Moral Motivation

Against the backdrop of Lerner's analysis of justice motivation, what can be said about moral motivation? Quite a bit, I believe, especially if we think about the origins of moral motivation in the light of the emergent-versus-received distinction that seems important in differentiating forms of justice motivation. Before considering origins, however, we need to have some idea of what we are talking about when we speak of moral motivation.

A Sketchy Map of the Moral Realm

Any analysis of moral motivation is heavily dependent on what one means by *moral*; so let me first sketch a map of the moral realm by offering definitions of six key concepts. These concepts are: moral precepts, being moral, moral motivation, moral hypocrisy, motivation not to be immoral, and moral integrity. I offer my definitions with no hope that they will fully satisfy others; they do not even fully satisfy me. My hope is that penciling them in may avoid needless misunderstanding about where we are and where we are going, and may make it easier to know if and when we get off track – or if the map needs to be redrawn.

Moral precepts. By moral precepts I mean *rules or principles of action that require consideration of the interests and desires of others.* I assume that, when contemplating action, an actor is likely to give consideration to his or her own interests and desires. Moral precepts add a further consideration, the interests and desires of at least some others. The degree of consideration given to one's own and to others' interests and desires can vary, producing a range of moralities. In some moralities, self-interest is dominant; consideration of the interests of others serves only to temper or constrain pursuit of self-interest. Other moralities are based on more equal weighting of own and others' interests. In still others, other-interest is dominant; self-interest serves only to temper or constrain pursuit of others' interests.

It may seem that self-interest-dominant moralities are the norm. But although they may be the descriptive norm in our society, they are clearly not the prescriptive norm. The moral precepts put forward by philosophers and religious teachers almost always involve giving at least equal weight to the interests and desires of others. Moralities of justice or fairness prescribe equal weights to the interests of self and others, whether the rules and principles are framed in terms of equality or equity, of distributive, retributive, or procedural justice. (Even Rand's [1964] morality of selfishness prescribes equality of opportunity to pursue self-interest.) Moralities of mercy or compassion are other-interest dominant; they prescribe that one be willing to put oneself out for others – to go the extra mile, turn the other cheek, and so on.

Each of the following could serve as a moral precept as defined here. Don't be greedy. (Or the self-interest-dominant version: Don't be *so* greedy.) Take turns. Give everybody a fair share. Give everybody an equal chance. Don't lie. Don't cheat. Don't steal. Do no harm. Do not kill. Help those in need. Be kind. Be nice. Note that many of these precepts are worded negatively, emphasizing the constraint on self-interest. Others are worded positively, emphasizing either the equal weighting of own and others' interests or a focus on the interests of others.

The term "rights" does not appear in the present definition of moral precepts. Here, rights are not inalienable attributes to be considered alongside (or instead of) interests and desires; they are products of the relative weighting of our own and others' interests and desires. Each person has a "right" to have his or her interests weighted as specified by the precept. According to a precept that assigns equal weights, I have a right to expect my interests to be considered on a par with yours – and I have an obligation (a "duty") to consider your interests on a par with mine. You have a parallel right and obligation. If I adopt an other-interest-dominated morality, as did Tolstoy (1908/1987), my rights are diminished and my obligations increased relative to the rights and obligations that I accord others.

By contrast to the elegant abstract universal prescription of Kant's (1785/1889) Kingdom of Ends, in which all people are treated as ends in themselves and not as means to other ends, the present definition of moral precepts confronts one with the difficult and confusing task of identifying the interests and desires of the people affected by one's action. How is this possible? The Golden Rule – "Do unto others as you would have them do unto you" (Matthew 7:12) – may serve as a rough guide. But even this celebrated rule begins to break down when the interests of those affected by my action differ from mine. What I would have them do to me may not be what they would have done to themselves. In such situations, we seem to need a different rule (platinum, perhaps?): "Do unto others as you would have them do unto you . . . if you had their interests and desires."

Being moral. Given the definition of moral precepts, being moral can be defined simply as *acting in accord with one or more moral precepts.* The term "acting" here implies both intention and choice. If a person behaves in accord with some moral precept by accident or because he or she cannot do otherwise, then I would not say this person is being moral.

Whether a given action is judged to be moral depends on the moral precepts held by the judge. My actions may be judged moral by me but not by you – or by you but not by me. Moreover, a given judge may apply different moral precepts at different times or in different situations – or to the actions of different people. Clearly, judgments about the morality of an action are highly subjective; yet they are not totally subjective. If a person accepts a particular moral precept, then an action that violates this precept is immoral. This is true even when the person denies it. If someone else effectively points out the discrepancy, the judgment of immorality should follow.

Moral precepts may contradict one another. When they do, the same action may be judged both as moral and as immoral, depending on which precept is applied. If a person simultaneously holds contradictory precepts, then the result is likely to be moral conflict and confusion when judging some act or when deciding how to act.

Moral motivation. Moral motivation is *a motivational state with the ultimate goal of being moral (i.e., of acting in accord with one or more moral precepts).* The term "ultimate" is not used here in a metaphysical sense; it is used in contrast to "instrumental." Instrumental goals are sought as means to reach other goals. Ultimate goals are sought as ends in themselves. Applying the present definitions, acting in accord with a moral precept (e.g., be nice) in order to gain and maintain friends is being moral, but it is not an example of moral motivation. The ultimate versus instrumental distinction is especially important because it serves to differentiate moral motivation from motives that may produce moral behavior in some situations but are not themselves moral.

Moral hypocrisy. Chief among such look-alikes is moral hypocrisy, which has been defined as *a motivational state with the ultimate goal of appearing moral while, if possible, avoiding the costs to self of actually being moral* (Batson et al., 1997). In situations in which the only way to appear moral is to be moral, moral hypocrisy and true moral motivation are impossible to disentangle. Both lead to an increased tendency to be moral. Results of experiments designed to disentangle these two motives by providing participants with an opportunity to appear moral without having to incur the costs of being moral indicate that many people are happy to avail themselves of such an opportunity (by, for example, flipping a coin to assign self and other to differentially desirable tasks, but fudging the flip outcome to give themselves the more desirable task). At least in the experimental situations studied so far, moral hypocrisy seems to be much more pervasive and powerful than true moral motivation (participants who have chosen to flip a coin to assign tasks, for example, have "won" the flip almost 90% of the time – Batson et al., 1997).

Motivation not to be immoral. It is also important to distinguish moral motivation from motivation not to be immoral. The latter may be defined as *a motivational state with the ultimate goal of not violating moral precepts.* For many of us, acting in accord with moral precepts and acting in a way that violates moral precepts do not exhaust the possibilities. One may do neither. Indeed, it seems that many of us are more strongly motivated not to be immoral than to be moral (see Baron's [1995] research on the "do no harm" principle). We aspire not to be bad more than we aspire to be good.

The distinction between these two motives seems to rest on an asymmetry in the perception of intention and choice when thinking about inaction and about action. Logically, if one could have acted in accord with a moral precept but did not, then this failure to act is a violation of the precept. From this purely logical perspective, motivation to be moral and motivation not to be immoral are the same. However, many of us apparently do not adhere to this pure logic. We cut ourselves – and others – some slack. We are less ready to call sins of omission sins, perhaps because as children we were punished only for sins of commission.

Moral integrity. Moral integrity is *congruence of a person's moral precepts, moral action, and moral motivation.* Said another way, a person displays moral integrity when he or she acts on motivation to uphold his or her moral precepts as an ultimate goal. Such a person is said to show *character*, especially if this action involves considerable cost to self.

Thinking about Moral Motivation in Light of What We Know about Justice Motivation

Working with this rough map of the moral realm, what insights into moral motivation can be gleaned from what Lerner has taught us about justice motivation? The first thing one notices is that Lerner's justice motive is not a moral motive, at least not as defined here. The goal of his justice motive is not to act in accord with a moral precept; the goal is to see the world as just. On the other hand, the second form of justice motivation identified by Lerner (1998), the motive to adhere to norms of justice, is a moral motive – if the adherence is an ultimate goal. If, instead, one adheres to norms of justice as an instrumental means to reach another goal (e.g., in order to deserve good outcomes or to avoid guilt or social censure), then the motivation is not moral, as defined here.

Moral Motivation as Received

It is ironic that the form of justice motivation that qualifies as moral is the form that is received, not emergent; rational, not experiential; and, as a result, one that is susceptible to rationalization and selective application. Yet this observation seems entirely congruent with the existing evidence on the relative weakness of moral motivation and on its susceptibility to rationalization (Darley, 1992; Todorov, 1996), disengagement (Bandura, 1991, 1999), exclusion (Staub, 1990), and exemption (Batson, 1996). The forms of moral motivation most frequently described and studied by psychologists are received, not emergent. The moral precepts on which they are based are products of socialization (Kurtines & Gewirtz, 1991).

To the extent that moral precepts are taught as rules to be remembered and followed, these precepts are likely to be perceived as oughts, not wants (Heider, 1958), as masters to be served. Learned in this way, one's moral principles and standards are apt to be perceived not as fully a part of oneself but as standing outside and over oneself, creating obligations rather than desires. In the language of Deci and colleagues (1994), the form of internalization that occurs is likely to be *introjection* (precepts are taken in as values or regulatory processes but are not accepted as part of one's core sense of self) rather than *integration* (precepts are accepted as part of one's core sense of self).

Nor are attempts to strengthen the inclination to act in accord with moral precepts by administering rewards and punishments likely to help. Theory and research on both cognitive dissonance (Festinger & Freedman, 1964) and the undermining of intrinsic motivation (Kunda & Schwartz, 1983; Lepper, 1983) provide compelling arguments against a carrot-and-stick approach. Not only is such an approach unlikely to increase moral motivation, it is likely to do the opposite. To perceive oneself to have acted morally due to anticipated rewards and punishments is likely to lead to the inference that one does not value being moral as an ultimate goal, but only as an instrumental means to obtain the self-benefits that come from being moral. With such a self-perception, if it is possible to obtain the self-benefits without actually being moral, then one should jump at the chance. And often, it is possible.

Moral Hypocrisy as Emergent

The forms of moral motivation most frequently described and studied by psychologists seem, then, to be received, not emergent; rational, not experiential; and, unless internalized to the point of integration, lacking in depth and centrality. Moral hypocrisy, on the other hand, appears to be an emergent motive. Our parents, teachers, and religious leaders are not likely to teach hypocrisy, at least not explicitly. We are far more likely to acquire this motive as a result of our experience in the world, experience whereby we learn, first, that being moral can at times be personally costly and, second, that appearance can at times be more important than reality.

A window through which to glimpse the emergence of moral hypocrisy may be provided by observational research on the adjudication by adults of conflicts among young children, whether at home (Dunn, 1987; Dunn & Munn, 1986, 1987) or in school (Walton & Sedlak, 1982). Darley and Schultz (1990) have analyzed this research using a legal metaphor. As if in a courtroom, each child pleads his or her case before the adult judge. ("She hit me first"; "Did not; he took my truck"; etc.) The judge then renders a verdict.

As in a courtroom, reality is not what determines the verdict. Whatever can be made to appear real to the judge will decide the case. No doubt the child is shocked and confused the first time that he or she, although innocent, is judged guilty because a sibling or peer was more adroit at juggling the evidence. But also a key lesson is learned: Adults – parents, teachers, others – are not omniscient. These adults who judge whether one has been good or bad, and who dispense rewards and punishments accordingly, can be deceived. Once this lesson is learned, it is only a short, natural step to convert any inclination to be moral – either as an instrumental goal, pursued to gain reward and avoid punishment, or as an ultimate goal – into a desire to appear moral while, if possible, avoiding the cost of being moral. The hypocrisy motive is born.

These lessons learned in the early courtrooms of life probably do not lie as close to the foundation of the psyche as does the personal contract; but they do lie deep, and they are emergent from direct experience, not received through didactic transmission from others. As a result, the hypocrisy motive may lie outside the realm of language, cognitive awareness, and rational control. Moreover, the hypocrisy motive has the virtue that, unlike true moral motivation, it does not conflict with self-interest. It is no surprise, then, that much behavior that appears to be a product of moral motivation can be seen, on closer inspection, to be a product of moral hypocrisy. It is also no surprise that we are prone to keep this truth even from ourselves (Batson et al., 1999).

Emergent Forms of Moral Motivation

Are there no emergent forms of truly moral motivation? I know of no good empirical evidence that there are. Still, I think there may be. Let me suggest two types of early childhood experience that may produce emergent moral motivation. These are the experience of playing games and the experience of being the recipient of exceptional niceness.

Playing Games

Piaget (1932) and Mead (1934) each point to the importance of playing games for moral development. Games create social realities, complete with rules and roles. If players ignore either the rules or the roles, a game quickly breaks down. In this sense, playing a game involves a social contract. The contract is not a defensive, negative social contract of the sort depicted by Hobbes (1651), whereby I allow constraints on my power in order to assure constraints on yours. It is a more positive contract that allows each of us to enter into and enjoy a socially constructed world that we otherwise could not experience.

Important lessons are learned from the experience of playing games, lessons that may lead to the emergence of moral precepts and moral motivation. We learn to take turns, to apply rules impartially, to be attuned to the effects of our actions on others, to adopt the perspective of other players in order to understand and anticipate their moves, to recognize that others are doing the same in order to understand and anticipate our moves, to understand that events that are good for us can be bad for others, and vice versa. Of course, not all games teach all of these lessons to the same degree. Formal, adult-regulated games (such as Little League baseball) probably teach more about following received rules than about making things fair or about perspective taking. Informal competitive games created on the spot with playmates tend to do the opposite.

Out of the lessons learned from playing games may emerge, over time, values of fair play, respect for others, honor, courage, self-discipline, and self-sacrifice for a common (team) good. These values may, in turn, provide the basis for moral precepts, especially precepts that focus on giving equal consideration to the interests and desires of each person in zero-sum situations. Motivation to enact these principles would seem to be an emergent form of moral motivation, an emergent morality of procedural justice. The game player may later want to "play fair" not simply because he or she has been taught that this is right, but because deep down it feels right.

The British were fond of saying that the Battle of Waterloo was won on the playing fields of Eton. Presumably, what they meant was that principles learned on the playing fields contributed in a lasting and powerful way to the character of future officers. Might the same be said of the effect of other fields of play on future performance in the moral fray? Is it possible that those children who play more games – especially informal competitive games where rules and roles are created and maintained by common consent – place a higher intrinsic value on procedural justice and fair play as adults? I do not know, but it seems possible (see Gilligan & Wiggins, 1987, for somewhat similar speculation).

Being the Recipient of Exceptional Niceness

Young children are likely to take for granted the effort that parents put into their care. All the food, clothes, toys, and love are just the way things are. When the child is old enough to form expectations, parental care is apt to be high on the list of what is expected – not noticed, not appreciated.

At times, however, the child is the recipient of exceptional niceness – beyond what is expected – that is noticed. One such occasion might be receiving gifts; another might be receiving special care when sick. These experiences may evoke feelings of gratitude and appreciation. They may also lead the child to value the role of giver. A desire to be thoughtful and nice to others may emerge. Playing with dolls, caring for a younger brother or sister, caring for a pet, or helping Mom all provide contexts for expression of this desire, which can apparently be quite powerful in children (Kagan & Lamb, 1987; Rheingold, Hay, & West, 1976; Zahn-Waxler et al., 1992).

Perhaps because it seems so pedestrian, the desire to be thoughtful or nice is rarely considered in discussions of morality. Yet it may be one of the most pervasive and powerful forms of emergent moral motivation. Note that this form of moral motivation is not focused on justice or equal consideration of the interests and desires of all; it is focused on compassion and care. When one is being thoughtful or nice, the interests of the other dominate.

Of course, being thoughtful or nice may not be an ultimate goal. It may simply be an instrumental means to secure gratitude, thanks, or reciprocity. If so, it would not reflect a form of moral motivation, as defined here. And even if being nice reflects a moral motive, the form may be received, not emergent. Certainly, few children escape being taught to be nice. Is there an emergent form of this motive as well? It seems possible – even likely.

Conclusion

How powerful are these two emergent forms of moral motivation – the desire for procedural justice arising from playing games, and the desire to be thoughtful and nice arising from being the recipient of exceptional niceness? Are there other emergent forms of moral motivation? I do not know. I do not even know if these two exist. What I would suggest is that, if they do exist, then they may be less vulnerable to rationalization, disengagement, exclusion, and exemption than are the more frequently discussed received forms of morality. I suggest this because these emergent forms – like Lerner's motive to believe in a just world – reflect truths learned from experience, not truths received secondhand from others. As such, they are at once more ingrained and internal, more closely tied to emotion, and less subject to rational manipulation than are moral precepts learned from others. They may also be more likely to be sources of moral integrity.

Using Lerner's insightful analysis of the nature and origins of justice motivation as a model for analyzing moral motivation has highlighted new issues and possibilities. It has suggested that his emergent motive to believe in a just world is not a moral motive, but that the received desire to adhere to norms of justice may be. It has led us to suspect the power and integrity of this and other received moral motives, and to look for emergent forms of moral motivation. In so doing, it may point to more effective, more practical ways to stimulate moral action – including action to redress injustice in our society. And redressing injustice has always been a focal concern of Lerner's profoundly productive career.

REFERENCES

Bandura, A. (1991). Social cognitive theory of moral thought and action. In W. M. Kurtines & J. L. Gewirtz (Eds.), *Handbook of moral behavior and development. Volume 1: Theory* (pp. 45–103). Hillsdale, NJ: Erlbaum.

(1999). Moral disengagement in the perpetration of inhumanities. *Personality and Social Psychology Review, 3*, 193–209.

Baron, J. (1995). Blind justice: Fairness to groups and the do-no-harm principle. *Journal of Behavioral Decision Making, 8*, 71–83.

Batson, C. D. (1996). Do prosocial motives have any business in business? *Social Justice Research, 9*, 7–25.

Batson, C. D., Kobrynowicz, D., Dinnerstein, J. L., Kampf, H. C., & Wilson, A. D. (1997). In a very different voice: Unmasking moral hypocrisy. *Journal of Personality and Social Psychology, 72*, 1335–1348.

Batson, C. D., Thompson, E. R., Seuferling, G., Whitney, H., & Strongman, J. (1999). Moral hypocrisy: Appearing moral to oneself without being so. *Journal of Personality and Social Psychology, 77*, 525–537.

Darley, J. M. (1992). Social organization for the production of evil. *Psychological Inquiry, 3*, 199–218.

Darley, J. M., & Schultz, T. R. (1990). Moral rules: Their content and acquisition. *Annual Review of Psychology, 41*, 525–556.

Deci, E. L., Eghrari, H., Patrick, B. C., & Leone, D. R. (1994). Facilitating internalization: The self-determination theory perspective. *Journal of Personality, 62*, 119–142.

Dunn, J. (1987). The beginnings of moral understanding: Development in the second year. In J. Kagan & S. Lamb (Eds.), *The emergence of morality in young children* (pp. 91–112). Chicago: University of Chicago Press.

Dunn, J., & Munn, P. (1986). Sibling quarrels and maternal intervention: Individual differences in understanding and aggression. *Journal of Child Psychology and Psychiatry, 27*, 583–595.

(1987). Development of justification in disputes with mother and sibling. *Developmental Psychology, 23*, 791–798.

Epstein, S., Lipson, A., Hostein, C., & Hub, E. (1992). Irrational reactions to negative outcomes: Evidence for two conceptual systems. *Journal of Personality and Social Psychology, 62*, 328–339.

Festinger, L., & Freedman, J. L. (1964). Dissonance reduction and moral values. In P. Worchel & D. Byrne (Eds.), *Personality change* (pp. 220–243). New York: Wiley.

Gilligan, C., & Wiggins, G. (1987). The origins of morality in early childhood relationships. In J. Kagan & S. Lamb (Eds.), *The emergence of morality in young children* (pp. 277–305). Chicago: University of Chicago Press.

Heider, F. (1958). *The psychology of interpersonal relations.* New York: Wiley.

Hobbes, T. (1651). *Leviathan: Or the matter, form, and power of a commonwealth, ecclesiastical and civil.* London: A. Crooke.

Kagan, J., & Lamb, S. (Eds.) (1987). *The emergence of morality in young children.* Chicago: University of Chicago Press.

Kant, I. (1889). *Kant's* Critique of Practical Reason *and other works on the theory of ethics*, 4th ed. (T. K. Abbott, Trans.). New York: Longmans, Green. (Original work published 1785.)

Kohlberg, L. (1969). Stage and sequence: The cognitive-developmental approach to socialization. In D. A. Goslin (Ed.), *Handbook of socialization theory and research* (pp. 347–480). Chicago: Rand McNally.

(1976). Moral stages and moralization: The cognitive-developmental approach. In T. Lickona (Ed.), *Moral development and behavior: Theory, research, and social issues* (pp. 31–53). New York: Holt, Rinehart, and Winston.

Kunda, Z., & Schwartz, S. (1983). Undermining intrinsic moral motivation: External reward and self-presentation. *Journal of Personality and Social Psychology, 45*, 763–771.

Kurtines, W. M., & Gewirtz, J. L. (Eds.) (1991). *Handbook of moral behavior and development* (Vols. 1–3). Hillsdale, NJ: Erlbaum.

Lepper, M. R. (1983). Social-control processes and the internalization of social values: An attributional perspective. In E. T. Higgins, D. N. Ruble, & W. W. Hartup (Eds.), *Social cognition and social development* (pp. 294–330). New York: Cambridge University Press.

Lerner, M. J. (1970). The desire for justice and reactions to victims. In J. Macaulay & L. Berkowitz (Eds.), *Altruism and helping behavior* (pp. 205–229). New York: Academic Press.

(1980). *The belief in a just world: A fundamental delusion.* New York: Plenum.

(1981). The justice motive in human relations: Some thoughts on what we know and need to know about justice. In M. J. Lerner & S. C. Lerner (Eds.), *The justice motive in social behavior: Adapting to times of scarcity and change* (pp. 11–35). New York: Plenum.

(1982). The justice motive in human relations and the economic model of man: A radical analysis of facts and fictions. In V. J. Derlega & J. Grzelak (Eds.), *Cooperation and helping behavior: Theories and research* (pp. 249–278). New York: Academic Press.

(1998). The two forms of belief in a just world: Some thoughts on why and how people care about justice. In L. Montada & M. J. Lerner (Eds.), *Responses to victimizations and belief in a just world* (pp. 247–269). New York: Plenum.

Lerner, M. J., & Goldberg, J. H. (1999). When do decent people blame victims? The differing effects of the explicit/rational and implicit/experiential cognitive systems. In S. Chaiken & Y. Trope (Eds.), *Dual-process theories in social psychology* (pp. 627–640). New York: Guilford.

Lerner, M. J., Miller, D. T., & Holmes, J. G. (1976). Deserving and the emergence of forms of justice. In L. Berkowitz (Ed.), *Advances in experimental social psychology* (Vol. 9, pp. 133–162). New York: Academic Press.

Lerner, M. J., & Simmons, C. H. (1966). Observers' reaction to the "innocent victim": Compassion or rejection? *Journal of Personality and Social Psychology, 4*, 203–210.

Mead, G. H. (1934). *Mind, self, and society* (posthumous; C. M. Morris, Ed.). Chicago: University of Chicago Press.

Piaget, J. (1932). *The moral judgment of the child*. London: Kegan Paul.

Rand, A. (1964). *The virtue of selfishness: A new concept of egoism*. New York: New American Library.

Rawls, J. (1971). *A theory of justice*. Cambridge, MA: Harvard University Press.

Rheingold, H., Hay, D., & West, M. (1976). Sharing in the second year of life. *Child Development, 47*, 1148–1158.

Rubin, Z., & Peplau, L. A. (1973). Belief in a just world and reactions to another's lot: A study of participants in the national draft lottery. *Journal of Social Issues, 29*, 73–93.

Shweder, R. A., & Haidt, J. (1993). The future of moral psychology: Truth, intuition, and the pluralist way. *Psychological Science, 4*, 360–365.

Staub, E. (1990). Moral exclusion, personal goal theory, and extreme destructiveness. *Journal of Social Issues, 46* (1), 47–64.

Todorov, T. (1996). *Facing the extreme: Moral life in the concentration camps* (A. Denner & A. Pollak, Trans.). New York: Henry Holt.

Tolstoy, L. (1987). The law of love and the law of violence. In *A confession and other religious writings* (J. Kentish, Trans.). London: Penguin. (Original work published 1908.)

Walton, M. D., & Sedlak, A. J. (1982). Making amends: A grammar-based analysis of children's social interaction. *Merrill-Palmer Quarterly, 28*, 389–412.

Zahn-Waxler, C., Radke-Yarrow, M., Wagner, E., & Chapman, M. (1992). Development of concern for others. *Developmental Psychology, 28*, 126–136.

VICTIM DEROGATION AND THE BELIEF IN A JUST WORLD

7. Why We Reject Innocent Victims

CAROLYN L. HAFER

In our daily lives, we are often confronted with individuals who suffer through little fault of their own. Common activities such as reading the newspaper, watching television, and walking down a crowded city street can expose us to instances of misfortune. These scenes are inescapable. Responses to these images, however, vary greatly – from sympathy and offers of help to derogation of the victims' character and behavior. The research presented in this chapter focuses on our tendency, under certain circumstances, to reject victims of misfortune – our tendency, for example, to derogate their character, to blame them for their fate, and to psychologically disassociate ourselves from their plight.

In a series of experiments in the 1960s and 1970s, Melvin Lerner and his colleagues addressed the tendency for observers, under certain conditions, to reject victims of innocent suffering (for a review, see Lerner & Miller, 1978). Lerner concluded from this work that people *need* to believe that the world is a just place, a place where individuals get what they deserve. Certain victims pose a threat to the belief in a just world (BJW) by providing information to the contrary. Strategies for coping with such a threat include attempts to restore justice by alleviating the suffering or providing compensation. Observers might also cope with innocent suffering by rejecting the victim. For example, people may choose to restore a sense of justice through psychological rationalization, such as blaming victims for their misfortune or derogating their character (i.e., labeling them as bad or unworthy individuals). Such rationalization restores justice by interpreting the suffering as deserved. As well, observers may choose to disassociate themselves from the victim – for example, by claiming that the victim and his or her situation bears no resemblance to their own. Disassociation allows observers to reduce the threat to the BJW by convincing themselves that similar injustices will not befall them; that is, that although injustice appears to occur in the larger world, at least their own immediate world is just. Disassociation may also reduce the threat posed by innocent suffering by providing a rationale for dismissing thoughts of the victim (e.g., she is not like me, therefore I do not have to concern myself with her fate). In sum, according to Lerner, rejecting innocent victims, whether by derogation, attributing blame, or disassociation, is often the result of our need to protect the BJW in the face of threat.

In this chapter, I draw on two sets of studies on the BJW to shed further light on why people reject innocent victims. These studies address the following questions. First, is it the *injustice* of innocent suffering that we find threatening, and, if so, does this threat motivate rejection of innocent victims? Though these propositions are predicted by Lerner's notion of the BJW, there has been little attempt to assess threat to the BJW (and its relation to rejection of victims) beyond inferring such a threat from presumed coping responses. In the first part of this chapter, I summarize a series of studies showing what I believe to be compelling evidence for these propositions, thus providing strong support for a BJW interpretation of the tendency to reject innocent victims.

Second, the BJW must fulfill an important function given that we seem to be motivated to defend this belief, sometimes by rejecting those who suffer innocently. What is the function of the BJW? Although Lerner (1980) and others have often commented on the possible functions of this belief, there have been few empirical tests of these arguments. In the second part of this chapter, I present a program of research providing evidence that the need to believe in a just world is fueled, in part, by our desire to invest in long-term goals and to achieve these goals through just means.

I. Injustice and the Rejection of Innocent Victims

In a typical study of the BJW and reactions to victims, experimenters manipulate a variable that should influence the magnitude of the threat to the BJW, then measure the effect of this manipulation on responses to the victim that are potential strategies for maintaining the BJW in the face of contradictory evidence (e.g., victim blame). The reaction(s) of interest should be stronger under conditions of presumably strong threat to the BJW than under conditions of weak threat. Findings from many such investigations show this pattern and, thus, support Lerner's notion that certain innocent victims threaten the BJW and that rejection of these victims (as well as other responses) can be a strategy for coping with that threat. However, most of these studies simply infer that the victim's situation threatens the observer's BJW from supposed responses to this threat (e.g., victim blame). That is, this research does not attempt to assess the presence and magnitude of a justice-related threat independent of presumed coping responses. Such an assessment could help to test whether it is specifically the injustice of innocent suffering that is threatening to observers, as well as whether justice-related threat (if it occurs) predicts responses presumed to be strategies for dealing with contradictions to the BJW, responses such as rejection of innocent victims. Results from such investigations would provide unique corroboration of Lerner's ideas regarding the BJW and its motivational properties.

In a series of recent studies, I have tried to provide this corroborating evidence. There are several methods one might use to assess the potential justice-related threat posed by an innocent victim. For example, one might ask participants for retrospective self-reports of their thoughts and emotions while they were observing an innocent victim. There are several problems with this methodology, however, including social desirability biases (e.g., it may be undesirable to report feeling threatened by innocent suffering) and the possibility that observers are unaware that they are threatened by innocent victims and, thus, may have difficulty reporting their relevant internal states (see Lerner, 1998; Lerner & Goldberg, 1999). Given the problems with such self-report measures, I decided to use an alternative technique for investigating justice-related threat.

The technique I used involves a modified Stroop task and was adapted from research on cognition and psychopathology (for a review, see Williams, Mathews, & MacLeod, 1996). In this research, participants are presented with words written in different colors of ink. Some words are affectively neutral, whereas others are related to events that threaten the participant (e.g., words like "embarrassment" and "insult" might be used if participants are socially anxious). Participants are asked to identify the color of the word stimulus as quickly and accurately as possible. The difference in color-identification latencies for threat-relevant words and color-identification latencies for neutral words is the contrast of interest. The greater the latencies for threat-relevant words versus neutral words, the more "interference" these words are said to have produced while the participant is attempting to identify the ink color. These studies show significantly greater color-identification latencies for threat-relevant words than for neutral words; that is, people demonstrate interference for words that are reminiscent of threatening concepts. It should be noted that this interference can occur both when the emotional concern is chronic, such as in clinical populations (e.g., Mogg et al., 1993), or when it is induced by situational pressures (e.g., Mogg et al., 1990).

Though there is disagreement over the mechanism underlying these Stroop effects in the psychopathology literature, one possibility is that, in the presence of threat, mental categories relevant to the threat become primed in preparation for coping responses (see Williams et al., 1996). This priming leads to increased activation of words associated with threat-relevant categories, and thus these words are more likely to capture attention during the Stroop color-identification task (see MacLeod & Hodder, 1998).

Studies 1 and 2: The Injustice of Innocent Suffering Threatens Observers

In Study 1 reported here (Hafer, 2000-a), I showed Stroop effects similar to those in the cognitive psychopathology literature for a supposed manipulation of threat to people's BJW. Participants were shown an edited television news clip portraying a victim of robbery and physical assault. Participants were then presented with a Stroop task in which they identified the ink color of several types of words that were presented on a computer screen. Each word was displayed for 16 ms, followed by a mask in the same color as the word (thus, the words were difficult to perceive consciously). Participants responded to each stimulus by pressing the appropriately colored key on the computer keyboard. The words belonged to one of five categories: justice-related (e.g., fair, unequal), physical harm (e.g., cancer, torture), social harm (e.g., hostile, insult), relevant to the victim's story but not inherently associated with justice or harm (e.g., railway, tent), and neutral (e.g., candles, sorted).

If it is specifically the *injustice* of innocent victims' suffering that is threatening to observers, as predicted by Lerner's theory of the BJW, then observers should show interference for justice-related words (i.e., color-identification latencies should be significantly greater for these words than for neutral words), but not for physical harm words, social

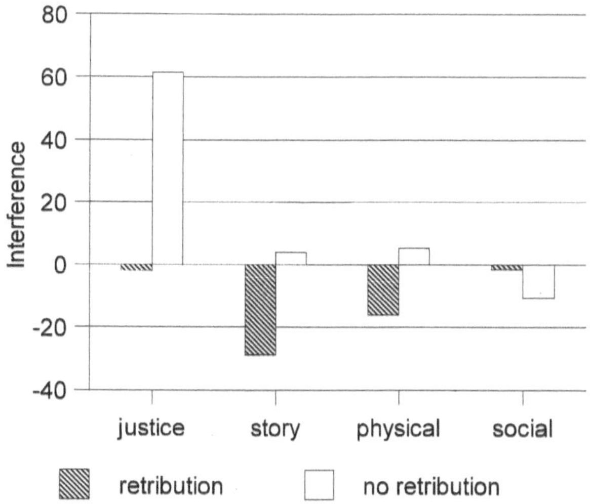

Figure 7.1. Interference as a function of retribution and word category.

harm words, or story-related words. The results supported this hypothesis. Moreover, interference for justice-related words was moderated by a presumed manipulation of the magnitude of threat to the BJW. In the strong threat condition, the perpetrators of the assault escaped punishment (i.e., there was no retribution for the crime). In the weak threat condition, the perpetrators were tried and sent to prison (i.e., there was retribution, which would presumably reduce the threat to the BJW). Justice-word interference occurred only when the perpetrators had escaped punishment. Interference for the other categories of words (i.e., physical harm, social harm, and story-related) did not differ by condition. Figure 7.1 demonstrates these findings.

These results corroborate Lerner's theory of the BJW by suggesting that it is the *injustice* of innocent victims' suffering that threatens observers and not, for example, a more general concern with negative outcomes (which might have resulted in similar interference effects for the physical and social harm words). Support for Lerner's theory would be stronger, however, if there were evidence that the injustice of the victims' suffering was threatening because it was counter to a BJW. The fact that the expected justice-word interference was moderated by a variable that should theoretically affect the magnitude of the threat to the BJW – retribution – lends some support to this idea; however, there are alternative explanations. For example, perhaps the injustice of the no-retribution victim's situation represented a perceived threat to the social order (e.g., the efficacy of government institutions) rather than a threat to a BJW.

We reasoned that, if the injustice of the victim's situation represented a threat to the BJW, then the interference for justice-related words that occurred after exposure to the innocent suffering should be moderated by individual differences in the BJW. Specifically, justice-word interference should occur primarily for observers with a strong versus a weak BJW, because innocent suffering is more discrepant with the former's beliefs and, thus, should present a greater threat. I tested this proposition in Study 2 (Hafer, 2000-c).

Participants in this study completed an initial session in which they filled out Rubin and Peplau's (1975) Just World Scale as well as several questionnaires for unrelated investigations. A few weeks later, they participated individually in an ostensibly separate study on perceptions of current events. This session was similar to Study 1, except that the words in the Stroop task were presented on the screen without a mask and disappeared from the screen only after participants had made a color identification; thus, the words were all perceived at a conscious level (for further comments on this variation on the Stroop procedure, see Hafer, 2000-c). Initial analyses indicated that the retribution manipulation had no effect on color-identification latencies; thus, results reported here are based on analyses conducted across the two levels of this variable.

Much as they were in the previous study, color-identification latencies were significantly greater for justice-related words than for neutral words; i.e., interference occurred for justice-related words. There were no significant interference effects for the other word categories.

Consistent with the predicted moderating effect of BJW, interference for justice-related words was significant for strong believers in a just world, but not for weak believers (see Figure 7.2). Similar results did not occur for the other word categories.

Study 3: The Threat of Injustice Motivates Rejection of Innocent Victims

Given this evidence that innocent suffering threatens the BJW, perhaps, as Lerner suggests, the rejection of innocent victims is a strategy for dealing with this threat. Study 3 reported here (Hafer, 2000-a) tests this proposition.

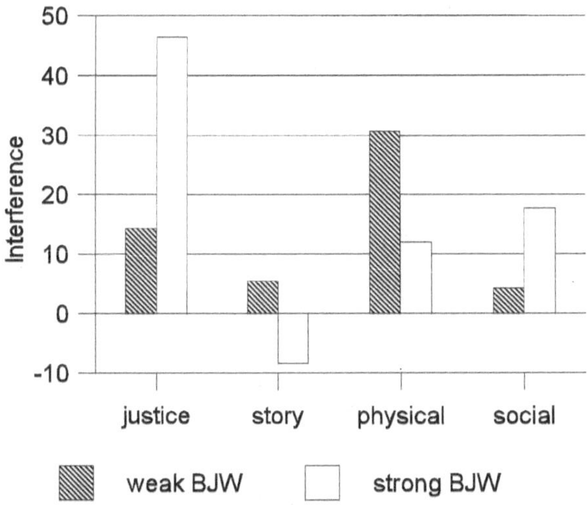

Figure 7.2. Interference as a function of belief in a just world (BJW) and word category.

The reasoning behind this study was as follows. If the rejection of innocent victims is a strategy for coping with the threat these victims pose to the BJW, then the more justice-word interference shown on the Stroop task (i.e., the greater the threat to the BJW), the greater should be one's rejection of the victim. This relation should be moderated by variables that presumably increase the threat that the victim poses to the BJW, such that justice-word interference should predict rejection of the victim primarily under strong threat conditions.

The procedure was identical to that for Study 1, except that immediately following the Stroop task, participants completed a questionnaire assessing two ways of rejecting an innocent victim – disassociation and derogation. Disassociation was measured by summing participants' assessment of how similar they thought the victim's attitudes and personality characteristics were to their own, and of how likely they thought it was that a mugging and/or assault might happen to them. Derogation of the victim's character was measured by summing ratings of the degree to which participants saw the victim as, in general, a responsible/irresponsible person, a careful/careless person, and of their overall impression of the victim.

The results of this study replicated the justice-word interference effect found in Studies 1 and 2, as well as the interaction between justice-word interference and retribution found in Study 1. Additionally, as hypothesized, the greater the interference for justice-related words, the greater the tendency both to disassociate oneself from the victim, $r(38) = .27$, and to derogate the victim's character, $r(38) = .26$ (though the latter correlation was only marginally significant). These relations were moderated, as expected, by the manipulation of retribution or threat to the BJW. Justice-word interference significantly predicted disassociation, $r(18) = .48$, and derogation, $r(18) = .52$, only when there was no retribution for the crime (i.e., when there was a strong threat to the BJW). None of the other interference scores (i.e., physical harm, social harm, story-related) showed this pattern of results.

In sum, participants in these studies showed interference for justice-related words on a Stroop task following exposure to an innocent victim, suggesting that it is the injustice of the victim's suffering that threatens observers. Also, consistent with the notion that this injustice threatens the BJW, justice-word interference was moderated by a situational variable that presumably affects the magnitude of the threat to the BJW – retribution for the injustice – as well as being moderated by individual differences in the BJW itself. Study 3 offered evidence that rejection of the innocent victim, specifically, disassociating oneself from the victim and derogating the victim's character, is a coping response to this threat. The more justice-word interference, the greater the rejection; and this was the case only under high-threat conditions.

Thus, there is strong evidence that we may reject innocent victims because we are disturbed by the injustice of their suffering; as Lerner proposes, this injustice threatens our BJW, and rejection helps to preserve this belief. Why, though, do we need to believe in a just world in the first place? That is, what is the function of a BJW, such that we are motived to preserve it, at times by rejecting innocent victims?

II. The Function of the BJW

Lerner (1980) suggests that the BJW helps fulfill a fundamental need to "know" that our psychological, material, and physical investments will be justly rewarded. Without this "knowledge," planning for any but the most immediate goals would appear to be futile. If we believe in a just world where individuals get what they deserve, however, we can carry on with our daily lives with a certain basic confidence in our future outcomes. Thus, an important function of the BJW may be to give us the confidence needed to invest in long-term goals.

I conducted three studies in which I attempted to find evidence for this function, primarily by investigating the implications this function might have for the rejection of innocent victims. Specifically, I manipulated or measured variables that, according to the function proposed here, should decrease the *need* to believe in a just world, or should reduce the extent to which the BJW serves a useful purpose. If the need to believe in a just world is weak (i.e., if the belief serves little purpose), then people should be less inclined to protect the belief in the face of contradictory evidence; for example, they should be less likely to reject victims whose situation challenges the BJW.

Study 4: Long-term Planning Drives the Need to Believe in a Just World

In Study 4, I manipulated people's focus on their long-term investments. If the BJW serves, in part, to encourage long-term planning, the need to protect the BJW (e.g., by rejecting victims who threaten this belief) should be stronger when individuals are more focused on their long-term goals. People who are less focused on long-term investments would have less need to believe that they will eventually get their just deserts and, therefore, less motivation to protect the BJW in the face of threat. Based on this rationale, I predicted that, when a victim poses a strong threat to the BJW, people who are highly focused on long-term investments should reject the victim more than those who are less focused on long-term investments.

Participants were given ten minutes to write down their thoughts in response to open-ended questions about their university experience. In the long-term focus condition, they were asked to write about their goals after graduation. In the no long-term focus condition, participants were asked to write about their current courses and other activities at the university. No mention of long-term goals was made.

Under the guise of a second and unrelated study, participants then watched a videotape of a student named "Sarah" being interviewed by a counselor. During the interview, Sarah reported several symptoms of depression that had begun shortly after she had been diagnosed with an STD. In the innocent victim condition, Sarah had contracted the STD as a result of a condom breaking during intercourse. In the noninnocent victim condition, Sarah had contracted the STD as a result of her partner's not using a condom.

Following the videotape, participants rated their responses to the victim. Three measures of rejection of the victim were created from these ratings. A measure of victim derogation was the sum of participants' ratings of the victim on twelve bipolar trait dimensions and a single question assessing their overall liking for the victim. A measure of victim blame was created by summing responses to six items assessing the extent to which participants believed that something about Sarah's character was to blame or was responsible for her situation, and the extent to which participants felt Sarah's behavior was to blame or was responsible for her situation. Finally, a composite measure of disassociation from the victim was the sum of three items: perceived similarity to the victim, the extent to which participants felt the victim was like them, and the extent to which participants identified with the victim.

As predicted, when the victim was innocent, participants showed more victim derogation, more victim blame, and disassociated themselves more from the victim when their long-term investments had been primed than when they had not been primed (see Table 7.1). There were no significant differences between the long-term focus groups when the victim was noninnocent, presumably because this victim posed little threat to the BJW.

These findings support the reasoning that people need to believe in a just world, in part, because the belief gives them confidence that their own long-term investments will be rewarded. If this function is important, then people who are focused on long-term investments should have a greater *need* to believe in a just world and, therefore, should be more motivated to preserve that belief when it is threatened by, for example, rejecting innocent victims.

Table 7.1. Derogation, blame, and disassociation as a function of victim innocence and long-term focus (Study 4)

	Innocent Victim		Noninnocent Victim	
Dependent Variable	**L-T**	**No L-T**	**L-T**	**No L-T**
Derogation	3.81 (18)	3.40 (21)	3.77 (19)	3.88 (22)
Blame	4.27 (19)	3.61 (22)	4.21 (20)	4.45 (21)
Disassociation	5.74 (19)	4.49 (22)	5.05 (19)	5.57 (21)

Note: L-T = Long-term focus condition. No L-T = No long-term focus condition. Numerical values are the averages of participants' ratings on a seven-point scale.

Studies 5 and 6: A Commitment to Just Means Also Drives the Need to Believe in a Just World

For Study 4, focus on long-term investments was experimentally manipulated. Of course, there are likely individual differences in the extent to which people invest in, focus on, and are concerned with long-term plans. The first purpose of Study 5 (Hafer, 2000-b) was to attempt to generalize the findings presented here to such individual differences.

A second purpose of Study 5 was to investigate an additional variable that should influence the need to believe in a just world (i.e., the extent to which the belief serves a useful purpose), given that one function of the BJW is to encourage investment in long-term goals. This variable was the extent to which people are committed to reaching their goals through just means. The more individuals plan to reach their goals through *un*just means, the less they should need to protect the belief that justice will prevail (in fact, they may even have a need to believe in an *un*just world). Thus, perhaps paradoxically, the more individuals plan to reach goals through unjust means, the less likely they should be to reject victims who contradict the BJW. Thus I predicted that, consistent with the results of Study 4, when a victim poses a strong threat to the BJW, the greater individuals' tendency to invest in and be concerned with long-term goals, the greater their rejection of the victim; I also predicted that the greater individuals' desire to obtain goals through unjust means, the *less* their rejection of the victim.

In an initial session, participants completed a booklet of questionnaires containing the individual difference measures for this study interspersed among several other measures for unrelated investigations. A scale measuring long-term investment orientation was created specifically for this research and consisted of sixteen items designed to assess the extent to which participants thought about their long-term goals following graduation as well as the importance and clarity of these goals (e.g., I try to choose my courses and other university activities according to how useful the experience will be for my future; I am not very concerned about what I will do with my degree once I have finished my university education [reverse-keyed]). The scale used to tap the extent to which participants would use unjust means to obtain their goals was Rushton and Chrisjohn's (1981) Self-Report Delinquency Scale (e.g., I have trespassed somewhere I was not supposed to go, like empty houses or private gardens; I have stolen money or goods from someone I worked for).

About two weeks later, under the guise of a separate and unrelated study, participants watched essentially the same videotape as that used for Study 4. The victim, however, was always innocent (i.e., she had always contracted the STD after a condom had broken), and threat to the BJW was manipulated by describing her suffering as either current (high threat) or in the past (low threat). In the past-suffering condition, participants were told that the student had continued with counseling and that her mental condition had improved. In the current suffering condition, participants were told that, due to government cutbacks, affordable counseling services were no longer available to her; therefore, Sarah had continued to suffer, although she would have improved if counseling had continued.

Following the videotape and experimental manipulation, participants completed a questionnaire containing the measures of victim rejection. Derogation was measured as in Study 4. Blame was the sum of six items regarding the extent to which Sarah could be held responsible or to blame for contracting the STD, and six items regarding the extent to which Sarah could be held responsible or to blame for her current emotional difficulties. The primary measure of disassociation was the sum of two items, one asking participants how likely they thought it was that a similar situation could happen to them, and another assessing how much they could identify with Sarah's negative experience.

As hypothesized, when the victim's suffering continued (i.e., posed a strong threat to the BJW), the greater participants' long-term investment orientation, the greater their tendency to reject the victim by blaming her for her fate, $r(28) = .35$, and by disassociating themselves from her suffering, $r(28) = .38$. Also as predicted, the higher participants' delinquency scores, the less their tendency to blame, $r(26) = -.40$, or to disassociate themselves from the victim, $r(26) = -.56$. When the victim's suffering had ended, that is, when the victim posed less of a threat to the BJW, the above relations were nonsignificant. These interaction effects were nonsignificant for character derogation.

The results of Study 5 further support the argument that an important function of the BJW is to allow investment in long-term goals. Given this function, the need to believe in a just world and, therefore, attempts to preserve the belief through rejection of the victim should be stronger (1) the more one invests in or focuses on long-term goals, and (2) the more one plans to reach these goals through just means.

Although the results of Studies 4 and 5 support this reasoning, neither tests the notion that rejection of a victim who threatens the BJW will be greatest when *both* long-term investments are of concern *and* one plans to reach these goals through just means (or when both long-term investments and just means are salient). The purpose of Study 6 (Hafer, Koumarelas, & Werthmiller, 2000) was to test this hypothesis.

As in Study 4, participants had ten minutes to write down their thoughts in response to open-ended questions. There were three versions of the essay questions for this study, however, rather than two. In the no long-term focus condition, participants were asked to write about their current courses and other activities at the university; there was no mention of long-term goals. In the long-term focus/just means condition, participants were asked to write about their long-term goals, and about how they might reach these goals in ways that are fair, just, or honest. In the long-term focus/unjust means condition, they were asked to write about their long-term goals, and about how they could reach these goals in ways that are less fair, just, or honest.

Participants were then exposed to the high-threat condition of Study 4; that is, they watched a videotape of an innocent victim who had contracted an STD after a condom had broken. Following the videotape, participants completed a questionnaire containing the dependent measures. As in Studies 3 and 4, derogation of the victim's character, victim blame, and disassociation were assessed. The derogation and disassociation measures were the same as those reported for Study 4. Blame was measured with a shorter version of the blame scale used for Study 5.

As predicted, participants who focused on reaching long-term goals through just means blamed ($M = 15.27$) and derogated the victim ($M = 50.36$) more than did participants in the other two conditions (blame, combined $M = 10.93$; derogation, combined $M = 42.47$). There was no significant effect for disassociation.

In sum, there was a greater tendency to reject the innocent victim (at least in terms of blame and derogation) when participants were focusing both on long-term investments *and* on reaching long-term goals through just means. Like the results for Studies 3 and 4, these findings support the notion that one of the primary functions of the

BJW is to give people confidence that their long-term investments will pay off.

Why Do We Reject Innocent Victims?

I have summarized two sets of studies that corroborate and extend previous work on Lerner's theory of the BJW in an attempt to better understand our tendency to reject innocent victims (through derogation of their character, disassociating ourselves from their suffering, etc.). What does this work tell us about why we reject such people? Almost four decades ago, Lerner suggested that we respond in this manner to innocent victims because the injustice of their suffering threatens a cherished belief – the BJW. Rejecting the victim helps to preserve the BJW in the face of this threat. Using a unique methodology, the first set of studies summarized here corroborates previous tests of Lerner's reasoning. I believe these studies provide compelling evidence that it is specifically the injustice of innocent suffering that is threatening and that this threat to the BJW motivates rejection of the victim.

Knowing that we may reject innocent victims to preserve the BJW raises the question of why we need to hold such a belief in the first place. Lerner has proposed that a belief that the world is a just place, where individuals get what they deserve (at least eventually), is essential for striving toward future goals; without this belief, we would have little hope that our efforts will pay off, and therefore any investment in the future would appear to be in vain. The second set of studies presented in this chapter is the first attempt to empirically test and support this proposed function of the BJW.

In sum, research on the BJW, including the studies presented in this chapter, suggests that we may reject innocent victims for the following reason. Rejection allows us to cope with the threat these victims pose to our BJW – a belief that is fundamental to our attempts to invest in long-term goals according to society's rules of fair play.

Is Rejection of Innocent Victims Inevitable?

This summary suggests, somewhat paradoxically, that rejecting innocent victims may be a product of our motivation to work toward future goals, and to do so in ways that are just, honest, and fair. What are the implications of this notion for modifying the tendency to defensively reject innocent victims? One obvious implication is that encouraging people to live "for the moment," with little attention to long-term goals, might reduce this response to suffering. However, given that striving toward long-term goals has been deemed by many to be a fundamental aspect of human personality (e.g., Allport, 1961; Funder, Block, & Block, 1983), as well as important for stable relationships and societies (e.g., Holmes, 1981; Platt, 1973; Thibaut & Kelley, 1959), such encouragement seems unrealistic and undesirable. Similarly, it seems inconceivable to suggest encouraging the achievement of goals through unjust means (which, according to the present research, might actually reduce defensive rejection of innocent victims), given the rather pervasive nature of the justice motive as well as its apparent adaptiveness for human social relations (see Lerner, 1977; Walster, Berscheid, & Walster, 1973). Another approach to reducing the rejection of innocent victims might be to decrease the motivation to defend the BJW in the face of contradictory evidence. As shown in the present research, however, this belief may be extremely important for long-term investment and, thus, important to preserve. It should also be noted that the BJW probably serves many other functions aside from encouraging long-term planning. For example, the belief might heighten well-being in times of stress by fostering a sense of order and hope for the future (e.g., Bulman & Wortman, 1977; Lambert, Burroughs, & Nguyen, 1999; Tomaka & Blaskovich, 1994; but see Dalbert, 1998; Hafer, Bogaert, & McMullen, in press, for negative effects of the BJW under similar circumstances). The BJW, therefore, might be classified as a "positive illusion" (Dalbert, 1998) that is too entrenched and too adaptive to give up.

A more reasonable approach toward modifying the rejection of innocent victims is to focus on the strategy for coping with threats to the BJW. Most research that examines reactions to victims within a BJW framework has focused on victim blame and derogation as methods of coping with innocent suffering (Maes, 1998; Reichle, Schneider, & Montada, 1998). There is less research on what Lerner (1980) refers to as "rational" strategies. For example, few studies have examined prosocial responses, such as helping and compensation, as methods of resolving the threat to the BJW posed by innocent victims (for examples, see Lincoln & Levinger, 1972; Lerner & Simmons, 1966; Miller, 1977). This work suggests that, when a victim threatens the BJW, people will help or compensate the victim to resolve the injustice if given a chance to effectively do so, and that this behavior might reduce the likelihood of rejection. Of course, it is not always possible to personally restore justice by helping or compensating the victim. However, even in such a situation, rejection of the victim is not inevitable. Lerner (1980) has suggested that one other rational way of dealing with injustices in the world is to accept that we can not resolve them all. Realizing this, we must set priorities regarding whom to help and then "do what we can." Increased use of these (and other) rational strategies for dealing with threats to the BJW may be a positive step toward reducing defensive rejection of victims.

Toward this end, future research should expand the focus on victim blame and derogation to examine the vast array of strategies that people may use to maintain the BJW when confronted with contradictory evidence, as well as to examine the situational and individual difference predictors of these behaviors. We have recently begun to study these issues in our own lab (see Hafer & SanCartier, 2000). Research findings and their implications could then be disseminated to lay audiences in an attempt to increase awareness of defensive rejection and to encourage more rational and compassionate responses to innocent victims. For example, such research could be used to create workshops for people who deal with victims in their work (e.g., police, social workers) or to augment existing "empathy training" programs (Stephan & Finlay, 1999). Increasing our understanding of both defensive and rational responses to innocent victims can ultimately help us to move toward a society that is more humane, constructive, and just in the way it treats those who suffer.

REFERENCES

Allport, G. W. (1961). *Pattern and growth in personality.* New York: Holt, Rinehart, and Winston.

Bulman, R. J., & Wortman, C. B. (1977). Attributions of blame and coping in the "real world": Severe accident victims react to their lot. *Journal of Personality and Social Psychology, 35,* 351–363.

Dalbert, C. (1998). Belief in a just world, well-being, and coping with an unjust fate. In L. Montada & M. J. Lerner (Eds.), *Responses to victimization and belief in a just world* (pp. 87–105). New York: Plenum.

Funder, D. C., Block, J. H., & Block, J. (1983). Delay of gratification: Some longitudinal personality correlates. *Journal of Personality and Social Psychology, 44,* 1198–1213.

Hafer, C. L. (2000a). Do innocent victims threaten the belief in a just world? Evidence from a modified Stroop task. *Journal of Personality and Social Psychology, 79,* 165–173.

(2000b). Investment in long-term goals and commitment to just means drive the need to believe in a just world. *Personality and Social Psychology Bulletin, 26,* 1059–1073.

(September, 2000c). *New evidence that innocent victims threaten justice beliefs.* Paper presented in a symposium at the Eighth Biennial Conference of the International Society for Justice Research, Tel Aviv, Israel.

Hafer, C. L., Bogaert, A. F., & McMullen, S. (in press). The belief in a just world and condom use in a sample of gay and bisexual men. *Journal of Applied Social Psychology.*

Hafer, C. L., Koumarelas, M., & Werthmiller, T. (2000). [Honesty, long-term striving, and the protection of the belief in a just world.] Unpublished raw data.

Hafer, C. L., & SanCartier, N. (September, 2000). *Individual differences in observers' responses to innocent victims.* Paper presented in a symposium at the Eighth Biennial Conference of the International Society for Justice Research, Tel Aviv, Israel.

Holmes, J. G. (1981). The exchange process in close relationships: Microbehavior and macromotives. In M. J. Lerner & S. C. Lerner (Eds.), *The justice motive in social behavior* (pp. 261–284). New York: Plenum.

Lambert, A. J., Burroughs, T., & Nguyen, T. (1999). Perceptions of risk and the buffering hypothesis: The role of just world beliefs and right-wing authoritarianism. *Personality and Social Psychology Bulletin, 25,* 643–656.

Lerner, M. J. (1977). The justice motive: Some hypotheses as to its origins and its forms. *Journal of Personality, 45,* 1–51.

(1980). *The belief in a just world: A fundamental delusion.* New York: Plenum.

(1998). The two forms of belief in a just world. In L. Montada & M. J. Lerner (Eds.), *Responses to victimization and belief in a just world* (pp. 247–269). New York: Plenum.

Lerner, M. J., & Goldberg, J. H. (1999). When do decent people blame victims: The differing effects of the explicit-rational and implicit-experiential cognitive systems. In S. Chaiken & Y. Trope (Eds.), *Dual process theories in social psychology* (pp. 627–640). New York: Guilford.

Lerner, M. J., & Miller, D. T. (1978). Just world research and the attribution process: Looking back and ahead. *Psychological Bulletin, 85,* 1030–1051.

Lerner, M. J., & Simmons, C. H. (1966). The observer's reaction to the "innocent victim": Compassion or rejection? *Journal of Personality and Social Psychology, 4,* 203–210.

Lincoln, A., & Levinger, G. (1972). Observers' evaluations of the victim and the attacker in an aggressive incident. *Journal of Personality and Social Psychology, 22,* 202–210.

MacLeod, C. M., & Hodder, S. L. (1998). Presenting two incongruent color words on a single trial does not alter Stroop interference. *Memory and Cognition, 26,* 212–219.

Maes, J. (1998). Immanent justice and ultimate justice: Two ways of believing in justice. In L. Montada & M. J. Lerner (Eds.), *Responses to victimization and belief in a just world* (pp. 9–40). New York: Plenum.

Miller, D. T. (1977). Altruism and threat to a belief in a just world. *Journal of Experimental Social Psychology, 13,* 113–124.
Mogg, K., Bradley, B. P., Williams, R., & Mathews, A. (1993). Subliminal processing of emotional information in anxiety and depression. *Journal of Abnormal Psychology, 102,* 304–311.
Mogg, K., Mathews, A. M., Bird, C., & MacGregor-Morris, R. (1990). Effects of stress and anxiety on the processing of threat stimuli. *Journal of Personality and Social Psychology, 59,* 1230–1237.
Platt, J. (1973). Social traps. *American Psychologist, 28,* 641–651.
Reichle, B., Schneider, A., & Montada, L. (1998). How do observers of victimization preserve their belief in a just world cognitively or actionally? In L. Montada & M. J. Lerner (Eds.), *Responses to victimization and belief in a just world* (pp. 55–64). New York: Plenum.
Rubin, Z., & Peplau, L. A. (1975). Who believes in a just world? *Journal of Social Issues, 31,* 65–89.
Rushton, J. P., & Chrisjohn, R. D. (1981). Extraversion, neuroticism, psychoticism and self-reported delinquency: Evidence from eight separate samples. *Personality and Individual Differences, 2,* 11–20.
Stephan,W. G., & Finlay, K. (1999). The role of empathy in improving intergroup relations. *Journal of Social Issues, 55,* 729–743.
Thibault, J. W., & Kelley, H. H. (1959). *The social psychology of groups.* New York: Wiley.
Tomaka, J., & Blascovich, J. (1994). Effects of justice beliefs on cognitive appraisal of and subjective, physiological, and behavioral responses to potential stress. *Journal of Personality and Social Psychology, 67,* 732–740.
Walster, E., Berscheid, E., & Walster, G. W. (1973). New directions in equity research. *Journal of Personality and Social Psychology, 25,* 151–176.
Williams, J. M. G., Mathews, A., & MacLeod, C. (1996). The emotional Stroop task and psychopathology. *Psychological Bulletin, 120,* 3–24.

8. Helping and Rationalization as Alternative Strategies for Restoring the Belief in a Just World: Evidence from Longitudinal Change Analyses

BARBARA REICHLE AND MANFRED SCHMITT

The need for justice is a core construct of Melvin Lerner's just world theory (Lerner, 1970, 1980). According to this theory, human beings want to believe that individuals get what they deserve and deserve what they get. They prefer to assume that bad deeds are punished and good deeds rewarded, and that good things happen to good people and bad things to bad people. The belief in just contingencies among character, behavior, and fate enables the person to maintain a sense of confidence and efficacy. If justice is a guiding principle in life, individuals can rely upon getting what they earn for their achievements and being respected for decency and moral integrity. This principle implies that they can prevent misfortune by conforming to social norms and ethical standards.

Injustice threatens this belief system and motivates the person to engage in activities that either restore justice directly or help to maintain the belief in a just world by other means. According to Lerner and his colleagues, this can be accomplished by acting prosocially on behalf of the victim, or by cognitively restructuring the situation in such a way that it appears just (Lerner, 1980; Lerner & Miller, 1978; Lerner, Miller, & Holmes, 1976). Acknowledging injustice and actively fighting it, for example, by helping innocent victims or punishing victimizers, have been called action strategies. Activities aimed at reinterpreting the situation so as to make it appear just after all, or at least less unjust than it seemed at first sight, have been termed cognitive strategies (Reichle, Schneider, & Montada, 1998). Reinterpretation may focus on the event, the causes of the event, the behavior of those who have committed an act of injustice or of those who have suffered from it, or the character of those who are involved in the incident. For example, when observers are confronted with disadvantaged groups, they may downplay the situation by arguing that happiness and wealth are unrelated. Or, when confronted with a violently aggressive situation, observers may reinterpret the perpetrator's behavior as an act of self-defense, or as retribution justified by a former offense committed by the current victim. Observers often justify misery and suffering by claiming that victims are responsible for their own fate (Montada, 1998; Ryan, 1971). Derogating the character of victims and less fortunate people is another way of distorting reality in order to defend the belief in justice (e.g., Dion & Dion, 1987). This mechanism is based on the assumption that character and fate are intrinsically interwoven, that is, that good things happen to good people and bad things to bad people (Heider, 1958; Lerner, 1970). Accordingly, ascribing favorable character traits and higher achievement to those who are fortunate by mere chance (e.g., even to those winning money on a random basis) can help to maintain the belief that people deserve what they get (Lerner, 1965; Schmitt, 1991).

Given the many ways of defending the belief in a just world, it is important to know which strategy will be used by which individuals under which conditions. It has been argued (Lerner, 1980; Lerner & Miller, 1978) that prosocial actions will be preferred if the observer is capable of restoring justice by direct action, such as compensating victims or punishing perpetrators. Observers will engage in prosocial actions provided that they are convinced that such actions will have lasting effects, and that the costs of such actions neither exceed a critical level nor interfere with what the observers feel they deserve. If these conditions are not met, that is, if concrete actions appear impossible, ineffective, or too costly, observers will more likely show cognitive responses such as blaming or derogating victims. Additional moderators have been suggested, although empirical evidence on their impact is limited. For example, Aderman, Brehm, and Katz (1974) asked participants in one experimental condition to imagine how they would feel if they received electric shocks for unavoidable errors. Under this condition of empathy, observers did not derogate others who received electric shocks. Although the psychological mechanism producing this effect is not entirely clear (Lerner & Miller, 1978), it appears logical to assume that the observers identified with the victims. If this was the case, then derogation would have implied self-derogation. Consequently, (implicit) self-derogation was avoided by refraining from victim derogation. Following this conjecture, empathy, role taking, and similarity of fate may lead observers to prefer prosocial actions instead of cognitive restructuring, even at the price of higher costs.

Two common research strategies have been used to test these assumptions. The first strategy has been to vary situational conditions *experimentally*, so that some participants were given the opportunity to end an observed injustice by compensating a victim or punishing a victimizer, while other participants had no ability to intervene directly. All other factors being identical, participants in the first type of situation were expected to prefer prosocial actions, while participants in the second type of situation should tend to rationalize what they saw. Several experiments used this design and yielded the expected results. In a classic experiment by Lerner and Simmons (1966), student participants were shown another student receiving painful shocks for unavoidable errors during a learning task. In one of the experimental conditions, participants were able to compensate by reassigning the victim to a reward condition. In another of the conditions, participants could not compensate the victim and knew that the painful shocks would continue in the second trial. Consistent with expectations, derogation was more pronounced in the latter condition than in the former. In another study, Miller (1977) gave students the opportunity to help families in need by donating some of the money they earned for participating in further experiments. In one condition, the family was portrayed as a single case with well-defined and manageable needs. In the other condition, participants were told that at least 300 other families in the area had similar needs. As expected, more help was offered in the former than in the latter condition. Although cognitive strategies such as blaming and derogation were not measured, the differing amounts of help depending on the number of families in need are consistent with the assumption that the likelihood of prosocial activities is a function of their effectiveness.

The second research strategy takes into account and explicitly uses the plausible idea that the moderators mentioned above (availability of means, costs, effectiveness) vary objectively and subjectively among individuals. Obviously, individuals differ in the availability of resources such as knowledge, power, money, and other means that are needed to act against injustice. In addition, control, efficacy beliefs, and optimism vary greatly among individuals. Individuals are less likely to attempt to restore justice by action when the resources needed for such actions are *subjectively* not available to them (although they *objectively* may be available), or when they believe that actions against injustice would not be effective, or when they expect that such actions would be too costly. In such a situation they would be more likely to cope cognitively. In a similiar vein, other individuals will perceive resources, effectiveness, and low costs although they are powerless and although their actions are ineffective from an objective point of view. Following this line of reasoning, the moderator hypothesis can also be tested by measuring the individual extent of the moderating variable (instead of varying it experimentally) and correlating it with indicators for prosocial actions and cognitive strategies. A recent study by Mohiyeddini and Montada (1998) may illustrate this approach. In this study, employed participants were confronted with unemployment in order to threaten their belief in justice. Participants were given an efficacy scale for measuring the extent of their (generalized) belief that they are able to contribute to a just world. Several indicators for prosocial actions and cognitive strategies were measured as dependent variables. Intentions to help the unemployed (e.g., by writing petition letters to politicians) and membership in social and political organizations committed to help disadvantaged groups such as the unemployed served as indicators for prosocial actions, while derogation (lack of sympathy) and blaming (self-infliction) were measured as cognitive strategies. As expected, self-efficacy had significantly positive regressive main effects on all indicators for prosocial actions and a negative (not significant) regressive main effect on the cognitive strategy of derogation. In addition, efficacy interacted with belief in a just world as measured by the Dalbert, Montada, and Schmitt scale (1987). For participants with high scores on the efficacy scale, belief in a just world tended to decrease victim derogation, whereas for subjects with low scores on the efficacy scale, belief in a just world tended to increase derogation. Similarly, the effect of believing in a just world on the willingness to fight unemployment was positive for high-efficacy participants and negative for low-efficacy participants.

This latter effect of the Mohiyeddini and Montada (1998) study corresponds to an effect reported earlier by Miller (1977). In this study (just described), an interactional design was implemented. In addition to the experimental variation of situational effectiveness (one versus 300 needy families), belief in a just world was measured with the Rubin and Peplau scale (1973, 1975). The impact of effectiveness on helping depended on belief in a just world. As expected, effectiveness made a difference for strong just world believers, but not for weak believers. This effect, the interaction effects reported by Mohiyeddini and

Montada (1998), and similar effects found in some (but not all) other studies (Schmitt, 1998) suggest that situational threats to the belief in a just world are more severe for individuals with a strong need for justice (i.e., with high scores on belief in a just world scales). According to the construct, the motivational force to restore justice is more powerful for these individuals than for individuals with a weak desire for justice.

Although the results of a large number of studies that implemented one of these (experimental, correlational, interactional) research strategies are consistent with the *implications* of Lerner's hypothesis that individuals use different strategies for maintaining their belief in justice, we are not aware of studies that have *directly* tested this assumed process. Such a direct test would require a longitudinal design in which belief in justice is measured at least twice. Belief in justice would have to be challenged at the first measurement instance or between the two occasions of measurement. In addition, strategies for defending the belief in justice against these challenges would need to be observed. The theory predicts that belief in justice decreases from wave 1 to wave 2 for individuals who do not employ defensive strategies, whereas no change or even an increase in justice belief can be expected for individuals who make use of restorative strategies such as helping, blaming, and derogation. Furthermore, the amount of positive or negative change in justice belief should depend on the intensity of the restorative efforts. This research strategy could be supplemented by including the moderator variables (effectiveness of action, cost of action, etc.) on which the type of restorative strategy presumably depends.

Two variations of this design seem appropriate. Belief in justice could be measured before and after *acute* threats to justice beliefs, such as those applied in the Lerner and Simmons (1966) experiment, the Miller (1977) experiment, and similar experiments. Measures for reactions to these threats, such as blaming (Lerner & Simmons, 1966) and helping (Miller, 1977), which served as dependent variables in these experiments, would then obtain the status of intervening variables and predictors for changes in justice belief from pre-test to post-test. A weakness of this procedure might be that it is too explicit and susceptible to response biases (memory effects, consistency effects, reactance, etc.). Well-designed cover stories and distraction procedures might help to disguise the purpose of the justice measures and increase internal validity. This experimental procedure seems adequate for simulating threats to the justice belief by finite incidences of injustice, such as accidents and crimes.

Longitudinal surveys are probably more appropriate than experiments for studying how individuals cope with *enduring* social inequalities that challenge the belief in justice over a long period of time. In cases of such a constant challenge to one's belief in justice, single acts of help may not suffice to defend the belief in a just world. Individuals are more likely to develop enduring action tendencies and attitudes to maintain their belief in justice. Action tendencies might include helping on a regular basis, such as donating part of one's income to disadvantaged groups or joining activity groups that regularly support the disadvantaged. According to the theory, such prosocial actions will be chosen by individuals who believe that these actions will be effective and that they can afford the costs of these actions. Individuals who are not convinced that such actions will be successful, or who fear they will come short of what they deserve by providing help repeatedly, are more likely to develop negative attitudes toward the victims, including derogation, blaming, and other rationalizations.

Empirical evidence from a large number of *cross-sectional studies* is consistent with this reasoning. It has been found in these studies that belief in a just world correlates with the willingness to help disadvantaged groups as well as with certain negative social attitudes, including blame and derogation (cf. Furnham & Gunter, 1984; Montada, 1998; Montada, Schmitt, & Dalbert, 1986; Montada & Schneider, 1989; Maes, 1994, 1998; Maes & Schmitt, 1999). Although these cross-sectional results are in accord with the assumption that different strategies are employed for preserving justice belief, they do not reflect the process of restoration itself, and they should not be interpreted causally. Intraindividual changes in justice belief and causal effects of individual differences in restorative efforts on intraindividual changes in justice belief can be uncovered only in longitudinal studies. Belief in justice has to be measured at least twice during the time it is being challenged by ongoing injustice. Furthermore, measures for traitlike restorative behaviors (ongoing help, membership in activity groups, forming stable attitudes toward victim groups) have to be implemented with sufficient distance from the second justice belief measurement. Given the slow intraindividual changes in action and attitude traits as well as in justice beliefs (Schmitt et al., 1993), the time span between two measurements needs to be sufficiently long to permit reliable detection of intraindividual changes in justice belief as well as longitudinal effects of restorative behaviors on these changes.

A longitudinal residual analysis is the appropriate statistical method for exploring whether restorative behavior has an effect on the changes in justice belief. Belief in justice measured at occasion 2 is first regressed on belief in justice measured at occasion 1. Given that belief in justice remains constant on the level of means (which has been demonstrated; Schmitt et al., 1993), residual values of belief in justice reflect intraindividual changes between the two occasions of measurement, part of which is measurement error, of course. If these residual values can be predicted by measures for restorative behavior (helping, blaming, derogation) obtained at occasion 1 or between the two occasions (with sufficient distance to occasion 2), this would mean that changes in justice belief depend on these restorative efforts. Furthermore, given the time order of the measurement occasions, a causal interpretation of the effect is possible under the additional assumption that restorative efforts are not confounded with any third variables that could have a (causal) effect on belief in justice (Steyer, 1984, 1985). Ideally, all confounded third variables would have to be measured and controlled statistically. This would require knowledge that we don't have at this point. Therefore, it seems appropriate to begin with testing whether longitudinal effects of restorative behavior on belief in justice can be obtained.

The longitudinal survey design can also be used to explore which restorative strategies are effective under which conditions. Looking at the reasons for choosing cognitive versus prosocial action strategies, groups of individuals (observers of injustice) who are confronted with different types of chronic injustice could be compared. Let us assume that one type of injustice is constructed in such a way that it can probably be ended by direct intervention, whereas concrete action seems ineffective or too costly to most observers when confronted with the other type of injustice. It is to be expected that under the former condition, interindividual differences in intraindividual change in justice belief would originate more from the individual differences in direct prosocial action, while under the latter condition, individual differences in cognitive restoration strategies would be more effective.

Using data from two longitudinal studies with different samples and different justice issues, we will implement the methodology outlined here and explore the effects of prosocial and cognitive restoration on changes in justice belief. Both studies were large-scale questionnaire studies. In the first study, reactions of privileged German citizens to the relative deprivation of three disadvantaged groups (people living in developing countries, migrant workers living in Germany, and unemployed Germans) were obtained. The design, the variables, and results from cross-sectional analyses have been reported by Montada (1998), Montada and Schneider (1989), and Schneider, Reichle, and Montada (1986). In addition, Reichle et al. (1998) presented longitudinal analyses that were performed according to the methodology explained earlier. They tested whether changes in justice belief, specifically related to the three groups of disadvantaged people, depended on helping and rationalization. In the current analysis, we explore the impact of these restorative strategies on general belief in a just world. These additional analyses are valuable for three reasons. The first reason is parsimony. It has been argued in the field of personality psychology that domain-specific constructs are undesirable from a theory of science point of view because they violate the principle of parsimony. A related argument is that the domain-specific measurement of psychological variables runs the risk of obtaining artificial correlations among variables due to the semantic similarity of item contents (method effects). The third reason is to make the results of Study I as comparable as possible to those of Study II, in which domain-specific belief in justice was not measured, but only justice belief in general.

The second study deals with relative deprivation in Germany after the reunification in 1990. The data for this study were collected during spring 1996 and spring 1998. International readers can find a description of the study and cross-sectional results in Schmitt and Maes (1998) and Maes and Schmitt (1999). A more detailed description in English of the design, variables, and sample is available upon request (Maes et al., 1998).

Study I

Method

In order to maximize the likelihood of threats to the justice beliefs of respondent observers, the first half of the sample was recruited randomly from adult citizens living in a relatively privileged neighborhood of a West German city; the second half of the sample consisted of university students of various majors (38% of the second-half sample) and two groups of employed citizens with varying job security. At the first wave of measurement, the sample consisted of 865 participants. Of these, 434 also participated in the second wave. The mean age of this subsample was $M = 35$ (SD = 17), with a minimum of 19 and a maximum of 84 years. Fifty-nine percent of the participants were male. As a consequence of the recruitment strategy, participants with a higher education are overrepresented.

Data were collected by means of questionnaires in fall 1985 and in spring 1986. The time difference between the occasions of measurement amounted to five months. Questionnaires containing a total of about 600 items were send by mail and answered anonymously by the participants (Schneider, Reichle, et al., 1986).

The main focus of the questionnaires was on social inequality, specifically differences in the quality of life between (West) German citizens and people living in developing countries, Turkish migrant workers living in (West) Germany, and unemployed (West) Germans. The disadvantageous living conditions of these groups were described in nine scenarios (three for each group). Deprivations were specified as financial problems, insecurity about the future, bad working conditions, low pay, low status, insufficient medical care, and poor housing. Participants were asked to give their perceptions, appraisals, and attributions regarding the differences between their own living conditions and the living conditions of the disadvantaged groups, including one statement of justice versus injustice for each of the nine scenarios (e.g., "I think it is not fair that unemployed people are that much worse off than myself"; "These big differences between the industrialized countries and the developing countries are not just"; 1 = agree completely – 6 = disagree completely).

On the average, participants evaluated the differences between their own living conditions and those of the disadvantaged groups as rather unjust. Most injustice was perceived in comparison to the poverty of developing countries, less when viewing the situation of Turkish migrant workers, and even less vis-à-vis the situation of unemployed (West) Germans. Consequently, a large majority of the respondents felt undeservedly privileged. Justice judgments were rather stable across the five months considered ($.61 \leq r \leq .71$). It thus can be safely assumed that the unequal living conditions represented a constant threat to the belief in justice of our participants.

In the present context, three groups of variables are relevant: (1) belief in a just world, (2) cognitive strategies to justify unequal living conditions, and (3) willingness to help the disadvantaged as a prosocial action strategy.

(1) Belief in justice was measured on both occasions with the Dalbert, Montada, and Schmitt (1987) scale. The internal consistency of this scale amounted to *Alpha* = .79. Factor analyses yielded a common factor (Schneider, Montada, Reichle, & Meissner, 1986). Therefore, all items were aggregated to obtain an index of general belief in a just world.

(2) Three cognitive strategies aimed at rationalizing or downplaying the living conditions of the disadvantaged groups were assessed at the time of first measurement: *perception of disadvantages as self-inflicted* (e.g., "Many unemployed have brought about their situation themselves"), *minimization of the disadvantage* (e.g., "One cannot generalize; many unemployed manage their situation pretty well"), *justification of own advantages* (e.g., "It is not just because I am lucky that I am better off, I really deserve what I have"). The items for measuring these three strategies were part of the existential guilt inventory that also included items for assessing other reactions to social inequalities (Reichle, Montada, & Schneider, 1985). Factor analyses were performed with the items for each disadvantaged group separately. One common factor always emerged that loaded the three cognitive strategies important here. It seemed acceptable, therefore, to aggregate these strategies to obtain a reliable indicator of rationalization for each disadvantaged group (*Alpha* > .80; Schneider, Montada, et al., 1986).

(3) With regard to each of the three disadvantaged groups, respondents had to indicate their willingness to engage in eight different activities aimed at improving the situation of the disadvantaged groups (spending money, signing a petition, participating in a march or demonstration, joining a group of activists) (Schneider, Reichle, et al., 1986). These activities appeared as homogeneous indicators in the factor analyses. Therefore, they were aggregated into scales (*Alpha* > .80; Schneider, Montada, et al., 1986).

Results

The retest correlation of belief in a just world was $r = .73$, which is lower than the estimated reliability of *Alpha* = .79. This indicates that despite substantial stability, true intraindividual changes in justice belief occurred across the five months. The theory predicts that such intraindividual changes result from cognitive and action strategies employed to defend one's belief in a just world against threats. We tested this hypothesis by regressing the belief in a just world measured in wave 2 on the belief in a just world measured in wave 1, as well as rationalization in wave 1 and helping in wave 1. This longitudinal causal change multiple regression analysis was performed as follows. First, the belief in a just world as measured in wave 1 was entered. Then, the three indicators for rationalization (one indicator for each disadvantaged group) and the three indicators for helping (one indicator for each disadvantaged group) were taken into the regression equation under the condition that their *unique* contribution to belief in justice variance of wave 2 was significant. Only rationalization of the disadvantages in developing countries appeared as a significant predictor of change in justice belief ($F_{1,409} = 18.32$; $p < .01$; 2% unique variance). This result means that participants who rationalized the disadvantages in developing countries at time 1 had a higher belief in a just world at time 2 compared to participants who did not rationalize the disadvantages in developing countries at time 1. None of the other rationalization scales (migrant workers, the unemployed) and none of the helping scales could explain significant proportions of just-world belief found in wave 2 – in addition to the rationalization scale for developing countries. Before discussing these results, we will describe Study II and the results obtained there.

Study II

According to most political scientists, the desire for better material living conditions was an important, and probably the most important, motivation for East Germans to stand up against the socialist regime of the former German Democratic Republic in 1989. Despite enormous efforts of the East German government to satisfy the consumer needs of the population, East Germans were confronted constantly with the much better living conditions in West Germany, Europe, and the United States. Almost all East Germans had access to West German TV, and almost all watched West German programs. Besides the large discrepancy between East and West Germany in the availability of consumer goods, East German industry was increasingly less able to compete with the West, and it was obvious that the economic gap would continue to increase. Between the revolution (November 1989) and the reunification (October 1990), West German politicians promised that the living conditions in East Germany would rapidly improve and soon be equal to those in West Germany. Although some politicians and economists were less optimistic, there was general agreement among a large majority of experts, the media, and the general population that it would take no more than five, at most ten years to turn East Germany into a prosperous part of a reunified Germany. Some even envisioned a reverse gap between former East and West Germany, with East Germany becoming the economically superior part of Germany.

History proved these optimistic forecasts wrong. Even today, ten years after the reunification, substantial differences in the quality of life between East and West Germany remain. In almost every domain of life, the living conditions are still considerably better in West Germany than in East Germany. For example, East Germans earn 14.5% less than West Germans for the same work; the average rate of savings is about three times higher in West Germany than in East Germany; and the unemployment rate is currently about twice as high in East Germany (16%) than in West Germany (8%). This situation is a constant topic of political discussion and in the media. More important, it is a major justice concern for East and West Germans alike (Schmitt & Maes, 1998). Most East and West Germans agree that the situation cannot be justified. This became evident when the participants in Study II compared the living conditions in East and West Germany on a large number of dimensions regarding work, income, property, housing, cities, and the natural environment. Participants were asked to indicate on rating scales how much better or worse they considered the living conditions in East Germany compared to West Germany. In addition, participants were asked to indicate what they would consider to be a fair or justified East–West difference. The difference between the two ratings (is – ought) was taken as an indicator of relative deprivation. In all domains of quality of life, except the natural environment, a substantial degree of relative deprivation of the East was perceived by both East German and West German participants. Accordingly, the unequal living conditions in united Germany should threaten the belief in justice of East and West Germans alike.

For the purpose of comparability with Study I, we will focus on the situation of West Germans who are relatively privileged in comparison to East Germans. How do West Germans cope with the situation? How will they protect their belief in a just world vis-à-vis the unjust situation they are reminded of almost daily by the media? And, more specifically, how effective are cognitive and action strategies?

Method

In order to maximize the demographic heterogeneity and the representativeness of the sample, participants were recruited on the basis of a geographical division of Germany into eighteen cells. The registration officers of two communities in each cell were asked to provide random samples from the population of all inhabitants between fifteen and seventy-five years of age. Additional respondents were randomly drawn from telephone directories. A total of 929 West Germans participated at the first wave of measurement. The mean age was $M = 45$ ($SD = 16$). Sixty-one percent of the participants were male. The sample is representative according to many but not all demographic variables. Most pronouncedly, participants with higher education are overrepresented. The current analyses are based on a subsample of 368 West Germans who had always lived in West Germany, who participated in both measurement waves, and who provided complete data on all variables that are included in the present analyses.

Data were collected using questionnaires in spring 1996 and in spring 1998. Questionnaires were sent by mail and answered anonymously. The items to measure the variables for the current analyses were embedded in a large set of about 2,500 items. The main focus of the questionnaire was on social inequalities in united Germany. Perceptions, appraisals, and attributions of East–West differences in quality of life were assessed over five domains (labor, prosperity, human relations, housing, natural environment). Participants were asked to estimate East–West differences in living conditions and to indicate whether and how much they considered these differences to be unjust (versus justified). Overall, participants unanimously agreed that the living conditions were much poorer in East Germany and that this was unjust. In other words, the majority of West Germans felt *undeservedly* privileged. These estimates were rather stable on the level of group means across two years, although slight improvements in the living conditions in East Germany were perceived by a majority of the participants. Given these finding, it can safely be assumed that the unequal living conditions in Germany provide a constant threat to the belief in justice.

Three variables are of primary interest in the present context: belief in a just world, victim derogation as a typical cognitive strategy, and willingness to help the disadvantaged as a prosocial action strategy. *Belief in justice* was measured as in Study I, *Alpha* (.73) being somewhat lower. *Derogation* was measured at occasion 1 as follows. Participants were asked to describe the typical East German on thirty-six evaluative adjective scales. Half of these adjectives were positive (friendly, polite, etc.), half of the adjectives were negative (arrogant, lazy, etc.). Factor analyses yielded two negatively correlated common factors. The first factor loaded only positive-trait adjectives, the second factor loaded only negative-trait adjectives. The items of the second factor were summed to obtain an index for derogation (*Alpha* = .93). *Willingness to help* was measured at occasion 1 with two sets of items. In one section of the questionnaire, participants were given a list of seven political, economic, and legal actions that could be taken to improve living conditions in East Germany. The actions included sending financial aid to East Germany, granting East Germans special tax deductions, and using tax money to create jobs in East Germany. Participants were asked to approve or disapprove of these activities, which all implied sacrifices by the West German population. Consecutively, respondents were given a list of four individual efforts they could make to support the actions they had approved. This list included donating money, signing petitions, writing letters to politicians, and going on strike. Participants were asked how much they were willing to commit themselves to engaging in these actions. The two sets of items were submitted to a common factor analysis. A common factor appeared that loaded twelve items from both sets of items and that could be interpreted clearly as *willingness to help improve the living conditions in East Germany*. The items were summed to obtain an index of willingness to help (*Alpha* = .80).

Results

The retest correlation of belief in a just world was .56. This value is lower than the corresponding value obtained in Study I, the most likely reason being the longer time interval between the times of measurement in Study II (two years) as compared to Study I (five months). As in Study I, however, the stability (.56) of the just world scale was considerably lower than its reliability (.73). This means that despite substantial stability, true intraindividual changes in justice belief occurred across the time span considered. The belief in justice became stronger for some individuals and weaker for others. As in Study I, we explored whether these intraindividual changes were systematically related to cognitive and action strategies. The same statistical procedure as in

Study I was used for this purpose. Belief in a just world measured in wave 2 was regressed on the belief in a just world from wave 1, as well as derogation measured in wave 1 and helping in wave 1. Willingness to help had a significantly unique effect on *changes* in justice belief ($F_{1,365} = 6.75$; $p < .01$; 1.5% unique variance). West German participants who committed themselves to help had a stronger belief in a just world two years later than participants who were not willing to sacrifice part of their advantageous living conditions for the sake of improving the living conditions of East Germans. We did not assess whether or not participants who indicated their willingness to help actually engaged in such helping. It is not possible, for this reason, to estimate the differential effectiveness of behavioral intentions and behavior. Given the high correlation found in many studies between behavioral intentions and behavior (Ajzen & Fishbein, 1980), it seems safe to assume that the effect of actual help on changes in justice belief are similar to the effects of helping intentions. Furthermore, it seems plausible on theoretical grounds that the positive effects of helping – if they are different at all from the effects of willingness – would be higher.

The effect of derogation was not significant, according to conventional criteria ($F_{1,364} = 2.14$; $p = .14$). However, consistent with theory, the sign of the regression weight was positive. To test whether the non-significant effect of derogation was due to a lack of reliability, a LISREL model was specified that corresponded to the regression analysis. However, regression parameters were estimated for latent variables. Latent variables were measured with two indicators each. These indicators were obtained by randomly splitting the items into test halves. The fit of the model was good ($\chi_{12} = 14.35$; $p = .28$). As expected, the standardized regression weights of the latent predictors were somewhat larger than the corresponding statistics for the manifest predictors. The regression weights for the latent belief in a just world measured in wave 1 and the latent willingness to help in wave 1 were .62 (instead of .55) and .14 (instead of .12), respectively. However, the regression weight for the latent derogation in wave 1 was about equal to the regression weight for the manifest derogation indicator in wave 1 (.05 instead of .07) and again was not significant.

Discussion

The results of the two studies have several interesting aspects. To begin with, they show that the justice issues addressed in the questionnaires were indeed justice concerns for the participants that challenged their sense of justice. Although these issues probably did not predominantly occupy our participants' way of thinking and feeling, they were made aware of them often enough by the media or in other ways to make the need for justice salient and to allow for an instigation of the restorative processes involved. Although we measured indicators for these processes at distinct points in time, they are not isolated acts but rather stable mind sets. This can be concluded from the retest correlation of willingness to help and coping, which amounted to .58 and .34 in Study II, respectively. Even higher stability coefficients were obtained for the coping strategies in Study I (the stability of helping between .73 and .77; the stability of rationalization between .84 and .89). Although the temporal stability of derogation is much lower in Study II than the temporal stability of helping, both stability coefficients and the stability coefficients obtained in Study I are high enough to warrant the conclusion that our indicators do not reflect ad hoc judgments, but rather slowly changing attitudes toward disadvantaged groups.

It seems unlikely that the justice issues addressed in the questionnaires were the only ones that the participants experienced during the time of our studies. However, they must have been important enough to require restorative efforts. The effects of these efforts on changes in justice belief were small in both studies. The proportions of belief in justice variance measured in wave 2, uniquely explained by the restorative strategies variables, are significant but low in both studies. This is not surprising, given that most respondents were probably confronted with additional kinds of injustice during our investigations besides the kinds of injustice we explored. These other injustices and the restorative strategies employed in these contexts were not investigated in our studies. It is therefore not possible to estimate their effects. The point is that the types of experienced injustice we considered in our studies were probably not the only ones that our participants experienced during our investigation. Therefore, the types of injustice we explored can hardly be expected to explain the majority of change variance of belief in justice. Nevertheless, the cases of injustice we looked at seem to have been important enough to show up as systematic effects of the two types of restorative strategies on changes in the belief in justice after five and twenty-four months, respectively.

Different restorative strategies proved to be successful in the two studies. While in Study I, blaming victims, but not being willing to help them, contributed to defending the belief in justice, actively helping was a successful strategy in Study II. The moderator hypotheses outlined earlier offer possible interpretations for this difference of results between the two studies. It seems likely that West Germans confronted with the disadvantages of their East German neighbors were convinced that their disadvantages would not be permanent but would disappear sooner or later. Furthermore, our participants were probably convinced that they and other West Germans can contribute effectively to reducing the East–West gap. In fact, both beliefs would correspond to the current position of most politicians and economists. Although how much time is needed for equalizing the living conditions is a matter of considerable disagreement, most experts are convinced that the East–West gap will disappear sooner or later. In addition, concrete measures have been taken by the government to reach this goal. More importantly, perhaps, every German who has an income (including interest from savings) has to contribute a certain percentage of his earnings to a so-called solidarity fund, which is used exclusively for building up the economy and infrastructure in East Germany. Although this contribution is forced by law and not submitted voluntarily, it may give West Germans a sense of efficacy and optimism. In addition, the amount that has to be contributed to this solidarity fund is small enough that it probably does not interfere with most West Germans' sense of getting what they deserve.

To summarize, the prosocial action strategy of helping was probably considered possible for most of the West German participants in Study II, and it is perhaps for this reason that willingness to help was a more effective strategy than derogating East Germans. Empathy may be an additional reason (Aderman et al., 1974). The division of Germany after World War II was decided by the Allied forces on the basis of military and political considerations, not according to the characteristics of the population. Consequently, it was a matter of chance who lived in what later became West Germany or East Germany. Today's social inequalities between East and West Germany are thus a late consequence of an arbitrary decision. It must be easy for any German to imagine of having lived on the other side of the wall, with the consequence of being deprived instead of privileged today or vice versa. Although since Lerner's experiment (1965) we know that a random distribution of advantages and disadvantages does not prevent blaming and derogation, role taking, empathy, and imagined similarity of fate seem to have been more likely for the participants in Study II (for whom the randomness of the distribution of advantages and disadvantages could have been much more salient) than for the participants in Study I.

The participants in Study I were confronted with the disadvantages of people living in developing countries, migrant workers living in Germany, and unemployed Germans living in Germany. Although these disadvantaged groups differ in many ways, each of them may have attributes that reduce the effectiveness of helping as a restorative strategy.

Foreign migrant workers came to Germany voluntarily, mostly because they wanted to achieve a better standard of living. Although most migrant workers in Germany are disadvantaged compared to Germans, most of these groups are rather successful economically and do not appear as needy. Italians were the first large group of migrant workers to come to Germany after World War II. Their living conditions were very poor in the beginning, but have improved consistently since then. Today, many Italians run prosperous businesses, and their standard of living is quite high. The subjects of Study I may have generalized this flourishing to other groups of migrant workers (such as the Turkish) who came to Germany later and who are still much less well-off than the Italians. Furthermore, empathy, role taking, and similarity of fate seem less likely for West German citizens vis-à-vis migrant workers than vis-à-vis East Germans. Both factors may explain why helping migrant workers was not an effective restorative strategy in Study I.

People living in developing countries (Study I) differ from East Germans (Study II) in several regards. First, their disadvantages seem much less limited in time. Everybody knows that the developing countries have been deprived for decades. And it seems rather likely that the situation in these countries will endure for a long time. Second, the gap between West Germany and these countries is much greater than the gap between West and East Germany. The amount of financial help needed to improve the living conditions in developing countries is much greater than the money needed to equalize the living conditions in Germany. Finally, empathy, role taking, and hypothetical fate similarity are certainly much lower vis-à-vis this group than vis-à-vis East Germans. Together with a lower sense of efficacy, this may be an important reason why helping is not an effective coping strategy when confronted with the bad living conditions in developing countries.

What are the differences between East Germans (Study II) and the *unemployed* (Study I) that may explain why helping was an effective restorative strategy in Study II but not in Study I? Unemployment was on the rise when Study I was conducted. Furthermore, none of the various economic and political programs to reduce unemployment had been successful. On the contrary, only large-scale economic and structural changes seemed to cause changes in the unemployment rate. Such changes cannot be influenced by individual citizens playing their roles as customers and voters. In addition, it is unclear what individual citizens can do to reduce unemployment. There is nothing like a solidarity fund for the unemployed to which an individual could contribute money. All of this may have reduced the sense of efficacy of the participants of Study I and may explain why helping was not an effective restorative strategy.

The just world theory predicts that cognitive strategies will be employed whenever prosocial actions fail. Indeed, blaming the people in developing countries was an effective strategy in Study I. Why did rationalization regarding the other two deprived groups not have a significant effect on changes in justice belief? Two interpretations are plausible. (1) The deprivation of inhabitants of developing countries was considered more unjust by our privileged German participants than was the deprivation of migrant workers and the unemployed. Consequently, the unfair deprivation of people living in developing countries posed the greatest threat to belief in justice and evoked the strongest need for restoration. (2) The three rationalization scales were highly correlated among each other (between $r = .78$ and $r = .91$), possibly leading to the problem that the partial rationalization scales (migrant workers, unemployed) did not contain sufficient information to explain changes in justice belief.

Our reasoning regarding possible causes for the different coping effects in the two studies cannot be tested directly, because the studies differ in many ways. The time spans between the two occasions of measurement were different. Different types of cognitive strategies were assessed (rationalization in Study I, derogation in Study II). The participants of Study I were explicitly confronted with the deprivation of the three disadvantaged groups via scenarios, whereas the participants of Study II were asked to rate East–West differences in the quality of life. All of these and additional differences between the studies are confounded with those variables (efficacy of help, amount of help needed, etc.) upon which according to the just world theory the selection of a restorative strategy depends. Therefore, the present research should not be regarded as a flawless test of these moderator hypotheses, but rather as preliminary evidence of this type of survey research. Despite these limitations, we consider the longitudinal change evidence that our studies provide to be stronger than cross-sectional correlations that have been obtained in past research.

Acknowledgments

This research was funded by the German Science Foundation, whose generous support is greately acknowledged, with grants to Leo Montada (Study I) and Manfred Schmitt (Study II).

REFERENCES

Aderman, D., Brehm, S. S., & Katz, L. B. (1974). Empathic observation of an innocent victim: The just world revisited. *Journal of Personality and Social Psychology, 29*, 342–347.

Ajzen, I., & Fishbein, M. (1980). *Understanding attitudes and predicting social behavior*. Englewood Cliffs, NJ: Prentice Hall.

Dalbert, C., Montada, L., & Schmitt, M. (1987). Glaube an eine gerechte Welt als Motiv: Validierungskorrelate zweier Skalen [Belief in a just world: Correlations of two scales with validation criteria]. *Psychologische Beiträge, 29*, 596–615.

Dion, K. L., & Dion, K. K. (1987). Belief in a just world and physical attractiveness stereotyping. *Journal of Personality and Social Psychology, 52*, 775–780.

Furnham, A., & Gunter, B. (1984). Just world beliefs and attitudes towards the poor. *British Journal of Social Psychology, 23*, 265–269.

Heider, F. (1958). *The psychology of interpersonal relations*. New York: Wiley.

Lerner, M. J. (1965). Evaluation of performance as a function of performer's reward and attractiveness. *Journal of Personality and Social Psychology, 1*, 355–360.

(1970). The desire for justice and reactions to victims. In J. Macaulay & L. Berkowitz (Eds.), *Altruism and helping behavior: Social psychological studies of some antecedents and consequences* (pp. 205–229). New York: Academic Press.

(1980). *The belief in a just world: A fundamental delusion*. New York: Plenum.

Lerner, M. J., & Miller, D. T. (1978). Just world research and the attribution process: Looking back and ahead. *Psychological Bulletin, 85*, 1030–1051.

Lerner, M. J., Miller, D. T., & Holmes, J. G. (1976). Deserving and the emergence of forms of justice. In L. Berkowitz (Ed.), *Advances in experimental social psychology* (Vol. 9, pp. 133–162). New York: Academic Press.

Lerner, M. J., & Simmons, C. H. (1966). The observer's reaction to the "innocent victim": Compassion or rejection? *Journal of Personality and Social Psychology, 4*, 203–210.

Maes, J. (1994). Blaming the victim – belief in control or belief in justice? *Social Justice Research, 7*, 69–90.

(1998). Immanent justice and ultimate justice: Two ways of believing in justice. In L. Montada & M. J. Lerner (Eds.), *Responses to victimization and belief in a just world* (pp. 9–40). New York: Plenum.

Maes, J., & Schmitt, M. (1999). More on ultimate and immanent justice: Results from the research project "Justice as a Problem within Reunified Germany." *Social Justice Research, 12*, 65–78.

Maes, J., Schmitt, M., Lischetzke, T., & Schmiedemann, V. (1998). *Effects of experienced injustice in unified Germany on well-being and mental health* (Berichte aus der Arbeitsgruppe "Verantwortung, Gerechtigkeit, Moral" Nr. 110). Trier: Universität Trier, Fachbereich I – Psychologie.

Miller, D. T. (1977). Altruism and threat to the belief in a just world. *Journal of Experimental Social Psychology, 13*, 113–124.

Mohiyeddini, C., & Montada, L. (1998). BJW and self-efficacy in coping with observed victimization: Results from a study about unemployment. In L. Montada & M. J. Lerner (Eds.), *Responses to victimization and belief in a just world* (pp. 41–54). New York: Plenum.

Montada, L. (1998). Belief in a just world: A hybrid of justice motive and self-interest? In L. Montada & M. J. Lerner (Eds.), *Responses to victimization and belief in a just world* (pp. 217–246). New York: Plenum.

Montada, L., Schmitt, M., & Dalbert, C. (1986). Thinking about justice and dealing with one's own privileges: A study of existential guilt. In H.-W. Bierhoff, R. L. Cohen, & J. Greenberg (Eds.), *Justice in social relations* (pp. 125–143). New York: Plenum.

Montada, L., & Schneider, A. (1989). Justice and emotional reactions to the disadvantaged. *Social Justice Research, 3*, 313–344.

Reichle, B., Montada, L., & Schneider, A. (1985). *Existentielle Schuld: Differenzierung eines Konstruktes* [Existential guilt: Differentiation of a construct] (Berichte aus der Arbeitsgruppe "Verantwortung, Gerechtigkeit, Moral" Nr. 35). Trier: Universität Trier, Fachbereich I – Psychologie.

Reichle, B., Schneider, A., & Montada, L. (1998). How do observers of victimization preserve their belief in a just world – cognitively or actionally? Findings from a longitudinal study. In L. Montada & M. J. Lerner (Eds.), *Responses to victimization and belief in a just world* (pp. 55–64). New York: Plenum.

Rubin, Z., & Peplau, L. A. (1973). Belief in a just world and reactions to another's lot: A study of participants in the national draft lottery. *Journal of Social Issues, 29* (4), 73–93.

(1975). Who believes in a just world? *Journal of Social Issues, 31* (3), 65–89.

Ryan, W. (1971). *Blaming the victim.* New York: Pantheon.

Schmitt, M. (1991). Ungerechtes Schicksal und Personbewertung [Unjust fate and person evaluation]. *Zeitschrift für Sozialpsychologie, 22*, 208–210.

(1998). Methodological strategies in research to validate measures of belief in a just world. In L. Montada & M. J. Lerner (Eds.), *Responses to victimization and belief in a just world* (pp. 187–215). New York: Plenum.

Schmitt, M., & Maes, J. (1998). Perceived injustice in unified Germany and mental health. *Social Justice Research, 11*, 59–78.

Schmitt, M., Reichle, B., Schneider, A., & Steyer, R. (1993). *Stability and occasion specificity of justice norms.* Paper presented at the Fourth International Conference on Social Justice Research, Trier.

Schneider, A., Montada, L., Reichle, B., & Meissner, A. (1986). *Auseinandersetzung mit Privilegunterschieden und existentieller Schuld: Item- und Skalenanalysen I* [Dealing with relative privileges and existential guilt: Item and Scale Analyses I] (Berichte aus der Arbeitsgruppe "Verantwortung, Gerechtigkeit, Moral" Nr. 37). Trier: Universität Trier, Fachbereich I – Psychologie.

Schneider, A., Reichle, B., & Montada, L. (1986). *Existentielle Schuld: Stichprobenrekrutierung, Erhebungsinstrumente und Untersuchungsplan* [Existential guilt: Sample, measurement instruments, and design] (Berichte aus der Arbeitsgruppe "Verantwortung, Gerechtigkeit, Moral" Nr. 36). Trier: Universität Trier, Fachbereich I – Psychologie.

Steyer, R. (1984). Causal linear stochastic dependencies: The formal theory. In E. Degreef & J. van Buggenhaut (Eds.), *Trends in mathematical psychology* (pp. 317–346). Amsterdam: North-Holland.

(1985). Causal regressive dependencies: An introduction. In J. R. Nesselroade & A. von Eye (Eds.), *Individual development and social change: Explanatory analysis* (pp. 95–124). Orlando, FL: Academic Press.

9. Violence in the Workplace – The Explanatory Strength of Social (In)Justice Theories

HERMAN STEENSMA

Introduction

Violence is one of the most troubling issues facing many organizations today. The Second European Survey on Working Conditions, based on 16,000 face-to-face interviews with workers throughout the European Union, indicated that each year about six million European workers (= 4% of all workers) are subjected to physical violence; twelve million workers (8%) are subjected to intimidation and bullying, and three million workers (2%) are subjected to sexual harassment. Highest exposures to sexual harassment were found in the catering services (hotels and restaurants), among female workers, and among employees with a precarious status, that is, employees with fixed-term contracts and temporary agency contracts. As for intimidation and bullying, high exposure rates were found in services (public administration, banking, and other services); and again, employees in precarious employment are among the most affected. Physical violence is one of the severe problems in public administration. The European Survey also found that violence at work clearly seems to lead to an increase in health complaints, in particular to stress. And health-related absenteeism increased at an alarming rate along with violence at work (Paoli, 1997). American society has the same problems of violence in the workplace. For example, homicide is one of the leading causes of death in the workplace. As for the less extreme forms of organizational violence, millions of workers in the United States are physically attacked with or without the use of weapons, while many more receive threats or are the target of some form of harassment (O'Leary-Kelly, Griffin, & Glew, 1996).

These high levels of violence create tremendous costs for both employees and employers. There are, of course, the direct consequences of death or injury. Beyond these obvious direct costs, many additional negative effects of organizational violence can be mentioned, including health problems and costs of absenteeism and health care, decreased productivity, damage to property, tarnished public image and reputation of the organization, weaker employee morale, and increased turnover. So it is quite clear: Organizational violence is a pressing problem and a meaningful area of study. To develop a successful antiaggression policy, it is necessary to gain insight into the intricate and complicated network of real and perceived causes and consequences of the several forms of violence in the workplace. Both descriptive and explanatory studies should be done to reach that goal. These studies should focus on the two different forms of violence in the workplace: "external" aggression and "internal" aggression. External aggression is the violent and threatening behavior of outsiders, such as robbers, dissatisfied customers, and the general public. Internal aggression, on the other hand, is that committed by colleagues, supervisors, and (sometimes) subordinates. This second form of workplace aggression includes behavior such as socially isolating a person, verbal threats, physical attacks, spreading rumors, and attacking the victim with organizational measures (e.g., assigning the person tasks far below his or her skills) (Leymann, 1993a, 1993b; Zapf, Knorz, & Kulla, 1996). In continental Europe, researchers often use the term "mobbing" to refer to these behaviors; in the English-speaking countries, bullying and harassment seem to be the concepts that are preferred. The name is not important; the explanation of the phenomenon surely is.

In this chapter, I will present some studies that shed more light on the phenomenon of violence in the workplace, its causes and consequences. I will show how theories and constructs developed by social justice researchers can be used to explain a substantial proportion of the variance of the problem, and to fill the gap of knowledge needed to handle and solve this societal problem. In doing so, it will become clear how important Mel Lerner's contributions have been to the field. A sizeable part of the nomological network could be built using ideas borrowed from Mel's work.

All studies that are reported here were done in close cooperation with former students of mine. Together with other researchers, we have founded a Dutch network of applied social scientists with the mission to study violence in the workplace, and to improve the quality of antiaggression programs.

The Causes of Violence in the Workplace

External violence can be explained as a function of the characteristics of both the perpetrator and the "environment" (and the interaction between these characteristics) (Steensma et al., 1997). There are four levels of environmental characteristics:

1. Macro-level characteristics, the most important being societal norms, cultural values, and legislation.
2. Characteristics and procedures of organizations; for example, organizations may use procedures that are perceived as frustrating and unfair by their customers. The perceived unfairness could lead to aggression.
3. Workplace characteristics, including not only the physical characteristics of the workplace but also factors like crowding.
4. Characteristics of the work itself. If you work with money, you could draw the attention of thieves and robbers. If your work includes many difficult social contacts, there is a higher risk that social conflicts will arise.

Relevant personal characteristics of the aggressor are emotional reactivity, weak impulse control, low frustration tolerance, and low tolerance for ambiguity. Of course, characteristics of workers affect the risk of becoming a victim of external aggression. If you are strong like a bull, angry customers will think twice before acting aggressively.

Environmental and personal factors are important in the explanation of internal violence, too. In this case, however, the victims tend to be somewhat shy, passive, timid, dependent persons, while perpetrators are described as active, impulsive, selfish, self-reliant persons. However, there are many exceptions to these "rules." Characteristics of managers and their leadership styles are also important explanatory factors, as will be illustrated later in this chapter. As for the environmental factors, low quality of job content seems to be the most important risk factor.

It should be stressed here that, although characteristics of the work, the workplace, the organization, and the society covary with violence in the workplace, these characteristics are not "aggressive" in and of themselves. Aggression is an act of people, not of things. So, researchers should try to explain why some workplace characteristics seem to affect aggressive behaviors of some people and not others.

External Aggression in a Casualty Ward

To prevent bullying and harassment, and to attend the victims effectively, information on the causes of the problem is needed. What should be done? The approach that is preferred strongly hangs on the analysis of causal factors. What should be done with environmental factors? Should we pay attention to the perpetrators, or are most problems in reality mainly caused by the behavior of victims? Let's assume that there are factors that lead to systematic biases in the perception and analysis of causes. To be effective, theoretical models and prevention programs should be designed bearing in mind the problems that may be created by such biases. So, it is important to know how and why causes are attributed to events. Therefore, I will describe some relevant variables. Psychologists know that almost all perceptions are in fact partly cognitive "constructions" (Neisser, 1967). Attribution research has demonstrated some well-known phenomena. The actor-observer effect, for example, states that observers interpret behavior in another way than it is interpreted by the actors themselves. Observers are inclined to "see" personal dispositions as the causes of the behavior of actors, whereas these actors point to the environmental characteristics (Jones & Nisbett, 1972). Attributional processes are not free from self-serving biases: People have a tendency to take credit for good outcomes, but they deny responsibility for negative events and outcomes (Bem, 1972; Snyder, Stephan, & Rosenfield, 1976). The self-serving bias has been observed at the aggregate level of perceived characteristics of groups (Forsyth & Schlenker, 1977), leading to the in-group favoritism described in a series of experiments by Tajfel (1972). It is well known that the groups to which we belong influence the way in which we see and interpret things and processes. The perception of reality often amounts to a "social construction." The "meaning" of a stimulus (object or event) appears to be a product of a process of social negotiations (Gergen, 1978). Social constructions differ from one group to another, creating a high potential for social conflict.

Other factors affecting or moderating attributions are individual differences, and these are of two kinds:

- characteristics of the person perceived (e.g., race, age of the actor)
- characteristics of the observer.

As for the observers, both external, visible characteristics and beliefs, norms, and values are important. One of the most important characteristics of a person is the strength of the just world belief.

Just World Belief

Piaget (1932) observed that children gradually develop a belief that they live in a world where the fates of persons corresponds to what they deserve. Bad people will suffer, and good ones will be rewarded – if not now, then at least in the future. In other words, children seem to believe in a "just world." They are not the only ones. Many adults believe in a just world, too. Research focusing on this belief has been stimulated in particular by the studies of Lerner (Lerner, 1980; Lerner, Miller, & Holmes, 1976). Lerner reasons as follows. A person must learn to forsake immediate gratification in order to orient herself toward future deserving. A child gradually makes a "personal contract" with himself in order to orient himself to the world on the basis of what he "deserves" via his prior investments rather than on the basis of what he can get at any given moment. This is the transition from living by the "pleasure" principle to living by the values and norms of society. If the person wants to maintain this personal contract, then any evidence that deserving efforts are not appropriately compensated presents a threat. Therefore, the person will be motivated to protect her belief that she lives in a world where each person's fate corresponds to what she deserves, or, in other words, the person believes in a just world. This belief in a just world is a tentatively held hypothesis, but it is backed by very strong motivational forces. This may lead to some rather unexpected consequences when people see other people suffer. Persons who witness an injustice and who cannot reestablish justice are inclined to think that the victim of injustice has done something for which he merits his sad fate. In this way, justice has been restored by cognitive work, and the just world belief can be maintained. In what is perhaps the first experimental test of the existence of the just world belief (JWB), Lerner and Simmons (1966) found evidence that – if victims cannot be helped – observers of victims alter their evaluations of victims' characteristics and attributes. Evaluations are more negative in these conditions. This finding has been reconfirmed in several other studies (see, e.g., the review by Lerner, Miller, & Holmes, 1976).

The belief in a just world is considered a relatively stable personality characteristic. People vary in the strength of this belief. The stronger their JWB is, the more motivated they are to eliminate threats to this belief. Such threats are posed by victims of aggression. Victims are living evidence that grim events can hurt innocent people. By believing that victims deserve their fate, however, the evidence is dismissed. Therefore, according to the theoretical notions of the just world theory, the strength of the JWB should covary with the attribution of responsibility and blame to victims of aggression in the workplace. However, there's a snag. To be sure, this hypothesis should be true for those third-party observers who "see" the events happening from a distance. Suppose, however, that you are a victim, or that you are working at a job with a well-known, rather high risk of becoming a victim of aggression. In such situations, reality itself creates a counterforce to the tendency to blame victims. Behavior is a function of the person and of the environment. The same is true for experience and perception. The environment in the present case – the job and the circumstances involved – presents the workers with evidence that they, and many of their colleagues, apparently run the risk of becoming victims of aggression. The sense of reality goes counter to the tendency to blame victims. This counterforce grows even stronger with the contribution of the self-serving bias: Why should you blame yourself? So, the effects of strong JWB on blaming the victims of aggression in the workplace should disappear or diminish for workers in workplaces with a high risk of aggression. This hypothesis was tested in a pilot study on aggression in the casualty (first aid) department of a large hospital (a joint research effort of Edwin Boom, George Evers, Kees Plug, and myself). Such casualty departments are notorious for the high risk of aggressive behavior by patients and their accompanying persons. The highest risks are run by the rank-and-file employees: the nurses. Their supervisors and managers have far less direct contact with potential aggressors. Therefore, we hypothesized that the relationship between strength of JWB and the tendency to attribute responsibility for aggression in the casualty ward to the victims should be strong for supervisors, while being weak or even completely absent for nurses. There were fourteen nurses, reporting to eight supervisors. The strength of participants' JWB was measured by ten items derived from the Just World Scale (Rubin & Peplau, 1975). Our hypothesis was supported: the JWB of supervisors correlated highly positively ($r = .83$) with their tendency to attribute the causes of aggression in the ward to the behavior of the employees, while this correlation approached the zero value among the nurses.

Now let's take a closer look at the parties in organizations. Employees are doing their work, while managers supervise and create conditions to enable the workers to do their jobs. So, in organizations, managers are held responsible for the work environment and the quality of working life (QWL). Therefore, avoidance of blame for low

QWL is very important for them. Unsafe conditions and aggression and harassment in the workplace are explicitly included as examples of low QWL in the Dutch Work Environment Act. Assuming that managers and supervisors feel a rather strong need to deny the existence of low QWL, we derived the following ad hoc hypotheses:

1. Supervisors will perceive a lower frequency of external aggression in the casualty ward than do the nurses.
2. Supervisors will perceive several forms of aggression as less threatening than do the nurses.
3. Supervisors will perceive there to be less necessity to take measures against external aggression in the casualty ward than do the nurses.

By and large, these hypotheses were supported by the data. There was a tendency for supervisors to report lower frequencies of aggressive behavior than did the nurses. Moreover, all forms of aggression studied – raising of voice, calling names, threatening gestures, verbal threats, threatening with weapons, physical violence – were perceived as less severe by the supervisors, resulting in a highly significant difference between supervisors and nurses after combining the scores ($p < .004$). And finally, both nurses and supervisors had to judge the necessity of ten measures to reduce aggression – a silent alarm, more male nurses during (high risk) night shifts, name badges with only the first names of the nurses, and so forth. Scores on the combined scale of "necessity" were indeed far lower for supervisors than for nurses ($p < .01$). So, here we have a situation which may easily lead to a conflict. Workers, formally the weaker party in organizations, perceive high risks of becoming victims of violence in the workplace. Their supervisors think the risks are not that high, and see less necessity to take measures against aggression. Applied scientists should think of methods to do justice to the feelings of the rank and file without antagonizing their supervisors. But before saying more about this subject, I will present some results of research into internal aggression.

Internal Aggression in the Workplace

One of the first studies focusing on internal violence in the workplace was published in 1976 by Brodsky. Still, it took some time before researchers developed a real interest in bullying in the workplace. Most researchers credit Heinz Leymann with stimulating psychologists to study harassment and victimization at work. Leymann began to study internal aggression ("mobbing") in the mid-1980s in Sweden, and since that time other research projects have been started in the (northern) European countries (see, for example, the special issue of the *European Journal of Work and Organizational Psychology*, edited by Zapf and Leymann, 1996). Gradually, relationships involving bullying, its causes, and its consequences were clarified, but much work remains to be done (see, e.g., Einarsen, 1996). From about the mid-1990s, many studies have been done in the Netherlands, and almost all researchers responsible for these studies are members of our network. I will now describe some results of these studies.

Attributional Styles, Self-esteem, and JWB of Victims of Bullying

Attributions may be classified using the dimensions of internality (the cause is seen as either an internal factor, like personality, or an external factor, like task characteristics), stability, and generality – specificity (causes are seen as present in all cases, or as present only in very specific situations) (Frieze, 1976; Weiner et al., 1972). Researchers of learned helplessness in humans have found evidence for the existence of the depressive attributional style (Abramson, Seligman, & Teasdale, 1978; Seligman et al., 1979). This style implies that internal, stable, and general factors are considered to be responsible for negative events. Combined with very important negative events, this attributional style may lead to chronic depression. Now bullying is, of course, a negative event. And in his review of "mobbing" research, Niedl (1996) describes the negative effects on well-being: bullied employees show more symptoms of depression and post-traumatic stress disorders than do nonbullied persons. So, bullied employees are victims of important negative events, and they often show the same symptoms of depression that are shown by persons who use the depressive attributional style. Therefore, on the face of it, it seems probable that victims of bullying are characterized by a depressive attributional style. If we assume that victims of bullying are characterized by a depressive attributional style, it should also be true that these victims attribute more internal (hypothesis 1A), stable (hypothesis 2A), and general (hypothesis 3A) causes to negative events than do nonvictims. But why should we assume that victims have a depressive attributional style? Attributional processes may be affected by the self-serving bias. Moreover, it is a well-known fact that people frequently overestimate the probability of pleasant events. This phenomenon is called the "positive illusion" (Taylor & Brown, 1988), a special case of a defensive attributional style. Self-serving bias and defensive attributional style lead to predictions exactly opposite to the hypotheses derived from the literature of the depressive attributional style: Victims of bullying will attribute more external (hypothesis 1B), unstable (hypothesis 2B), and specific (hypothesis 3B) causes to negative events than do nonvictims. Some learned helplessness theorists think that "importance" is a contingency factor, that is, that helplessness and depressive mood reactions will follow only after negative events and situations that are seen as very important (Metalsky et al., 1993; Stiensmeijer-Pelster, 1989). Therefore (hypothesis 4): Victims of bullying behavior will attach more importance to negative events than do nonvictims.

Earlier in this chapter, I described why persons who witness an injustice often think that the victim of injustice has done something for which he merits his fate and how this protects their just world belief. So far, so good, for the perceptions of the observing bystanders. But what about the victims? For them, believing in the justness of their fate can't be a comforting thought. These victims have good knowledge of what they did and why, and they are in a perfect position to compare their own fate to that of colleagues. This comparison should lead to a lower belief in a just world among victims of bullying (hypothesis 5).

Self-esteem is a more traditional concept in personality psychology. Being bullied over a long period of time implies a more or less permanent attack on the self-esteem of the victim, leading to the hypothesis (6) that victims of bullying have a lower level of self-esteem than do nonvictims. It should be noted, though, that a recent reformulation of the learned helplessness theory, known as the "hopelessness theory of depression," leads to the same prediction. However, the causal path is completely different, since in the hopelessness theory lowered self-esteem is seen as a causal factor, coacting with the negative event (Metalsky et al., 1993).

All hypotheses were tested in a joint research effort with Richard van Dijke. Finding cooperative victims of bullying turned out to be very difficult. We were helped by the Dutch Occupational Safety Inspection. The Inspection had registered twenty-seven complaints of victims of severe bullying. All victims were asked by safety inspectors to cooperate. In the end, ten victims (37%) participated by filling out a questionnaire. A random sample ($N = 90$) from a list of employees (nonvictims) were asked for their cooperation; $N = 30$ (33%) agreed to cooperate. Their answers to "bullying items" were inspected to check if these nonvictims indeed could not be classified as victims. (All participants were correctly categorized.)

The Questionnaire

Bullying was measured using fifteen items borrowed from a Dutch translation of the Leymann Inventory of Psychological Terrorization (LIPT). Scores were combined to form a (bullying) victim scale.

The questionnaire contained an adapted Dutch version of the Extended Atribution Style Questionnaire (EASQ; Metalsky, Halberstadt, & Abramson, 1987). Participants were presented with descriptions of ten situations in which a negative event occurred. All events showed a resemblance to some form of bullying. For example, a situation was described in which a participant should imagine that she is taking part in a team sport (for example, soccer) and gradually becomes aware of the fact that her teammates are ignoring her. After reading this description, the subject had to answer five questions:

1. What is the most probable cause of this behavior? (open-ended question)
2. Can this cause be attributed to yourself, or to others/the situation? (seven-point scale, from "completely to others" to "completely to myself")
3. Suppose you are ignored again in the future; is the same cause involved again? (seven-point scale, from "no, never" to "yes, always")
4. In real life: In how many situations is the cause that you have mentioned playing a role? (seven-point scale, from "not in any situation" to "in all situations")
5. Suppose that the situation as described happened in reality. How important is this for you? (seven-point scale, from "not important at all" to "very important")

Items 2–5 are measures of, respectively, the internality dimension, stability dimension, "generality" dimension and, of course, importance. Scores were combined to construct scales for, respectively, internality, stability, generality and importance.

The strength of participants' belief in a just world was measured by the abbreviated Dutch version of Rubin and Peplau's Just World Scale

(Rubin & Peplau, 1975; Steensma, den Hartigh, & Lucardie, 1994). The Dutch version of Rosenberg's Self-Esteem Scale (1965) was used to measure the self-acceptance aspect of self-esteem.

Results

Scores of victims on the "internality" dimension of attribution did not differ significantly from the scores of nonvictims. Mean scores of victims and nonvictims on the "stability" and "generality" scales did not differ significantly either. So, neither the "self-serving defensive" nor the "depressive" hypothesis received empirical support. However, the dispersion of "stability" scores among victims was much larger than among nonvictims. There seem to be two subtypes of victims: those who attribute causes to negative events in a self-defensive, "unstable" way, and those victims who make use of a depressive attributional style.

Finally, victims of bullying attached higher importance to negative situations than did the nonvictims. "Importance" may be seen as a conditional factor, a necessary (but not sufficient) cause of feelings of helplessness, hopelessness, and depression. But, of course, another explanation is that once you are a victim, you simply know better that negative events are indeed very painful – which implies that you attach high importance to being able to prevent such situations in the future. And once again, it may be true that there are two subgroups of victims: a group with high scores on the importance dimension "from the beginning," and a group of victims who developed high attributions to importance only after becoming victims.

Personality Characteristics: JWB and Self-esteem

Both the hypothesis about the just world belief and the hypothesis about self-esteem received empirical support from the research data. Mean scores of victims on the JWB scale were far lower than scores of nonvictims ($p < .001$). Also, self-esteem of victims of bullying was lower than self-esteem of nonvictims ($p < .05$).

Bullying frequently goes on for a rather long time. And, although personality characteristics are by definition rather stable, they are not completely unchangeable. Apparently, a long-continued series of negative experiences can undermine and weaken one's just world belief. The same reasoning can be applied to the lower self-esteem scores found among victims of bullying. There is a problem here, however. It seems logical that victims' self-esteem is gradually lowered after many negative events. However, it is also possible that persons with low self-esteem are "easy prey," and therefore run a higher risk of becoming victims of bullying. Data on self-esteem scores in the pre-bullying period were not available, so we can't be sure which of the two possible explanations is true. Personally, we think that both causal routes are partially true, and that each route explains a part of the variance of self-esteem scores in the group of victims. It should be clear that the second path – low self-esteem as one of the causes of becoming a victim – fits rather well into the "hopelessness theory of depression." Longitudinal research with self-esteem scores, measured at several times, may shed more light on this problem.

Risky Leadership Styles: The Boss as a Bully

Together with my colleagues Adrienne Hubert and Jur Furda, I was involved in a large-scale survey study, specially designed to test a theoretical model of the relationships between work characteristics (job decision latitude and job demands), leadership style, mobbing, and health complaints. The model postulates that negative work characteristics and low quality of leadership contribute to high "bullying risks," and that health complaints may be caused both by bullying and by low quality of working life (QWL) and poor leadership. In all, 3,011 employees working in a banking and insurance company participated. Briefly, the model stood its test well. Bullying, low QWL, and poor leadership covaried with health problems; and bullying could be explained by lack of decision latitude, high workload, and poor socioemotional leadership – which was exactly what we had predicted (Hubert, Furda, & Steensma, 1997). Statistically significant relationships between the variables were rather weak. But in another survey study with 427 employees working in a publishing company, the same model was tested. This time, workload contributed only weakly (and not significantly) to mobbing, but both poor leadership and lack of decision latitude covaried strongly with mobbing, and mobbing correlated strongly with sickness absenteeism (Hubert, 1997). Now, there are two ways by which leadership may cause bullying. First, leaders may neglect group dynamics. Mounting tensions in the group of subordinates may result in the bullying of one or more employees by (some of) their colleagues. The bullying goes on, unnoticed by the supervisor, and/or the leader does not intervene successfully. A second, and very alarming, possibility is that there is the direct causal path: The leader/supervisor is the initiator of the bullying behavior, and/or is participating actively in bullying one or more victims. We were unpleasantly surprised when we found out that more than one-third of the victims participating in our survey studies indicated that their supervisor was a perpetrator of bullying! (Hubert, 1997; Hubert, Furda, & Steensma, 1997). To gain more insight into this problem, we planned a series of in-depth interviews with victims of bullying. This time we had no difficulty in finding victims. Dutch mass media had by now paid a lot of attention to violence in the workplace, and many victims apparently felt less ashamed to talk about their experiences. In fact, our research group was often approached by victims of bullying who wanted to talk about their experiences. Some fifty-five in-depth interviews with victims were held; and in about thirty-five of these interviews, special attention was paid to the behavior of leaders and supervisors.

I will now summarize some of the main findings. Parts of these data have been presented already in an article (Vermunt, Oskam, & Steensma, 1998). Some data are completely new, however; they are based mainly on the results of victim interviews by Jeroen Mulder, a former student of mine. Before presenting the results, it should be pointed out that not all mistreatment is bullying. Bullying is the continual and deliberate repeated malicious treatment of a targeted person (or small group of individuals). It is treatment that persistently provokes, pressures, frightens, intimidates, or otherwise causes discomfort (Brodsky, 1976; Einarsen, 1996). Many interviewees had been bullied both by their colleagues and by their supervisors; many were bullied only by their colleagues; and about one-third of our interviewees had been bullied mainly or only by their supervisor(s). Supervisors occupy hierarchically higher positions, so it is interesting to see whether their bullying behavior differs from the bullying behavior of peers. And indeed, some differences were found. Supervisors have more structural "bullying resources" at their disposal than have the colleagues of the victims, and bosses who bully frequently use these resources. For example, they may use performance appraisals to frustrate ambitions of victims, or to damage the public image of victims. Another way in which bullying supervisors use their legitimate power is the "systematic" allocation of unpleasant tasks to the same person – the victim – time and again. Refusal to delegate responsibility to some subordinates and publicly demonstrating a lack of trust is rather frequently seen in organizations. Emphasizing existing status differences is rather popular, too. Neglecting the ideas and suggestions offered by unpopular subordinates is another effective way to lower the status of victims, and sometimes the quality of the workplace, the furniture and equipment of the victims is lower than the quality of the workplace and equipment of their colleagues. A rather rigid application of formal rules without concern for the needs of subordinates and without consideration of their views is not unusual behavior for many managers. So, supervisors are in a better position to take organizational measures against subordinates they don't like; and unfortunately, many bosses don't hesitate to use these opportunities to expand their stock of bullying behaviors. Of course, there are a lot of similarities in the bullying behaviors of supervisors and employees. For example, social isolation of victims is one of the preferred ways of hurting people, and both supervisors and colleagues often use the isolation option.

Transgressions of Social Justice Norms

All interviewed victims mentioned many examples of stress-causing behaviors by their supervisors. Many examples amount to transgressions of norms of procedural and/or interactional justice. Procedural justice focuses on the methods, the procedures by which outcomes (tasks, money, rewards in general) are distributed. Perceptions of fair procedures may be influenced by several aspects: clarity, absence of bias, apprehensiveness (understandable rules), fact-based decision making, correctability, respect for rights, and so forth (Leventhal, Karuza, & Fry, 1980; Sheppard, Lewicki, & Minton, 1992; Tyler & Lind, 1992). Interactional justice is the quality of the interpersonal treatment people receive during the enactment of organizational procedures (Bies & Moag, 1986). Frequently, interactional justice is seen as a subset of norms and rules of procedural justice.

Most authors seem to recognize that the control of procedures is of central importance in procedural justice. People want to have a say in the procedures. This "say" or "voice" guarantees concern for their needs and consideration of their views (Folger, 1977; Thibaut & Walker, 1975; Tyler & Lind, 1992). The striving for control as the common ground of several procedural justice theories had already been noticed by Lerner and Whitehead (1980). They developed an alternative theoretical approach, based on Lerner's theory of the justice motive in social behavior, and using relations people have with each other and processes in which people can engage with others as building blocks for a model of eighteen "emergent activities." This surely is an interesting model, and it is a fine example of integrating notions from procedural justice theories, distributive justice, and motivation theories. It must be admitted, though, that at the moment the majority of procedural justice studies are based on the relational model of procedural justice, developed by Tyler and Lind (1992). The structure of their model (in a slightly adapted version also known as the group-value model) is as follows. Judgments of procedural fairness indicate a person's value to the group. This group-value belief is, in turn, a determinant of group- and authority-oriented attitudes and behaviors. Judgments of procedural fairness are influenced by three types of relational judgments about authorities. Neutrality is perceived when decision-making procedures are unbiased, honest, and based on facts. The second relational judgment focuses on trust or trustworthiness, indicated by authorities' concern for the needs of group members. Finally, status recognition or "standing" involves assessments of politeness, treatment with dignity, and respect for the rights of people. Think of the complaints of our victims, and it will be clear that a framework of a procedural (in)justice theory might do a good job in explaining perceptions and reactions of victims of violence in the workplace. I will now describe such a model.

The Injustice Stress Theory

Together with my colleague Riel Vermunt, I am in the process of developing the injustice stress theory. Theories of justice demonstrate a striking resemblance to the general stress model: Distributions and procedures are compared to reference criteria. If deviations from the norm are perceived, an attempt is made to reduce the perceived deviation. Until now, we have presented some slightly different versions of this theory (Steensma, 1999; Steensma, Vermunt, & Allegro, 1997; Vermunt and Steensma, 2001). This new model may be used to explain at least parts of both external and internal aggression. Therefore, the core characteristics of the injustice stress model will be outlined in this section of the chapter. The version described here is the "Helsinki" version, which was applied to explain employees' perceptions and negative outcomes of bullying by supervisors.

Objective procedures and behaviors are perceived as more or less adhering to norms of fairness, and may thus contribute to perceptions and feelings of procedural and interactional injustice. Whether procedural injustice will be felt depends, however, not only on the objective and the subjective, perceived characteristics of the procedures, but also on (1) the moderating effects of just world beliefs, (2) the outcomes that have been allocated, and (3) the goals of the person who is the target of the procedures. The felt (in)justice may affect feelings of commitment to leaders, groups, organizations, and even the society positively in the case of perceived justice, but may cause stress in the case of perceived injustice. Levels of commitment and stress are affected not only by the "amount" of injustice, but also by moderating effects flowing from the rather stable self-esteem of the target: The higher the self-esteem is, the lower the stress will be. There are several ways to cope with stress, and these ways have different effects on the health of the target. Coping may be problem-oriented, a way of coping that is healthy. Other ways are emotional coping, with generally less positive effects, and cognitively changing the reality (perception-oriented coping), with sometimes positive, sometimes negative effects on the health of employees.

Some Concluding Remarks

In this chapter I have proposed that elements from social justice theories are excellent candidates for filling positions in the nomological network of causes and consequences of violence in the workplace. Mel Lerner's concept of just world belief and basic tenets from procedural justice theories were used to support this claim. Important progress in theoretical knowledge could be made in this way. Creating and developing theoretical knowledge is necessary but not sufficient for applied social scientists.

Our "aggression in the workplace" group tries to develop methods to reduce violence. Our general approach might be called the IDPIE model, after its five core elements (phases):

- Intention (all parties involved, and particularly the managers, must be willing to do something to reduce violence)
- Diagnosis (data gathering and trying to develop a body of knowledge of causes and consequences of aggression)
- Prioritize (you can't always do all things that are desirable, so you must make choices: what to do first?)

- Implementation of actions
- Evaluation (both of results and of the processes used to reach results)

It should be added that in our projects great importance is attached to the participative change approach. We give people a say in our projects, and this seems important in making the projects a success. So, once again, a social justice principle is useful, this time not only for scientific explanation, but also for the purpose of humanization of the workplace. A nice thought with which to conclude this chapter.

REFERENCES

Abramson, L. Y., Seligman, M. E. P., & Teasdale, J. D. (1978). Learned helplessness in humans: Critique and reformulation. *Journal of Abnormal Psychology, 87* (1), 49–74.

Bem, D. J. (1972). Self-perception theory. In L. Berkowitz (Ed.), *Advances in experimental social psychology* (Vol. 6, pp. 1–62). New York: Academic Press.

Bies, R. J., & Moag, J. S. (1986). Interactional justice: communication criteria of fairness. In R. J. Lewicki, B. H. Sheppard, & M. H. Bazerman (Eds.), *Research on negotiation in organizations* (Vol. 1, pp. 43–55). Greenwich, CT: JAI Press.

Brodsky, C. M. (1976). *The harassed worker.* Toronto: Lexington Books.

Einarsen, S. (1996). *Bullying and harassment at work: Epidemiological and psychological aspects.* Dissertation, University of Bergen.

Einarsen, S., Raknes, B. I., & Matthiesen, S. B. (1995). *Bullying and harassment at work and its relationships to work environment quality: An exploratory study.* Paper, presented at the Seventh European Congress of Work and Organizational Psychology, Györ, Hungary.

Folger, R. (1977). Distributive and procedural justice: Combined impact of "voice" and improvement of experienced inequity. *Journal of Personality and Social Psychology, 35,* 108–119.

Forsyth, D. R., & Schlenker, B. R. (1977). Attributing the causes of group performance: Effects of performance quality, task importance, and future testing. *Journal of Personality, 45,* 220–236.

Frieze, I. H. (1976). The role of information processing in making causal attributions for success and failure. In J. S. Carroll & J. W. Payne (Eds.), *Cognition and social behavior* (pp. 95–112). Hillsdale, NJ: Erlbaum.

Gergen, K. J. (1978). Toward generative theory. *Journal of Personality and Social Psychology, 36* (11), 1344–1360.

Jones, E. E., & Nisbett, R. E. (1972). The actor and the observer. In E. Jones et al. (Eds.), *Attribution: Perceiving the causes of behavior* (pp. 79–94). Morristown, NJ: General Learning.

Lerner, M. J. (1980). *The belief in a just world.* New York: Plenum.

Lerner, M. J., Miller, D. T., & Holmes, J. G. (1976). Deserving and the emergence of forms of justice. In L. Berkowitz & E. Walster (Eds.), *Equity theory: Toward a general theory of social interaction.* (*Advances in experimental social psychology*, Vol. 9, pp. 133–162.) New York: Academic Press.

Lerner, M. J., & Simmons, C. H. (1966). Observers' reaction to the "innocent victim": Compassion or rejection? *Journal of Personality and Social Psychology, 4*, 203–210.

Lerner, M. J., & Whitehead, L. A. (1980). Procedural justice viewed in the context of justice motive theory. In G. Mikula (Ed.), *Justice and social interaction* (pp. 219–256). Bern: Huber.

Leventhal, G., Karuza, J., & Fry, W. R. (1980). Beyond fairness: A theory of allocation preferences. In G. Mikula (Ed.), *Justice and social interaction* (pp. 167–218). Bern: Huber.

Leymann, H. (1993a). Ätiologie und häufigkeit von Mobbing am Arbeitsplatz – eine Übersicht über die bisherige Forschung. *Zeitschrift für Personalsforschung, 7*, 271–283.

(1993b). *Mobbing – Psychoterror am Arbeitsplatz und wie man sich dagegen wehren kann.* Reinbeck: Rohwolt.

Metalsky, G. I., Halberstadt, L. J., & Abramson, L. Y. (1987). Vulnerability to depressive mood reactions: Toward a more powerful test of the diathesis–stress and causal mediation components of the reformulated theory of depression. *Journal of Personality and Social Psychology, 51*, 435–442.

Metalsky, G. I., Joiner, T. E., Jr., Hardin, T. S., & Abramson, L. Y. (1993). Depressive reactions to failure in a naturalistic setting: A test of the hopelessness and self-esteem theories of depression. *Journal of Abnormal Psychology, 102* (1), 101–109.

Neisser, U. (1967). *Cognitive psychology.* New York: Appleton Century Crofts.

Niedl, K. (1996). Mobbing and well-being: Economic and personnel development implications. *European Journal of Work and Organizational Psychology, 5* (2), 239–249.

O'Leary-Kelly, A. M., Griffin, R. W., & Glew, D. J. (1996). Organization-motivated aggression: A research framework. *Academy of Management Review, 21* (1), 225–253.

Paoli, P. (1997). *Second European survey on the work environment 1995–1996.* Dublin: European Foundation for the Improvement of Working and Living Conditions.

Piaget, J. (1932). *The moral judgment of the child.* London: Routledge & Kegan Paul.

Rosenberg, M. (1965). *Society and the adolescent self-image.* Princeton, NJ: Princeton University Press.

Rubin, Z., & Peplau, L. A. (1975). Who believes in a Just World? *Journal of Social Issues, 31* (3), 65–89.

Seligman, M. E. P., Abramson, L. Y., Semmel, A., & Baeyer, C. (1979). Depressive attributional style. *Journal of Abnormal Psychology, 88* (3), 242–247.

Sheppard, B. H., Lewicki, R. J., & Minton, J. W. (1992). *Organizational justice: The search for fairness in the workplace.* New York: Lexington Books/Macmillan.

Snyder, M. L., Stephan, W. G., & Rosenfield, D. (1976). Egotism and attribution. *Journal of Personality and Social Psychology, 33*, 435–441.

Steensma, H. (1999). *Injustice stress and the bullying leader: A new research model.* Paper presented at the Ninth European Congress on Work and Organizational Psychology, Espoo–Helsinki, Finland.

Steensma, H., Hartigh, E. den, & Lucardie, E. (1994). Social categories, Just World Belief, locus of control, and causal attributions of occupational accidents. *Social Justice Research, 7,* 281–299.

Steensma, H., Hubert, A., van Duijn, S., & Evers, G. (1997). Geweld op het werk. Omgevings- en persoonskenmerken, verklarende modellen. *Tijdschrift voor toegepaste Arbowetenschap, 10* (2), 24–29.

Steensma, H., Vermunt, R., & Allegro, J. (1997). *Toward a new model of social justice to explain reactions to organizational restructuring.* Paper presented at the Sixth Biennial Meeting of the International Network for Social Justice Research, Potsdam, Germany.

Stiensmeier-Pelster, J. (1989). Attributional style and depressive mood reactions. *Journal of Personality, 57* (3), 581–599.

Tajfel, H. (1972). La catégorisation sociale. In S. Moscovici (Ed.), *Introduction à la psychologie sociale* (Vol. 1, pp. 272–302). Paris: Larousse.

Taylor, S. E., & Brown, J. D. (1988). Illusion and well-being: A social-psychological perspective on mental health. *Psychological Bulletin, 103,* 193–210.

Thibaut, J., & Walker, L. (1975). *Procedural justice: a psychological analysis.* Hillsdale, N.J.: Erlbaum.

Tyler, T. R., & Lind, E. A. (1992). A relational model of authority in groups. In M. P. Zanna (Ed.), *Advances in experimental social psychology* (Vol. 25, pp. 115–191). San Diego, CA: Academic Press.

Vermunt, R., Oskam, M., & Steensma, H. (1998). Van baas tot bazig: stress als gevolg van onheuse bejegening door de baas. *Gedrag en Organisatie, 11* (6), 354–371.

Vermunt, R., & Steensma, H. (2001). Stress and justice in organizations – An exploration into justice processes with the aim to find mechanisms to reduce stress. In R. Cropanzano (Ed.), *Justice in the workplace* (Vol. 2, pp. 27–48). Mahwah, NJ: Erlbaum.

Weiner, B., Heckhausen, H., Meyer, W., & Cook, R. E. (1972). Causal ascriptions and achievement behavior: Conceptual analysis of effort and reanalysis of locus of control. *Journal of Personality and Social Psychology, 21,* 239–248.

Zapf, D., Knorz, C., & Kulla, M. (1996). On the relationship between mobbing factors, and job content, social work environment, and health outcomes. *European Journal of Work and Organizational Psychology, 5* (2), 215–237.

Zapf, D., & Leymann, H. (Eds.) (1996). Mobbing and victimization at work. *European Journal of Work and Organizational Psychology, 5* (2) (special issue).

10. The Just World and Winston Churchill: An Approach/Avoidance Conflict about Psychological Distance When Harming Victims

ROBERT FOLGER AND S. DOUGLAS PUGH

How do people respond when they observe a victim's undeserved suffering, such as when competent, hardworking employees are laid off for reasons that have nothing to do with their performance? Lerner's famous just world hypothesis (e.g., Lerner, 1980; Lerner & Simmons, 1966) addressed reactions by non-harmdoing observers, such as outsiders who learn about the suffering of laid-off employees. We instead address the case of harmdoing observers, such as the managers who lay off the employees.

In the Lerner analysis, witnesses to a victim's undeserved suffering "will be increasingly likely to reject that victim as a function of the degree of *injustice* associated with the victim's fate" (Lerner, 1980, p. 56). Because victims received derogatory ratings under the predicted conditions, this form of rejection is known as victim derogation. Other possible responses – such as prevention, restitution, and acceptance of one's limitations – Lerner called *rational* tactics. *Non*rational tactics that involve variations on the theme of ego defense, of course, constitute the more interesting category from a psychological perspective. These include denial/withdrawal and reinterpretation. Derogating a victim is a special case of the latter – namely, a reinterpretation of the victim's character. Other psychological defenses in the same category (nonrational tactics) include reinterpreting the outcome and reinterpreting the cause.

In the original Lerner and Simmons (1966) paradigm, the observer was innocent and powerless. We instead focus on observers who are *not* completely powerless with regard to the victim's suffering, especially because the observer's actions might in some ways alleviate that suffering or at least mitigate some of its severity. The types of observers whose actions we address (e.g., managers reacting to the victims of workplace layoffs) are also less than totally innocent (at least in the eyes of some of those laid-off employees). We note that this special category of observers also sometimes displays a victim-derogation tendency and related responses. As with Lerner's (different) category of observers, however, some of the most challenging issues involve trying to specify the conditions under which derogation and related tendencies will occur, in contrast with conditions under which quite different (victim-positive, nonderogatory) responses occur instead.

For simplicity, we collapse reactions to victims into two broad categories: *approach* versus *avoidance* orientations. Prevention, restitution, and other amelioration-related actions qualify as approach-oriented in the sense of identifying empathically with the victim and wanting to reduce the suffering or to help the victim cope with it. Lerner put it this way: "Sometimes we react automatically to a cue which elicits a sense of identity, concern, compassion, outrage, the desire to ameliorate the unjust suffering and deprivation of these victims" (1980, p. 25). Derogating victims, however, is an avoidance response that emphasizes an exclusion of the victim from the good-person category presumably occupied by the observer (in the latter's eyes). As Lerner noted, "at other times they [observers of victims] appear to go through considerable effort to avoid any involvement, any recognition of the hint of any possible relation – they avoid, ignore and possibly revile [victims]" (1980, p. 26). Like denial/withdrawal, therefore, derogating is a way of creating some psychological *distance* between the victim and oneself as observer. We will refer to the general orientation or family of responses that includes avoid, ignore, and revile (derogate) as those characterized by an avoidance orientation and manifested in various forms of *psychological distancing*. Distancing responses are those in which the observers seek separation from victims – physically, psychologically, emotionally, characterologically (in terms of traits attributed to self versus the victim), and so on. The opposite orientation (approach) shows concern, considerateness, and interpersonal sensitivity toward victims.

Churchill and Distancing as the Criticism of Politeness toward Victims (Enemies)

We think that victims create approach-avoidance conflicts for harmdoing and non-harmdoing observers, although we focus only on the former. As an introduction to possible sources of tension in the role of harmdoer, consider the following sequence of events. On the day after the bombing of Pearl Harbor, Winston Churchill telegrammed the Japanese ambassador in London to notify him that Great Britain had declared war on Japan. The text, contained in Churchill's memoirs, took the form of a very proper British letter, complete with the following closing: "I have the honour to be, with high consideration, Sir, Your obedient servant, Winston S. Churchill" (Churchill, 1950, p. 610). In reacting to public outcry about that letter's tone, Churchill replied, "When you have to kill a man, it costs nothing to be polite" (1950, p. 611).

The public's response, consistent with avoidance, distancing, and derogating the enemy's status of (future) victim, contrasts with Churchill's use of politeness and consideration even for one's enemy or those one would harm. We call interpersonal distancing by harmdoers the *Churchill effect* in reference to the effect of Churchill's letter on the public (e.g., criticism of civility toward victims). A Churchill effect involves denying the need for, or legitimacy of, any politeness or considerateness toward those one would harm or has harmed. We identify the Churchill effect as a special case of an avoidance orientation consistent with victim derogation.

Churchill was referring to the absence of *financial* cost associated with politeness as considerate interpersonal treatment, but his comment ignores the potential costliness in emotional and psychological terms. The public's outcry against Churchill's politeness shows that the British people wanted to maintain psychological distance from the Japanese as an avoidance orientation, rather than to experience some unresolved approach-avoidance tension potentially aroused by simultaneously being polite and trying to kill.

At the level of anecdote, however, two opposite kinds of responses can be seen in the everyday orientations of harmdoers toward their victims. On the one hand, Churchill's remark echoes the sentiment expressed when even those guilty of the most heinous crimes in past epochs, about to face a firing squad, were politely asked "Cigarette? Blindfold?" (In a modern counterpart, guards offer those condemned to death a choice of last meals.) On the other hand, conventional advice calls for harmdoers to distance themselves from victims. Farmers are cautioned against having family members make pets out of animals to be slaughtered, for example, just as surgeons are warned against too much emotional involvement with terminally ill patients.

Sticking close to the lines of Lerner's analysis, of course, would tend to eliminate any sense of inconsistency in such examples, because they confound clear-cut guilt or innocence with the nature of the response. That is, perhaps little or no psychological discomfort results from kindness shown to one's victim who clearly deserves harm, as in the case of the condemned criminal. Other anecdotal evidence, however, again clouds the picture. In particular, managers in charge of laying off employees sometimes exhibit signs of considerable distancing from those employees (including victim derogation), but at other times managers in such a position exhibit great interpersonal sensitivity. As social psychologists, we would feel inclined to charge ourselves with committing the fundamental attribution error if we simply assumed that "bad" managers are insensitive in such cases, whereas "good" managers act in a more kindly fashion. Are there characteristics of the situation associated with the likelihood of Churchill effects? The rest of our discussion presents a preliminary attempt to answer that question.

The Harmdoer's Social Predicament Caused by the Victim's Unjust Suffering

Our starting point is an analysis by Bies (1987) of unjust harm, potential threats to the harmdoer, and the use of social accounts as self-defense on the part of harmdoers. As Bies observed, "When people feel harmed wrongfully . . . , they are likely to become morally outraged – that is, they will experience such emotions as anger and resentment" (1987: 290). Thus, Bies noted that unjust treatment creates a predicament for the harmdoer based on the potential for retaliation. Facing evidence that they have harmed another, harmdoers may also experience threats to their social identities as moral and just persons. Their threatened self-esteem is analogous to what innocent observers (nonharmdoers) experience as a threat to their belief in a just world; in this case, it is a threat to the belief in a just self.

An injustice thus creates a social predicament for the harmdoer, an aversive state marked by fear of retaliation and threats to the harmdoer's social identify (Bies, 1987). In Goffman's (1971) terms, the social predicament can represent a strong threat to the "face" or social identity of both the victim and the harmdoer. The result is an awkward social situation, marked by high levels of tension, disrupted interactions, and threats to the esteem of all participants (Goffman, 1971). Bies (1987) suggested that in response, harmdoers are motivated to offer social accounts (e.g., explanations, excuses, justifications, apologies) to extract themselves from the predicament created by the injustice. Such social accounts represent the type of interpersonal communication that is a major part of what Bies called *interactional justice*. More broadly, interactional justice refers to the quality of interpersonal treatment received during the implementation of a procedure (Bies, 1987, 2001). As such, it fits under our broad heading of an approach orientation.

At first it might seem as if Bies implied that managers will ordinarily work to repair or restore damaged relationships with laid-off employees by offering social accounts (e.g., apologies, justifications), but sometimes as harmdoers they do the opposite: they distance themselves from employees unjustly harmed by layoffs, offer no explanation, and, in extreme cases, derogate and even mistreat these victims. Consider, for example, across-the-board layoffs despite acceptable employee performance, which might violate the social norms of an implicit psychological contract (Rousseau, 1989). Across-the-board cuts might also be considered inequitable when they are administered without regard to employee contributions. Because a layoff is a social predicament, social accounts would be expected, but often they do not materialize. Sutton, Eisenhardt, and Jucker, for example, describe the treatment of workers during a downsizing at Atari's Silicon Valley plant as "humiliating" (1986, p. 21). Workers were dismissed without warning upon arriving at work one morning – their badges were collected and they were escorted from the premises. Management later went on to denigrate the former employees: "Now we've gotten rid of all the rummies . . ." (1986, p. 23).

Atari is not an isolated incident. On Take Your Daughter to Work Day, eight-year-old Marisa Means saw her father abruptly dismissed without warning, as a security guard escorted him from the site (Working in the 1990s, 1995). When Middlebury College staff found their jobs eliminated, the only communication was an impersonal form letter from the college president informing them that their benefits would continue, but only if they cooperated with the outplacement firm hired by the college (Greenberg & Baron, 1993). When Tenneco laid off 1,200 employees over a six-week period, many learned about the layoff only when confronted by armed guards carrying boxes to be used for removing personal effects from offices. Department heads at Allied Bank of Texas called meetings and then read the names of laid-off employees in front of their coworkers (Marks, 1993). We think such actions have a remarkable potential for being dysfunctional. At Middlebury College, for example, a consultant recommended conducting the layoffs in the implemented fashion so that employees could not go back to their offices and vent their hostility. We suspect that in actuality, most such venom might have been avoided if the layoffs had instead been handled in a more sensitive manner.

We do not claim that these examples reflect a norm in organizations. They do represent cases where social accounts such as excuses and apologies would be expected, however, whereas behaviors with the opposite effect occurred instead. We argue that both social accounts and aloof or even abusive behavior can be understood from a social predicament perspective. Although social accounts provide one means of exiting the predicament of injustice, management behaviors with quite the opposite effect on employees can also serve the same function.

Managing Social Predicaments: Approach/Avoidance and the Mitigation–Aggravation Continuum

Konovsky and Folger call social accounts "explanations aimed at extracting the actor from a social predicament" (1991, p. 632). A predicament's severity is a function of the harmdoer's responsibility for the unjust outcome, the perceived undesirability of the outcome, and the extent to which the harm contradicts important aspects of the harmdoer's social identify (Bies, 1987). Social accounts might influence victim perceptions of any or all of those factors, allowing escape from the predicament by diffusing moral outrage. If an explanation indicates that mitigating circumstances caused the harmdoers' unjust behavior, for example, victims will be less outraged, less likely to retaliate, and the harmdoer's self-identity will also be protected. We argue, however, that a harmdoer can also exit a social predicament without doing anything to decrease moral outrage. Consider, for example, the manager who takes a two-week vacation while the organization dismisses a large number of employees. By physical and psychological isolation, such managers (a) remove themselves as targets of retaliation and (b) decrease the salience of the layoff victims, thus decreasing self-sanctions and threats to self-identity.

To understand harmdoers' competing motivations in social predicaments, we return to Goffman's (1971) idea that injustice threatens the social identity or "face" of all participants in a social predicament. Social accounts serve as a corrective mechanism, repairing the face damage of the participants (Hodgins, Liebeskind, & Schwartz, 1996).

Yet there are competing demands present in restoring equilibrium to damaged social relationships. Social accounts that benefit victims most (e.g., concessions) may at the same time be threatening to the harmdoer, as they acknowledge the harmdoer's responsibility for the act. The tension between addressing harmdoers' and victims' needs has led researchers to conceptualize social accounts as varying along a *mitigation-aggravation* continuum (McLaughlin, Cody, & O'Hair, 1983; Hodgins, Liebestand, & Schwartz, 1996). Concessions, at the mitigation end, typically "involve acknowledgement of the predicament as defined by others, assumption of full responsibility for the offense and its consequences, and often expression of regret and embarrassment or offers of restitution" (Gonzales, Manning, & Haugen, 1992, p. 959). Refusals, at the aggravation end, "involve a denial of any personal responsibility for the offense or its consequences, or a denial of the right of anyone to reproach or question actors" (p. 959). Concessions show the most concern for victims but are also the most threatening to the harmdoer in terms of social identity, the psychological costs of becoming close to the victim, and being vulnerable to reproach or moral outrage (Bies, 1987). Justifications and refusals, at the continuum's other end, are more protective of the offender, yet show less concern for the victim's needs – hence, they can aggravate an already damaged social relationship (and be consistent with victim derogation). The mitigation-aggravation continuum of social accounts thus reveals a tension for the harmdoer: a desire to protect or restore the self-identity of the victim, and a desire to protect the self.

In extending our focus beyond social accounts to include more broadly all interpersonal treatment of employees, we mean to equate the approach orientation at least loosely with high levels of perceived interactional justice (Bies, 2001; Bies & Moag, 1986). Moreover, we consider other interpersonal behaviors beyond accounts, because behaviors that physically or psychologically distance the harmdoer from the victim also provide ways to exit social predicaments. Thus, we refer to *managerial distancing* as actions that psychologically or physically remove harmdoers from social predicaments. We refer to approach behavior as managerial actions that increase contact with victims and attempt to repair damaged relationships (e.g., interpersonal sensitivity, timely communications, apologies, explanations). Thus, the approach-distancing (or approach-avoidance) continuum parallels the mitigation-aggravation continuum.

The conceptualization of managerial distancing as self-protective behavior comes from several literatures on approach-avoidance orientations toward victims – including research on equity restoration, dissonance, guilt-induced compliance, and empathic distress after harmdoing. For example, equity theory predicts that an individual who harms or exploits another will feel distress about that inequitable relationship. Subsequently, the harmdoer might attempt to reduce the distress by restoring equity in any of several ways (Walster, Walster, & Berscheid, 1978), including self-deprivation and compensating the victim (cf. related findings from guilt-induced compliance studies such as Freedman, Wallington, & Bless, 1967). Similarly, Batson (1994) has reviewed research linking the harmdoer's empathic concern for a victim to reparations by the harmdoer (e.g., alleviating suffering, expressing remorse). On the other hand, dissonance research (e.g., Davis & Jones, 1960; Glass, 1964) reveals instances in which harmdoers derogate victims.

Indeed, the review of helping behavior by Batson, Early, and Salvarani (1997) described two possible reactions toward victims that have rather opposite implications: empathy and personal distress. Empathy is an other-oriented emotion consistent with an altruistic motivation to relieve others' suffering. Personal distress, on the other hand, produces an egoistic motivation to reduce one's own distress (Batson, 1994). A mix of empathy and personal distress creates tension between altruistic and egoistic motivations when dealing with victims, similar to the distress of an approach-avoidance conflict.

Research on guilt and shame reveals a similar tension. Although often used as synonyms, guilt and shame are distinct emotional states with different behavioral outcomes (Neidenthal, Tangney, & Gavanski, 1994; Tangney, 1991, 1992; Tangney et al., 1992). Guilt and shame both involve negative reactions to violations of internal standards, but the focus of negative affect differs. Guilt focuses externally on a "bad thing" that was done, a specific act or failure to act (Tangney, 1992; Tangney et al., 1992). Shame focuses on the self; the "bad thing" is experienced as "a reflection of a 'bad self'" (Tangney et al., 1992, p. 670). The resulting motivations and actions also differ. Guilt creates a desire to repair the damage done, to "confess, apologize, make amends," whereas shame creates a desire to withdraw or hide, to "remove himself or herself from any interpersonal situation that may have given rise to this experience" (Tangney et al., 1992, p. 670). In the extreme, shame may also motivate anger, a lashing out at others as a defensive mechanism to repair damage to the self (Lewis, 1971).

We postulate an approach/avoidance conflict to account for the otherwise contradictory findings from different streams of research. For example, research associated with equity theory (Walster, Walster, & Berscheid, 1978) referred to the distress that comes from harming another as guilt. Baumeister, Stillwell, and Heatherton's review (1994) found considerable evidence that feelings of guilt motivate helping, prosocial, and compliant behavior. This evidence fits our description of the approach tendency. That is, the manager who terminates subordinates may experience guilt feelings if he or she focuses on the harm done to them. As a result, the manager may take reparative actions to heal the relationship and to "make it up" to the fired employees (e.g., giving a healthy severance package and advance notice so that they can prepare for a new job, or at least handling the layoffs in a sensitive, caring manner so as to diminish further stress on the fired employees). In such cases, guilt would mediate between the harm (firing) and the reparative action (viz., a humane manner of conducting the layoff process). Baumeister and colleagues also note, however, that causing harm is sometimes associated instead with antisocial effects directed against victims–in particular, "a tendency for transgressors to want to avoid their victims" (1994, p. 258). Thus, evidence about harmdoers' behavior indicates both approach and avoidance responses.

In sum, several theoretical traditions point to a tension, when dealing with victims, between an other-oriented focus leading to approach (e.g., offering apologies, concessions, and sympathy) and a self-protective focus leading to avoidance (e.g., denial of responsibility, distancing from victims). At first glance, the behaviors suggested as responses to the approach-avoidance conflict fit with those suggested by Bies (1987). Excuses, for example, are mentioned in the framework of causal accounts used by Bies (1987) and by Hodgins and colleagues (1996). An excuse is "an explanation containing a reason to mitigate the harmdoer's responsibility for some action" (Bies, 1987, p. 298). Because an excuse is an attempt to reduce the harmdoer's responsibility for an event, Bies reasons that it should also decrease victims' feelings of moral outrage. Other researchers (Hodgins et al., 1996; Gonzales, Manning, & Haugen, 1992) concur that excuses reduce personal responsibility for an act, but Gonzales and colleagues note that excuses may actually *increase* threat to the victim's face, in comparison to a concession (apology). "Excuses represent a greater threat to [victim's] face concerns than do concessions, for although excuses acknowledge the damage done, they question other's inference about the degree of offender's personal responsibility for the predicament" (Gonzales et al., 1992, p. 959).

The aggravation-mitigation continuum, therefore, makes it clear that certain social accounts may actually increase tension in the relationship rather than repairing the relationship and diffusing moral outrage. The contrast becomes most clear in the social accounts closest to the aggravation end of the continuum: refusals. Refusals "involve a denial of any personal responsibility for the offense or its consequences, or a denial of the right of anyone to reproach or question actors" (Gonzales et al., 1992, p. 959). Refusals may also include silence: offering no social account (Hodgins et al., 1996). Refusals are thus maximally threatening to victims: they fail to acknowledge the injustice and the victim's right to reproach or sanction the offender (Gonzales et al., 1992). Further, refusals are likely to infuriate victims because they fly in the face of the "intuitive jurist" assumption – the need for a victim to know why an injustice has occurred.

We argue that refusals do reduce the severity of social predicaments in a manner consistent with Bies (1987), however, when they protect the harmdoer's social identity: "[I]f there is no predicament or if the offender played no role in it, there is no tarnished identity to be restored" (Gonzales et al., 1992, p. 959). A refusal (a) decreases the harmdoer's responsibility, (b) may deny that the outcome is undesirable, and (c) restores and protects the social identity of the harmdoer. Thus, the intensity of the predicament is decreased *in the eyes of the harmdoer*. It is not that the moral outrage of victims has been diminished; the predicament is less intense because the harmdoers have removed themselves from the victims.

Thus, consistent with Bies (1987), we argue that refusals defend the harmdoer by creating *psychological distance* between the harmdoer and the victim. Milgram (1974) referred to psychological distance in his work on obedience to authority. Kelman and Hamilton (1989) and Bandura (1990) give similar functional analyses of distancing. In each case, the analysis suggests that offenders use distancing as a mechanism for reducing the adversity of contact with their victims. Although we refer to these self-protective actions as psychological distancing, they clearly may involve actual physical distancing as well.

In some cases, distancing also may include victim derogation. Bandura (1990) gives the example of the operators of gas chambers in

Nazi prison camps, who found it necessary to derogate and dehumanize their victims in order to avoid being overwhelmed by distress. In discussing how harmdoers selectively disengage self-sanctions for inhumane conduct, Bandura noted that perceiving a victim as another human being activates empathetic and vicarious emotional reactions. To disengage moral control, harmdoers divest the victim of human qualities, blunting empathetic responses. Lewis's (1971) research on shame also found an aggressive lashing out at victims. Shame is a self-focused negative emotion that arises in response to a transgression or a failure. Redirecting negative emotions toward one's victim is viewed as a defensive maneuver (Lewis, 1971) – "an attempt to turn the tables and to right the self, which has been impaired in the shame experience" (Tangney et al., 1992).

In sum, a harmdoer fears retaliation from his or her victim, and the injustice also poses a threat to the harmdoer's social identity. Social accounts can be defensive, protecting the harmdoer and providing an exit from the predicament. Bies asserts that accounts decrease the intensity of the predicament because they diffuse moral outrage – making it less likely that victims will retaliate, and posing less threat to the harmdoer's social identify. We agree that this fits the use of mitigating accounts, such as apologies or excuses. We extend this perspective, however, by noting that aggravating accounts also decrease the intensity of the predicament of injustice. Refusing to acknowledge responsibility preserves self-identity. Social distancing from the victim further protects the harmdoer from victim retaliation and from the personal distress caused by proximal contact with the victim. Rather than diffusing moral outrage, however, these social accounts are more likely to stoke its fires.

AGGRAVATION OR MITIGATION

We argue that offending parties react to social predicaments along an approach-avoidance continuum. Consistent with research on social accounts (Bies, 1987; Greenberg, 1990), they may provide explanations and show sympathy (approaching the victim, reducing interpersonal distance). But they may instead distance themselves (an avoidance response), which can include victim derogation and abuse. Trying to predict the tactic harmdoers will adopt essentially makes justice (e.g., the interactional justice or injustice of a manager's behavior toward layoff victims) another type of dependent variable in our analysis.

Although many factors might influence harmdoers' orientations toward their victims, Hodgins and colleagues (1996) highlight (a) the degree of threat to the harmdoer's face, (b) motivation to maintain the relationship, and (c) perceived ability to repair the relationship.

In the following section, we will follow Hodgins and colleagues' lead and review a number of studies that investigate the determinants of harmdoers' orientations toward their victims. Most of the research we review is experimental, using vignettes and scenarios. Although experimental scenarios do not invoke the type of strong emotions in participants that an actual encounter with a victim would produce, scenario studies have proved useful for studying harmdoer reactions. As Folger and Skarlicki noted, in defending their choice to study this phenomenon using experimental methods, "a person need not experience any vicarious emotions to recognize that someone about to leap over a deep chasm would be more afraid (and more likely to want to avoid the experience) than someone about to hop over a pothole" (1998, p. 83). Stated differently, even in laboratory settings, study participants can anticipate the aversive consequences and cues associated with encountering someone who has just been harmed.

Harmdoer's Face Threat

In a study of offenders' use of social accounts, Hodgins and colleagues (1996) operationalized face threat as offender blameworthiness for a transgression. This is consistent with Bies's (1987) conceptualization of offender responsibility as a primary determinant of predicament severity – to the extent that an offender is seen as personally responsible for the transgression, he or she may expect greater moral outrage from those harmed. Hodgins and colleagues' results showed that highly blameworthy participants gave shorter accounts, used more aggravating accounts, and told more lies in their social accounts than did the less blameworthy. Gonzales and colleagues (1992) presented similar evidence, finding fewer concessions (apologies) among highly blameworthy subjects than among those less culpable. When offenders are highly blameworthy, salvaging their own social identities appears to take priority over taking reparative actions toward the victim. Gonzales and associates noted that "when offenders are forced to choose in the aftermath of serious transgressions, others' face concerns pale in comparison with offender motives to salvage their own identities, and they dismiss others' face concerns in favor of their own" (1992, p. 967).

Thus, our analysis implies a positive relationship between (a) threat to the harmdoer's face or social identity (independent variable), and (b) the use of distancing strategies in communication (dependent variable).

Folger and Skarlicki (1998), using a sample of masters of business administration students and working managers, found evidence consistent with this prediction when studying the effect of prior mismanagement (blameworthiness) on layoff communications. The research procedure involved an in-basket exercise, a technique in which respondents role-play a manager's duties by answering memos addressed to that manager. During this exercise, the respondents designated time allocations for various management duties, including sessions with employees being laid off. Blameworthiness was manipulated in a letter from the CEO that either blamed the layoffs on the participant's mismanagement, or said that the layoffs occurred because of market forces beyond anyone's control. The authors operationalized managerial distancing as time dedicated to dismissal sessions. Managers who designate less time for dismissal sessions may have a greater tendency (than when longer times are used) not to provide a complete and adequate explanation – a variable shown to be related to fairness perceptions of both layoff victims and layoff survivors. The amount of time allocated to the dismissal also may be seen by both layoff victims and layoff survivors as symbolic of the company's relative priorities. Consistent with our analysis, Folger and Skarlicki's results showed significantly greater distancing as a function of blame: Low-blame managers dedicated an average of almost forty minutes to each of ten laid-off employees, whereas high-blame managers dedicated an average of only 28.3 minutes to each.

Other evidence (Folger & Skarlicki, 1998) also supports the role that blameworthiness plays in managerial distancing. Recall that when a harmdoer is highly responsible for damage done, the social predicament is proposed to be more severe, because greater anger, and possibly revenge, may be expected from victims (Bies, 1987), a concept also known as the harmdoer's "retaliation distress" (Walster, Walster, & Berscheid, 1978). To assess retaliation distress, Folger and Skarlicki (1998) included questionnaire items regarding the respondents' feelings of discomfort associated with administering the layoff (e.g., "I would feel uncomfortable when giving the . . . employees their layoff notices"). As expected, high-blame managers reported significantly greater emotional discomfort than did low-blame managers. Folger and Skarlicki (1998, study 2) also explored concepts related to retaliation distress using a sample of managers who were experienced in conducting layoffs (a mean of three layoffs over five years). During the in-basket exercise, high-blame managers were significantly more likely to anticipate criticism when encountering laid-off employees, as assessed by agreement to items such as "I expect them to put me on the spot with questions that might be hard to answer in ways that they would readily accept." Highly blameworthy managers also expected more trouble from laid-off employees, as assessed by agreement with items such as "Laid-off employees might steal, embezzle, sabotage, commit arson, or otherwise serve as a threat to the company's property and goods."

Motivation to Maintain the Relationship

A harmdoer's communication strategy has been described as reflecting the strength of the preference to protect and repair one's own social identity versus the social identity or face of the harmed party (Gonzales et al., 1992; Hodgins et al., 1996). To the extent that a relationship is valued and the harmdoer wishes the relationship to continue, the harmdoer will be more willing to pursue account strategies that threaten his or her own social identify while repairing damage to the relationship and to the victims' identity (Hodgins et al., 1996). Hodgins and colleagues' (1996) scenario-based study operationalized motivation to maintain the relationship through the manipulation of two factors: closeness (victim as a friend versus victim as an acquaintance) and status of the victim (greater motivation to maintain the relationship is assumed when the victim is of higher status). Results generally supported their hypotheses, demonstrating that harmdoers gave longer and more mitigating social accounts to friends than to acquaintances (supporting an "approach" orientation) and more mitigating (but not longer) accounts to high-status victims. Our analysis generalizes such results as the following prediction: The motive strength to maintain the relationship should relate negatively to the use of distancing strategies in communication.

Research on the interpersonal treatment received by harmed parties has often focused on harmdoers who provide explanations and expressions of sympathy and regret (i.e., approach strategies). We suspect that distancing, rude, or abusive communication has been relatively neglected because such research has dealt with social predicaments where it is desirable to repair or maintain the relationship (e.g., relationships between friends). Yet sensitive interpersonal communication requires effort and can be threatening to the harmdoer. At some point, it is likely that such communication strategies simply are not worth the effort to the harmdoer, whereupon distancing may begin to occur.

Bies (1987) argued for the management of moral outrage about injustice in ongoing relationships. In ongoing relationships, however, the desire to maintain the relationship can vary. A professor attacked for grading practices, for example, could explain those practices, justify the marks, and listen to individual concerns and complaints. On the other hand, the professor could disallow questions, ignore complaints, and criticize the students as spoiled. The classroom is clearly an ongoing faculty-student relationship, but certain factors (e.g., the time during the semester when complaints surface) can affect the desire to maintain the relationship and, subsequently, the account strategy used. If complaints come late in the semester, the professor might calculate that the students will be gone soon enough, and that they are of insufficient status to warrant the time-consuming task of providing considerate interpersonal treatment.

Perceived Ability to Repair the Relationship

Finally, if a harmdoer is to offer a social account in an attempt to repair a damaged relationship, he or she must perceive that the account will have some beneficial effect. In some cases, the damage done may simply be too great to merit an attempt at relationship repair. For an excuse to be effective, for example, it must be perceived as adequate and sincere (Bies & Shapiro, 1987; Bies, Shapiro, & Cummings, 1988). Whether an apology will be accepted by the harmed party also depends on the severity of the offense (Greenberg, 1990). Indeed, an offending party might believe that, in the face of a serious transgression willingly committed, an excuse or apology will serve only to enrage an already agitated victim. As noted by Gonzales and colleagues, "to proffer concessions is at once to admit guilt for a serious offence and to appear insincere or downright mendacious when expressing dismay or remorse over an intentional offense" (1992, p. 967). Thus, to the extent that a harmdoer perceives that a social account will be rejected, he or she can be expected to use a more distancing approach in interactions with victims. Such reasoning can be generalized as the following prediction: The harmdoer's perception of his or her ability to repair the relationship with the victim will relate negatively to the harmdoer's use of distancing strategies in communication.

Conclusion

In the tradition of Lerner's analysis of the reactions of innocent observers to the undeserved suffering of victims, we have analyzed the reactions of not-so-innocent observers: those in a position to observe the undeserved suffering of victims whose harm they caused (or in the case of managers ordered to lay off employees, those associated with the harmdoing in the victims' eyes). We have argued that this situation creates a social predicament for harmdoers, with an inherent conflict between approach-oriented and avoidance-oriented tendencies. Following the parallel analysis of a mitigation-aggravation continuum, determinants of approach-versus-distancing include (a) threat to the harmdoer's face, (b) motivation to maintain the relationship, and (c) perceived ability to repair the relationship. We suspect that a bad combination of these factors can easily occur during organizational downsizings when hardworking and competent employees lose jobs.

Indeed, perhaps a combination of factors accounts for the particularly harsh treatment sometimes given to downsized employees. When such employees are dismissed, the face threat to managers may be high. Even if the managers responsible for carrying out the downsizing are not directly responsible for the decisions, they will probably view themselves as targets of their subordinates' moral outrage. Folger and Skarlicki (1998) found, for example, that most managers expected to be targets of some criticism from employees, with the expectation of criticism increasing as managers became more culpable for the offense. Because the dismissed employees soon will be leaving, motivation to maintain the relationship also may be low. Although employees who are to be laid off may stay on the job for weeks or months as the organization makes a full transition, managers may fall into an "out of sight, out of mind" orientation toward them with the knowledge that they will soon be out of the organization. Finally, we suspect that many managers view the possibility of repairing a relationship following a layoff as remote.

Why should managers care about hostile reactions from their victims if any immediate danger from hostility can be avoided simply by distancing? Perhaps, one argument might go, such managers would make the best use of their time not by worrying about being sensitive to the victims of layoffs, but by concentrating on the normal business responsibilities associated with maximizing shareholder wealth. We can think of several counterarguments, but none so conclusive as to offset with finality the case for ignoring layoff victims – one reason why distancing tendencies might be generated to begin with! First, we suggest that although avoiding laid-off employees might remove managers from immediate danger, some chance of long-term danger from retaliatory hostility can persist. Second, the chance of physical danger is not the only costly consequence for managers and their firms. Avoiding victims also means keeping one's own emotional turmoil from approach-avoidance conflict bottled up, with potentially damaging consequences for managers' health, as suggested by research on inhibiting emotional expression (Pennebaker, 1997). Detrimental consequences can also stem from loss of morale, lowered productivity, and even possible retaliatory responses by layoff survivors when they see their former coworkers mistreated (cf. Brockner et al., 1994).

We have speculated about some of the factors that increase distancing behavior during layoffs, and certainly others can exist. Legal concerns, for example, might argue for swift, dispassionate separations. But the abusiveness that can occur, as in the case of Atari's downsized employees (Sutton, Eisenhardt, & Jucker, 1986), extends far beyond organizational concerns for protection of property. Speaking to the prevalence of poor downsizing practices in organizations, Cameron, Freeman, and Mishra (1993) note that the best ways to handle downsizing simply represent good management practices under normal circumstances (e.g., keeping employees informed, treating employees with respect). What makes good management rare during downsizing, however, is "that managers experience enormous pressure to abandon these management principles" (1993, p. 50). We hope that further study of these pressures can address how to increase the prevalence of good management practices even during tough times.

REFERENCES

Bandura, A. (1990). Selective activation and disengagement of moral control. *Journal of Social Issues, 46*, 27–46.

Batson, C. D. (1994). Prosocial motivation: Why do we help others? In A. Tesser (Ed.), *Advances in experimental social psychology* (pp. 333–381). Boston: McGraw-Hill.

Batson, C. D., Early, S., & Salvarani, G. (1997). Perspective taking: Imagining how another feels versus imagining how you would feel. *Personality and Social Psychology Bulletin, 23*, 751–758.

Baumeister, Stillwell, A. M., & Heatherton, T. F. Guilt: An interpersonal approach. *Psychological Bulletin*, 115, 243–267.

Bies, R. J., (1987). The predicament of injustice: The management of moral outrage. In L. L. Cummings and B. M. Staw (Eds.), *Research in organizational behavior* (Vol. 9, pp. 289–319). Greenwich, CT: JAI Press.

(2001). The sacred and the profane: Toward a new understanding of interactional justice. In J. Greenberg & R. Cropanzano (Eds.), *Advances in organizational justice* (pp. 89–118). Stanford, CA: Stanford University Press.

Bies, R. J., & Moag, J. S. (1986). Interactional justice: Communication criteria of fairness. In R. J. Lewicki, B. H. Sheppard, and M. H. Bazerman (Eds.), *Research on negotiations in organizations* (Vol. 1, pp. 43–55). Greenwich, CT: JAI Press.

Bies, R. J., & Shapiro, D. (1987). Interactional fairness judgments: The influence of causal accounts. *Social Justice Research, 1*, 199–218.

Bies, R. J., Shapiro, D., & Cummings, L. L. (1988). Causal accounts and managing organizational conflicts: Is it enough to say it's not my fault? *Communications Research, 15*, 381–399.

Brockner, J., Konovsky, M. A., Cooper, R., Folger, R., Bies, R. J., & Martin, C. (1994). The interactive effects of procedural justice and outcome negativity on job loss victims and survivors. *Academy of Management Journal, 37*, 397–409.

Cameron, K. S., Freeman, S. J., & Mishra, A. K. (1993). Downsizing and redesigning organizations. In G. P. Huber and W. H. Glick (Eds.), *Organizational change and redesign* (pp. 19–63). New York: Oxford University Press.

Churchill, W. S. (1950). *The grand alliance*. Boston: Houghton-Miflin.

Davis, K. E., & Jones, E. E. (1960). Changes in interpersonal perception as a means of reducing cognitive dissonance. *Journal of Abnormal and Social Psychology, 61*, 402–410.

Folger, R., & Skarlicki, D. (1998). When tough times make tough bosses: Managerial distancing as a function of layoff blame. *Academy of Management Journal, 41*, 79–87.

Freedman, J. L., Wallington, S. A., & Bless, E. (1967). Compliance without pressure: The effect of guilt. *Journal of Personality and Social Psychology, 7*, 117–124.

Glass, D. (1964). Changes in liking as a means of reducing cognitive discrepancies between self-esteem and aggression. *Journal of Personality, 32*, 531–549.

Goffman, E. (1971). *Relations in public*. New York: Basic Books.

Gonzales, M. H., Manning, D. J., & Haugen, J. A. (1992). Explaining our sins: Factors influencing offender accounts and anticipated victim responses. *Journal of Personality and Social Psychology, 62*, 958–971.

Greenberg, J., (1990). Looking fair vs. being fair: Managing impressions of organizational justice. In B. M. Staw & L. L. Cummings (Eds.), *Research in organizational behavior* (Vol. 12, pp. 111–157). Greenwich, CT: JAI Press.

Greenberg, J., & Baron, R. A. (1993). *Behavior in organizations*, 4th ed. Boston: Allyn and Bacon.

Hodgins, H. S., Liebestand, E., & Schwartz, W. (1996). Getting out of hot water: Facework in social predicaments. *Journal of Personality and Social Psychology, 71*, 300–314.

Kelman, H. C., and Hamilton, V. L. (1989). *Crimes of obedience*. New Haven, CT: Yale University Press.

Konovsky, M. A., & Folger, R. (1991). The effects of procedures, social accounts, and benefits level on victims' layoff reactions. *Journal of Applied Social Psychology, 21*, 630–650.

Lerner, M. J. (1980). *The belief in a just world*. New York: Plenum.

Lerner, M. J., & Simmons, C. H. (1966). The observer's reaction to the "innocent victim": Compassion or rejection? *Journal of Personality and Social Psychology, 4*, 203–210.

Lewis, H. (1971). *Shame and guilt in neurosis*. New York: International Universities Press.

Marks, M. L. (1993). Restructuring and downsizing. In P. H. Mirvis (Ed.), *Building the competitive workforce*. (pp. 66–94). New York: Wiley.

McLaughlin, M. L., Cody, M. J., & O'Hair, H. (1983). The management of failed events: Some contextual determinants of accounting behavior. *Human Communication Research, 9*, 208–224.

Milgram, S. (1974). *Obedience to authority*. New York: Harper and Row.

Neidenthall, P. M., Tangney, J. P., & Gavanski, I. (1994). "If only I weren't" versus "if only I hadn't": Distinguishing shame and guilt in counterfactual thinking. *Journal of Personality and Social Psychology, 67*, 585–595.

Pennebaker, J. W. (1997). *Opening up: The healing power of expressing emotion*. New York: Guilford Press.

Rousseau, D. M. (1989). *Psychological contracts in organizations*. Thousand Oaks, CA: Sage.

Sutton, R., Eisenhardt, K. M., & Jucker, J. V. (1986). Managing organizational decline: Lessons from Atari. *Organizational Dynamics, 14*, 17–29.

Tangney, J. P. (1991). Moral affect: The good, the bad, and the ugly. *Journal of Personality and Social Psychology, 61*, 598–607.

(1992). Situational determinants of shame and guilt in young adulthood. *Personality and Social Psychology Bulletin, 18*, 199–206.

Tangney, J. P., Wagner, P. E., Fletcher, C., & Gramzow, R. (1992). Shamed into anger? The relation of shame and guilt to anger and self-reported aggression. *Journal of Personality and Social Psychology, 62*, 669–675.

Walster, E., Walster, G., & Berscheid, E. (1978). *Equity: Theory and research*. Boston: Allyn and Bacon.

Working in the 1990s. (1995). *Atlanta Journal and Constitution*, May 16, p. A8.

THE JUSTICE MOTIVE AND PROSOCIAL BEHAVIOR

11. Just World, Social Responsibility, and Helping Behavior

HANS-WERNER BIERHOFF

This chapter attempts to integrate research on belief in a just world and social responsibility. First, the concepts of belief in a just world and social responsibility are described in some detail, and common aspects and differences are pointed out. On the basis of this discussion, two hypotheses are derived that refer to the overlap between just world belief and social responsibility and to the prediction of prosocial behavior. In the second part, empirical results that bear on the hypotheses are reported. Finally, some variations in the meaning of belief in a just world are considered, and a possible explanation is offered for the finding that belief in a just world is sometimes positively and sometimes negatively related to prosocial behavior.

Belief in a Just World

Just world theory is one of the key theories in social psychology (Lerner, 1980), and a central component of this is the belief in a just world construct. The belief in a just world may be defined as a belief system that rests on the premise that in general people get what they deserve. This assumption – which certainly is not confirmed in reality – is a positive illusion (cf. Taylor & Brown, 1988) and serves as a protection against the possibility that fate is uncontrollable and arbitrary.

The development of the belief in a just world is closely linked to the development of a personal contract (Lerner, 1974). The child assumes that the world is a just place. This immanent justice is based on the assumption that wrongdoing will be punished automatically. It is part of moral realism (Piaget, 1932). Other characteristics of moral realism include the tendency to blame people on the basis of objective damage rather than on the basis of their intent, and approval of authorities who maintain the social order by administering sanctions for misconduct (Lickona, 1976).

The belief in a just world is rooted in the emergence of a personal contract between the person and society that promises fair treatment in the future in exchange for the willingness to delay gratification in the present (Lerner, 1977). This personal contract is feasible as long as it is applied to oneself and to people in general. Therefore, just world thinking is not only a resumption of the child's conception of immanent justice, which was described by Piaget as a tendency to attribute justice to social events that have occurred, but also the conclusion following from the assumption that people must follow the rules of the game dictated by society.

In children, acceptance of immanent justice and belief in a just world are two sides of the same coin (Jose, 1990). In adults, acceptance of immanent justice and severity of punishment are linked together (Maes & Schmitt, 1999). Whereas Piaget assumed that the stage of moral realism gives way to the stage of moral cooperation, which is based on the acceptance of the norm of reciprocity and emphasizes intentions instead of consequences, traces of the child's worldview continue to exist. In some cases, the stage of moral cooperation is not reached. As a consequence, the belief in a just world determines the social reasoning of adults as well, but to a lesser extent than in children. In addition, specific situations may influence the belief in immanent justice, with some situations calling for more immanent justice than others (Medinnus, 1959). This observation leads to the assumption that belief in a just world is stronger in some situations than in others.

Piaget (1932) assumed that moral development refers to two main domains: respect for the rules of the social order, and the sense of justice (Lickona, 1976). Whereas the child's sense of justice is represented by the belief in a just world, respect for the rules of the social order means that social norms are taken seriously and are adopted as standards of behavior. This focus of moral development refers to social responsibility, which will be discussed later.

Individual Differences

The belief in a just world can be conceptualized and measured as an individual-difference variable. Whereas some people tend to agree that the world is basically a just place, others disagree. The first questionnaire to measure general belief in a just world was developed by Rubin and Peplau (1975). The revised German questionnaire, which measures general belief in a just world independent of the endorsement of the equity principle (Dalbert, 1999; Dalbert, Montada, & Schmitt, 1987), was used in the research reported in this chapter.

Strong believers in a just world admire successful people and derogate the victims of bad fate and underprivileged people in general (Dalbert, 1996). In addition, they report more life satisfaction than weak believers (Lipkus, Dalbert, & Siegler, 1996). Belief in a just world is also positively related to mental health and self-esteem (Dalbert, 1999).

High believers in a just world and high authoritarians have in common an admiration of successful people. Therefore, a positive correlation between the two constructs is expected (Rubin & Peplau, 1975). Whereas belief in a just world implies an optimistic worldview, authoritarianism takes on a more pessimistic perspective (Dalbert, 1996). The results of factor analyses including both constructs are informative (Lerner, 1980): Belief in a just world and authoritarianism load on different factors. The dimension of authoritarianism is characterized by prejudice and ethnocentrism. The just world dimension is described as a winner–loser factor.

Belief in a just world may be understood as an attempt to exert control (Mikula, 1984). As a consequence, the belief in a just world is positively correlated with internal locus of control (Furnham & Procter, 1989). The overlap between belief in a just world and internal locus of control is based on the emphasis on personal decision control in both concepts.

Strong believers in a just world tend to perceive personal deprivation as fair (Hafer & Olson, 1989). In addition, they are less involved in self-improvement and collective action in the context of discrimination (Hafer & Olson, 1993). These results are explained by the assumption that a strong belief in a just world implies that the world is fair.

Strong believers in a just world are more concerned about the undeserved suffering of others than are weak believers (Miller, 1977). For strong believers, it is important to construe the social world as just. Undeserved suffering challenges their worldview. In principle, two strategies are available for the reduction of distress elicited by the undeserved suffering of others. On the one hand, perceived injustice may be reduced by compensation, which may be provided by the government, other observers, or by the person him- or herself. This strategy is applicable as long as the undeserved suffering of the victim is successfully reduced. In general, when limited problems cause the suffering of the victim, prosocial action may completely restore the well-being of the victim.

On the other hand, if the victim's suffering is caused by complex, big, or unknown problems (= unlimited need case), or if a large number of victims suffer in the same way when help is available only for a few (= unlimited number of victims), other strategies for the maintenance of the general belief in a just world may be adopted that are less humane and more egocentric. These strategies can be subsumed under the term "derogation of the victim" (Lerner & Simmons, 1966). The subjective logic is as follows: If the victims deserve their bad fate, then this no longer challenges the belief in a just world. On the contrary, their suffering bolsters the principle of justice, because apparently it is people who have done wrong who find themselves in a bad situation. It is in this way that the derogation of victims contributes to the construction of a meaningful social world in cases where there are numerous victims or victims with unlimited needs.

Social Responsibility

Several meanings are attached to the term "social responsibility" in the social sciences. One of these meanings pertains to the attribution of responsibility. Why did an accident happen? Who was responsible? According to this perspective, responsibility is a social construct that is understood on the basis of attributional principles (Weiner, 2001). A second meaning of responsibility, which is pursued in this chapter, is based on the sense of personal obligation that results from the internalization of the norm of responsibility. Berkowitz and Daniels (1963) originally proposed the existence of a norm of responsibility that is evoked by the perception that another person is dependent on help in order to achieve a positive goal. The willingness to spend time and effort on behalf of the dependent person is assumed to be a direct function of the amount of perceived dependency, which depends on the objective level of dependency as well as on the number of potential helpers (Berkowitz, 1978). If responsibility is diffused among several bystanders, the individual willingness to act prosocially is reduced (Latané & Darley, 1970).

Berkowitz and Daniels (1964) assumed that social responsibility varies not only as a function of the need situation but also as a function of individual differences in the sense of personal obligation. Whereas some people take the norm of responsibility seriously and treat it as a personal standard, others ignore society's prescriptions, considering them either generally irrelevant or relevant for others but not for themselves. On the basis of these assumptions, a twenty-two-item responsibility scale was developed.

This concept of responsibility is quite broad, and as a consequence the items of the responsibility scale are very heterogeneous in content. Bierhoff (2000) suggested that the concept of responsibility is based on two dimensions that are positively related but that differ in content. On the one hand, the term "responsible" refers to the moral fulfillment of the justified expectations of others, which is related to moral orientation (cf. Piaget, 1932). The basic concern is serving humanity in the sense of enhancing the well-being of others and inflicting the minimum of pain. On the other hand, it refers to the inclination to follow the social rules of the game, which society dictates. The basic concern is adherence to social prescriptions. Piaget (1932) already called attention to this aspect when he noted that moral orientation includes respect for the rules of the social order. In the public debate about the responsible citizen, both meanings of responsibility are articulated – acting in accordance with the spirit of humanity, and acting in accordance with social rules.

Just World and Responsibility: Common Aspects and Differences

The just world hypothesis and the norm of social responsibility hypothesis share a focus on the perception of the suffering of others. The just world hypothesis specifies that assistance depends on the likelihood that the suffering will be reduced by giving help. The norm of social responsibility specifies that assistance is a function of the perceived dependency of the victim and the extent to which this appeals to an individual's sense of moral obligation. Therefore, just world theory and the norm of social responsibility make similar predictions with respect to prosocial behavior in cases where there is limited victim need and high victim dependency, but not in cases where there is unlimited victim need and high victim dependency. In the case of limited need and low responsibility, the two theories actually make opposite predictions, with just world theory predicting helping and the norm of social responsibility predicting nonhelping. In the case of unlimited need and low responsibility, both approaches predict a low level of helping. Note that the norm of responsibility is silent with respect to the issue of derogation of victims, which the just world framework predicts will occur when unlimited need situations are encountered by observers.

The two-dimensional framework of social responsibility offers new insights into the differences between belief in a just world and responsibility, as well as their common aspects. Whereas the moral fulfillment of the justified expectations of others and just world thinking have little in common, adherence to social prescriptions and just world belief seem to overlap considerably in their meaning. People who adhere to social prescriptions are predisposed to think in terms of the belief in a just world, because their own adherence to social prescriptions is based on the expectation that people in general follow social rules of conduct. For them, the social order is based on adherence to the norms of society by all members of society, which is rewarded by positive feedback. In addition, they assume that sanctions are imposed when social rules are broken in order to ensure that the norm is reinforced.

Hypotheses

I assume that the meaning of just world belief and adherence to normative standards overlap in part because in modern society adherence to the rules of the game implies that the world is a just place. The meaning of the belief in a just world is broader than that, because it refers to a genuine sense of justice. But I assume that the adherence-to-the-rules-of-the-game component predicts help in the case of limited emergencies. In the case of unlimited need situations, help is suppressed by the insight that it is not possible fully to compensate for the suffering of the victims. However, if this is not the case, the adherence to social rules is assumed to dominate the planning of action.

Based on the presumption that the just world belief is rooted in a commitment to a stable and orderly social world, it can be predicted (Hypothesis 1) that belief in a just world will be positively related to adherence to social rules of conduct, but will be independent of the moral fulfillment of duties that derive from a humanitarian orientation. Additionally, it can be predicted (Hypothesis 2) that the effect of belief in a just world on prosocial behavior for limited need situations (Miller, 1977) will be mediated by the level of adherence to the social rules.

A Test of Hypothesis 1

Participants

Hypothesis 1 was tested in several samples. Sample 1 included 82 students (27 male, 55 female; mean age = 24 years), and Sample 2 included 59 female students (mean age = 24 years), all from the University of Marburg. Sample 3 included 110 students from the University of Bochum (29 male, 81 female; mean age = 26 years). Finally, Sample 4 included 394 respondents whose data had been previously reported by Bierhoff, Klein, and Kramp (1991). Sample 4 consisted in turn of three subgroups: (1) 186 respondents who took part in a door-to-door survey in a small town in Germany, (2) 90 respondents who came from different parts of Germany and included a majority of professional drivers, and (3) 118 respondents who participated in a course at the national training center of St. John's Ambulance Brigade in Germany. Three-fifths of the sample was male. The average age of respondents was thirty-one.

Measures

Measures of belief in a just world and social responsibility were obtained in all samples. The belief in a just world was measured using the six-item scale of Dalbert, Montada, and Schmitt (1987), which contains the following items (English translation by Dalbert, 1999):

I think basically the world is a just place.
I believe that, by and large, people get what they deserve.
I am confident that justice always prevails over injustice.
I am convinced that in the long run people will be compensated for injustice.
I believe that injustices in all areas of life (e.g., professional, family, politics) are the exception rather than the rule.
I think that people try to be fair when making important decisions.

Answers were obtained on six-point scales. The alpha coefficients of internal consistency were .68, .78, and .73, respectively, in three consecutive studies by Dalbert (1999), which is sufficient considering the small number of items. All six items loaded above .40 on a general-belief-in-a-just-world factor in principal component analyses (Dalbert, 1999).

Social responsibility was measured by the German translation of the Berkowitz and Daniels (1964) twenty-two-item scale. On the basis of principal component analysis, two subscales were formed: moral fulfillment of the expectations of others (eight items) and adherence to social prescriptions (eight items). Once again, six-point response scales were used. Internal consistencies ranged between .65 and .70 in several studies. Considering the small number of items, this level of reliability is satisfactory.

Sample items on the moral fulfillment subscale are:

It is no use worrying about current events or public affairs; I can't do anything about them anyway. (Disagree)
When I work on a committee, I usually let other people do most of the planning. (Disagree)
I am the kind of person that people can count on. (Agree)
I would never let a friend down when he expects something of me. (Agree)

Sample items on the adherence to social prescription subscale are:

In school my behavior has gotten me into trouble. (Disagree)
I have been in trouble with the law or police. (Disagree)
When a person does not tell all his income in order to get out of paying some of his taxes, it is just as bad as stealing money from the government. (Agree)
When given a task I stick to it even if things I like to do better come along. (Agree)

Results

Table 11.1 summarizes the correlations between belief in a just world and the social responsibility subscales. As expected, the two subscales of the social responsibility measure, moral fulfillment of the expectations of others and adherence to social prescriptions, were correlated positively. Consistent with Hypothesis 1, there was a positive relationship between belief in a just world and adherence to social prescriptions, but no relationship between belief in a just world and moral fulfillment of the expectations of others.

Table 11.1. Correlations between belief in a just world and social responsibility subscales

	Belief in a Just World		
Sample	(1) Moral Fulfillment of Expectations	(2) Adherence to Social Prescriptions	Social Responsibility (1) with (2)
1	−.129 (81)	.249* (82)	.139 (81)
2	−.115 (58)	.358** (54)	.257 (55)
3	.000 (109)	.245* (101)	.346*** (101)
4	−.060 (391)	.382*** (381)	.194*** (380)

* $p < .05$, ** $p < .01$, *** $p < .001$.
Note: N in parentheses. Number of respondents is reduced because of missing data.

A Test of Hypothesis 2

Sample

Two groups comprised the sample used to test Hypotheses 2. One group was based on 34 (26 male, 8 female; mean age = 35 years) qualified first-aiders (who were met by an ambulance team at the scene of the accident and who were identified as first-aiders). A second, control group (C) consisted of 36 respondents (26 male, 10 female; mean age = 31 years) who reported that they actually had witnessed a car accident but had not helped. Comparisons between these two groups with respect to personality variables were reported by Bierhoff, Klein, and Kramp (1991). They found that qualified first-aiders scored higher on the six-item belief in a just world scale and the twenty-two-item social responsibility scale than the control group. This was interpreted as evidence for the altruistic personality.

Results

Preliminary analyses. The data were first reanalyzed on the basis of the formation of two subscales of responsibility. First, a MANOVA was conducted using the scores on the just world scale and the two responsibility subscales as the dependent variable, and group (first aiders vs. control) as the independent variable. As expected, the overall test was significant, Wilks Lambda = .788, $mF = 5.824$, $df = 3/65$, $p = .001$. Specifically, first aiders scored significantly higher on belief in a just world

($M = 3.12$) than did control respondents ($M = 2.56$), $F(1, 67) = 6.83$, $p = .011$. In addition, first aiders scored higher on moral fulfillment of expectations ($M = 5.07$) than did control respondents ($M = 4.82$), $F(1,67) = 4.65$, $p = .035$. Finally, first aiders scored higher on adherence to social prescriptions ($M = 4.24$) than did control respondents ($M = 3.51$), $F(1,67) = 15.35$, $p < .001$.

Next, logistic regressions were conducted, with group as the dependent variable and belief in a just world, moral fulfillment of expectations, and adherence to social prescriptions as predictors. As expected, the overall prediction is significant, $df = 3$, $chi^2 = 16.34$, $p = .001$. The classification table indicates that 74.3% of control respondents and 73.5% of first-aiders were classified correctly (overall, 73.9% correctly classified). Among the three predictors, only adherence to social prescriptions is significant ($df = 1$, $p = .02$).

Testing Mediation. To examine the mediation of the influence of belief in a just world on group via adherence to social prescriptions, the analytical procedure suggested by Baron and Kenny (1986) was applied. This procedure permits us to test the hypothesis that a mediator explains the relationship between the independent and the dependent variable. Mediation is tested by three successive regression analyses:

- The mediator (adherence to social prescriptions) is regressed on the independent variable (belief in a just world).
- The dependent variable (group membership) is regressed on the independent variable (belief in a just world).
- The dependent variable (group membership) is simultaneously regressed on the independent variable (belief in a just world) and the mediator (adherence to social prescriptions).

Mediation is indicated if the first two analyses reveal significant predictions and if the dependent and independent variables are no longer significantly interrelated after controlling for the mediator, whereas only the mediator significantly affects the dependent variable. These conditions for mediation were met (see Figure 1).

These results are confirmed by a logistic regression analysis with adherence to social prescriptions as predictor of group membership. The prediction is highly significant ($df = 1$, $chi^2 = 14.15$, $p = .0002$). In this analysis, 73.9% of respondents are classified correctly. This indicates the same efficiency that was observed in the logistic regression

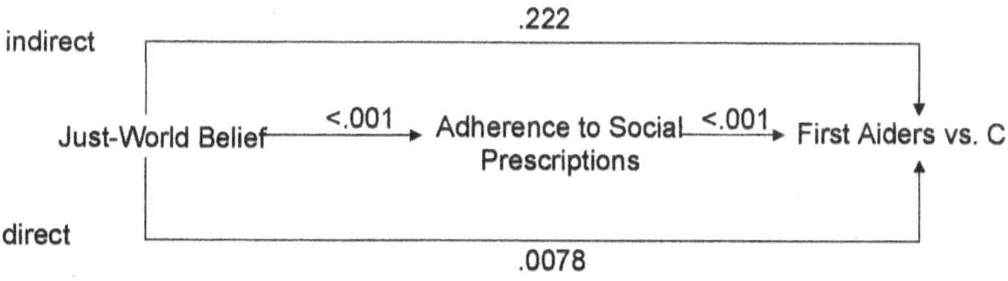

Figure 11.1. Group membership (first aiders vs. control group) as a function of just world belief and adherence to social prescriptions.

with the three predictors reported earlier. As a single predictor, adherence to social prescriptions is highly significant ($df = 1$, $p < .001$).

Note that the preconditions for the mediation of the influence of belief in a just world on group via moral fulfillment of expectations are not given, since the mediator (moral fulfillment of expectations) and the independent variable (belief in a just world) are independent of each other across respondents in the two groups ($p > .30$). The logistic regression with moral fulfillment of expectations and belief in a just world as predictors of group membership is significant ($df = 2$, $chi^2 = 10.11$, $p = .0064$). Whereas belief in a just world is a significant predictor in this analysis ($p = .019$), moral fulfillment of expectations is not ($p = .094$), indicating that it is not a mediator of belief in a just world.

Discussion

This investigation examined the relation between belief in a just world, as measured by the scale of Dalbert, Schmitt, and Montada (1987) based on the classical Rubin and Peplau (1975) scale, and the norm of social responsibility first described by Berkowitz and Daniels (1964). More specifically, it examined the relation between the belief in a just world and two recently identified distinct facets of social responsibility, moral fulfillment of justified expectations of others and adherence to social prescriptions. It was hypothesized that variance in belief in a just world overlaps with variance in adherence to social prescriptions, but not with moral fulfillment of justified expectations of others. This hypothesis was confirmed in four samples. It appears that citizens who follow society's rules of the game tend to believe in a just world, supporting Hypothesis 1.

A mediational analysis of the present results revealed another striking finding. As predicted by Hypothesis 2, the relationship between just world belief and group membership (first-aiders vs. control respondents) was nearly completely accounted for by adherence to social prescriptions. Moral fulfillment of justified expectations, by contrast, did not function as a mediator. In conclusion, adherence to social prescriptions is the main predictor of prosocial behavior in field settings.

A Comparison to Other Conceptions of the Belief in a Just World

Whereas this research has focused on the core meaning of belief in a just world, other researchers have followed a different strategy by distinguishing different meanings of the belief in a just world. Considering the present results in relation to these other conceptualizations is instructive. Maes and Schmitt (1999) have contrasted immanent and ultimate justice. Whereas immanent justice is in correspondence with the original just world concept (e.g., "Misfortune is the just punishment for a bad character"), ultimate justice refers to the restitution or compensation of current suffering in the far future (e.g., "Those who have suffered will be compensated one day"). Our results may hold more for the concept of immanent justice than for the concept of ultimate justice. The tendency to believe that forthcoming events will settle any injustice that occurs is derived from religion, which promises a greater justice in the long run. This orientation is likely to contribute to the willingness to endure injustice without complaining.

Dalbert (1999) distinguished between the general and the personal belief in a just world. General beliefs correspond to the classical meaning of belief in a just world, whereas personal beliefs are tapped by statements like "I am usually treated fairly," which emphasize the personal relevance of fairness. The personal belief in a just world is especially relevant for predicting mental health (Lipkus, Dalbert, & Siegler, 1996). The more personal the perceived injustice, the more threatening it will be.

According to Dalbert (1999), injustice is denied more on a personal than on a general level. As a corollary, fairness is attributed more to one's own actions than to the actions of others (Bierhoff, 1996; Messick et al., 1985). Whereas personal belief in a just world is positively related to subjective well-being, positive mood, and self-esteem, general belief in a just world (the just world scale employed here) is positively related to the use of defensive strategies to justify one's own privileges in society (Montada, Schmitt, & Dalbert, 1986). General belief in a just world is a good index of fairness considerations in the broad societal context, whereas personal belief in a just world seems to be a good index of individual considerations. The common variance between belief in a just world and prosocial behavior seems to reflect the fact that the general belief in a just world includes an adherence-to-the-rules-of-the-game component.

A Final Thought

Why does the just world scale fail to predict prosocial behavior when no means are available to reduce the injustice completely (cf. Miller, 1977)? Is it possible to integrate the results that indicate that belief in a just world is sometimes positively and sometimes negatively related to prosocial behavior? The answer may lie in another component of the belief in a just world, which centers around justice as a value in itself (cf. Hafer & Olson, 1989, 1993). As a first step, people who believe in a just world seem to be interested in the establishment of justice. If an unlimited need situation is met, they retreat to psychological methods of establishing justice by defensive strategies. As a second step, which is optional in the case where the need situation is limited, people consider the importance of adhering to society's rules of conduct as a way to make sure that people get what they deserve (e.g., helping when they are involved in a traffic accident).

REFERENCES

Baron, R. M., & Kenny, D. A. (1986). The moderator-mediator variable distinction in social psychological research: Conceptual, strategic, and statistical considerations. *Journal of Personality and Social Psychology, 51*, 1173–1182.

Berkowitz, L. (1978). Decreased helpfulness with increased group size through lessening the effects of the needy individual's dependency. *Journal of Personality, 46*, 299–310.

Berkowitz, L., & Daniels, L. R. (1963). Responsibility and dependency. *Journal of Abnormal and Social Psychology, 66*, 429–436.

Berkowitz, L., & Daniels, L. R. (1964). Affecting the salience of the social responsibility norm: Effects of past help on the response to dependency relationships. *Journal of Abnormal and Social Psychology, 68*, 275–281.

Bierhoff, H. W. (1996). Egozentrische Verzerrungen bei Fairness-Urteilen [Egocentric bias in fairness judgments]. Paper presented at the Fortieth Conference of the German Society of Psychology, Munich.

Bierhoff, H. W. (2000). Skala der sozialen Verantwortung nach Berkowitz und Daniels: Entwicklung und Validierung [Scale of social responsibility according to Berkowitz and Daniels: Development and validation]. *Diagnostica, 46*, 18–28.

Bierhoff, H. W., Klein, R., & Kramp, P. (1991). Evidence for the altruistic personality from data on accident research. *Journal of Personality, 59*, 263–280.

Dalbert, C. (1996). *Über den Umgang mit Ungerechtigkeit. Eine psychologische Analyse* [Dealing with injustice: A psychological analysis]. Bern: Huber.

(1999). The world is more just for me than generally: About the personal belief in a just world scale's validity. *Social Justice Research, 12*, 79–98.

Dalbert, C., Montada, L., & Schmitt, M. (1987). Glaube an eine gerechte Welt als Motiv: Validierungskorrelate zweier Skalen [Belief in a just world: Validity correlates of two scales]. *Psychologische Beiträge, 29*, 596–615.

Furnham, A., & Procter, E. (1989). Belief in a just world: Review and critique of the individual difference literature. *British Journal of Social Psychology, 28*, 365–384.

Hafer, C. L., & Olson, J. M. (1989). Beliefs in a just world and reactions to personal deprivation. *Journal of Personality, 57*, 799–823.

(1993). Beliefs in a just world, discontent, and assertive actions by working women. *Personality and Social Psychology Bulletin, 19*, 30–38.

Jose, P. E. (1990). Just-world reasoning in children's immanent justice judgments. *Child Development, 61*, 1024–1033.

Latané, B., & Darley, J. M. (1970). *The unresponsive bystander: Why doesn't he help?* New York: Appleton.

Lerner, M. J. (1977). The justice motive: Some hypotheses as to its origins and forms. *Journal of Personality, 45*, 1–52.

(1980). *The belief in a just world: A fundamental delusion*. New York: Plenum.

Lerner, M. J., & Simmons, C. H. (1966). Observer's reaction to the "innocent victim": Compassion or rejection? *Journal of Personality and Social Psychology, 4*, 203–210.

Lickona, T. (1976). Research on Piaget's theory of moral development. In T. Lickona (Ed.), *Moral development and behavior: Theory, research, and social issues* (pp. 219–240). New York: Holt.

Lipkus, I. M., Dalbert, C., & Siegler, I. C. (1996). The importance of distinguishing the belief in a just world for self versus for others: Implications for psychological well-being. *Personality and Social Psychology Bulletin, 22*, 666–677.

Maes, J., & Schmitt, M. (1999). More on ultimate and immanent justice: results from the research project "Justice as a Problem within Reunified Germany." *Social Justice Research, 12*, 65–78.

Medinnus, G. R. (1959). Immanent justice in children: A review of the literature and additional data. *Journal of Genetic Psychology, 94*, 253–262.

Messick, D. M., Bloom, S., Boldizar, J. P., & Samuelson, C. D. (1985). Why we are fairer than others. *Journal of Experimental Social Psychology, 21*, 480–500.

Mikula, G. (1984). Justice and fairness in interpersonal relations: Thoughts and suggestions. In H. Tajfel (Ed.), *The social dimension: European developments in social psychology* (Vol. 1, pp. 204–227). Cambridge: Cambridge University Press.

Miller, D. T. (1977). Altruism and threat to a belief in a just world. *Journal of Experimental Social Psychology, 13,* 113–124.

Montada, L., Schmitt, M., & Dalbert, C. (1986). Thinking about justice and dealing with one's own privileges. In H. W. Bierhoff, R. L. Cohen, & G. Greenberg (Eds.), *Justice in social relations* (pp. 125–143). New York: Plenum.

Piaget, J. (1977). *The moral judgement of the child.* Harmondsworth: Penguin. (Originally published 1932.)

Rubin, Z., & Peplau, L. A. (1975). Who believes in a just world ? *Journal of Social Issues, 31* (3), 65–89.

Weiner, B. (2001). An attributional approach to perceived responsibility for transgressions: Extensions to child abuse, punishment goals, and political ideology. In A. E. Auhagen & H. W. Bierhoff (Eds.), *Responsibility: The many faces of a phenomenon* (pp. 49–59). London: Routledge.

12. Policies to Redress Social Injustice: Is the Concern for Justice a Cause Both of Support and of Opposition?

D. RAMONA BOBOCEL, LEANNE S. SON HING, CAMILLA M. HOLMVALL, AND MARK P. ZANNA

As documented by the research in the current volume, people are profoundly affected by social injustice. Fortunately, efforts to remedy many forms of social injustice have been undertaken by our legal and political institutions. Yet, despite many well-intentioned efforts to remedy injustice at the societal level, a paradox exists: Often the policies designed to redress injustice are themselves criticized as unfair and, in turn, are opposed. As a result, there is mounting polarization at the societal level in terms of support for, or opposition to, the policies designed to redress social injustice. There is also a rising divergence of opinion among researchers in the psychological literature, due to evidence demonstrating that there are both possible benefits (see Crosby & VanDeVeer, 2000) and burdens (e.g., Heilman, Block, & Lucus, 1992) associated with such policies. In the hope of closing the chasm, we believe that it is necessary to better understand the basis of this paradox. As society diversifies and people question what is or is not fair, research in this vein is especially relevant.

In one line of research at the University of Waterloo, we have been investigating the basis of the paradox, following in the tradition of Mel Lerner, both theoretically and methodologically. Theoretically, our overarching approach derives from what is perhaps Lerner's central legacy: his firm conviction that people have a fundamental or core justice motive (Lerner, 1974; Lerner, 1977; Lerner, 1980; Lerner & Lerner, 1981; Lerner & Miller, 1978). Specifically, our research has been guided by the assumption that researchers can better understand both positive and negative reactions to social policies designed to redress injustice by adopting a justice perspective. In one series of studies, we have examined whether people's concern for justice can be a genuine determinant of opposition to certain policies designed to redress social injustice. In a second line of research, we have examined whether objections rooted in the concern for justice can be mitigated by situational variables; from a justice perspective, we have focused on the role of situational variables that highlight unfairness in the status quo – in particular, the violation of meritocracy in the distribution of outcomes. The principal argument we hope to make in the present chapter is this: By truly appreciating the idea that justice matters to people, researchers can better understand why people sometimes oppose certain social policies designed to redress injustice; on the basis of that knowledge, they can then elucidate conditions under which people's reactions will be less polarized. From a methodological perspective, Lerner advocated the importance of studying justice issues within situations that are highly psychologically involving, in order to allow researchers to uncover the complexities of the justice motive. As we will describe in the next sections, we have followed Lerner's tradition in the design of our research, as well as in our theoretical analysis.

The chapter is divided into three main sections. In the first section, we describe an initial series of studies in which we set the stage by asking whether the concern for justice can be a genuine cause of opposition to social policies. In the second section, we describe a more recent line of research examining whether justice-based opposition can be mitigated. In particular, we describe two sets of studies using different research paradigms that converge on the idea that opposition may be reduced when people perceive a violation of meritocracy in the status quo. In the third section, we summarize and highlight the central implications of the research program.

Can the Concern for Justice be a Genuine Cause of Opposition?

As stated earlier, for almost every public policy decision that claims to redress social injustice, there are people who express opposition to it on the grounds that the policy is unfair. A common rejoinder by advocates is that opponents are in fact being disingenuous. One argument is that opponents' claims of unfairness are a cover-up for prejudice, self-interest, or other variables related to maintaining an unfair status quo.

Perhaps the context that best exemplifies the debate over justice-versus prejudice-based sources of opposition to social policies is affirmative action. On one side of the debate are people who claim that they oppose affirmative action because it is unfair. In particular, these people argue that affirmative action is unfair because it violates the merit principle of distributive justice. According to the merit principle, outcomes are fair when they are distributed among people in proportion to their relative contributions or inputs (e.g., Deutsch, 1975; Lerner, 1974). Thus, to the extent that an affirmative action policy advantages less qualified target-group members (according to traditional indices of qualifications), it is perceived in the eyes of most people as violating the merit principle of distributive justice. Moreover, even when a policy upholds traditional definitions of the merit principle, it may be perceived as violating the consistency principle of procedural justice. According to the consistency principle of procedural justice, allocation procedures should treat all potential recipients identically (e.g., Leventhal, 1980). Thus, to the extent that an affirmative action policy treats target-group members and nonmembers differently in hiring and promotion decisions, it is perceived as violating the consistency principle of procedural justice. Numerous studies are consistent with the idea that justice considerations are a relevant predictor of reactions to affirmative action (for two examples, see Kravitz et al., 1997; Nacoste, 1987). According to a *justice hypothesis*, then, opposition to policies aimed at redressing injustice may be derived, at least in part, from people's fundamental concern over the violation of valued justice principles.

On the other side of the debate is the *prejudice hypothesis*, which suggests that people who oppose affirmative action do so because of negative attitudes toward the potential beneficiaries. Indeed, there is evidence to show that the more negative people's attitudes toward women or blacks, the more they oppose the general concept of affirmative action (e.g., Kluegal & Smith, 1983; Sidanius, Pratto, & Bobo, 1996). It has further been suggested that opposition to affirmative action on the grounds that it is unfair may itself reflect a rationalization of prejudice. The idea that prejudice may manifest itself in this manner is consistent with theorizing and research on the "modern" forms of prejudice (e.g., Murrell et al., 1994; Tougas et al., 1995; Gaertner & Dovidio, 1986).[1]

[1] It is noteworthy, however, that in some of the past research demonstrating links between the modern forms of prejudice and opposition to the general concept of affirmative action, the items purportedly measuring the more subtle forms of prejudice often solicit people's attitudes toward policies such as affirmative action. In other words, people's attitudes toward affirmative action are sometimes taken as an indicator of prejudice. Although the latter operationalization is consistent with the conceptualization of a more subtle form of prejudice, it raises an obvious construct validity problem in research on attitudes toward affirmative action (for more details, see Davey et al., 1999).

Whereas undoubtedly prejudice is one determinant of negative attitudes toward some social policies designed to help the disadvantaged, is prejudice the entire story? If justice-based opposition is merely a manifestation of prejudice, then this casts doubt on the validity of the paradox outlined earlier. That is, we could attribute people's justice-based objections to motivations other than the concern for justice per se. This is an important issue, because the interpretation of the causes of people's opposition ultimately influences how social and organizational psychologists study attitudes in this domain and how society develops and implements policies designed to redress injustice.

It is interesting to note that, in the broader psychological literature on procedural and distributive justice, there is virtually no debate about the validity of people's justice-based objections to a number of different kinds of workplace or public policies, such as drug testing, performance monitoring, and smoking bans (for reviews, see Folger & Cropanzano, 1998; Lind & Tyler, 1988). Nor is there debate on the effects of such perceptions on work attitudes and behaviors. From a theoretical perspective, it is not clear why justice concerns should have a lesser role to play in the domain of affirmative action than in other domains. Thus, in the same way that adopting a justice perspective has advanced researchers' understanding of reactions to work policies that do not necessarily involve group membership (or which involve lines of group categorization other than sex and race), we believe that adopting a justice perspective can advance researchers' understanding in the domain of affirmative action.

On the basis of the preceding concerns, our primary objective in a first series of studies was to test whether people's concern for justice can indeed be a *determinant* of their attitudes toward affirmative action, or whether objections in the name of fairness are necessarily rooted in people's prejudices toward those who purportedly benefit most from the policy (e.g., women, the disabled, visible minorities).

If the concern for justice is a genuine cause of opposition rather than solely a rationalization of prejudice, then by deduction two predictions follow. First, we would expect that the extent to which people value a particular justice principle should predict their opposition, but only when evaluating a policy that violates the relevant justice principle. For example, the more strongly people endorse the idea that outcomes ought to be distributed according to the merit principle of distributive justice, the more strongly they should oppose a policy that violates this principle. By contrast, people's endorsement of the merit principle should not predict opposition to a policy that upholds the merit principle (indeed, it could predict support for the policy). Second, the effect of justice values should be independent of people's prejudice level. In fact, whereas it may seem counterintuitive, we reasoned that prejudice level might have a relatively small or no significant effect on attitudes when a policy explicitly violates a justice principle. If (a) justice values and prejudice are independent constructs, and (b) justice-based objections are genuine, then, depending on people's justice values, it is possible for those who are relatively nonprejudiced and those who are relatively prejudiced to be equally opposed to a justice-violating policy. Our prediction regarding the role of prejudice is supported by two prior studies. In one study investigating students' attitudes toward four affirmative action programs designed to increase representation of black students at their university, Nosworthy, Lea, and Lindsay (1995) found that racism contributed as a predictor of opposition to only the mildest of the four possible programs (e.g., targeted ads versus enrollment quotas). In addition, in a large survey aimed at validating a unidimensional conceptualization of forms of racism, Kleinpenning and Hagendoorn (1993) found that Dutch secondary school students' scores on racism were correlated more highly with their opposition to a question about equal opportunity in society than to a question about preferential treatment in job hiring. In summary, the data from these studies are consistent with our idea that, for policies that violate valued justice principles, prejudice may have a lesser or nonsignificant role as a predictor of attitudes.

By contrast, if prejudice were the whole story of opposition, then there should be no independent effect of people's justice values over and above their prejudice level, nor should justice values predict differentially as a function of whether the policy violates or upholds the relevant justice principles.

We have conducted a series of experiments to test this logic (see Bobocel et al., 1998). For example, in one study, in an initial phase, we assessed University of Waterloo students' endorsement of two justice principles, using measures we had created in some of our previous research. One measure (fifteen items) was designed to tap people's preference for allocations that are based on the distributive justice principle of equity or merit, which states that to be fair outcomes or "goods" ought to be distributed on the basis of people's relative contributions (i.e., the Preference for the Merit Principle Scale; for details, see Davey et al., 1999). An example item (rated on a five-point scale with end points labeled disagree and agree) is: "In organizations, people who do their job well ought to rise to the top" (positively keyed). The other measure (twenty items) was designed to tap, in a variety of social domains, people's preference for the consistency principle of procedural justice, which states that to be fair people ought to be treated identically in decision making (Son Hing, 1997). An example item (rated on a five-point scale with end points labeled extremely unfair and extremely fair) is: "To treat everyone the same, all taxpayers ought to pay for highway maintenance even though some people use the roads more than others" (positively keyed). Finally, we also assessed people's level of prejudice, using existing measures of sexism (e.g., Tougas et al., 1995) and racism (e.g., McConahay, 1986). To provide a clearer test of the hypotheses, we designed our justice measures to be free of content of constructs related to prejudice and the desire to maintain the status quo, such as social dominance orientation, authoritarianism, and the belief that the world is currently just (for scale details, see Bobocel et al., 1998; Davey et al., 1999). In addition, we deleted items from previous prejudice measures (e.g., sexism) that appeared to have substantial content overlap with the criterion of interest: attitudes toward affirmative action (see note 1, p. 206).

In a separate experimental session held about one month later, a random sample of these participants were invited to participate in what was ostensibly an unrelated corporate survey. In brief, participants were told that a local company was gathering reactions from several constituents regarding various workplace policies that they were considering implementing, and that because University of Waterloo students are potential "employees of the future," the company was interested in their views. To make the situation as psychologically involving as possible, we bolstered the cover story by conducting the study outside of the psychology building; the experimenter was dressed in a business suit; the experimental materials were professionally designed; and we told participants that their opinions would determine whether or not the company implemented the policies in question. Indeed, we further created the sense that participants were providing the company with their "vote" by having them seal their ratings in an envelope and drop them in what appeared to be a ballot box.

Participants evaluated the following three specific workplace affirmative action policies (counterbalanced in order), which by design did or did not violate the relevant justice principles. A *preferential treatment* policy violated the merit principle of distributive justice by stating that, as long as they were minimally qualified, women, visible minorities, and the physically challenged would be hired or promoted over nontarget-group members even if the former were relatively less qualified. A *tie-break* policy violated the consistency principle of procedural justice by stating that target-group members would receive preference in jobs or promotions in instances of "tied" merit. This policy thus treats people differently as a function of group status, but it does not violate the merit principle per se because in no case would a less qualified target-group member be advantaged. Finally, an *equal treatment* policy violated neither justice principle by stating that new programs such as flexible hours, maternity/paternity leaves, and mentorship programs would be available to all employees as a means of removing systemic barriers.

Not considering individual differences for the moment, we found that participants were in general most opposed to the preferential treatment policy and most favorable toward the equal treatment policy. Attitudes toward the tie-break policy fell in between (at about the neutral point on the scale). The principle results – predicting opposition to each policy as a function of individual differences – are presented in Table 12.1. In line with the justice hypothesis, we found that, over and above people's prejudice level, strength of endorsement of justice principles predicted opposition, but only when the policy violated the relevant justice principle. That is, when the policy violated the merit principle (preferential treatment policy), opposition was significantly and uniquely influenced by participants' preference for the merit principle of justice. The more strongly people endorsed the merit principle, the more they opposed this policy. When the policy violated

Table 12.1. Standardized regression coefficients (betas) for the within-cell regressions of opposition on the predictors

	Affirmative Action Policy		
Predictor	Equal Treatment	Tie-break	Preferential Treatment
Prejudice	.34**	.16	.12
Endorsement of the consistency principle	−.03	.18†	.03
Endorsement of the merit principle	−.01	.05	.35**

Note: Adapted from Bobocel et al., 1998. $N = 86$. ** $p < .01$, † $p < .10$.

the consistency principle (the tie-break policy), opposition was predicted by participants' preference for the consistency principle. The more strongly people endorsed the consistency principle, the more they opposed this policy. Finally, when the program violated neither justice norm, attitudes were not influenced by justice values; rather, it was in this case that prejudice significantly distinguished those who were relatively more opposed from those who were relatively more supportive.

Thus, in line with the prejudice hypothesis, we indeed found that the greater the prejudice, the more the opposition. Yet this was true only for the policy that did not explicitly violate justice principles. It is of further interest to note that, in follow-up mediation analyses, we found that prejudiced individuals were more opposed to the equal treatment policy compared to less prejudiced individuals because they construed it as justice-violating. This finding is consistent with the idea that, for prejudiced people, justice concerns may indeed serve as a rationalization for opposition to the equal treatment policy. In two related follow-up studies, we have replicated the prejudice effect on attitudes toward the *global concept of affirmative action*, which, as noted earlier, is the dependent variable most often examined in past research examining the role of prejudice. In one study, 455 University of Waterloo students completed the measures of justice values and prejudice, as well as providing their attitudes toward and construal of a "typical affirmative action program." The results showed that prejudice, but not justice values, predicted opposition to the undefined program. In an effort to test whether this effect of prejudice generalizes to a nonstudent population, we included a shortened version of our measures (in this case, only modern racism, attitudes, and justice construal were assessed) as part of the Kitchener–Waterloo Metropolitan Area Survey 1998 (Bobocel, Son Hing, & Zanna, 1998). This was a larger community survey that was mailed to a random sample of adults whose names were obtained from the tax assessment rolls for the local area. The primary sample details are as follows: 62% response rate; $N = 307$; mean age of respondents = 47 years; 53% women; 60% employed full-time. Again, we found that prejudice predicted attitudes toward the undefined affirmative action program. Moreover, as in the case of the equal treatment policy, in both of the latter studies mediation analyses confirmed that prejudiced people were more opposed than were their less prejudiced counterparts in part because of their construal of the undefined affirmative action policy as justice-violating.

The data from our initial line of research thus clearly indicate that, for some policies – those that are non-justice-violating or are undefined – opposition on the grounds that the policy is unfair may derive from motivations other than the concern for justice per se – in this case, prejudice. People who have negative attitudes toward the beneficiaries may oppose social policies aimed at redressing injustice with the claim that the policies are unfair. Whether this claim of unfairness is applied after the fact to cover up their dislike of the policy, or whether prejudice directly influences people's beliefs about the fairness of the policy is not clear from our data. Likely, both processes occur. What is clear, however, is that prejudice was most likely to predict reactions when the policy is – in the minds of most people – not explicitly justice-violating.

By contrast, when the policy did violate traditional justice principles, we were unable to predict attitudes simply by knowing participants' levels of prejudice; people were generally more opposed to these policies, regardless of their level of prejudice. However, rather than prejudice level, attitudes were predicted by participants' justice values. Participants were more opposed to policies that violate norms of merit and consistency as a result of their endorsement of those justice principles. This implies that, when policies explicitly violate certain justice norms, we can expect people who most strongly endorse those norms to be especially opposed. In other words, in line with the justice hypothesis, sometimes people will reject policies aimed at redressing social injustice out of a genuine concern for justice.

Can the Concern for Justice Reduce Opposition?

Our initial studies revealed that people who strongly endorse certain justice principles tend to be particularly opposed to policies that violate those principles. Yet, is this always the case? We believe that the answer is no. Whereas the concern for justice may affect attitudes in this manner under ordinary circumstances, we also believe that there are conditions, derived from a justice framework, in which the typical effect is reduced.

In brief, if people object to social policies that violate certain justice norms as a result of their endorsement of those norms, then opposition should be reduced under conditions that highlight the unfairness or potential unfairness of the status quo. For instance, if bias exists in the manner in which merit is assessed in an organization's selection procedures, then this situation should offend people who strongly endorse the merit principle, because the existence of such bias would violate meritocracy. Under these conditions, we propose that people who strongly value the meritocratic distribution of outcomes will face a conflict: Ordinarily, they would oppose a merit-violating policy like our preferential treatment policy, because it offends their justice principles; however, the existence of bias in the workplace also offends their justice principles, because it too is merit-violating. In this set of "dual justice-violating" conditions, it is possible that people's typical justice-based objections to the policy would be overridden by their more specific beliefs about unfairness in the status quo. Indeed, in line with previous theorizing by Crosby and her colleagues (e.g., Crosby, 1994), it is possible that, in this situation, people will be more supportive of the policy because it is perceived as enhancing meritocracy. In the next two subsections, we review two sets of studies that converge on these ideas.

The Effect of the Perception of Workplace Discrimination in Mitigating Opposition to Affirmative Action

In one series of studies (see Son Hing, Bobocel, & Zanna, 2000), we used the same methodology as in our earlier research and examined the role of the perception of workplace discrimination in moderating justice-based opposition to an affirmative action policy. In particular, we focused on potential moderation of the effect of participants' endorsement of the merit principle of distributive justice on opposition to the preferential treatment policy. In a first study, in addition to assessing students' endorsement of the merit principle in an initial session, we measured their perceptions of discrimination in the workplace, using an eighteen-item scale that we had previously developed. On the basis of our conceptualization of workplace discrimination as a form of merit violation, a subset of the scale items was designed to tap people's perceptions of bias in the assessment of minority group members' merit. An example item (rated on a five-point scale with the end points labeled disagree and agree) is: "Typically, the criteria used to measure employee performance reflect male-dominated norms of professional behavior (e.g., competitiveness) and thus criteria are biased against female employees" (positively keyed). As in our earlier studies, we obtained participants' attitudes toward the preferential treatment policy one month later.

The results showed that, as before, participants' justice values predicted opposition to the preferential treatment policy; the more strongly participants endorsed the merit principle of distributive justice, the more they opposed the policy. As predicted, however, there was a significant interaction between justice values and perceptions of workplace discrimination. As shown in Figure 12.1, the effect of justice values on opposition was significant only among people who perceive little workplace discrimination; by contrast, among those who perceive high workplace discrimination, the effect of justice values was entirely mitigated.

In a second follow-up study, we used the same general methodology except that, rather than measuring participants' perceptions of workplace discrimination, we experimentally manipulated this variable before participants evaluated the affirmative action policy. We induced the perception of workplace discrimination by altering the wording of a subset of the items in the measure we had used in the preceding study. Specifically, in one condition (low workplace discrimination), the items were difficult to agree with by virtue of the qualifiers used in the items; by contrast, in the other condition (high workplace discrimination), the items were worded so that they were easy to agree with (e.g., "[Typically/Sometimes], the criteria used to measure employee performance reflect male-dominated norms of

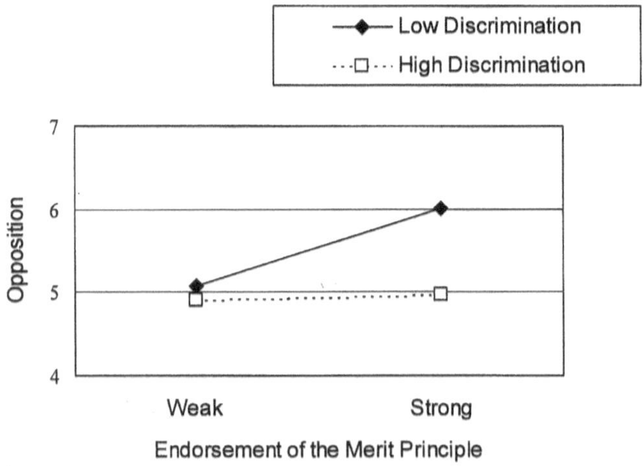

Figure 12.1. Relation between participants' endorsement of the merit principle and their opposition to the preferential treatment policy, as a function of perceived workplace discrimination ($N = 107$) (adapted from Son Hing et al., 2000).

professional behavior and, thus, criteria [are nearly always/may be] biased against female employees"). By inducing people to either systematically disagree with or endorse these items, we expected to manipulate their beliefs about the existence of workplace discrimination through a self-persuasion mechanism (Salancik & Conway, 1975; Schwarz, 1994).

The results, shown in Figure 12.2, were virtually identical to those of the previous study. That is, we found a significant interaction between justice values and experimental condition, such that the usual effect of justice values on opposition to the merit-violating policy was observed, but only in the low discrimination condition. By contrast, in the condition in which participants were induced to perceive high discrimination, people who strongly endorse the merit principle of distributive justice were no longer especially opposed (indeed, the pattern of these data suggests that they were slightly in favor of the preferential treatment policy compared to people who endorse the merit principle less strongly). In addition, we also found that, when induced to perceive high discrimination, people who strongly endorse the merit principle believe that qualified target-group members are more likely to be identified by the policy. Thus, it is possible that the reason why people who strongly endorse meritocracy are less opposed to the preferential treatment policy in conditions of high discrimination is that

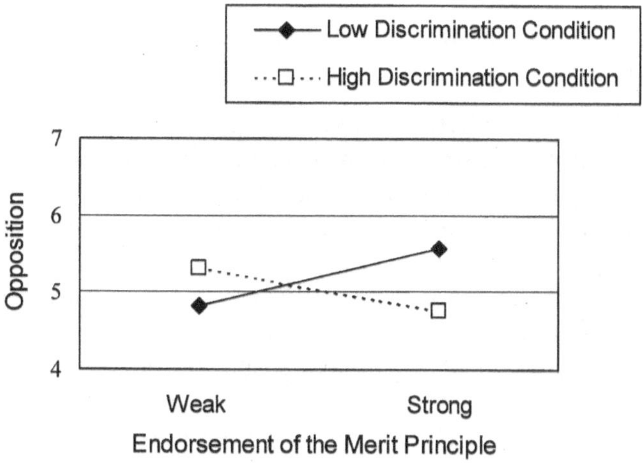

Figure 12.2. Relation between participants' endorsement of the merit principle and their opposition to the preferential treatment policy, as a function of experimental condition ($N = 82$) (adapted from Son Hing et al., 2000).

these individuals believe that the policy increases the probability that deserving candidates will be hired.

To summarize thus far, whereas we have found that justice-based objections to certain social policies can be genuine, our more recent research suggests that the usual effect of justice values on opposition is not absolute. The preceding studies show that, under conditions in which people perceive that there is workplace discrimination – in particular, bias in the assessment of minority group members' merit – those who strongly endorse the merit principle of distributive justice object substantially less to the preferential treatment policy compared to when they perceive little workplace discrimination.

It is noteworthy that the results were the same whether we measured people's preexisting beliefs about bias in the workplace or whether we experimentally manipulated these beliefs. Thus, we can more firmly conclude that the preference for the merit principle of distributive justice and the perception of bias in the measurement of merit in organizations are independent constructs. In other words, it is not the case that those people who value the merit principle are necessarily less likely to perceive bias in the status quo. These findings add further support for the construct validity of our Preference for the Merit Principle Scale as an index of people's preference for how outcomes *ought* to be distributed versus how they are perceived to be distributed *at present* (see Davey et al., 1999).

The Effect of Disadvantage in Mitigating Opposition to the Violation of Procedural Justice

In the preceding set of studies, we found that people who strongly value the merit principle of distributive justice and who were ordinarily most opposed to a merit-violating policy (preferential-treatment affirmative action) were less opposed under situational conditions in which they perceived that bias exists in the measurement of merit.

In a related experiment (see Bobocel et al., 2000), we have examined the effect of a similar situational variable on people's reactions to the violation of procedural justice. The primary goal of this study was to directly test the idea that people may in general (regardless of justice values) be less opposed to policies that violate procedural justice when the policies enhance the likelihood of achieving the meritocratic distribution of outcomes. We reasoned that, in the context of allocating resources such as pay, promotions, and selection decisions, most people are predominantly concerned with distributive justice, and in particular with the equitable distribution of outcomes (Deutsch, 1975; Lerner, 1974). In this situation – where distributive justice concerns are paramount – people may object less to procedural justice violations to the extent that such violations enhance the likelihood of achieving meritocracy. Indeed, one might argue that one reason why people ordinarily prefer consistent treatment during outcome allocations is because being treated in the same way as all others is most likely to yield the fair distribution of outcomes (Rawls, 1977; Thibaut & Walker, 1975). In other words, it is possible that, at least in certain contexts, people's concerns for traditional procedural justice norms may be secondary to their concern for achieving distributive justice. This idea could also help to explain another justice paradox: that is, why sometimes people want to be treated identically to others during allocation decisions (procedural consistency), but at other times want to be treated differently than others (procedural inconsistency; Crosby, 1994; Folger, 1994; Folger, Sheppard, & Buttram, 1995).[2]

Thus, our goal in this study was to examine whether violating one principle of procedural justice – namely, procedural consistency – is more acceptable to people when it has implications for the meritocratic distribution of outcomes. As in our earlier studies, we sought to create a psychologically involving situation in the lab. To accomplish this, we brought participants into the lab individually, under the guise of conducting a study to examine the link between people's personalities and the basic cognitive abilities that are presumed to predict successful job performance. Accordingly, in a first phase, the participants completed a three-page personality inventory, ostensibly to assess their personalities; in a second phase, they completed a visual-spatial test under time pressure, ostensibly to assess their cognitive abilities. (The latter test comprised fifty problems derived from cognitive ability measures in the literature.) As part of the cover story, we told participants that, to simulate real-world conditions in which people are paid for on-the-job performance, participants would be financially rewarded on the basis

[2] Researchers sometimes conceptualize people's concerns about procedural justice and distributive justice as reflecting concerns about microjustice (the fairness of rewards to individual recipients) and macrojustice (the aggregate fairness of rewards in a society), respectively (see Brickman et al., 1981). Whereas it is possible to conceptualize the procedural–distributive justice and micro–macrojustice distinctions in this manner, it is also possible to consider them independently. In the present study, our goal was to present participants with a conflict between two forms of microjustice concerns.

of their performance on the visual-spatial task (i.e., the better they performed relative to others, the more money they would earn).

Participants were University of Waterloo students who had indicated in an earlier mass-testing booklet (administered to all introductory psychology students) that English was their first language. They were led to believe that we were running the study in small groups, and, on their arrival to the lab, they encountered an accented female Asian confederate, who presumably was another participant. Following the introduction to the study, participants completed the personality inventory. For half of the participants (in the *disadvantage condition*), the confederate expressed difficulty with the English language during this phase. (She asked for the meaning of several adjectives on the inventory and took five minutes longer to complete the test.) For the other half of the participants (in the *control condition*), the confederate expressed no such difficulty. Following the manipulation of disadvantage in phase one, participants were then asked to complete the visual-spatial task under time pressure. We had altered the visual-spatial test so that it required participants to read rather lengthy written instructions in order to understand how to complete the problems. We told participants that, given the nature of the test, difficulty with the English language could affect one's performance on the visual-spatial test; accordingly, more time and a dictionary would be granted to participants, namely the Asian confederate, who in mass testing had reported English as a second language. Participants were told that they and the confederate would thus have twenty and twenty-eight minutes respectively for the test, and the participant and confederate were separated, ostensibly to minimize distractions. Thus, procedural consistency was violated in both conditions, because the confederate always received a dictionary and (40%) more time to complete the visual-spatial test. The potential implications of the procedural inconsistency for distributive justice varied, however, as a function of the experimental condition. In the disadvantage condition, in which the confederate exhibited difficulty understanding English, allowing the confederate more time and access to a dictionary could in fact enhance the assessment of merit. By contrast, in the control condition in which the confederate exhibited no disadvantage, these additional resources could hinder the assessment of merit. To the extent that participants are concerned with ensuring the fair and, in this case, meritorious distribution of outcomes, we expected that they would object less to the violation of procedural consistency in the disadvantage condition relative to the control condition.

After participants' twenty-minute work period had elapsed, they were asked to respond to a questionnaire, ostensibly to provide anonymous feedback to the researchers on a variety of aspects of the study while the experimenter scored their tests. Embedded within a number of non-fairness-related questions, we asked participants to report (on seven-point rating scales) their attitudes toward the experimental procedures and their perceptions of the likelihood that the procedures would ensure the fair distribution of rewards. Once the measures were completed, the true purpose of the study was explained to participants, and their names were entered into a lottery for a cash prize.

The results showed that, as expected, participants were significantly less opposed to the procedural inconsistency in the disadvantage condition compared to the control condition. In addition, as shown in Figure 12.3, a mediation analysis revealed that this effect of the disadvantage manipulation on opposition ($r = -.34$, $p < .05$) was due to participants' enhanced perceptions of distributive fairness. In other words, when the confederate was disadvantaged, participants perceived that inconsistent treatment was more likely to be distributively fair; in turn, the greater participants' perceptions of distributive justice, the less they opposed the procedures. Finally, when perceptions of distributive justice were controlled, the effect of the disadvantage manipulation on opposition was no longer statistically significant (beta = –.20, *ns*). These data are in line with the notion that people may object less to the violation of consistency in procedures during outcome allocation,

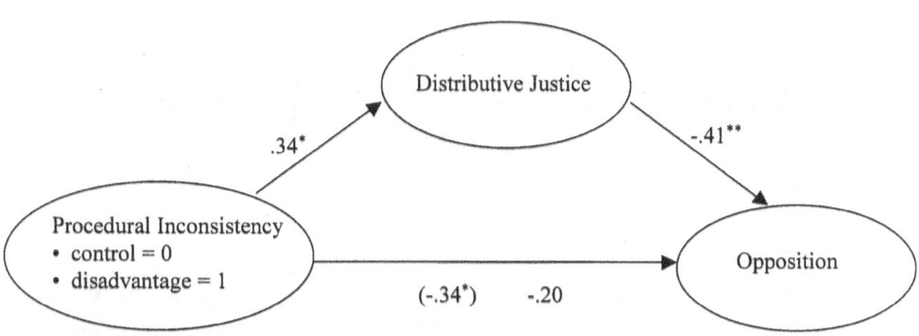

Figure 12.3. Path analysis depicting the mediating role of perceived distributive justice. Inconsistent treatment is constant across experimental conditions (coded 0,1). The total effect between condition and opposition is given inside parentheses; the direct effect (controlling for justice perceptions) is given outside parentheses ($N = 41$) (adapted from Bobocel et al., 2000). *$p < .05$ **$p < .01$

under conditions that enhance the likelihood of achieving distributive justice.

As a follow-up to this study, we recently conducted a second experiment using the same paradigm and the same manipulation of disadvantage; the only difference was that the confederate did not receive the extra resources. In other words, our procedures treated the participant and the confederate *consistently* by giving them the same amount of time to complete the visual-spatial task (and neither received a dictionary). If people are indeed concerned with distributive justice, then we reasoned that they should be more *opposed* to procedural consistency when the confederate is, in fact, disadvantaged in the way that merit is assessed. The results are in line with this prediction. In addition, a mediation analysis is consistent with the idea that the effect of the manipulation of disadvantage on attitudes was due to the perception that maintaining procedural consistency under these circumstances would reduce the likelihood of achieving meritocracy.

To summarize, the findings of the two sets of studies reported in this section converge on the idea that objections to policies that violate traditional justice principles are not necessarily absolute. The first set of studies showed that, when people perceive or are induced to perceive discrimination in the workplace (in particular, bias in the assessment of minority group members' merit), those who strongly value the merit principle of distributive justice were less opposed to a policy that violates this principle than ordinarily would be the case. Our data suggest that this is because these individuals perceive that the policy will identify deserving target-group members. Similarly, the second set of experiments showed that, in a situation in which another person was disadvantaged in terms of how merit was assessed, participants (a) objected less to the violation of the consistency principle of procedural justice and (b) objected more to the maintenance of procedural consistency, compared to a situation in which there was no disadvantage. Our data suggest that this occurs because of the perception that distributive justice would be enhanced.

One interesting difference between the two sets of studies reported in this section deserves to be highlighted. In the first set of studies, not all participants were affected by the perception of workplace bias; only people who most strongly value the merit principle reduced their opposition to the policy. By contrast, in the second set of studies, we found similar effects regardless of justice values. Although it is premature to draw firm conclusions, we believe that reactions may differ depending on the "strength" of the justice violation in the policy. Further consideration of this issue in our future research will undoubtedly add to the present analysis.

Conclusion and Implications

We began this chapter with the problem of understanding why people sometimes object to policies aimed at redressing social injustice on the grounds that the policies are themselves unfair. We have taken a justice perspective in approaching this problem, guided by Lerner's fundamental theoretical assumption: justice matters deeply to people. On the basis of our research, we have argued that, first, such objections can be genuine. Our findings that (a) people's endorsement of procedural and distributive justice principles significantly predicts their opposition to affirmative action, but only when the policy explicitly violates the relevant justice norm, and that (b) the effect of justice values holds over and above any effect of prejudice are, taken together, consistent with the idea that justice-based objections can be genuine. Yet we have also found that justice-based objections are not necessarily absolute. Indeed, we have begun to illuminate conditions under which objections to social policies can be mitigated, as a result of people's concern for justice. Taken as a whole, our data suggest that reactions to policies – which ordinarily may be opposed because they violate traditional justice norms – will be more favorable in the context of other conditions that highlight the violation of meritocracy in the status quo. It is interesting to note, however, that depending on the norm that is violated by the policy (e.g., procedural versus distributive justice), the effects could be more or less sweeping in terms of who is most affected. This is a question for future investigation.

What are the broader implications of our analysis for understanding the paradox we began with? We believe that, by adopting a justice framework, we can offer two central contributions, of both theoretical and practical significance. In Figure 12.4, we provide a heuristic device to highlight the implications of our analysis. We close the chapter with these implications.

First, most importantly, we suggest that both strong opposition to and strong support for social policies aimed at reducing social injustice can stem, at least in part, from the same underlying process: people's concern for justice. As shown in the top path of Figure 12.4, when people encounter a policy that violates traditional norms of

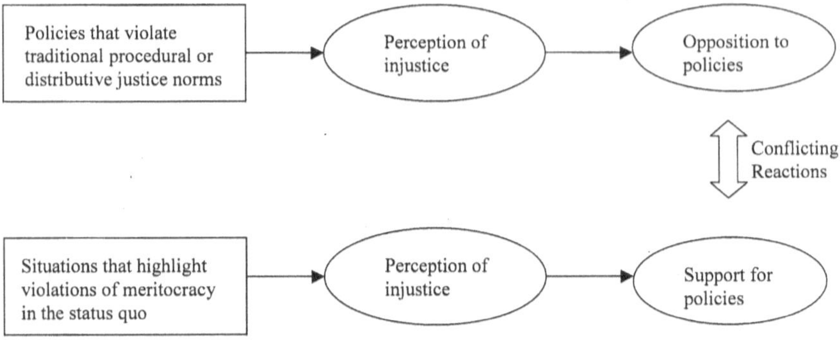

Figure 12.4. Heuristic framework derived from the present analysis.

distributive or procedural justice, they will, all else being equal, perceive an injustice; in turn, due to people's fundamental concern for justice, they will strongly *oppose* the policy. As shown in the bottom path, when people encounter situations that potentially violate meritocracy in the status quo – they will also, all else being equal, perceive an injustice, and, due to a concern for justice, they will strongly *support* the policy designed to redress the injustice. But consider both paths together. When both of these conditions are salient, people may experience conflicting reactions: opposition and support. As a consequence of these conflicting reactions, people's attitudes toward the policy may become more moderate or less polarized. Thus, by adopting the view that the concern for justice can indeed be a genuine determinant of opposition as well as of support, our research begins to delineate conditions that might help to reduce backlash against certain policies on the grounds of perceived unfairness.

Second, our analysis may help to explain the rising divergence in the literature on attitudes toward social policies (such as affirmative action) aimed at redressing social injustice. It is our contention that researchers have most often focused their research and theorizing on the processes depicted by either the top or the bottom path in our heuristic framework. But there has been relatively little consideration of the two paths in conjunction with each other. This may, in turn, account for a rising divergence of opinion at the societal level. It is our hope that, by adopting more complex theoretical and research approaches, social and organizational psychologists will gain a better understanding of how we as a society might balance the equally desirable goals of maintaining people's sense of justice and at the same time attempting to redress social injustice.

REFERENCES

Bobocel, D. R., Holmvall, C. M., Zdaniuk, A., & Son Hing, L. S. (2000, September). Is it always fair to treat people the same? Paper presented in a symposium at the Eighth Biennial Conference of the International Society for Justice Research, Tel Aviv, Israel.

Bobocel, D. R., Son Hing, L. S., Davey, L. M., Stanley, D. J., & Zanna, M. P. (1998). Justice-based opposition to social policies: Is it genuine? *Journal of Personality and Social Psychology, 75*, 653–669.

Bobocel, D. R., Son Hing, L. S., & Zanna, M. P. (1998). Examining the link between prejudice and attitudes toward affirmative action in a community sample. Unpublished raw data, University of Waterloo.

Brickman, P., Folger, R., Goode, E., & Schul, Y. (1981). Microjustice and macrojustice. In M. J. Lerner & S. C. Lerner (Eds.), *The justice motive in social behavior* (pp. 173–202). New York: Plenum.

Crosby, F. J. (1994). Understanding affirmative action. *Basic and Applied Social Psychology, 15*, 13–41.

Crosby, F. J., & VanDeVeer, C. (Eds.) (2000). *Sex, race, and merit: Debating affirmative action in education and employment*. Ann Arbor: University of Michigan Press.

Davey, L. M., Bobocel, D. R., Son Hing, L. S., & Zanna, M. P. (1999). The preference for the Merit Principle Scale: An individual difference measure of distributive justice preferences. *Social Justice Research, 12*, 223–240.

Deutsch, M. (1975). Equity, equality, and need: What determines which value will be used as the basis of distributive justice? *Journal of Social Issues, 31*, 137–149.

Folger, R. (1994). Workplace justice and employee worth. *Social Justice Research, 7*, 225–240.

Folger, R., & Cropanzano, R. (1998). *Organizational justice and human resource management*. Beverly Hills, CA: Sage.

Folger, R., Sheppard, B. H., & Buttram, R. T. (1995). Equity, equality, and need: Three faces of social justice. In B. Benedict Bunker & J. Rubin (Eds.), *Conflict, cooperation, and justice: Essays inspired by the work of Morton Deutsch*. San Francisco, CA: Jossey Bass.

Gaertner, S. L., & Dovidio, J. F. (1986). The aversive form of racism. In J. F. Dovidio & S. L. Gaertner (Eds.), *Prejudice, discrimination, and racism* (pp. 61–89). Orlando, FL: Academic Press.

Heilman, M. E., Block, C. J., Lucus, J. (1992). Presumed incompetence? Stigmatization and affirmative action efforts. *Journal of Applied Psychology, 77*, 536–544.

Kleinpenning, G., & Hagendoorn, L. (1993). Forms of racism and the cumulative dimension of ethnic attitudes. *Social Psychology Quarterly, 56*, 21–36.

Kluegel, J. R., & Smith, E. R. (1983). Affirmative action attitudes: Effects of self-interest, racial affect, and stratification beliefs on whites' views. *Social Forces, 61*, 797–824.

Kravitz, D. A., Harrison, D. A., Turner, M. E., Levine, E. L., Chaves, W., Brannick, M. T., Denning, D. L., Russell, C. J., & Conrad, M. A. (1997). *Affirmative action: A review of psychological and behavioral research*. Bowling Green, OH: Society for Industrial and Organizational Psychology.

Lerner, M. J. (1974). The justice motive: "Equity" and "parity" among children. *Journal of Personality and Social Psychology, 29*, 539–550.

(1977). The justice motive: Some hypotheses as to its origins and its forms. *Journal of Personality, 45*, 1–51.

(1980). *The belief in a just world: A fundamental delusion*. New York: Plenum.

Lerner , M. J., & Lerner, S. C. (1981). *The justice motive in social behavior: Adapting to times of scarcity and change*. New York: Plenum.

Lerner, M. J., & Miller, D. (1978). Just world research and the attribution process: Looking back and ahead. *Psychological Bulletin, 85*, 1030–1051.

Leventhal, G. S. (1980). What should be done with equity theory? New approaches to the study of fairness in social relationships. In K. Gergen, M. Greenberg, & R. Wills (Eds.), *Social exchange: Advances in theory and research* (pp. 27–55). New York: Plenum.

Lind, E. A., & Tyler, T. R. (1988). *The social psychology of procedural justice*. New York: Plenum.

Murrell, A. J., Dietz-Uhler, B. L., Dovidio, J. F., Gaertner, S. L., & Drout, C. (1994). Aversive racism and resistance to affirmative action: Perceptions of justice are not necessarily color blind. *Basic and Applied Social Psychology, 15*, 71–86.

Nacoste, R. W. (1987). But do they care about fairness? The dynamics of preferential treatment and minority interest. *Basic and Applied Social Psychology, 8*, 177–191.

Nosworthy, G. J., Lea, J. A., & Lindsay, R. C. L. (1995). Opposition to affirmative action: Racial affect and traditional value predictors across four programs. *Journal of Applied Social Psychology, 25*, 314–337.

McConahay, J. B. (1986). Modern racism, ambivalence, and the modern racism scale. In S. F. Dovidio & S. L. Gaertner (Eds.), *Prejudice, discrimination and racism: Theory and research*. New York: Academic Press.

Rawls, J. (1971). *A theory of justice*. Cambridge, MA: Harvard University Press.

Salancik, G. R., & Conway, M. (1975). Attitude inferences from salient and relevant cognitive content about behavior. *Journal of Personality and Social Psychology, 32*, 829–840.

Schwarz, N. (1994). Judgment in a social context: Biases, shortcomings, and the logic of conversation. In M. P. Zanna (Ed.), *Advances in experimental social psychology* (Vol. 26, pp. 123–162). New York: Academic Press.

Sidanius, J., Pratto, F., & Bobo, L. (1996). Racism, conservatism, affirmative action, and intellectual sophistication: A matter of principled conservatism or group dominance? *Journal of Personality and Social Psychology, 70*, 476–490.

Son Hing, L. S. (1997). *Opposition to affirmative action based on program type, prior attitudes, and construals.* Unpublished master's thesis, University of Waterloo.

Son Hing, L. S., Bobocel, D. R., & Zanna, M. P. (2000). Meritocracy and opposition to affirmative action: Making concessions in the face of discrimination. Manuscript under review.

Thibaut, J., & Walker, L. (1975). *Procedural justice: A psychological analysis.* Hillsdale, NJ: Erlbaum.

Tougas, F., Brown, R., Beaton, A. M., & Joly, S. (1995). Neo-sexism: Plus ça change, plus c'est pareil. *Personality and Social Psychology Bulletin, 2,* 842–849.

13. Justice and Empathy: What Motivates People to Help Others?

STEVEN L. BLADER AND TOM R. TYLER

A core premise of the social psychology of justice is that people's attitudes, feelings, and behaviors are shaped by their subjective judgments about what is right or wrong, just or unjust, ethical or unethical (Tyler et al., 1997). This fundamental argument is now supported by a large and diverse body of literature. However, this was not always the case, and the work of Mel Lerner, both in his influential just world hypothesis (Lerner, 1980) and through several influential theoretical articles pointing out the broader implications of the justice motive (Lerner, 1981, 1982), has had a great deal to do with encouraging social psychologists to think seriously about the nature and importance of justice. Our goal in this chapter is to build upon Lerner's articulation of the existence of the justice motive, as well as upon the now large literature documenting the range and importance of the influence of people's concerns about justice. We do so by considering one core distinction within social psychology that we feel is underdeveloped at this time – the distinction between justice and empathy.

Justice and empathy share (at least) one important behavioral influence. Both lead those who possess resources and/or power to help others who are needy or in distress. Understanding justice and empathy therefore also helps us to understand when and why people come to the aid of victims. These prosocial activities can take a variety of forms, from providing direct assistance, such as money and other resources, to the needy, to less direct approaches, such as supporting policies that direct government resources to the poor, ensuring fair representation, and providing equal access to opportunity. In all cases, prosocial behaviors involve individual efforts and actions targeted at the needs and welfare of others (Batson, 1999). Such helping not only assists its intended beneficiaries, but also can have critical effects on the healthy functioning of society (Smith & Tyler, 1996) insofar as it ensures some degree of prosperity for all, forestalls social unrest, and fosters the cohesion of communities.

However, both lay people and social scientists can readily agree that such prosocial or helping behavior cannot be assumed or taken for granted. Many obstacles stand in the way of people stepping up and helping victims, not the least of which is that they may feel little motivation to do so. Nevertheless, most people can think of particular situations that have compelled them to act, often in cases where they may even have surprised themselves. In this chapter, we consider the distinction between empathy and justice by examining their relationship to prosocial behavior.

Motivations for Prosocial Behavior

Many social psychologists have considered the problem of what motivates prosocial behavior. One consistent finding is that people are more likely to come to the aid of victims when that aid will also result in personal benefits, or at least has minimal personal costs, for the helper (e.g., Latane & Darley, 1970; Piliavin, Piliavin, & Rodin, 1975). So one answer to the question of how people decide whether to act prosocially is that they do so with regard to the costs and benefits to their own welfare. Benefits that encourage helping can be affective as well as material in nature, such as the relief or avoidance of guilt and other forms of aversive arousal (Cialdini et al., 1987; Schaller & Cialdini, 1988). It has even been suggested that helping can be related to one's own welfare via an intermingling of the distinction between self and other (Cialdini et al., 1997). All these approaches share the notion that people will act prosocially when doing so is in their self-interest. This egoistic, self-interest perspective is in accord with the predominant view among social scientists that humans are essentially resource-oriented, rational-choice beings who act purely out of self-interest.

In contrast to the self-interest perspective, two largely unrelated bodies of research have investigated alternative motives for prosocial action. The first line of research develops from the concept of justice (Tyler et al., 1997). This research emphasizes that justice motivations play an important part in determining our reactions to events and situations, both behavioral and psychological. When the plight of victims is perceived as unjust, the justice motive prompts prosocial behavior targeted at alleviating that injustice. This justice motive is often conceptualized as affective or emotional, although it is aroused by a principled judgment made using abstract criteria of justice. People feel psychological distress when they experience or observe situations that they judge to represent injustice, and they act to relieve this emotional distress. The distress from experiencing or observing injustice comes from the cognitive evaluation that principles or rules of justice are being violated. Importantly, justice theory suggests that we are disturbed even when a loathsome person, for whom we feel little empathy, is the victim of injustice. These reactions are distinct from self-interest concerns, insofar as benefits to oneself play little role in these responses to perceived injustice.

Second, research on empathy has extensively documented the robust effect that empathic distress can have on helping (Batson, 1991). Empathy researchers have found that people are much more likely to come to the aid of those toward whom they are empathically oriented and who are in need of help. Furthermore, and critical for distinguishing empathy from the self-interest perspective, it has been demonstrated that this helping can be distinct from any consideration of the personal benefits that may be associated with helping (e.g., Batson et al., 1989; Batson et al., 1991). This body of research indicates that empathic concern motivates prosocial action on behalf of victims, and that this helping is not completely self-interested in nature.

The empathy and justice-based models of prosocial behavior both paint a rather different picture of human nature than that advanced by the dominant, instrumentally oriented self-interest model. They are predicated on the idea that people can and do look beyond their own interests and act on behalf of others. Given the novelty of this notion in the social and academic ethos of our times, these two bodies of research have directed most of their attention to distinguishing themselves from instrumental models of helping. That is, the popularity of the egoistic perspective has established models of self-interest as the baseline against which other approaches prove themselves. This has prompted research on both (1) the empathy model and (2) the justice model to validate their distinction from the self-interest model, with little emphasis on comparisons between them. In this chapter, we review evidence for the prosocial consequences of empathy and the justice motive, and begin to consider the interrelationship between them.

Justice and Prosocial Behavior

A large body of research demonstrates the pervasive influence of justice on feelings, attitudes, and behaviors (for a review, see Tyler et al., 1997). This body of work provides compelling evidence that justice is a core criterion by which people judge and approach their social worlds, and that these judgments evoke strong reactions in them. Further, it has been shown that the potency of justice considerations can override those of self-interest. Studies show that people distinguish between what is fair and what benefits them and that, when evaluating outcome distributions, people prefer fairness even in situations where it decreases their own outcomes. For instance, workers who believe themselves to be fairly compensated are more satisfied than those who believe that they are overpaid (Adams, 1965; Pritchard, Dunnette, & Jorgenson, 1972), who may act to restore equity by changing their inputs in light of the outcomes they receive (Greenberg, 1988). Research also shows that people have a propensity to utilize fairness concerns over self-interest in their decision making, with regard to both resources (Diekmann et al., 1997) and access to opportunities (Jost & Ross, 1999).

These findings support the early arguments of Lerner (1980, 1981, 1982), who noted that people are intrinsically motivated to be fair, to believe that justice exists in the world, and to uphold justice. In addition to behavioral effects, Lerner demonstrates that people engage in cognitive distortions of their beliefs and evaluations in order to make them consistent with their justice principles. Justice research supports the notion that people value fairness and will act both behaviorally and in constructing their model of the world so as to perceive and promote fairness.

In terms of helping, empirical evidence confirms that even uninvolved nonvictims or "unaffected observers" (Mikula, 1994) will act prosocially on behalf of victims of injustice in the interest of promoting justice. For instance, Montada and Schneider (1989) found that advantaged individuals showed an increased willingness to support redistribution of resources to favor the disadvantaged to the extent that they felt existential guilt and moral outrage over the plight of the disadvantaged. Since both of these emotions conceptually depend on a recognition of unjust allocations, they are both justice-related emotions (Montada & Schneider, 1989). Chen and Tyler (2001) likewise found that advantaged individuals will support policies that redistribute resources in society to the disadvantaged to the extent that they endorse ideologies that advocate such redistribution (e.g., social responsibility and moral outrage). These ideologies provide the framework within which the plight of the disadvantaged is perceived as an injustice. Furthermore, an important finding for demonstrating the primacy of the justice motive is that the decision *not* to support prosocial policies is also related to justice-based evaluations that the policies are unfair, as opposed to alternative possibilities, such as prejudice against the beneficiaries of those policies (Bobocel et al., 1998).

Justice principles are especially important for helping in situations where people are not linked by strong emotional bonds. Consider the situation examined by Kelman and Hamilton (1989): soldiers killing civilians during the Vietnam War. In this situation, the soldiers did not generally feel an emotional connection to the civilians, whom they regarded as being, or at least aiding, the enemy. What, therefore, stopped the soldiers from killing civilians? One factor that was important was soldiers' views that killing civilians was a morally inappropriate behavior in which they should not engage. Those soldiers who held these abstract moral views about what is just were less likely to engage in killing civilians, irrespective of whether they knew, liked, or empathized with the particular civilians they encountered. The actions of such justice-motivated soldiers were influenced, however, by evidence that particular civilians were fighting for the enemy, thereby shaping judgments about whether they were noncombatants and within the soldiers' scope of justice or could legitimately be regarded as threats and attacked.

Limits to the Justice–Prosocial Behavior Hypothesis

The association between injustice and helping, however, is not inevitable. Cohen (1991) suggests that individuals are perceived as entitled to a fair distribution of material and symbolic resources to the extent that they are included within the "moral community" of one's justice concerns (Deutsch, 1985). Those outside these boundaries are subject to "moral exclusion" (Opotow, 1990), and justice is applied less strongly, if at all, to judgments about their situation. Identification is a primary determinant of these boundaries of the scope of justice (Huo, 1994; Nagata, 1990); people's scope of justice may therefore depend on whether they identify most strongly with their subgroup or superordinate group (e.g., Americans). Consequently, identification can influence whom people will help. However, attempts to shift the level of one's identification can promote justice-based prosocial behavior.

Self-serving biases may also decrease the likelihood that justice concerns will provoke helping, since they may deter the subjective perception of injustice (Tyler et al., 1997). That is, cognitive distortion may preclude seeing the victim's situation as an injustice. By justifying the conditions of the victim, people are able to avoid negative feelings of inequity (Taylor & Moghaddam, 1994) and to avoid the costs associated with helping. In such situations, justice is said to have been restored psychologically rather than behaviorally (Tyler et al., 1997). Lerner (1996a) cautions that the influence of costs and benefits on concerns for justice may not be as strong as is widely suspected; the same may or may not be true of their influence on perceptions of justice. Interestingly, the inability of the nonvictim to eliminate the injustice may foster these cognitive distortions. For instance, Lerner and Simmons (1966) found that when people are powerless to alter a victim's fate, they are more likely to reject and devalue the victim. This derogation of the victim enables them to maintain their belief that the world is just (Lerner, 1980) in the face of the victim's suffering.

If self-serving biases cloud justice perceptions, how can justice be a useful motive for the promotion of helping behavior? Some have discounted the utility of justice as a prosocial motive because of its susceptibility to influences stemming from the individual's goals, needs, and concerns (e.g., Batson, 1996). However, although there may be a tendency toward biased perception, such bias is far from inevitable or complete. Even a flexible justice motive is constrained by reality, as are justice evaluations and judgments. Further, justice provides a framework of general principles around which thinking can be guided and persuasion directed; in other words, it provides a common ground for considering these issues, and rational appeals will often override self-serving biases. For instance, attempts to shift one's identification may broaden their scope of justice (Smith & Tyler, 1996). Both research and the everyday experiences of people acting to help others whom they believe deserve their help tell us that the influence of biases is incomplete. People are still motivated to react behaviorally when they observe others being treated unjustly.

Factors Facilitating the Justice-Helping Hypothesis

Counter to these limitations on justice-based helping, other factors may actually enhance this assistance. For instance, to the extent that nonvictims perceive their own position as unjustly overadvantaged, they may react more strongly to the injustice of the disadvantaged. A recent article in *The New Yorker* captures this drive on behalf of the "overbenefited." It describes the notable philanthropy of a highly affluent woman who donates a half-million dollars a year to organizations actively engaged in the redistribution of wealth in society. When queried about the irony of her supporting groups whose success would lead to a loss of her own wealth, she replied: "It's nice to be rich, I would never argue otherwise. But the great thing about giving some away is that it makes me feel less guilty about my portfolio" (Mayer, 2000). Chen and Tyler (2001) find that the prevalence of these reactions depends on the extent to which these "unfairly advantaged" individuals do or do not subscribe to ideologies that justify their advantage.

Summary

Evidence clearly suggests that justice considerations lead individuals to engage in prosocial behaviors on behalf of victims. Such justice-based prosocial behavior cannot be taken for granted, however, as it is susceptible to situational factors as well as to cognitive biases. Nevertheless, it is found to be robust across a wide variety of issues and situations. Research demonstrates many instances where potential benefits to the self do not interfere with justice-based prosocial activity. These actions are critical to the alleviation and prevention of victimization in society.

Empathy and Prosocial Behavior

Empathy refers to the psychological processes that lead one to have feelings that are more congruent with the situation of another than with one's own situation (Hoffman, 2000). More specifically, empathy is "an affective response that stems from the apprehension or comprehension of another's emotional state or condition and is similar to what the other person is feeling or would be expected to feel" (Eisenberg, 2000, p. 671). Given our current concern with empathy as a prosocial motive, we restrict ourselves to the case where the life situation of the target of empathy is negative, as opposed to cases where positive vicarious emotion is felt. As a result, the empathic emotion we consider here is always negatively valenced, an emotion often referred to as empathic distress (Hoffman, 2000).

Research has shown empathy to have a robust effect on motivating prosocial behavior toward others perceived to be in distress (for reviews, see Batson, 1991; Eisenberg & Miller, 1987; Hoffman, 2000), although its effect size is regarded as only moderate (Eisenberg, 2000). The relationship between empathy and helping has been replicated in a wide range of studies. In early research, Krebs (1975) found that subjects in a high-empathy condition demonstrated higher levels of helping than did other subjects. Coke, Batson, and McDavis (1978) compellingly demonstrated that helping increases only when the physiological arousal associated with empathy is interpreted as such, showing that it is the sense that one feels empathy that promotes helping. More recent research has continued to replicate these basic findings and to further explore the relationship between empathy and prosocial motivation. One advance has been to consider whether empathy-based helping may be more prevalent for some individuals. For instance, altruistic personality, a dispositional variable closely related to empathy, has been shown in many instances to be related to helping behaviors such as volunteerism (Carlo et al., 1991; Penner & Finklestein, 1998), due at least in part to the heightened experience of empathic feelings (Eisenberg et al., 1989).

The Nature of the Empathic Motive

The link between empathic feelings and prosocial behavior is well replicated and largely undisputed (although the particular emotions involved are less clear; see Eisenberg, 2000). Considerably more debate surrounds the underpinnings of this prosocial motivational state. If empathy is associated with helping primarily because of positive affective consequences for the helper (Cialdini et al., 1987), it becomes conceptually indistinguishable from egoistic motivators of prosocial behavior. However, if empathy produces an ultimate concern with the welfare of the other individual, without particular regard to self-benefits that may, though need not, derive as a consequence of helping (for a review, see Batson, 1991), it represents a separate, altruistic basis of prosocial behavior.

Whether empathy-based prosocial behavior is egoistically or altruistically rooted can have important consequences for its reliability as a prosocial motivator. Since helping usually involves costs to the self, a self-interested basis for empathy-based helping should motivate the elimination of empathic distress via less costly methods. However, helping would be the only way to alleviate empathic distress if empathy has an altruistic basis.

Batson and colleagues have conducted a comprehensive program of research addressing this question (Batson et al., 1989; Batson et al., 1981; Batson et al., 1991; Batson & Weeks, 1996). The results of that work indicate that empathy-induced helping is, at least to some degree, altruistic in nature, although the theoretical and empirical debate persists (Cialdini et al., 1997). Batson has termed the relationship between empathy and helping the "empathy-altruism hypothesis." His findings suggest that empathic arousal can be reliably expected to prompt prosocial behavior, since it derives from a genuine concern for the welfare of the target and, as such, is less likely to be influenced by egoistic concerns and obstacles. Thus, like justice, empathy exists independent of self-interest.

Limitations on Empathy as a Prosocial Motive

Clearly, certain factors can intervene in the link between empathy and prosocial behavior. First, the utility of the empathy-altruism hypothesis for predicting prosocial behavior is contingent on the arousal of empathic distress in the first place. Several factors may impede the arousal of empathic feelings toward victims. For instance, empathy is less likely in situations that are not highly salient to the individual (the "here and now bias," Hoffman, 2000), and it is thus difficult to feel empathy toward people who have suffered in the past or who are suffering in locations remote from the nonvictim.

Familiarity is another important determinant of empathy (Hoffman, 2000). Empathic emotions are less likely toward individuals with whom we do not feel close or whom we regard as dissimilar to us (Batson, 1991, p. 209). We are more likely to feel empathy toward friends and family than toward strangers who may be more needy in objective terms. This limit on empathy is analogous to the effects of identification on justice.

Weiner, Perry, and Magnusson (1988) show that prosocial emotions and behavior are not aroused for victims who are deemed responsible for their predicaments and for whom overcoming the predicament is regarded as within the victim's control, consistent with other work showing that attributions can determine the onset of empathic emotion (Weiner, 1980). However, other research has shown empathy to be largely unaffected by ascriptions of responsibility (Batson et al., 1997).

One possibility for reconciling these differences may be that when empathic emotion precedes casual attribution (as it likely did in the 1997 study), it is unaffected by those attributions. Further, empathy may influence attributions of responsibility when it precedes those attributions, leading nonvictims to make attributions more similar to those made by victims themselves.

Even when empathic distress is experienced, situational factors may weaken the link between empathy and prosocial behavior. For instance, expectations regarding the cost of helping can hinder the empathy-altruism link (Batson, 1991, pp. 88–89), as was the case in a study where increased costs of helping had the potential to shift the focus of highly empathic subjects to a concern for their own welfare (Batson et al., 1983). Excessive levels of empathic emotion can also lead to empathic overarousal, which prompts a shift in focus to one's own needs and thus prevents empathy from expressing itself in prosocial behavior toward another (Eisenberg, 2000; Hoffman, 2000). Ascription of responsibility for another's plight to that individual may interfere with empathy's link to prosocial motivation, even if it doesn't interfere with the onset of empathic emotion. People may be less likely to act on their feelings of empathy and help someone who is suffering but responsible for their own fate (Kohn, 1990, pp. 125–126).

Empathy and Justice as Prosocial Motivators

To summarize, research supports the distinctions between justice, empathy, and self-interested, egoistic motivations. While empathy represents genuine altruistic motivations, justice relates to a moral, rule-based (albeit subjective) motive, or what Batson (1999, p. 303) refers to as "principalism." This leads to a framework consisting of three prosocial motives: egoism, altruism, and principalism/justice (cf. Batson, 1999). Both empathy and justice can lead people to act prosocially, and prosocial behavior may be a function of both of them, since the same behavior can certainly stem from multiple motives. But what is the relationship between them?

Two approaches can be taken regarding their interrelationship. On the one hand, their relative influence can be compared to see how they differentially affect helping. This approach assumes that the motives are relatively independent of one another (i.e., the association between them is nonexistent or minor). This may be an overly simplistic model because of its assumption that the two motives, and their underlying cognitions, exist in some pure form, untainted by one another. Nevertheless, we discuss this approach for two reasons: (1) because it strikes us as the first logical question to pose when comparing two constructs that are antecedents of the same outcome, and (2) because it has been the perspective adopted in past research.

A second approach is to consider their reciprocal influence. That is, we can explore how the experience of empathic emotion affects one's justice judgments and the justice motive, and also how justice judgments, and the justice motive, influence the experience of empathic emotion. This is a more dynamic approach to the relationship between these constructs. To the extent that these two motivations do shape one another, they will be empirically correlated. That correlation, however, will reflect a causal influence rather than a perfect empirical association.

No systematic program of research has attempted to connect these nonegoistic prosocial motives, despite the extensiveness of the literature on each one individually. By presenting this discussion, we hope to raise awareness of the idea that in order to understand prosocial behavior we should focus on all that is known regarding its multiple motivational antecedents, and proceed with research in an integrative manner.

Empathy and Justice as Independent Motives

The first approach considers empathy and justice as two independent motives underlying prosocial behavior, and questions how they differ. It assumes that any particular behavior can satisfy multiple motives and, furthermore, that there is nothing inherently incompatible between empathy and justice. Empathy is linked to emotional connections. Justice, on the other hand, evokes a motivation to uphold general moral/ethical principles. Clearly, one can be motivated by both empathic and justice concerns, as when people feel empathic distress for a victim of injustice.

Strength of Influence

If empathy and justice are independent of one another, there should be instances where they exert conflicting influences on behavior. An example of such a conflict would be when empathy-based partiality opposes justice-based neutrality. This leads to the conclusion that altruistic behavior may sometimes be unjust, and likewise that acting fairly may be regarded as "heartless" or "unaltruistic" (cf. Batson, 1996).[1] This approach serves as the premise of three studies by Batson and colleagues (1995) that directly compared the influence of morality (justice) and empathy on prosocial behavior. In these studies, the authors placed empathy and morality-based goals in conflict with one another. Their results indicate that high-empathy subjects distributed resources on the basis of their empathic emotion, while low-empathy subjects did so on the basis of justice principles, leading the authors to conclude that empathy overrode justice principles in determining the distribution strategy when there was a conflict between them. While these results are suggestive, several aspects of the studies leave reason to think that any such conclusion is premature, including the lack of a manipulation of justice concerns (i.e., there was no independent variable reflecting the strength of justice or moral motivation). This makes any definitive conclusions regarding the role of justice, and its influence relative to empathy, difficult to verify.

There are many instances where justice and empathy conflict, such as the conflict that professors sometimes face when students appeal low grades that they "deserved" to receive (Hoffman, 2000). Although they may care for these students as people, and empathy may drive them to want to raise a student's grade, doing so creates unfairness in the grading system and is thus unfair to the other students. However, such situations may also be framed as dilemmas of empathy toward different targets within a larger group (i.e., multiple claimants), where empathy toward both the student with the low grade and the student who worked hard to earn an A are in conflict, since raising the lower grade diminishes the value of receiving an A. Decisions between these multiple claimants may ultimately be made using principles of justice. No empirical research exists to verify how such dilemmas are actually conceptualized or negotiated by people in real situations. However, the example demonstrates that such a decision can be thought of as a conflict between empathy and justice, as a clash of empathies, or perhaps even as a clash of justice principles.

The relative influence of justice and empathy can also be examined in situations in which the two motivations are not in conflict. Montada

[1] We note with interest the awkwardness of the word "unaltruistic," reflecting the centrality of an egoist perspective in our language, where the semantic opposite of altruistic is selfish.

and Schneider (1989) took this approach and found that justice-related emotions prevailed over sympathy (an empathy-like emotion) in influencing prosocial behavior. Specifically, they found that sympathy no longer had any significant effect on prosocial outcomes once the two justice-related emotions (existential guilt and moral outrage) were considered, indicating that the justice constructs accounted for the effects of sympathy. This dominance of justice is in accord with the findings of Messick and colleagues (1985), who emphasized that people are primarily motivated by justice principles.

Nature of Influence

Empathy and justice may also differ in the nature of their prosocial consequences. Empathy is very much an individual-level concept. Indeed, it involves a bridging of the gap between self and other. Feelings of empathy are directed toward other people as individuals (Batson, 1996), and empathy-based helping may occur even when it harms the collective good (Batson, Batson et al., 1995). Although empathy for particular members of groups has been shown to improve attitudes toward the group, these attitudinal effects are small in magnitude and have not been shown to relate to prosocial helping (Batson et al., 1997). Thus, prosocial behavior based on empathy requires an emotional connection with a particular individual, and only that individual will be the recipient of that help.

Justice does not have this exclusive focus on the individual, and, if anything, group-level fairness evaluations may be made more easily, since fewer potential confounds exist to cloud those judgments. The justice-based prosocial behavior reviewed in the prior section of this chapter is behavior that is meant to address a particular issue of injustice, not just a particular victim of injustice. Help is therefore linked to the injustice of the situation; need without injustice will not lead to helping.

Thus, empathy and justice differ with regard to their requisite conditions (emotional connection vs. perception of injustice) and in the beneficiaries of their prosocial consequences (the individual or all who suffer from a particular injustice). Empathy will be relatively more predictive of prosocial helping when the victim is an individual, while justice may be relatively more predictive of helping when the victims are regarded as a group (Tyler, 2001). Other work has confirmed this notion that the antecedents of prosocial behavior may vary as a function of whether the intended beneficiary is an individual or a group (McNeely & Meglino, 1994). Importantly, the nature of prosocial action may also shift. Helping individuals in distress may involve providing them with assistance or money, while helping groups escape victimization may lead to attempts to change government policies and programs and thereby to assist entire groups of people.

Consider the prior discussion of the work of Kelman and Hamilton (1989) on the willingness of soldiers to kill civilians during the Vietnam War. In contrast to the *general* unwillingness of some soldiers to kill civilians because they felt it was morally wrong, other soldiers were found to help *particular* civilians. They did so because those civilians, as individuals, had characteristics that led particular soldiers to feel an emotional attachment toward them. As an example, soldiers who themselves had children sometimes felt an emotional attachment toward children they encountered, and made efforts to save those children from harm.

A similar distinction is found in studies of those who helped Jews during the Second World War. One strong predictor of the willingness to help Jews was having the moral belief that killing Jews was immoral, regardless of the Jewish victim in question. However, many Germans were willing to help particular Jews whom they knew from before the war and toward whom they felt empathy. These Germans, while not necessarily opposing the government policy against Jews, had personal attachments to specific people, and acted to help hide and save those particular individuals.

Empathy and justice may also differ in the temporal durability of their effects. Empathy is a highly affective, charged emotion; at the same time, as an emotion, it is also relatively short-lived, although its consequences may be more enduring when empathy transforms itself into a persistent concern for the other's welfare (Batson et al., 1995). This concern, however, may not instigate the same degree of motivation toward prosocial behavior shown to occur in the case of affective empathy. Justice concerns may not be so short-lived. They may persist over time, until the injustice is corrected.[2] As such, it may be that empathy is a stronger prosocial motive at the immediate onset of

[2] It is important not to overstate this argument, since studies show that, over time, the desire to restore actual equity is supplanted by the psychological restoration of equity. This change in the form of reaction to feelings of injustice does not mean that such feelings disappear over time, but it suggests that the nature of justice concerns changes over time.

empathy, but that justice's motivating effects are more enduring over time.

Summary

There is research evidence to suggest that either empathy or justice may prevail in predicting prosocial behavior within particular situations. Given the paucity of empirical research directly examining this question, no definitive conclusions either way should be drawn at this point. Further work is needed to clarify their relative impact on prompting prosocial behavior, and potential moderators of those effects should also be investigated.

Reciprocal Effects between Empathy and Justice

The other approach we propose considers the influence that justice and empathy may have on one another. That is, rather than considering whether empathy outdoes justice, or vice versa, it considers the causal influence that each may exert on the other. As such, it poses a more dynamic and complex approach to considering the association of either motive with prosocial behavior.

The Effects of Empathy on Justice Motivations

We will first consider the potential influence of empathy on the strength or nature of people's concerns about justice. Empathy may shape whether people care about justice and/or the way they define what is fair (for example, whether they use equity or equality to fairly distribute outcomes). For example, people may think about what constitutes justice, in part, by reference to the impact of a principle on people toward whom they have emotional ties. Greenberg (2001) further notes that empathy may make justice salient in the first place, since the negative outcomes of others become more prominent, and it is negative outcomes that especially lead to concerns about justice.

Some researchers have suggested just such an influence. For instance, Hoffman (1989, 2000) postulates that empathy can drive the use of distributive justice norms away from equity and toward need-based allocations of resources. More generally, it may be said that the selection of moral principles (i.e., justice norms) is determined in part by empathic reasoning and feeling, and thus that moral judgments may be shaped by empathic emotion. However, the effects of empathy may not always consist of a drive toward need-based principles; victimization may also be rooted in denying to victims what they deserve based on other distributive norms, and, as such, empathy for victims could also invoke equity or equality norms. For example, cases of workplace gender discrimination in pay and promotions may invoke equity norms. The influence empathy exerts on the selection of justice principles may therefore depend on the nature of the perceived victimization.

In addition to considering the effects of empathy on the choice of justice principle, empathy could affect perceptions related to the application of a single justice principle. For instance, in the evaluation of the adequacy and fairness of social welfare programs, which are based on need principles, empathy may shift perceptions of whether a person's needs are being met. That is, as empathy toward victims is aroused, judgments of the sufficiency of allocations in meeting the needs of the victim may become more stringent. The same dynamic may hold in cases where equity is the justice principle used; valuations of inputs and outputs may vary as empathy shifts. Empathy can thus lead people to regard distributions and situations that they may previously have regarded as just to be unjust, without a change in the justice principle utilized.

Research on retributive justice supports this prediction. People tend to advocate harsher punishments, such as the death penalty, if asked to sentence a "murderer" than if asked to sentence a particular person convicted of murder and given a dossier describing that person's background and life history (Tyler et al., 1997). In this case, information about the individual, which allows empathy to develop, attenuates the moral drive to punish harmdoers.

Empathy may also affect the perception of justice by counteracting the self-serving biases in justice evaluations that were discussed earlier, since it bridges the gap between victim and nonvictim. Since self-interest can bias justice perceptions and lead to psychological justifications for injustice, empathy may be a crucial element in promoting actual restoration of justice to some victims. For instance, Aderman, Brehm, and Katz (1974) showed that empathy-inducing instructions deterred subjects from blaming victims for their plight. By instructing subjects to take the perspective of a victim, subjects were led to see the plight of victims as an instance of injustice. Lerner and Goldberg (1999) come to a similar conclusion; they reference the findings of research by

Simons and Piliavin (1972) as suggesting that when the norms of appropriate reactions toward innocent victims are induced (which can be regarded as a superficial empathy induction), the derogation of victims disappears. Empathy may thus shape the nature of the activation of the justice motive.

Not only can empathy help promote a consensus between victim and nonvictim by breaking down self-serving perceptions, it may also foster agreement among empathizing nonvictims. Hoffman (2000) interprets Hume's writings as specifying a similar consensus-building effect of empathy:

> Hume argued further that . . . because most people respond empathically to events in similar ways, talk to each other about these events, and respond empathically to each other's descriptions of relevant acts and their consequences, empathy provides the information input needed by impartial observers to achieve a reliable consensus on moral judgments. (p. 246)

In other words, empathy with victims may lead all empathizing nonvictims to adopt a common perspective – that of the victim – and thereby to develop an unbiased and perhaps more consensual understanding of the injustice of the victim's situation (Galinsky & Moskowitz, 2000). This leads their perceptions of the situation to become more similar to each other, and also more similar to the victim's own perception.

Empathy and adopting the perspective of the victim has important links to the influence of identification on the scope of justice. People have stronger concerns about justice for those with whom their identification is strong. Strength of identification, in turn, is conceptually related to feeling that another person is similar, to the ability to adopt the perspective of that other person, and thus to feeling empathy for them. So the effects of identification on the scope of justice are suggestive of the effects of empathy on justice. As an example of these effects, research has found that the survivors of corporate layoffs reacted much more strongly to the fairness or unfairness of those layoffs when they felt a strong prior attachment to the victims (Brockner, 1990). Opotow (1993) similarly notes that when we think that someone else is similar to us, we are more concerned about whether they are receiving their rights and entitlements.

The influence of empathy on justice perceptions is also supported by more basic social psychological research on the interface of affect and cognition. The primary findings of this work are that affect typically exerts an influence on cognitive processing (Forgas, 1995). More specifically, negative affect tends to foster more systematic, careful processing of information (Schwarz, 1990; Schwarz & Bless, 1991), while positive affect has the opposite effect, leading to more top-down, superficial processing (Bodenhausen, 1993). So empathic distress, a negative affective state, may actually lead to more systematic processing of information and, therefore, to more thoughtful (and perhaps less biased) justice judgments. This basic research suggests a strong and largely unconscious influence of empathy on justice, with an intermingling of both leading to behavior (Epstein & Pacini, 1999).

What are the implications of this influence of empathy on justice? One implication is that empathy can help create distributions and situations that are regarded as just by all. That is, if empathy leads nonvictims to view needs, inputs, outcomes, and so forth more along the lines of how they are viewed by victims, the justice judgments of victims and nonvictims are more likely to converge. For instance, empathy may lead both victim and observer to take into account the difficult life situation of a criminal defendant (parents who were drug users and beat their children, a horrific life in reform school, etc.) and to agree on a punishment that reflects these considerations.

The Effects of Justice on Empathy

It is also possible to consider the influence of principles of justice on feelings of empathy toward others. For instance, empathy and its prosocial behavioral consequences may be heightened when the plight of the victim is contrasted with the life circumstances of others in ways that emphasize the injustice of their situation. When such strong contrasts emerge, the injustice of the situation becomes salient and may fuel feelings of empathic injustice (Hoffman, 1994), an empathic affect exceeding that of empathic distress. When empathic injustice motivates prosocial behavior, justice and empathy can be said to be working in concert, evoking stronger reactions than either might individually.

A large body of great literature is centered around innocent victims, whose plight gains our sympathy due to their innocence. Consider one example of many such plots, the famous *Count of Monte Cristo*, whose hero emerges from a lifelong quest for revenge as a sympathetic figure because his original imprisonment was unjustified. Our sympathy is considerably diminished when the revenge seeker is morally responsible for the original crime and its subsequent punishment. Since responsibility judgments may determine empathic arousal when they precede them (Weiner, 1980; Weiner et al., 1988), justice evaluations may thus shape empathic reactions to criminals seeking revenge. More generally, justice may impact empathy through its close association with attributions of responsibility.

Justice principles can also temper the bias associated with empathic emotions and shape later responses to those emotions. Empathic motivations are inherently partial in the sense that they are linked to the situations of particular people, and empathic emotion creates a motivation to help the specific target of one's empathy. This helping, however, may often come at a cost to others and may violate principles of justice. Consider a common example described by Hoffman (2000): the decision to write a letter of recommendation for a student toward whom a professor may be empathically disposed, but who is nonetheless undeserving. The empathic stance toward the student may lead the professor to want to write a positive recommendation. However, this bias may be mitigated by the motivation to be fair. Thus, justice can dampen the influence of empathy on helping.

Kohn (1990) explains why the influence of justice on empathy may be especially important. Empathic emotions are inherently linked to partiality. This partiality requires a framework of justice principles to counter its biasing effects and to keep social allocation behaviors in check. As he notes,

> "Impartiality may be overrated, but even the most caring individual will often be troubled by its absence. John Stuart Mill warned us about people who 'may be very amiable to those with whom they sympathize, and grossly unjust and unfeeling to the rest of the world'." (p. 263)

Kohn attributes justice principles' capacity to balance the influence of empathy to the higher level of abstraction in thinking that they prompt. Justice defuses the saliency of the situation of those whose suffering and needs provoke empathy and refocuses a person's thinking on the broader picture of long-term social interaction within a system of rules. This abstraction in thinking is crucial if justice is to be served. This same idea underlies John Rawls's well-known justice principle of making justice judgments behind the "veil of ignorance" (Rawls, 1971), which defends against the motivational force of empathy for oneself or others by a procedure that minimizes the influence of one's emotions. Principles of justice thus serve to stabilize our empathic reactions toward specific others and to minimize the influence of those emotions on our behaviors and policy decisions.

Summary

In this section, we have attempted to develop some proposals for the influence that empathy and justice may exert on one another. In developing these proposals, we have drawn on past theorizing and have attempted to point out relevant empirical work. Unfortunately, very little research has directly examined the interface of empathy and justice, and so we stress the tentative nature of our proposals. Nevertheless, our review suggests several likely possibilities for how justice and empathy may shape one another.

Conclusion

In this chapter we have reviewed evidence for two nonegoistic motives of prosocial behavior: justice and empathy. In contrast to past approaches that emphasize the distinctness of each motive from self-interest, we have expanded the discussion to a consideration of how these motives relate to one another. In addressing this topic in this volume, it was our intention to demonstrate the relevance of this approach to studying the justice motive in social life. Justice researchers should attempt to consider prosocial affective constructs, such as empathy, in their work. Empathy can be relevant to all areas of justice research, including investigations of distributive, procedural, and retributive justice. In all cases where general rules or norms are applied, they are likely to be influenced by empathic affect.

Despite the potential reciprocal effects of justice and empathy explored here, they remain separate motives for prosocial helping. When the two motives conflict, negative reactions linked to the unfulfilled motive are likely to ensue. For instance, consider the problem of corporate downsizing addressed by Lerner (1996b). Managers in these situations must decide which employees to retain and which to lay off. Although they may feel quite justified in making those decisions using justice criteria, such as merit, doing so may make them feel guilty about the fate of laid-off employees toward whom they felt empathic emotion. Lerner (1996b) observes that such managers are often plagued by guilt despite believing that their actions were normatively justified and morally acceptable.

Ideally, of course, the two motives would work in concert with one another, resulting in a joining of "head and heart" (Batson, 1996, p. 63). Together, they can more reliably inspire prosocial behavior than either can singly. The conclusion we draw is that their working in concert with one another is far more likely than not, given the reciprocal influences between them. Of course, empirical research is needed to more closely examine, and to test, these ideas.

REFERENCES

Adams, J. S. (1965). Inequity in social exchange. In L. Berkowitz (Ed.), *Advances in experimental social psychology* (Vol. 2, pp. 267–299). New York: Academic Press.

Aderman, D., Brehm, S. S., & Katz, L. B. (1974). Empathic observation of an innocent victim: The just world revisited. *Journal of Personality and Social Psychology, 29*, 342–347.

Batson, C. D. (1991). *The altruism question: Towards a social psychological answer.* Hillsdale, NJ: Erlbaum.

(1996). Empathy, altruism, and justice: Another perspective on partiality. In L. Montada & M. J. Lerner (Eds.), *Current societal concerns about justice* (pp. 49–66). New York: Plenum.

(1999). Altruism and prosocial behavior. In D. T. Gilbert, S. T. Fiske, & G. Lindzey (Eds.), *Handbook of social psychology* (Vol. 2, pp. 282–316). Boston: McGraw Hill.

Batson, C. D., Batson, J. G., Griffit, C. A., Barrientos, S., Brandt, J. R., Sprengelmeyer, P., & Bayly, M. J. (1989). Negative state relief and the empathy-altruism hypothesis. *Journal of Personality and Social Psychology, 56*, 922–933.

Batson, C. D., Batson, J. G., Slingsby, J. K., Harrell, K. L., Peekna, H. M., & Todd, R. M. (1991). Empathic joy and the empathy-altruism hypothesis. *Journal of Personality and Social Psychology, 61*, 413–426.

Batson, C. D., Batson, J. G., Todd, R. M., Brummett, B. H., Shaw, L. L., & Aldeguer, C. M. R. (1995). Empathy and the collective good: Caring for one of the others in a social dilemma. *Journal of Personality and Social Psychology, 68*, 619–631.

Batson, C. D., Duncan, B., Ackerman, P., Buckley, T., & Birch, K. (1981). Is empathic emotion a source of altruistic motivation? *Journal of Personality and Social Psychology, 40*, 290–302.

Batson, C. D., Klein, T. R., Highberger, L., & Shaw L. L. (1995). Immorality from empathy-induced altruism: When compassion and justice conflict. *Journal of Personality and Social Psychology, 68*, 1042–1054.

Batson, C. D., O'Quin, K., Fultz, J., Vanderplas, M., & Isen, A. (1983). Self reported distress and empathy and egoistic versus altruistic motivation for helping. *Journal of Personality and Social Psychology, 45*, 706–718.

Batson, C. D., Polycappou, M. P., Harmon-Jones, E., Imhoff, H. J., Mitchener, E. C., Bednar, L. L., Klein, T. R., & Highberger, L. (1997). Empathy and attitudes: Can feeling for a member of a stigmatized group improve feelings toward the group? *Journal of Personality and Social Psychology, 72*, 105–118.

Batson, C. D., Turk, C. L., Shaw, L. L., & Klein, T. R. (1995). Information function of empathic emotion: Learning that we value the other's welfare. *Journal of Personality and Social Psychology, 68*, 300–313.

Batson, C. D., & Weeks, J. L. (1996). Mood effects of unsuccessful helping: Another test of the empathy-altruism hypothesis. *Personality and Social Psychology Bulletin, 22*, 148–157.

Bobocel, D. R., Son Hing, L. S. S., Davey, L. M., Stanley, D. J., & Zanna, M. P. (1998). Justice based opposition to social policies: Is it genuine? *Journal of Personality and Social Psychology, 75*, 653–669.

Bodenhausen, G. V. (1993). Emotions, arousal, and stereotypic judgments: A heuristic model of affect and stereotyping. In D. M. Mackie & D. L. Hamilton (Eds.), *Affect, cognition, and stereotyping* (pp. 13–37). San Diego, CA: Academic Press.

Brockner, J. (1990). Scope of justice in the workplace: How survivors react to coworker layoffs. *Journal of Social Issues, 46*, 95–106.

Carlo, G., Eisenberg, N., Troyer, D., Switzer, G., & Speer, A. L. (1991).The altruistic personality: In what contexts is it apparent? *Journal of Personality and Social Psychology, 61*, 450–458.

Chen, E. S., & Tyler, T. R. (2001). Cloaking power: Legitimizing myths and the psychology of the advantaged. In A. Lee-Chai & J. Bargh (Eds.), *The use and abuse of power* (pp. 241–262). Philadelphia: Psychology Press.

Cialdini, R. B., Brown, S. L., Lewis, B. P., Luce, C., & Neuberg, S. L. (1997). Reinterpreting the empathy-altruism relationship: When one into one equals oneness. *Journal of Personality and Social Psychology, 73*, 481–494.

Cialdini, R. B., Schaller, M., Houlihan, D., Arps, K., Fultz, J., & Beaman, A. L. (1987). Empathy-based helping: Is it selflessly or selfishly motivated? *Journal of Personality and Social Psychology, 52*, 749–758.

Cohen, R. L. (1991). Membership, intergroup relations, and justice. In R. Vermunt & H. Steensma (Eds.), *Social justice in human relations: Societal and psychological origins of justice.* (Vol. 1, pp. 239–258). New York: Plenum.

Coke, J. S., Batson, C. D., & McDavis, K. (1978). Empathic mediation of helping: A two-stage model. *Journal of Personality and Social Psychology, 36*, 752–766.

Deutsch, M. (1985). *Distributive justice.* New Haven, CT: Yale University Press.

Diekmann, K. A., Samuels, S. M., Ross, L., & Bazerman, M. H. (1997). Self-interest and fairness in problems of resource allocation: Allocators versus recipients. *Journal of Personality and Social Psychology, 72*, 1061–1074.

Eisenberg, N. (2000). Emotion, regulation, and moral development. *Annual Review of Psychology, 51*, 665–698.

Eisenberg, N., & Miller, P. A. (1987). The relation of empathy to prosocial and related behaviors. *Psychological Bulletin, 101*, 91–119.

Eisenberg, N., Miller, P. A., Schaller, M., Fabes, R. A., Fultz, J., Shell, R., & Shea, C. L. (1989). The role of sympathy and altruistic personality traits in helping: A reexamination. *Journal of Personality, 57*, 41–67.

Epstein, S., & Pacini, R. (1999). Some basic issues regarding dual process theories from the perspective of cognitive-experiential self theory. In S. Chaiken & Y. Trope (Eds.), *Dual process theories in social psychology* (pp. 462–482). New York: Guilford.

Forgas, J. P. (1995). Mood and judgment: The affect infusion model. *Psychological Bulletin, 117*, 39–66.

Galinksky, A. D., & Moskowitz, G. D. (2000). Perspective-taking: Decreasing stereotype expression, stereotype accessibility, and in-group favoritism. *Journal of Personality and Social Psychology, 78*, 708–724.

Greenberg, J. (1988). Equity and workplace status: A field experiment. *Journal of Applied Psychology, 73*, 606–613.

(2001). The seven loose ca(n)nons of organizational justice. In J. Greenberg & R. Cropanzano (Eds.), *Advances in organizational justice* (pp. 245–272). Stanford, CA: Stanford University Press.

Hoffman, M. L. (1989). Empathy and prosocial activism. In N. Eisenberg & J. Reykowski (Eds.), *Social and moral values: Individual and societal perspectives* (pp. 65–85). Hillsdale, NJ: Erlbaum.

(1994). The contribution of empathy to justice and moral judgment. In B. Puka (Ed.), *Reaching out: Caring, altruism, and prosocial behavior* (Vol. 7, pp. 161–195). New York: Garland.

(2000). *Empathy and moral development: Implications for caring and justice.* New York: Cambridge University Press.

Huo, Y. J. (1994). Are there limits to justice? Exclusionary effects in justice attitudes. Paper presented at the 102nd Annual Convention of the American Psychological Association, Los Angeles, California.

Jost, J. T., & Ross, L. (1999). Fairness norms and the potential for mutual agreements involving majority and minority groups. In R. Wageman, *Research on managing groups and teams: Groups in context* (Vol. 2, pp. 93–114). Stamford, CT: JAI Press.

Kelman, H. C., & Hamilton, V. L. (1989). *Crimes of obedience: Towards a social psychology of authority and responsibility.* New Haven, CT: Yale University Press.

Krebs, D. L. (1975). Empathy and altruism. *Journal of Personality and Social Psychology, 32*, 1134–1146.

Kohn, A. (1990). *The brighter side of human nature: Altruism and empathy in everyday life.* New York: Basic Books.

Latane, B., & Darley, J. M. (1970). *The unresponsive bystander: Why doesn't he help?* New York: Appleton-Century-Crofts.

Lerner, M. J. (1980). *The belief in a just world.* New York: Plenum.

(1981). The justice motive in human relations: Some thoughts on what we know and need to know about justice. In M. J. Lerner & S. C. Lerner (Eds.), *The justice motive in social behavior* (pp. 11–35). New York: Plenum.

(1982). The justice motive in human relations and the economic model of man. In V. J. Derlega & J. Grzelak (Eds.), *Cooperation and helping behavior: Theories and research* (pp. 249–278). New York: Academic Press.

(1996a). Doing justice to the justice motive. In L. Montada & M. J. Lerner (Eds.), *Current Societal Concerns about Justice* (pp. 1–8). New York: Plenum.

(1996b). Victims without harm doers: Human casualties in the pursuit of corporate efficiency. In L. Montada & M. J. Lerner (Eds.), *Current societal concerns about justice* (pp. 155–170). New York: Plenum.

Lerner, M. J., & Goldberg, J. H. (1999). When do decent people blame victims? In S. Chaiken & Y. Trope (Eds.), *Dual process theories in social psychology* (pp. 627–640). New York: Guilford.

Lerner, M. J., & Simmons, C. H. (1966). Observer's reaction to the "innocent victim": Compassion or rejection? *Journal of Personality and Social Psychology, 4*, 203–210.

Mayer, J. (2000). The heiress and the anarchists. *The New Yorker*, March 6, pp. 32–34.

McNeely, B. L., & Meglino, B. M. (1994). The role of dispositional and situational antecedents in prosocial organizational behavior: An examination of the intended beneficiaries of prosocial behavior. *Journal of Applied Psychology, 79*, 836–844.

Messick, D. M., Bloom, S., Boldizar, J. P., & Samuelson, C. D. (1985). Why we are fairer than others. *Journal of Experimental Social Psychology, 21*, 480–500.

Mikula, G. (1994). On the experience of injustice. In W. Stroebe & M. Hewstone (Eds.), *European review of social psychology* (Vol. 4, pp. 223–244). Chichester: Wiley.

Montada, L., & Schneider, A. (1989). Justice and emotional reactions to the disadvantaged. *Social Justice Research, 3*, 313–344.

Nagata, D. K. (1990). The Japanese American internment: Perceptions of moral community, fairness and redress. *Journal of Social Issues, 46*, 133–146.

Opotow, S. (1990). Moral exclusion and injustice: An introduction. *Journal of Social Issues, 49*, 71–85.

(1993). Animals and the scope of justice. *Journal of Social Issues, 50*, 49–63.

Penner, L., & Finklestein, M. A. (1998). Dispositional and structural determinants of volunteerism. *Journal of Personality and Social Psychology, 74*, 525–537.

Piliavin, I. M., Piliavin, J. A., & Rodin, J. (1975). Cost, diffusion, and the stigmatized victim. *Journal of Personality and Social Psychology, 32*, 429–438.

Pritchard, D., Dunnette, M. D., & Jorgenson, D. O. (1972). Effects of perceptions of equity and inequity on worker performance and satisfaction. *Journal of Applied Psychology, 56*, 75–94.

Rawls, J. (1971). *A theory of justice.* Cambridge, MA: Harvard University Press.

Schaller, M., & Cialdini, R. B. (1988). The economics of empathic helping: Support for a mood management motive. *Journal of Experimental Social Psychology, 24*, 163–181.

Schwarz, N. (1990). Feelings as information: Informational and motivational functions of affective states. In E. T. Higgins & R. Sorrentino (Eds.), *Handbook of motivation and cognition* (Vol. 2, pp. 527–561). New York: Guilford Press.

Schwarz, N., & Bless, H. (1991). Happy and mindless, but sad and smart? The impact of affective states on analytic reasoning. In J. P. Forgas (Ed.), *Emotion and social judgments* (pp. 55–71). Oxford: Pergamon Press.

Simons, C., & Piliavin, J. A. (1972). The effect of deception on reactions to a victim. *Journal of Personality and Social Psychology, 21,* 56–60.

Smith, H. J., & Tyler, T. R. (1996). Justice and power: When will justice concerns encourage the advantaged to support policies which redistribute economic resources and the disadvantaged to willingly obey the law? *European Journal of Social Psychology, 26,* 171–200.

Taylor, D. M., & Moghaddam, F. M. (1994). *Theories of intergroup relations.* New York: Praeger.

Tyler, T. R. (2001). Social justice. In R. Brown & S. Gaertner (Eds.), *Blackwell handbook of social psychology* (Vol. 4: Intergroup processes, pp. 344–366). London: Blackwell.

Tyler, T. R., Boeckmann, R. J., Smith, H. J., & Huo, Y. J. (1997). *Social justice in a diverse society.* Boulder: Westview.

Weiner, B. (1980). A cognitive (attribution)-emotion action model of motivated behavior: An analysis of judgments of help giving. *Journal of Personality and Social Psychology, 39,* 186–200.

Weiner, B., Perry, R. P., & Magnusson, J. (1988). An attributional analysis of reactions to stigmas. *Journal of Personality and Social Psychology, 55,* 738–748.

14. The Justice Motive and Altruistic Helping: Rescuers of Jews in Nazi-Occupied Europe

JANUSZ REYKOWSKI

There are good reasons to contend that the existence of a moral order is an important precondition for predictability of the social world and meaningfulness of personal actions. If people have doubts about the moral order in their society, the feeling of anomie is likely to ensue (Merton, 1957; Korzeniowski, 1994). The basis of the moral order is a normative system supported by authorities, social institutions, and members of the society at large. It implies a general societal consensus about what is good and what is evil, as well as a stable pattern of societal behavior – the society upholds the good and repudiates the evil in its declarations and practical actions. Although there are some exceptions, good behaviors and good people (as defined by the normative system) meet with positive reactions from the society, while bad behavior and bad people meet with negative ones.

People are interested in maintaining the moral order. One of the manifestations of this interest is the belief in a just world. Melvin Lerner, who formulated and together with his coworkers developed the just world hypothesis, contends that "people have a need to believe that their environment is a just and orderly place where people usually get what they deserve" (Lerner & Miller, 1978, p. 1030).

There is a large body of data supporting this hypothesis (Lerner, 1970, 1977; Lerner & Miller, 1978). Lerner and his associates show that the belief in a just world can be extended beyond the social world and may include the physical order as well. That is, many people operate on the implicit assumption of immanent justice in the universe: Good acts are rewarded and evil acts are punished by nature itself – if not immediately, then after some delay.

People try to protect their belief in a just world. One general strategy that they use is a cognitive reconstruction of the available information about social events. They tend to construe the meaning of these events in such a way as to protect their belief that "justice wins." Another strategy, a very important one, is undertaking corrective actions – attempts at modifying the social world in order to protect justice. In fact, a significant part of human effort is devoted to maintaining or restoring justice.

The fact that striving for justice is such a pervasive tendency should make the social world a very congenial place. But it does not. And one important reason for this failure is the difference in people's conceptions of the moral order.

Moral order is a group or rather a societal phenomenon. And societies have quite divergent interpretations of good and evil. First, they tend to define moral good in terms of the well-being of a particular social organization – a smaller or larger community – and its members. Hence, good is defined as something that contributes to the protection or enhancement of the community, and evil as something that is disadvantageous or threatening to it, whether the threat is real or imagined. By the same token, the division between "us" (in-group) and "them" (out-group) becomes a boundary – more or less permeable – for application of the norms of justice: Justice for "us" is different from justice for "them."

The classification of the social world into an "in-group" and "out-group" is a ubiquitous phenomenon. An equally ubiquitous phenomenon is the uneven treatment of "in-group" members and "out-group" members. And this unevenness ranges from minor manifestations of biased judgments and subtle discriminative practices, to horrifying acts of persecution and genocide. A relatively recent example of the extreme instance of this phenomenon is the mass killing of the Tutsi by the Hutu and its justification in a Hutu radio broadcast, which said about the Tutsi: "Those are rats that should be extinct, even infants. When you kill rats do you save their infants?"

Some of these classifications into in-group and out-group are more important than others. In particular, the categorization of a social world into national, religious, or ethnic communities tends to define the most significant aspects of people's social identities and their sense of group belonging, and is the basis for the delineation of the limits of the moral order. Hence the division along national, religious, or ethnic lines has a major effect on the range of applications of the norm of justice. The differences in these respects generate a variety of biases and discriminative practices. In other words, they generate ethnocentrism.

The uneven treatment of an in-group and an out-group is regarded as deeply rooted in human nature. Strong theoretical support for such a contention is provided by the social categorization (social identity) theory of H. Tajfel and J. Turner (1979). This theory is based on extensive empirical evidence that points to the fact that mere categorization of participants in a social situation into an in-group and an out-group produces bias and discrimination. Evidently, ethnocentrism in its broad sense is an inevitable consequence of people's identification with their own national, ethnic, and other social groups.

However, this conclusion is apparently contradicted by some well-known facts indicating that there are quite a few people who do not discriminate against members of other religious, national, or ethnic groups, and, moreover, that they treat them as members of the same moral community and protect their rights. In other words, for these people, religious, ethnic, and national affiliations do not define the borders of a community. Should we interpret these facts as mere errors of perception, implying that in these cases ethnocentrism is merely less apparent?

Many observations show that the majority of people are able to cooperate with members of out-groups in a variety of everyday situations. They even help each other, to some extent. Cooperation and help tend to disappear, however, when some more significant decisions are at stake: the allocation of important goods, decisions in which the interests of in-group and out-group members are pitted against each other, requests for help that may require a major effort or sacrifice, and so forth. But not always. We may wonder therefore how is it possible that for some people their ethnic, religious, and national identities do not define the borders of their moral community?

To analyze this issue I focus on some specific examples of altruistic helping where the recipients of this help belong, due to their religious and/or ethnic affiliations, to the category of an out-group. The basis of my analysis is the Altruistic Personality Project – a large-scale international study of rescuers, that is, the people who helped Jews to survive during the Holocaust. The study was originated and devised by Professor Samuel Oliner of Humboldt State University in California (himself a survivor of the Holocaust). It encompassed a large group of rescuers from Poland, France, Holland, Germany, and some other countries (Oliner & Oliner, 1988).

The Study

In the framework of the study more than 400 persons – bona fide rescuers – were interviewed, in addition to 126 nonrescuers who served as controls. The participants were chosen from the Yad Vashem files, as well as from files of local scientific institutions (in Poland, from documentation of the Jewish Historical Institute). The rescuers were selected on the basis of four criteria: their help was voluntary; it involved a high risk to the actor; there was no external reward for this act; and it was directed toward helping a Jewish person. The control group was selected on the matching-pair basis: for an individual rescuer, a matched person not involved in helping Jews was chosen. This person was of the same age, sex, and education as the rescuer and lived in the same neighborhood during the war.[1] Some people included in the control group were involved in resistance action – we called them "active controls" – and the rest were classified as "passive controls" (or "bystanders"); there were respectively fifty-three active and seventy-three passive controls.

Each participant was interviewed between 1983 and 1985 in his or her native language by means of a special questionnaire that included approximately 450 items (75% of them were forced choice) and dealt with personal history from early childhood, a detailed history of rescuing, and a number of attitudinal issues. In addition, some psychological scales were employed (Rotter I/E Locus of Control Scale, Rosenberg Self-Esteem Scale, Mehrabian and Epstein Empathy Scale, Berkowitz and Lutterman Social Responsibility Scale).

The data gathered in the project, albeit very rich, do not meet stringent methodological requirements. It was, therefore, appropriate to apply rather "soft" methodology in their analysis and interpretation.

Rescuing

The critical characteristic of the rescuers' behavior was involvement in an altruistic action where the goal was to help and protect another human being. The action entailed an extreme risk as well as a very high personal sacrifice. It was not a momentary (impulsive) response to the situational demands, but an effort extended over a long period of time

[1] Quantitative comparisons of rescuers and nonrescuers were performed on the reduced sample of rescuers for whom there were matched pairs of controls.

(lasting weeks, months, or even years). It was, indeed, a very dangerous and very difficult task. In the Western European countries (France, Holland) it entailed a high risk of imprisonment in a concentration camp; in Eastern Europe it meant the death sentence (sometimes on the spot) for both the "perpetrator" and his or her family.

The risk was real. For example, almost every rescuer interviewed in Poland reported an episode of dealing with so called "*szmalcownik*" (*shmaltzovnik*) – an individual who hunted for Jews and attempted to blackmail the rescuers. And the difficulties of the task were formidable. For example, the rescuers had to find and maintain the hiding place (often in crowded apartment houses), feed additional people (trying at the same time to avoid the attention of neighbors, who may have wondered about an unusual amount of food bought every day), solve problems related to everyday interactions in a small space with the same people for months or years, find or forge false documents.

Having all this in mind one can ask the question: What makes some people undertake actions of this kind?

Recognition of the Needs of Others – The Prerequisite of a Prosocial Goal

The essential feature of the behavior of the rescuers was its orientation toward the protection and maintenance of other people in spite of the fact that such action entailed high personal costs. To undertake and sustain such an activity one had to form a goal that was focused on the needs and interests of other people, that is, a prosocial goal (Staub, 1980). To form a prosocial goal, one has to have at least some recognition of the needs of another person. (Latane & Darley, 1970; Schwartz, 1977).[2]

In many everyday situations recognition of the needs of others is difficult, because information about needs is often quite ambiguous. But there are circumstances when the needs of others may seem to be obvious, for example, when a person sees that other people's survival is at stake, that they are being abused and deprived of their elementary rights and possessions. It is commonly assumed that such witnesses must be fully aware of the needs of the other. This does not have to be the case, however.

[2] We may leave aside the problem of accuracy of the perception of the needs.

Studying our participants' responses to questions that were supposed to probe their reactions to the fate of the persecuted Jews, we have noticed that the great majority of participants were, more or less, aware of the most conspicuous acts of oppression. They could recall such facts as the stigmatization of the Jews (e.g., that they were compelled to wear the armband with the Star of David), expropriation (e.g., expulsion from their home places), physical abuse, and murders. But there were major differences in the way this information was processed in the subjects' minds.

For some people (mainly from the "passive control" group), it was a kind of information about "facts of life." They were merely observers of these facts. Their reaction was apparently cold and detached, as in the case of looking at a falling tree or a hunted animal, where the concept of a need is not appropriate. Such a reaction does not necessarily mean that these people were exceptionally cruel or generally indifferent to the fate of others. They simply did not perceive the situation of the Jewish victims as related, in any way, to their own world. As a matter of fact, there is nothing extraordinary in this reaction. Quite recently, many Americans and Europeans who read about the massive bombing of Iraqi towns (or saw it on television) did not think about humans being mutilated, maimed, and feeling pain and terror. They did not think about the needs of these people.

The second kind of reaction was a negative, often strong affect. When telling stories about the persecution of Jews, the respondents reported their emotional arousal (e.g., crying, agitation), feelings of compassion, horror, repulsion, and their evaluative judgments, such as disapproval of the acts of persecution, moral contempt for the oppressors, and so on. These reactions, although quite common in the control group, did not imply a clear concept of a need, and did not lead to the formation of a prosocial goal. No wonder that these reactions had practically no consequences as far as helping activity was concerned.

This conclusion may require some additional explanation. The fact that people have negative emotional reactions to their own or someone else's predicament does not entail automatically that they will think about such a situation in terms of a need. In other words, it does not have to occur to them that there is a necessity for doing something about it. In fact, not infrequently people tend to accept their (or other people's) fate as a disturbing but unavoidable component of human life. For example, many people (including some physicians) treat physical pain as a sad but inescapable human condition that has to be humbly accepted – they do not invoke the concept of a need (for a painkiller). Instead, they produce various rationalizations to explain why such pain is unavoidable. The tendency to produce and accept such rationalizations differs across cultures.

The third kind of reaction appeared in people who perceived the events in terms of needs. These people interpreted the situation as a demand for a hiding place, or false documents, or food. Once such specific needs were perceived, formation of the prosocial goal could begin (that is, the person could start to think about how to get and provide food, where to find a hiding place, and so on).

The transition from the affective reaction to the need recognition is neither easy nor automatic. It requires some intellectual capabilities – particularly, the capability for cognitive transformation of the existing situation into another one. Not everybody could easily do it. For people who didn't do it, the situation of persecuted Jews was a kind of horrifying spectacle: One could be deeply moved by it but still have nothing to do about it.

Perceiving a situation in terms of a need is probably a necessary but not a sufficient condition for taking a helping action. It has been shown (Schwartz, 1977) that the observers of the situation do not undertake such an action if they do not attribute to themselves responsibility for alleviating the need. Some rescuers did it themselves. But in quite a few instances, the whole process was facilitated when an individual received a request for help. Many would-be rescuers were approached by a victim or by intermediaries who formulated a concrete demand. In such situations, a need was clearly defined as well as a prosocial goal; moreover, the request implied that it was the given individual's responsibility to deal with the need. If the individual accepted the responsibility, his or her task was reduced to finding concrete solutions for a practical problem. When an individual met with a request for a help, in most cases he or she had to define the specific goal (how to provide the effective help).

A good illustration of such a situation is provided by Samuel Oliner in his autobiographical book. He describes the first hours after his escape from the execution of the Jewish community in the Bobowa ghetto (in southern Poland). He came to his Polish neighbor asking for help. One of the first things she did was to give him a Christian name and teach him a Catholic prayer (Oliner, 1986). Apparently, that was not what the little boy was asking for. She herself diagnosed his situation and, understanding what would increase the chances of his survival, chose an appropriate action.

Whatever the origin of the need represented – whether it was generated by each individual or provided (in more or less complete form) by others – the rescuers faced a problem: Should they accept the need of the other as a legitimate and compelling reason for action? Should they decide that saving the lives of the victims was more important than their personal (and their families') safety and justified heavy burdens for themselves and those close to them?

The rescuers concluded that they should. We may wonder why they reached such a conclusion.

Sources of Motivation for Rescuing

The fact that someone's misfortune can evoke an affective reaction among witnesses is not at all surprising – it is a quite common phenomenon. Such a reaction can sometimes lead to an impulsive helping that is a momentary act of short duration (Piliavin et al., 1981). On the basis of Piliavin and colleagues' data, we can conjecture that in an emergency many people react to the immediate demands of the situation. They do not have time to think about the victim's group affiliation, or to ponder whether the norm of justice can or cannot be applied in the given circumstances. Most probably, the helping act is mediated by some basic affective mechanisms, and the higher mental processes are not involved in the action-initiating process. But the situation is different when helping becomes a long-lasting action that entails enduring stress and poses a grave threat for the actor. What are the psychological factors that initiate and maintain such actions? In other words, what is their motivation?

In an attempt to find the more general answer to the question about motivation, we took into consideration several kinds of information as indices of motivation (See Table 14.1).

There is no room here for a more elaborate discussion of the rationale for the selection of these indices. It can be pointed out only that the set contains various kinds of data: self-report; description of situational factors that could instigate, facilitate, or inhibit the given kind of activity; information about cognitive and affective concomitants of the activity, especially in its crucial stages (initiation, termination, or an

Table 14.1. Indices of motivation

- Self-report about motives (an answer to the question: "Now, can you summarize for me the main reasons why you became involved in this first activity?").
- Structure of the action: the conditions of initiation, the forms of activity, the conditions of termination.
- Attitudes and behavior of the subject's reference group.
- Types of arguments the rescuers used when they met with opposition or with criticism of their activity.
- Forms of contact between rescuers and rescued persons.
- Focus of attention of the rescuers (as revealed in their accounts of their actions and their relationships with other people, especially with rescued persons).
- The role of other people in undertaking and sustaining the rescuing activity.
- Behavior in situations when interests of different people (including the rescuer, his or her family, the rescued persons, and other victims) were at stake.

encounter with major obstacles); and data concerning relationships with people who were involved in the activity.

We must admit that our data are not complete enough to provide us in every case with information concerning all of the issues mentioned in Table 14.1. Nevertheless, the analysis of our material has convinced us that we have obtained a sufficient amount of information to reconstruct, in a hypothetical form, the motivational structure of the activity of our subjects. On this basis we were able to identify three major classes of motives that apparently instigated the rescuing activity. They can be described as allocentric, normocentric, and axiological.

The allocentric motives appeared as the result of a focus of the individual's attention on the situation of the persecuted person (or persons), especially in the case of direct exposure. The situation evoked a kind of cognitive and/or affective concentration on the fate of the person in need. Such concentration facilitated affective reactions of empathy and compassion, and prompted the individual to take the perspective of the person in need. It led to an arousal of a desire to do something to protect the needy person. When asked for a justification of their rescuing action, such individuals mentioned the situation of the victim as a primary factor (see Table 14.2).

Table 14.2. Allocentric motives

The main feature of the allocentric motives is a focus on another person's (or group's) predicament. They were expressed in the subjects' reports concerning, first of all, the needs, situations, or emotional states of others. For example:

- *"I knew they needed help. It was the most important."*
- *"Those Jews came and cried, so what could my mother do? She didn't have a choice."*
- *"A human being was in distress. I had to help."*
- *"Because we wanted to rescue her. We did not want her to get caught. We were sorry for her. We knew that if we sent her away she would not know where to go."*
- *"When I saw a mother with a child, how could I refuse? The child made up my mind."*

The motivational potential of the allocentric motives seems to originate in empathy. According to Hoffman, the author of the most elaborate theory of the development of empathy, there are different developmental levels of this reaction, from the very global emotional response of an infant to a highly articulated one based upon advanced forms of cognitive representation of another person. According to Hoffman, there is "empathy for another's feeling" and "empathy for another's life conditions" (Hoffman, 1977, 1982, 1989). In the latter case, however, empathy is not merely a spontaneous affective reaction to emotional cues; it is based on an elaborate cognitive representation of an external social object. Such representation can generate strong affective responses if exposed to incongruent input (Markus & Zajonc, 1985; Zajonc, 1968); in the case of representation of a person, this can be exposure to information about events that impinge upon his or her physical or psychological integrity (Reykowski, 1982a, 1982b).

The *normocentric motives* appeared as a result of the actualization of the norm of helping. For some people, the situation of mistreatment of the Jews was relevant to the norms of "helpfulness," solidarity, and so forth. The norm could have a religious interpretation (e.g., the Christian requirement to "love your neighbor") or a secular one. The actualization of such a norm evoked a feeling of obligation to act; an individual was more or less aware that inaction might evoke feelings of guilt and remorse. This kind of reaction was, quite often, based upon an explicit reference to the will or opinion of some external authority,

Table 14.3. Noromocentric motives

Normocentric motives are likely to be actualized when individuals perceive the situation as relevant to a given norm. Such an interpretation of the situation is facilitated when other in-group members or authorities define it in the given way. Quite often, individuals can themselves reconstruct what authorities would expect from them. For example:

- *"Because I was Christian. It was our duty."*
- *"I am a Christian and I want to do for Jesus what He wants us to do to the needy."*
- *"I was raised with the philosophy that I should always help."*
- *"We are such people. We help always. My mother taught us to help people when they need help."*

such as a reference group, a spiritual leader, or God; and its initiation and continuance was related to the moral and organizational support of members of the reference group (see Table 14.3).

The motivational potential of the normocentric motives stems from societal sources (Reykowski, 1989) – the individual reacts to the direct or indirect normative demands of the society. While in some cases these demands are formulated by in-group authorities who define what is positive and negative in the given situation, in others the normative requirements are formulated by the individual alone on the basis of internalized norms. Breaking the societal norms evokes inevitably strong affective consequences (shame, guilt). Anticipation of such consequences related to the possibility of breaking the norm provides an affective meaning for the action.

The explanation of prosocial (altruistic) actions in terms of conformity to social norms has been very popular among social psychologists (Bar-Tal, 1976; Berkowitz, 1972; Krebs & Miller, 1985). Many authors have suggested that the internalized norms are the only mechanism of such an action. This position is questioned by the structural-developmental approach (1976), which suggests that societal normative control over moral action is characteristics of people who represent the "conventional level" of the moral development. According to Kohlberg: "What fundamentally defines and unifies the characteristics of the conventional level is its social perspective, a shared viewpoint of the participants in a relationship or a group" (Kohlberg, 1976, p. 33).

Axiological motives appeared as the result of actualization of the subject's moral principles – "justice," "the sanctity of human life," and

Table 14.4. Axiological motives

Axiological motives appear as a result of discrepancies between certain general principles and reality; an elimination of such a discrepancy or its reduction is the main source of motivational potential. For example:

- *"The reason is because each man is equal. We should all live . . . It was plain murder and I couldn't stand that. I would help a Mohammedan just as well as I did a Jew."*
- *"Atmosphere of . . . respect for each other and people of the world, humanism. Religion could have also played a role. The same God creates all people."*
- *"The main reason is that I was a patriot. I was for my country. I was for law and order – the Germans robbed the people of their freedom . . . They took innocent people and I wanted to help."*

the like. If an individual noticed that some basic social values were being violated, he or she felt aroused in their defense. The reaction of such an individual was independent of reactions of other people or of any authority, since it was based upon his or her own moral convictions (see Table 14.4).

The motivational potential of axiological motives seems to originate from a well-developed network of principles. Principles can be described as abstract concepts having an evaluative content "built in" to their meaning. Principles differ from other (descriptive) abstract concepts in their origin and in their functions: We postulate that principles develop as the higher-order concepts for the coordination of evaluative standards in an individual (Reykowski, 1989). Thus, they provide a more general perspective regarding what is good (desirable) and what is bad (undesirable); as a rule, it is a perspective that transcends an individual point of view and takes into account a broader range of interests than the welfare of a particular person.

In some people, principles tend to attain the dominant position in the regulatory system. This means that evaluations generated by principles can have a major impact upon an individual's attitudes. Such evaluations can determine the affective qualities of prosocial goals and prosocial action.

The three motivational mechanisms of altruistic acts described here have been considered by some other authors. For example, Eisenberg in characterizing her five "stages" of moral reasoning mentions such categories as "needs of other orientation," "approval and interpersonal orientation," "the desire to maintain individual and contractual obligations, and the belief in the dignity, rights and equality of individuals" (Eisenberg, 1982). These categories resemble our classification of the rescuers' motives. There is, however, an important difference between the categories of reasoning and motivational mechanisms. While the former refer to the structure of thought, the latter refer to complex regulatory systems. This means that the various motivational mechanisms differ with respect to a variety of affective and behavioral characteristics, such as:

- *Instigating factors*: the aspects of the situation that tend to instigate the given motivation. In case of the allocentric motivation, it is a direct exposure to a person in distress that evokes an empathic reaction – in some cases, even an image of such distress can instigate such a reaction in an individual. Normocentric and axiological motivations are activated when an individual interprets the situation as relevant to his or her normative beliefs or to his or her principles. Especially in the case of axiological motivation, the rescuing action is instigated by a sense of injustice that, according to Deutsch, involves one as a member of a moral community whose moral norms are being violated (Deutsch, 1985, p. 195).
- *Facilitating factors*: the conditions that contribute or are necessary for the sustaining of an action controlled by a given motivation. For example, in the case of normocentric motivation, an important role in sustaining the rescuing action was moral support from other people, at least in the form of an example; such support was unnecessary in the case of axiological and allocentric motivation.
- *Affective concomitants* of the helping action: In the case of allocentric motivation, individuals often described their personal feelings for the rescued people, while in the case of the axiological and normocentric behaviors the feelings were more likely to be rather impersonal, focused on a norm or a principle (e.g., bad feelings that there is such injustice in the world, fear of feeling guilt).
- *Typical forms* of action: In the case of allocentric motivation, the action was aimed most likely at helping a particular person or group of persons with whom an individual was in direct contact. When axiological motivation was involved, the action was focused instead on unknown people (or on a group) with whom an individual did not have any personal ties. In the case of the normocentric motivation, the action tended to depend on an organizational structure or a social network. For example, the help

was extended to individuals indicated by an organization or recommended by some authority.

A good example of the axiological motivation is a case of a French woman who initiated large-scale activity to help the Jews – taking care of Jewish children whose parents had been sent to concentration camps, collecting infants' clothing, and so forth. In the course of her action, which lasted over three years, she helped, in various ways, several hundred people. All of them were unknown to her. The action was undertaken upon her own initiative (she was not asked by anybody to do it). She worked independently. She had no previous experience with Jews. In her report about her activities she did not mention any personal feelings of compassion, friendship, or the like. She also did not mention the feelings of people whom she helped – her helping was impersonal. Instead, she focused on the fact that French government had issued a law against the Jews. She regarded this as a great injustice – a violation of some basic principles.

It should be stressed that in many instances the motivation for action was quite complex. In other words, the same person could manifest more than one kind of motive. Moreover, the motivation could change in the course of action.

Extensivity

The motivation for altruistic helping can have different sources, and the structure of action can have various characteristics depending on the kind of motivation involved. But, as I argued at the beginning of this chapter, such motivation is likely to be inhibited, or not at all aroused, if the needy person is perceived as an out-group member. In such cases, indifference or detachment is likely to occur. We may ask, therefore, why such inhibitory processes did not appear in the rescuers.

This is, in fact, the most intriguing question for many people who have become acquainted with the activities of the rescuers. They seem to be puzzled by the motivation for this activity. Such motivation was also sometimes puzzling to those who received the help. This can be illustrated by a conversation that took place between Rabbi X and the French woman who made an extraordinary effort to save him (and reports this conversation): "*Just after the war he took me aside and told me: ⟩Now you say to me, are you Jewish or not?⟨ And I answered: ⟩I am not, not at all⟨. And he told me: ⟩You are definitely crazy⟨.*"

For Rabbi X, the behavior of his rescuer would have been intelligible had they belonged to the same religion or ethnic group. He implied that self-sacrifice for a compatriot (a member of the same moral community) is something natural. But for him, and for many other people, it was hard to understand that such behavior could appear in relation to the members of another "moral community" (as the Jews were perceived to be).

In such situations, the question of "deserving" becomes a very prominent one: Should I or should I not extend my help to this person or this category of persons? Is the Christian injunction to "love your neighbor" (or the similar injunctions of other religious and ethical systems) applicable in this instance? It is an issue that Deutsch describes as defining the scope of a moral community (Deutsch, 1985, p. 4).

One possible explanation for when and how a reaction such as rescuing can appear is a hypothesis of lack of, or low level of, identification of rescuers with their own particular ethnic or religious group. Individuals who are not affiliated with such groups would not use ethnic or religious categories for classification of other people into in-group and out-group. Therefore, the fact that the person in need is of a specific religious persuasion or belongs to a particular ethno-cultural category is irrelevant for helping (or not helping). This line of thinking was corroborated by the findings reported by London (1970) and Tec (1986). These authors claim that the dominant characteristic of rescuers was "marginality," or as Tec prefers to say, "individuality." However, our study does not provide supportive evidence for this claim. According to the Oliners, 80% of rescuers and 81.5% of nonrescuers declared their sense of belonging in community (Oliner & Oliner, 1988, p. 306). Nevertheless, one may agree that the person who is lacking strong ties with the in-group defined in ethnic or religious terms may be less sensitive to the barriers between him- or herself and others who formally belong to other groups.

The Oliners' data show that lack of identification with a religion or a national in-group (the characteristic of marginal people) is not the necessary precondition for involvement in rescuing. Instead, the authors suggest that a critical role can be attributed to a factor that they describe as an extensive conception of a moral community. Such a broad conception can be characteristic of an individual or of a normative system and moral ideology that a person espouses. Thus, some people tend to construe their moral community in such a way that it includes other ethnic and religious groups. One rescuer explained this in the following words: "*I am Polish patriot and the persecuted Jews are . . . Polish citizens.*" But this phenomenon can take a more general form – a construction of a moral community that includes persons of different religious, ethnic, and other social backgrounds. In fact, many rescuers revealed a tendency to downplay the importance of group belonging in their attitudes toward other people. For example, their friendship choices were less affected by differences in religion than the choices of controls (63% of rescuers vs. 38% of controls reported having close friends of a different religion). The same can be said about differences in social class (61% of rescuers and 43% of controls had friends from a different social class) and ethnic background (respectively 46% and 37% had Jewish friends). The rescuers and controls also differed in their perceived similarity to others. In response to the question, *"In general, did you think the people were very much like you, or not like you at all?"*, the rescuers more often than the nonrescuers asserted their similarity to several categories of people (the rich, Jews, Gypsies). The rescuers were also less likely to hold negative stereotypes of other people. In their responses to the question concerning their general opinions about people, far fewer rescuers than nonrescuers mentioned negative opinions related to nationality, religion, or ethnicity.

One implication of these findings is the postulate that an important characteristic of the rescuers is "extensivity" – the tendency to include in their concept of moral community a broad range of people belonging to various groups. The concept of extensivity was proposed by Pearl and Samuel Oliner (Oliner & Oliner, 1988, 1992). It describes a stable characteristic that plays an important role as the prerequisite of altruistic action. It affects the person's judgment of who is and who is not entitled to altruistic help.

I should add that an extension of a concept of moral community can sometimes be limited to specific persons. That is, some rescuers did not respond to the fate of Jews in general but only to the fate of certain specific people with whom they were well acquainted. The formation of affective bonds – the feelings of friendship, love, or esteem toward a person – tends to reduce ethnic and religious barriers. Such an attitude can be generalized to other people related in some way to the person: relatives, friends, compatriots. We found a number of cases where help was extended to someone because he or she was a relative or friend of a person who was perceived by the rescuer to be a close friend. One may conjecture that allocentric motivation could not fully be aroused if not for the fact that some personality characteristics or affective bonds "desensitized" people to the in-group/out-group differences.

The extension of a moral community can also be a characteristic of a moral ideology or a normative system with which a person is affiliated. In this case, the behavior of members of a reference group or legitimate authority defines the meaning of the norms in such way that they embrace a more or less broad class of people (e.g., Jews). Participation in such a group entails helping action. Thus, for example, in Poland some people became rescuers because they belonged to the resistance movement (*Armia Krajowa*) and were assigned their tasks in an underground organization (under the name *Zegota*) that had been established for helping Jews. In Holland there were a number of such organizations. In Germany, one particular Protestant denomination interpreted the Christian demand to help the needy as a requirement to aid people in dire conditions regardless of their belief systems.

Such an extensive interpretation of the norm of helping or the norm of social responsibility can originate in a specific family upbringing. A number of rescuers were brought up in an environment where some basic normative requirements were interpreted as universal ones. Hence, we can assume that normocentric motivation can be applied to ethnic or religious out-group members if socialization procedures or organizational definitions of the relevant norms facilitate a broad range of application.

A lack of barriers to altruistic action can also be a characteristic of people who perceive the social world in terms of abstract, general principles. Those probably are people who in terms of Kohlberg's theory of moral development represent the postconventional level (Kohlberg, 1981) – universality is an immanent characteristic of their moral judgment. In other words, the lack of ethnic or religious barriers is the very consequence of their moral outlook. This does not mean that everybody who attains the postconventional level of moral reasoning is eager to engage in altruistic helping. It only means that motivation to help, if aroused, is not limited by religious or ethnic considerations. In other words, axiological motivation of altruistic action is the least likely to be inhibited by in-group versus out-group differences in such people.

Concluding Remarks

There are some implications of the reasoning presented in this chapter. I focus on three of them.

First, our data seem to suggest that some altruistic actions may come about without any reference to normative considerations, including the consideration of justice. They are probably mediated by advanced forms of empathy – I have described this mechanism as allocentric motivation.

Second, the justice motive seems to be embedded somewhat in both normocentric and axiological motivations, but there are some important differences between them. While the former provides more or less clear prescriptions of desirable behavior and is highly dependent on social support, the latter involves abstract concepts (that do not indicate what should be done) and implies a high level of autonomy in moral actions.

Third, justice theory seems to suggest that the concept of deserving plays an important role in the initiation of altruistic action. In a number of our cases, this was an implicit or explicit theme of the rescuers' thinking. But the concept of deserving here has a double meaning. In one way, it was expressed in the form of the conviction that the treatment of the Jews by the fascists was a big injustice – they did not deserve such treatment (nor does anyone else). In fact, rescuers and most of the controls shared this conviction. However, the concept of deserving also had another meaning. It took the form of a question: Do these people deserve my involvement (and sacrifice) in helping them? In other words, the perception of injustice itself was not a sufficient condition for remedial action. One had to believe that it was an injustice in *his or her* own world, not in some remote place – physically or psychologically. As it was put by Lerner and Miller (1978, p. 1031): "[P]eople will be concerned primarily with their own world, the environment where they must live and function." The critical point in rescuing Jewish victims during the Holocaust was a more extensive interpretation of the borders of one's own world. It was a world that included people of different religious and ethnic belongings.

The answer to the question, what are the borders of one's own world – in other words, who is and who is not a member of one's moral community – is not at all obvious for people living in the contemporary world. For many people, it makes an enormous difference whether you are a Serb or an Albanian, a Hutu or a Tutsi, a Protestant or a Catholic, a German or a Turk, a Pole or a Gypsy, a Jew or a Gentile, an Arab or an Israeli. People are continually concerned with the question of "who deserves what." In pursuing justice and fighting for a just world (where people get what they deserve), they bring about a lot of injustice and make the world a dangerous and unhappy place for a great many of human beings.

REFERENCES

Bar-Tal, D. (1976). Prosocial behavior. Theory and research. New York: Wiley.

Berkowitz, L. (1972). Social norms, feelings, and other factors affecting helping and altruism. In L. Berkowitz (Ed.), *Advances in experimental social psychology* (Vol. 6, pp. 63–108). New York: Academic Press.

Deutsch, M. (1985). *Distributive justice. A social-psychological perspective.* New Haven, CT: Yale University Press.

Eisenberg, N. (1982). The development of reasoning regarding prosocial behavior. In N. Eisenberg (Ed.), *Developement of prosocial behavior* (pp. 219–251). New York: Academic Press.

Hoffman, M. (1977). Empathy, its development and prosocial implications. In *Nebraska Symposium on Motivation* (Vol. 25, pp. 169–218). Lincoln: University of Nebraska Press.

(1982). Development of prosocial motivation: Empathy and guilt. In N. Eisenberg (Ed.), *Developement of prosocial behavior* (pp. 281–313). New York: Academic Press.

(1989). Empathy and prosocial activism. In N. Eisenberg, J. Reykowski, & E. Staub (Eds.), *Social and moral values: Individual and societal perspectives.* Hillsdale, NJ.: Erlbaum.

Kohlberg, L. (1976). Moral stages and moralization: The cognitive developmental approach. In T. Lickona (Ed.), *Moral development and behavior* (pp. 31–53). New York: Holt.

(1981). *Essays on moral development. Volume 2: The psychology of moral development.* New York: Harper and Row.

Korzeniowski, K. (1994). Political alienation in Poland in days of systemic transformation. *Polish Psychological Bulletin, 25* (3), 187–200.

Krebs, D. L., & Miller, D. T. (1985). Altruism and aggression. In G. L. Lindzey & E. Aronson (Eds.), *The handbook of social psychology* (Vol. 2). New York: Random House.

Latane, B., & Darley, J. M. (1970). Social determinants of bystander intervention in emergencies. In J. Macaulay & L. Berkowitz (Eds.), *Altruism and helping behavior.* New York: Academic Press.

Lerner, M. J. (1970). The desire for justice and reactions to victims. In J. Macaulay & L. Berkowitz (Eds.), *Altruism and helping behavior.* New York: Academic Press.

(1977). The justice motive: Some hypotheses as to its origin and forms. *Journal of Personality, 45,* 1–52.

Lerner, M. J., & Miller, D. T. (1978). Just world research and the attribution process: Looking back and ahead. *Psychological Bulletin, 85,* 1030–1051.

London, P. (1970). The rescuers: Motivational hypothesis about Christians who saved Jews from the Nazis. In J. Macaulay & L. Berkowitz (Eds.), *Altruism and helping behavior.* New York: Academic Press.

Markus, H., & Zajonc, R. B. (1985). The cognitive perspective in social psychology. In G. Lindzey & E. Aronson (Eds.) *The handbook of social psychology.* (Vol. 1, pp. 137–230). New York: Random House.

Merton, R. K. (1957). *Social theory and social structure.* New York: The Free Press.

Oliner, S. P. (1986). *Restless memories: Recollections of the Holocaust years*. Berkeley, CA: Judah L. Magnes Memorial Museum.

Oliner, S. P., & Oliner P. (1988). *Altruistic personality*. New York: Wiley.

Oliner P., & Oliner, S. P. (1992). Promotive extensive altruistic bonds: A conceptual elaboration and some pragmatic implications. In P. Oliner, S. Oliner, L. Baron, L. A. Blum, D. L. Krebs, & M. Z. Smolenska (Eds.), *Embracing the other* (pp. 369–389). New York: New York University Press.

Piliavin, J., Dovidio, J. F., Gaertner, S. L., & Clark, R. D. III. (1981). *Emergency intervention*. New York: Academic Press.

Reykowski, J. (1982a). Social motivation. *Annual Review of Psychology, 33*, 123–155.

(1982b). Motivation of prosocial behavior. In V. J. Derlaga & J. Grzelak (Eds.), *Cooperation and helping behavior: Theories and research* (pp. 352–375). New York: Academic Press.

(1989). Dimensions of development in moral values. In N. Eisenberg, J. Reykowski, & E. Staub (Eds.), *Social and moral values: Individual and societal perspectives* (pp. 23–44). Hillsdale, NJ.: Erlbaum.

Schwartz, S. H. (1977). Normative infulences on altruism. In L. Berkowitz (Ed.), *Advances in experimental social psychology* (Vol. 10, pp. 221–279). New York: Academic Press.

Staub, E. (1980). Social and prosocial behavior: Personal and situational influences and their interactions. In E. Staub (Ed.), *Personality: Basic aspects and current research* (pp. 236–294). Englewood Cliffs, NJ.: Prentice-Hall.

Tajfel, H., & Turner, J. (1979). An integrative theory of intergroup conflict. In W. G. Austin & S. Worchel (Eds.), *The social psychology of intergroup conflict* (pp. 33–49). Monterey, CA: Brooks/Cole.

Tec, N. (1986). *When light pierced the darkness*. Oxford and New York: Oxford University Press.

Zajonc, R. B. (1968). Cognitive theories in social psychology. In G. Lindzey & E. Aronson (Eds.), *The handbook of social psychology* (Vol. 1). Reading, MA: Addison-Wesley.

15. Acting Righteously: The Influence of Attitude, Moral Responsibility, and Emotional Involvement

JOSEPH DE RIVERA, ELENA GERSTMANN, AND LISA MAISELS

Many people feel that nuclear weapons are potential sources of injustice. Even if used to prevent an attack or to retaliate, they would kill thousands, indiscriminately and undeservedly. Yet the Senate of the United States has refused to ratify the Comprehensive Test Ban Treaty, the Department of Energy is restarting tritium production, and a congressional committee has called for an immediate start on the designing of new nuclear warheads (Defense Monitor, 1999).

While some citizens believe the United States should continue to maintain its nuclear superiority, polling data repeatedly show that a majority favor nuclear disarmament (Kay, 1998). Given their majority status, why do the many citizens who are opposed to nuclear weapons fail to press for nuclear disarmament? Why is it hard for peace organizations to mobilize individuals to demand nuclear disarmament, or to make it an issue in election campaigns? One reason involves a relationship between perceived efficacy and justice. If people believed that they could convince the government to move toward nuclear disarmament, then many might demand disarmament in order to avoid the possibility of killing hundreds of thousands of innocent people. However, most people doubt that they can influence governmental policy and prevent nuclear war. Hence, to engage in any individual action advocating nuclear disarmament implies the possibility that nuclear war might really occur. This requires relinquishing the belief that the person is living in a just world (Lerner, 1980). When people feel powerless to influence the government in order to prevent a nuclear war, it is easier to maintain a belief in a just world by assuming that nuclear war is so unthinkable that it will not occur. Hence, individual action for disarmament is not perceived as necessary. This is but one example of the gap between moral reasoning (thinking that nuclear war is bad) and moral action (acting to prevent it). As Bandura (1999) emphasizes, understanding moral agency requires us to link moral reasoning to moral engagement and action.

What leads some persons to face injustice, become morally engaged, and act? In a previous study (de Rivera, Gerstmann, & Maisels, 1994), we have demonstrated that when we made a nuclear test ban salient and provided conditions that facilitated writing to congressional representatives, some people became emotionally engaged and wrote letters. This occurred without a specific victim with whom they could empathize and in the absence of normative pressure. In the analysis of Reykowski (this volume), they were motivated by axiological rather than allocentric or normocentric motives. We argued that it would be fruitful to distinguish between such prosocial righteous behavior (involving impersonal justice) and prosocial behavior that involved personal helping.

We found, as did Montada and Schneider (1989), that righteous behavior was predicted by anger rather than by the sympathy or personal distress, which is often involved in helping individual persons (Batson, Early, & Salvarani, 1999; Batson, Fultz, & Schoenrade, 1987; Eisenberg, 1989). That is, the tendency to write was predicted by the extent of moral outrage that was reported rather than by either sympathy or fear. We argued that the emotion of anger was particularly suited to facilitate righteous behavior, because the structure of that emotion is characterized by an "instruction" to remove any challenge to what a person asserts ought to exist (see de Rivera, 1977). We presumed that the material reminded people of the possibility of nuclear war and posed a challenge as to what ought to exist. Those who had become angry had accepted the responsibility of writing as a way of removing this moral challenge. However, we lacked evidence that the anger of the writers was related to their acceptance of moral responsibility.

A number of empirical studies support the idea that righteous behavior is a function of personal responsibility. For example, Schwartz (1977) showed that donating blood depends as much on an acceptance of personal responsibility as on attitudes toward donating, and Tyler and McGraw (1983) showed that anti–nuclear war activism is as strongly related to a sense of moral responsibility as to feelings of citizen efficacy. Theoretically, the importance of responsibility may be due to the fact that the acceptance of responsibility is an aspect of a person's identity; Blasi and Oresick's (1985) analysis of self-consistency suggests that morally responsible action occurs as an expression of this sense of identity. They argue that when a person has made a personal commitment to a set of values, that person's identity is at stake if action (or lack of action) is inconsistent with those values. However, persons may or may not be aware that their actions are inconsistent with their values (Batson et al., 1999), and we must ask if a general acceptance of responsibility will lead people to accept responsibility in particular situations. Reylowski (this volume) suggests that emotional involvement leads to prosocial action only when a person accepts responsibility. Might the inverse also be true? Might a person's general sense of moral responsibility lead to action only when the person is emotionally involved? In the case of righteous behavior, axiologically motivated, will this usually involve anger?

In the study reported here, we attempted to arouse emotion in one group of subjects and have another group be passive bystanders. While our experimental manipulation was not completely successful, we were able to show that the arousal of anger was related to moral responsibility and was an important predictor of action.

To investigate the effects of emotional involvement, we wanted to create ideal conditions for a person to act on his or her beliefs with minimal social pressure. We wanted the possibility of action to be clear and yet for it to involve some real cost. Our earlier work had established that most students had not previously written a political letter and found it to be a difficult task. Hence, we attempted to give subjects clear reasons for a nuclear test ban, a hope that it could be obtained by congressional action that could be spurred on by citizen advocacy, and the opportunity to write a letter to their congressional representative. A week before, we had obtained measures of attitudes toward a nuclear test ban and toward the behavior of writing letters to congressional representatives, and a measure of the degree to which persons felt morally responsible for preventing nuclear war. By comparing the predictive power of the different measures when persons were or were not emotionally involved, we could examine how involvement affected moral action.

We believed that action would occur only if persons were emotionally involved in the issue. However, we were not sure of the best way to constitute a control group. We wanted the group to have the same information, yet lack emotional motivation. If we simply presented information about a test ban and congressional advocacy, subjects might not act because of a relative lack of salience (see Fiske, 1987; Fox & Schofield, 1989). Yet we wanted to show that emotional involvement did not simply create salience, but rather *moved* people to act by engaging their moral responsibility. Hence, we attempted to create salience without emotional involvement by using technical writing about the Hiroshima and Nagasaki bomb drops. We hoped to raise the issue of Hiroshima and remind people of the horror of nuclear weapons, and yet leave them detached rather than moved. We reasoned that even those with moral responsibility would not act under these conditions; they would still live in a just world, unconnected to the injustice of a world with nuclear weapons.

Method

Participants

Participants were thirty-eight undergraduates recruited from an introductory psychology course as volunteers to help science (and with the possibility of winning a $100 raffle). Subjects who indicated an interest in participating in a study on "the effects of different media presentations on attitudes" were given a preliminary questionnaire on their beliefs about nuclear war, attitudes toward political participation, and past participation in behaviors opposing or supporting the development of nuclear weapons. About half of the subjects who took questionnaires returned them. Most indicated that they supported a comprehensive nuclear test ban. Those who did not support a test ban or were not U.S. citizens were not used in the study. Thus, all thirty-eight participants were U.S. citizens who supported a comprehensive test ban. They were randomly assigned to either an emotion or a detached condition.

Preliminary Questionnaire

Attitude toward a test ban. Participants were asked whether they agreed or disagreed with the statement: "Congress should support an agreement with the Soviet Union and all other countries to ban the testing and production of nuclear weapons." This was scaled from +5 (agree completely) to –5 (disagree completely) with no midpoint. It was followed by a question that asked about the importance of such an agreement (scaled from 1 to 10).

Attitude toward writing representatives scale. A scale measuring attitudes toward communicating with congressional representatives used six items (answered on ten-point Likert scales labeled "exactly" to "not at all") with a Cronbach's Alpha of .85. Three of the items were normative (e.g., "My family would respect me if I were to write to my congressperson") and three concerned the effectiveness of writing. The item with the highest item-total correlation was, "I think it would be a waste of time for someone to write to his/her congressperson" (reverse scored).

Moral responsibility scale. A scale measuring the extent to which a subject felt responsible for preventing nuclear war used five items with alpha = .87. The most highly correlated item was, "It is my responsibility to care for our Earth by working to ensure that nuclear war never occurs."

Promotional Material

A week after the preliminary questionnaire, participants came to the lab individually and were given the following:

Congressional aide video. All participants viewed a ten-minute videotape of an interview with a congressional aide. The aide discussed how U.S. congressional representatives are heavily influenced by the letters they receive from their constituents and how representatives could not adequately represent their constituents without knowing how the constituents felt. He mentioned that if a representative were voting in a way that the person did not like, the person should write a letter expressing displeasure, while if the representative were voting in a way that the person wanted, the representative should be thanked.

Information on test ban. All participants read an op-ed piece from the *Christian Science Monitor* (Schrag, 1989) that argued that a test ban would delay the spread of nuclear weapons and prevent the development of new weapons. An "update," written by the experimenters, was attached and mentioned that a test ban bill had lost, 207–211, but would be voted upon in Congress again in a few months.

Intellectual material. In the "detached" condition, participants (N = 19) read fourteen pages on the *physical* effects of the Hiroshima and Nagasaki bombs. These pages were taken from the first two chapters of a work on the bombings (Committee for the Compilation of Materials, 1981). While people were mentioned in passing, the pages used were written for a scientifically oriented reader and mainly discussed calculation of the time and altitude of the bomb drops and their sudden and immense thermal effects.

Emotional material. In the "emotion" condition, participants ($N = 19$) saw a videotape, *The Lost Generation*, produced by a committee of Japanese citizens. This twenty-minute tape juxtaposed contemporary interviews with survivors of the Hiroshima and Nagasaki bombings with army film footage taken days after the bombing. In some cases survivors were interviewed as they *watched themselves* on early films. Thus, a middle-aged woman might recognize herself in footage taken of a badly burned fifteen-year-old. Scenes of schoolchildren playing in modern day Hiroshima were contrasted with footage of the totally desolated city, and the narrator stated that such suffering should not be allowed to happen again. It seemed to embody a compelling emotional appeal for action.

Emotion Questionnaires

Emotional response to the material about the test ban and Hiroshima was measured in two different ways. First, four special "depth of feeling" items were created in order to tap the intensity of the subject's emotional experience.[1] The "angry and frustrated" and "miserable and mad" items (see Table 15.1) were summed to create a measure of anger, and the "sorrowful and overwhelmed" and "sorrowful and depressed" items were summed to yield a measure of sadness. Second, participants were asked to indicate the extent they to which were feeling each of twenty-three different feelings (on seven-point scales.) This list of feelings included satisfaction, outrage, sympathy, fear, guilt, and hopelessness (six feelings used in earlier studies), as well as feelings that reflected empathy or self-distress, and feelings that had been reported by other subjects exposed to the stimulus material.

[1] We want to express our appreciation for Dr. Thomas Snyder, who worked with data from Emotional Mining Company to generate these items.

Waiting Room Material

After participants had seen or read the promotional material, they were taken to a different room where they filled out questionnaires and waited to be interviewed by a different experimenter. This room contained: (1) a number of current magazines, catalogues, and copies of the student newspaper; (2) a list of addresses for the authors or producers of all the media that were utilized; (3) a list of congressional representatives and records as to whether they had voted for or against a comprehensive nuclear test ban; (4) writing material and a sample letter format (without content).

Procedure

All participants were randomly assigned to one of the experimental conditions. In order to minimize social influence, they were seen individually and by two experimenters. The first met the participant and gave a consent form stating that one could leave at any time that one wished. Participants were told that the experimenters were interested in evaluating the effects of different media presentations, that different people would be receiving different presentations, and that the best way to be helpful was to answer all questions as honestly as possible. All participants then watched the congressional aid video and completed questions that remeasured their attitude toward communicating with the government. They were then asked to read the op-ed piece on the nuclear test ban and read or view the material on Hiroshima. When participants notified the experimenter that they were finished, they were taken to the waiting room and given the emotional response questionnaires and the same items about moral responsibility and attitude toward a test ban that they had answered a week before.

Social influence to take political action was deliberately minimized by means of carefully constructed instructions. Participants were told, "When you are finished with this [the questionnaires] you will have your interview and debriefing. [Name of the *second* experimenter] will come knock on the door in about twenty minutes. If you get done early, there's some magazines over there to look at. Some people have told us that they want to see how their congressperson voted, so you can look that up over there if you want to, and some people want to write to their congressperson, or the author, or the film producer, or whatever, so there's envelopes and addresses and paper and a sample letter over there. Okay? [Name of the second experimenter] will knock on the door in twenty minutes." A clock was on the wall, and the instructions were successful to the extent that it was not until later, when the interview began to focus on what the participant actually did in the waiting room, that most participants began to realize that whether or not they had written, or had thought about writing, was of any concern to the first experimenter.

Thirty minutes later, the second experimenter came to the room and stated that she would be busy for a few more minutes but that the participant could get started answering a question. She then gave the participant a sheet of paper with the simple statement: "Though we are interested in how you felt during the whole experiment, we are especially interested in the last media presentation on Hiroshima you received. Please write down, as exactly as you can, how it made you feel, during the presentation and afterwards. *What did you do and think about and feel in this room?* (Please be exact.)" Five minutes later, she interviewed the participant about his or her experience in the waiting room and then debriefed the subject.

Behavioral Index. The participant's behavior was scored on the following six-point scale: reported only reading magazine = 0; reported checking representative's voting record = 1; reported checking voting record and thinking of writing but dismissing the idea = 2; reported checking record and intention to write = 3; reported intention to write and took envelope or copied down address = 4; wrote letter in waiting room = 5.

Results

Behavior varied widely, ranging from eight participants who simply read magazines in the waiting room to three who immediately wrote letters. The mean score on the behavioral index was 1.87.

Participants in the emotion condition were more inclined to act ($m = 2.3$) than those in the detached condition ($m = 1.5$), but the difference might be attributed to chance, $t(36) = 1.55$, $p < .065$ (single tail value). We therefore explored the results in three different ways. First, we assumed that the emotion condition created more emotional involvement and a greater propensity to act in accord with one's beliefs and investigated why this might be so. Second, we avoided that assumption and contrasted those subjects who were emotionally affected with those who were not. Finally, we contrasted those who acted (regardless of the experimental condition) with those who failed to act.

Emotion versus Detached Condition

An examination of emotional responses revealed a significant difference between the experimental conditions. The four items that attempted to measure depth of response by inquiring about imagined duration were particularly effective, both in distinguishing between conditions and in predicting behavior. The items and their means, standard deviations, and correlations with the behavioral index are displayed in Table 15.1.

While not as effective, the more traditional emotion items also revealed differences between the conditions. All twenty-three items were in the expected direction on the seven-point scales. In the emotion condition, there were significantly ($p < .05$) higher means for distressed

Table 15.1. Measuring the depth of emotional response and its correlation with the behavioral index

Regarding the bombing on Hiroshima and how it makes you feel, how well does the following statement represent your feelings? 1 = not at all 7 = very much so	Condition					
	Emotion			Detached		
	M	SD	R	M	SD	R
You are feeling angry and frustrated, and you can imagine feeling angry and dismay for a long time.	4.9a	1.7	.51*	3.7	1.6	.44
You are feeling sorrowful and overwhelmed, but you can imagine feeling rage.	4.9	1.8	.45	4.4	2.0	.24
You are feeling sorrowful and depressed, but you can imagine feeling dread.	5.3b	1.6	.41	3.8	1.5	.11
You are feeling miserable and mad, and you can imagine feeling uncomfortableness and anger for a long time.	5.1c	1.7	.59**	3.3	1.5	.16

Note: a, b, c = difference between means in different conditions significant at $p < .05$, .01, .001 levels.

* $p < .05$. ** $p < .01$.

(M = 5.0 vs. M = 3.9), moved (M = 5.3 vs. M = 3.6), and outrage (M = 5.1 vs. M = 3.7), and a significantly lower means for bored (M = 1.5 vs. M = 2.5). All correlations with the behavioral index were in the expected direction, and those with alarmed, ashamed, contented, disturbed, and moved were statistically significant at beyond the .05 level.[2]

A "personal distress" scale was formed by adding the ratings on alarmed, distressed, disturbed, grieved, perturbed, upset, and worried. An "empathic concern" scale was formed by adding the ratings on compassion, moved, softhearted, sympathy, tender, and warm. Neither scale discriminated between the emotion and detached group. The personal distress scale was somewhat predictive of behavior: emotional condition $r(19) = .31$, detached condition $r(19) = .25$, overall $r(38) = .33$, $p < .04$. The empathic concern scale was not predictive of behavior.

A series of 2 × 2 repeated measure analyses of variance explored the before-and-after effects of the two experimental conditions. As expected, since we deliberately used only persons who had favorable attitudes toward a test ban, neither attitude toward a nuclear test ban nor importance of a test ban showed significant increases or interactions. As we had hoped, attitude towards communicating with representatives improved under both conditions, ($F[1,36] = 5.97$), and the interaction did not approach significance. As anticipated, there was a significant interaction between experimental condition and pre-post measures of personal responsibility, $F(1,35) = 4.9$, $p = .034$. The acceptance of personal responsibility increased in the emotion condition (M = +3.3), while it slightly decreased in the detached condition (M = −1.4).

We then correlated the final scores on attitude toward communicating with representatives, acceptance of responsibility, anger, and sadness with the behavioral index, comparing the correlations when subjects were in the emotion and detached conditions. The results are shown in Table 15.2.

While attitude toward communicating with representatives predicted behavior in both conditions, moral responsibility significantly predicted behavior in the emotion but not in the detached condition.

[2] An analysis by gender revealed that females reported significantly more anxiety, distress, sadness, upset, and worry, and significantly less boredom and satisfaction. However, female scores on the behavioral index were not significantly higher than those of males ($t[36] = .12$). It seemed possible that females might be more influenced in the emotion condition, and males more influenced in the detached condition.

Table 15.2. Correlations between predictive factors and the behavioral index in different conditions

	Predictive Factors			
	Attitude toward Writing	Moral Responsibility	Anger	Sadness
Emotion condition	.59**	.72***	.57**	.45
Detached condition	.62**	.11	.33	.20

Note: ** $p < .01$. *** $p < .001$.

Thus it appears that moral responsibility is activated or made relevant in a particular situation in which a person is emotionally involved. Anger also significantly predicted behavior in the emotion condition.

Emotionally Affected versus Nonaffected Subjects

Examination of the participants' written statements about their feelings revealed that fourteen of the nineteen persons in the emotion condition expressed the intense emotion we had predicted. Anger, outrage, and disgust were expressed by most (as one participant wrote, "I was repulsed, disgusted, and very angry"). However, four of the fourteen who were emotionally involved expressed only intense sorrow, sympathy, or sadness, and one became upset and angry at the film producer! The four persons who did not report intense emotions appeared to defend by intellectualizing (One wrote, "I found the presentation interesting").

As expected, ten of the nineteen subjects in the detached condition showed little or no emotional response (e.g., "I was curious to read about the technical details"). However, to our surprise, nine subjects were emotionally affected by the article. In most of these cases, the article stimulated affect-laden thoughts about atomic war that were unrelated to the article per se. (One participant wrote, "I felt sad . . . because . . . families were split up . . . doesn't the government have any feelings . . .") One subject became angry (and wrote a letter) because she was "taken back by how technical the article was . . . it made me feel that the U.S. wasn't concerned about the people involved."

A comparison between the twenty-three participants from both conditions who reported being affected and the fifteen who were not revealed a highly significant difference in behavior ($M = 2.6$ vs. 0.7, $t(36) = 4.29$, $p < .0001$). For the thirty-eight participants, behavior was correlated +.57 ($p < .001$) with anger and +.45 ($p < .02$) with sadness.

Actors versus Nonactors

Since the attempt to experimentally control emotional involvement was only partially successful, we made an independent analysis of when subjects acted on their beliefs. First, we compared the ten subjects who scored 3 or above on the behavioral index (wrote or intended to write) to the twenty-eight who scored below 3. Seven of the ten actors were in the emotion condition; all four "depth" of emotion measures were significantly greater at $p < .01$; and the extent of their emotional arousal was evidenced by significantly greater ($p < .05$) scores on alarmed, distressed, disturbed, moved, upset, and personal distress. T-tests also revealed significant differences on positive attitude toward writing representatives, $t = 3.09(36)$, $p < .001$, and degree of moral responsibility, $t = 2.08(36)$, $p < .05$.

To investigate whether high scores on any one of these three factors sufficed to insure action, we selected participants who were in the upper quartile of attitude toward writing representatives, participants in the upper quartile of moral responsibility, and participants in the upper quartile of emotional arousal (as indicated by the four depth-of-emotion measures). In each case, it was clear that the factor was necessary but not sufficient to insure action. Of the eleven subjects highest in attitude toward writing, five failed to act, and four of these showed no emotional arousal. Of the ten subjects highest in moral responsibility, five failed to act, and four of these showed no emotional arousal. Of the eleven subjects highest in emotional arousal, five failed to act, and three of these were below average in attitude toward writing representatives and/or moral responsibility.

To investigate the relative importance of attitude toward writing, moral responsibility, and the arousal of anger, we entered these variables into a multiple regression equation to predict the behavior of writing. Although, taken alone, each of the three variables significantly predicted behavior, only attitude and anger contributed to the final multivariate equation, $R(37) = .66$, with beta weights of .43 and .36 respectively.

While it is anger, rather than personal responsibility, that combines with attitude to predict the moral action of writing, this anger was predicted by the moral responsibility scores that were obtained a week before participants viewed or read the material about Hiroshima ($r(37) = +.41$, $p < .01$). Hence, we may postulate that the acceptance of personal responsibility for doing something to prevent nuclear war led to anger when the participants were challenged by the material on the continued testing of weapons and the evidence of their destructive effects. Nevertheless, it is the degree of anger rather than the degree of responsibility that best predicts the extent to which moral action occurred.

Discussion

Since anger is a more direct predictor of moral action than personal responsibility, we must modify Blasi's (1999) argument that emotion does not explain moral motivation. While we may agree that moral behavior requires the acceptance of moral responsibility and the intentionality that this implies, the motivation that is required for moral action may require emotion, and emotion of a particular sort.

It is interesting to note the limitations of our experimental manipulation. On the one hand, the very powerful video appears to have provoked a defensive reaction in five of the nineteen subjects. On the other hand, the apparently innocuous scientific article stimulated latent feelings of resentment toward government or sorrow over atomic war in nine of the nineteen subjects. Nevertheless, it is clear that on average the video produced more emotional involvement and, particularly, deeper feelings of anger.

Of course, the stimulus materials differed in ways other than their emotional evocativeness. Some of these other differences may have accounted for the some of the differences in behavior we observed. Further, while the video created emotional involvement by leading the viewer to empathize with the victims of Hiroshima, it also made a moral appeal. Hence, we cannot be sure whether either one of these components of emotional involvement is sufficient, or whether both are necessary to stimulate action. Future studies should attempt to separate these features. The study also suffers from the fact that, because few participants actually wrote letters while they were in the waiting room, our measure of prosocial behavior was partly based on reports of intention. In the future, it would be desirable to find behaviors that a larger percentage of the subjects would objectively perform.

In spite of these limitations, the study clearly suggests that emotional involvement (as contrasted with mere intellectual awareness) is necessary if a person is to act on his or her beliefs in the absence of social pressure. Nine of the ten persons who acted in the study reported 5 or higher on the seven-point "angry and frustrated" item. No matter how much a person favored a nuclear test ban or had a positive attitude toward communicating with the government, if emotional energy in the form of anger was not aroused, the person did not act.

Yet it is also true that emotional motivation is not sufficient for action. There were eleven other subjects who reported 5 or higher on the "angry and frustrated" item yet failed to act. Compared to subjects who did act, these subjects had significantly lower scores on attitude toward writing their representative, $t(18) = 2.30$, $p < .05$.

The role of attitude toward writing seems clear. We would expect that people with more positive attitudes toward writing would be more likely to write to their congressperson. But how are we to understand how that attitude interacts with moral responsibility and emotional arousal? There has been continued debate as to whether moral obligation adds predictive power to that provided by attitude toward behavior and social norms (Gorsuch & Orthberg, 1983; Pomazal & Jaccard, 1976; Schwartz & Tessler, 1972; Zuckerman & Reis, 1978). The data reported here suggest that moral obligation adds predictive power *when emotion is involved*. Thus, in this study the proclaimed responsibility for preventing nuclear war did not lead a person to act on these beliefs unless emotion was involved. Only five of the ten subjects in the upper quartile of moral responsibility acted. Four of these five subjects were in the emotion condition, and all five reported high levels of arousal. The five subjects who did not act were all in the detached condition, and only one reported some arousal.

Yet it is also true that emotional motivation is not, in itself, sufficient reason to act. Of the nineteen participants in the emotional condition, fourteen showed appropriate levels of emotional involvement, yet only seven acted. When we contrasted these actors with the nonactors, we did not find significant differences in attitude toward behavior, or in evaluation of the importance of a test ban. We did find a significant difference in their moral responsibility, $t(12) = 2.86$, $p < .022$.

On the one hand, these data support Blasi and Oresick's (1985) view that moral action depends on personal commitments rather than on simple emotional forces. On the other hand, it seems clear that the motive to maintain a consistent identity (and, hence, to act in accord with one's commitments) is challenged only when one becomes emotionally involved. Participants with high moral responsibility failed to act in the detached condition unless, despite the experimenters' intentions, they became emotionally involved. Hence, we postulate that, in the absence of normative forces, emotional involvement in a particular situation is necessary if latent moral responsibility is to lead to action.

How may we reconcile findings that stress the importance of emotion with a rational approach toward action, such as that proposed by Fishbein (1980)? A rational approach stresses that action is motivated by intention and that these intentions are affected by a person's attitude toward the behavior and the normative forces acting on the person. We considered the possibility that emotional involvement might increase positive attitudes toward the behavior of writing or the normative forces for a test ban. However, these were already strong and were not increased by emotional involvement. How then does emotional motivation exert its affect? We propose that emotion influences the *formation* of the intention to act. There is a good deal of evidence from the early experiments of the Lewinian school (see de Rivera, 1977) that intentions are not automatically produced, but are created by the person. It seems reasonable to propose that the motivational energy involved in intention formation may come from emotion.

Certainly, the statements made by subjects while they were in the waiting room support this conjecture. For example, here are reflections from two subjects who had positive attitudes toward communicating with government and high moral responsibility, but who were in the detached condition:

(1) "I was relaxed and browsed through the library catalogue. I also looked up my congressperson and how he voted. I was pleased with his vote. However, I didn't feel any urge to write him."
(2) "If I had been more angered, moved, scared and sad, I believe I would have written . . . He voted 'yes' on the issue and I would like to thank him. But as I sit here, I think there are many causes (on) which my energy would have a greater positive affect."

By contrast, subjects with equivalent attitudes who were in the emotion condition decided to write.

Note that we are not proposing that emotion propels people to action apart from their intentions, rationality, and moral responsibility. Rather, we propose that emotion (which may or may not be in touch with reality) influences the creation of intentions that are based on rational attitudes and moral responsibility.

What is the nature of the emotional energy in the situation with which we are dealing? The data suggest that it is anger (in the form of moral outrage) – rather than sympathy, sorrow, guilt, or fear – that is motivating the political action of writing a letter to a congressperson. While this action is clearly prosocial behavior, it is "righteous" behavior rather than the "personal helping" behavior that is more frequently studied. It is the energy involved in restoring justice, in removing a challenge to what ought to exist. The situation in which humans find themselves when they face the presence of nuclear weapons is inherently distressing and a challenge to the existence of a just world. While some may be able to take political action out of compassion, many may require the energy of righteous anger in order to overcome the challenge posed by uncaring governments, and to avoid the political passivity implicit in assuming that the world is just. Of course, this willingness to face political distress may itself be motivated by an underlying empathetic concern. Such a possibility must be investigated in future research.

REFERENCES

Batson, C. D., Early, S., & Salvarani, G. (1997). Perspective taking: Imagining how another feels versus imagining how you would feel. *Personality & Social Psychology Bulletin, 23* (7), 751–758.

Batson, D., Fultz, J., & Schoenrode, P. (1987). Distress and empathy: Two qualitatively distinct vicarious emotions with different motivational consequences. *Journal of Personality, 155*, 19–39.

Batson, C. D., Thompson, E. R., Seuferliing, G., Whitney, H., & Strongman, J. A. (1999). Moral hypocrisy: Appearing moral to oneself without being so. *Journal of Personality and Social Psychology, 77* (3), 525–548.

Blasi, A. (1999). Emotions and moral motivation. *Journal for the Theory of Social Behaviour, 29* (1), 1–19.

Blasi, A., & Oresick, R. J. (1985). Emotions and cognitions in self-inconsistency. In D. Bearison & H. Zimiles (Eds.), *Thoughts and emotion* (pp. 147–165). Hillsdale, NJ: Erlbaum.

Chapman, M., Zahn-Waxler, C., Cooperman, G., & Iannotti, R. (1987). Empathy and responsibility in the motivation of children's helping. *Developmental Psychology, 23*, 140–145.

Committee for the Compilation of Materials on Damage Caused by the Atomic Bomb in Hiroshima and Nagasaki (1981). *Hiroshima and Nagasaki: The physical, medical and social effects of the atomic bombings*. New York: Basic Books.

The Defense Monitor (1999). *Two giant steps closer to a new nuclear arms race* (Vol. 28, no. 8, p. 6). Washington, DC: Center for Defense Information.

de Rivera, J. H. (1977). *Field theory as human-science: Contributions by Lewin's Berlin Group*. New York: Gardner Press.

(1994). The emotional motivation of righteous behavior. *Social Justice Research, 7* (1), 91–106.

Eisenberg, N., Fabes, R. H., Miller, P. A., Fultz, J., Shell, R., Mathy, R. M., & Reno, R. (1989). Relation of sympathy and personal distress to prosocial behavior: A multimethod study. *Journal of Personality and Social Psychology, 57*, 55–66.

Fishbein, M. (1980). A theory of reasoned action: Some applications and implications. In M. M. Page (Ed.), *Nebraska Symposium on Motivation* (Vol. 27, pp. 65–116). Lincoln: University of Nebraska Press.

Fiske, S. T. (1987). People's reaction to nuclear war: Implications for psychologists. *American Psychologist, 42*, 207–217.

Fox, D. C., & Schofield, J. W. (1989). Issue salience, perceived efficacy and perceived risk: An experimental study of the origins of pro-arms control behavior. *Journal of Applied Social Psychology, 19*, 805–827.

Gorsuch, R. L., & Ortberg, J. (1983). Moral obligation and attitudes: Their relation to behavioral intentions. *Journal of Personality and Social Psychology, 44* (5), 1025–1028.

Kay, A. F. (1998). *Locating consensus for democracy*. St. Augustine, FL: American Talk Issues.

Lerner, M. J. (1980). *The belief in a just world: A fundamental delusion*. New York: Plenum.

Leventhal, H. (1970). Findings and theory in the study of fear communications. In L. Berkowitz (Ed.), *Advances in experimental social psychology* (Vol. 5, pp. 120–181). New York: Academic Press.

Locatelli, M. G., & Holt, R. R. (1986). Antinuclear activism, psychic numbing, and mental health. *The International Journal of Mental Health, 15*, 143–161.

The Lost Generation. Chicago: Documentaries Plus.

McClenney, L., & Neiss, R. (1989). Psychological responses to the threat of nuclear war. *Journal of Applied Social Psychology, 19*, 1239–1267.

Montada, L., & Schneider, A. (1989). Justice and emotional reactions to the disadvantaged. *Social Justice Research, 3*, 313–344.

Pomazal R. J., & Jaccard, J. J. (1976). An informational approach to altruistic behavior. *Journal of Personality and Social Psychology, 33* (3), 317–326.

Radke-Yarrow, M., & Zahn-Waxler, C. (1986). The role of familial factors in the development of prosocial behavior: Research findings and questions. In D. Olwens, J. Blà6ck, & M. Radke-Yarrow (Eds.), *Development of antisocial and prosocial behavior* (pp. 207–234). New York: Academic Press.

Sarbin, T. (1989). Emotion as situationed action. In L. Cirillo, B. Kaplan, & S. Wapner (Eds.), *Emotion and ideal human development* (pp. 77–99). Hillsdale, NJ: Erlbaum.

Schrag, P. G. (1989). Banning nuclear tests – it's Bush's move. *Christian Science Monitor*, April 24.

Schwartz, S. H., & Tessler, R. C. (1972). A test of a model for reducing measured attitude-behavior discrepancies. *Journal of Personality and Social Psychology, 24* (2), 225–236.

Tyler, T. R., & McGraw, K. M. (1983). The threat of nuclear war: Risk interpretation and behavioral response. *Journal of Social Issues, 39*, 25–40.

Zuckerman, M., & Reis, H. T. (1978). Comparison of three models for predicting altruistic behavior. *Journal of Personality and Social Psychology, 36* (5), 498–510.

JUSTICE-BASED REACTIONS TO TRANSGRESSORS

16. Retributive Justice: Its Social Context

NEIL VIDMAR

As for the social character of [penal] reaction, it comes from the social nature of the offended sentiments. Because they are found in all consciences, the infraction committed arouses in those who have evidence of it or who learn of its existence the same indignation. Everybody is attacked; consequently, everybody opposes the attack. Not only is the reaction general, but it is collective, which is not the same thing. It is not produced isolatedly in each one, but with a totality and a unity, nevertheless variable, according to the case.

Emile Durkheim, 1893/1964, p. 102

Emile Durkheim, George Herbert Mead (1918), Thomas and Znaniecki (1945), and, in more recent times, Harold Garfinkel (1956) and Kai Erikson (1966) have commented extensively on the fact that deviant acts evoke group responses. In Erikson's summary phrasing:

The deviant act, then, creates a sense of mutuality among the people of a community by supplying a focus for group feeling. Like a war, a flood, or some other emergency, deviance makes people more alert to the interests they share in common and draws attention to those values which constitute the "collective conscience" of the community. (1966, p. 4)

Until relatively recently, social psychologists have given less attention to retributive justice than to other forms of justice, such as distributive and procedural justice (see Vidmar, 2000a). Although interest in retributive justice is increasing, the fact remains that social psychological research on retribution has tended to ignore, or at least to downplay, the insights of sociologists in deference to an approach that examines how individuals respond to deviant acts. Without rejecting psychological analyses, this chapter draws attention to the social context and social consequences of retributive justice. Group dynamics are at play in a wide array of settings in which people respond to rule or norm violations, but in this chapter I will draw primarily upon more than a quarter-century of research, much of it previously unpublished, that examines community reactions to criminal events. However, at the end of the chapter I argue that the issues raised by the research can and should be tested in more mundane settings in which rule violations occur.

The theme of this chapter is quite consistent with Mel Lerner's more general theorizing about the social psychology of justice (Lerner, 1981). Lerner argued that justice is a universal motive and that humans care deeply about justice. Justice judgments invoke evaluative and emotional assessments. Lerner (1987) persuasively argued that much research on justice has been carried out in experimental settings that minimize affective-motivational processes, and that there is an important need to test theoretical notions of justice in more complex settings that give sway to these inherent human factors. Lerner's research has also focused on the sequelae of justice judgments as well as on their antecedents. To wit, justice judgments have behavioral consequences (e.g., Lerner, 1977). Finally, Lerner argued that identity relationships are very important, that is, persons perceived to be members of in-groups are treated differently than members of out-groups.

I. A Social Psychological Perspective

I have no quarrel with the view that retributive justice reactions are represented in the minds of individual persons and involve attributional responses, but there is much more to the phenomenon. In a recent writing (Vidmar, 2000a), I proposed a six-stage model of the social psychological dynamics of retribution: (1) there is a perceived rule or norm violation; (2) the rule violator's intention is perceived as blameworthy; (3) the combination of (1) and (2) threatens or actually harms values related to the perceiver's personal self, status, or internalized group values; (4) the emotion of anger is aroused; (5) the cognitions and emotions foster reactions against the violator; (6) during or following punishment the anger dissipates, cognitions return toward homeostasis, and the rule or norm is perceived to be vindicated.

The model posits emotion as a core component of retributive justice reactions. It allows for the fact that some of the stages may occur out of sequence. It also takes cognizance of Heider's (1958) observation that justice reactions are often in an amorphous, inchoate form in the minds of responders, and that articulation of them typically takes the form of "oughtness" words and phrases such as "deserves," "do justice," and "right a wrong."

The model also contains the codicil that, in some circumstances, punishment of the offender may actually increase psychological and social tension because the act of punishing the offender serves to validate the perception of harm to the values that the rule incorporates. Although I know of no research that has directly tested this hypothesis, it is often argued indirectly in criticisms of the effect of capital punishment. The writings of Rene Girard (1986, 1987) analyzing scapegoating from the twelfth century to the present suggest that threats to social organization and norms evoke punitive responses that are transformed into beliefs and rituals that see the community as victimized and reinforce that sense of victimhood.

Now, while the model clearly recognizes that retributive impulses arise in individual psyches and are represented and expressed in the behaviors of individuals, there is also a social context. More than two decades ago, Dale Miller and I (Vidmar & Miller, 1979; see also Vidmar, 2000a) drew upon writings by the sociologists cited earlier as well as by Fritz Heider (1958) to insist upon the importance of norms in understanding retributive impulses. We argued that studies of retributive justice must consider motives involving group membership functions as well as punishment targeted at the offender. While rule offenders are punished in order to change the rule offender's belief system vis-à-vis the victim or societal rule, to reaffirm the self-image of the victim, to assert power over the offender, and to differentiate the offender from other members of the group, punishment also serves important functions bearing on group cohesion, particularly in solidifying support for the legitimacy of group norms among the nonoffending members of the group. Punishment vindicates societal rules; it helps to establish social consensus about the validity and legitimacy of the rules; it releases social tension about the rule violation through social comparison processes; and it serves to restore group cohesion. A second quotation from Durkheim (1893/1964, p. 102) is useful at this point, because it helps to set the stage for the discussion that follows:

> Crime brings together upright consciences and concentrates them. We have only to notice what happens, particularly in a small town, when some

> moral scandal has just been committed. They stop each other on the street, they visit each other, they seem to come together to talk of the event and to wax indignant in common. From all the similar impressions that are exchanged, for all the temper that gets expressed, there emerges a unique [public] temper.

Durkheim's observation has been endorsed by other sociologists. Thomas and Znaniecki (1945) concluded that in Polish peasant communities, punishment served the important purpose of obtaining consensus about the rules that were violated. Kai Erikson's (1960) study of the Salem witch trials explored the social context in which Puritan society was embedded. He concluded that a central dynamic of the phenomena that led to the trials was social change that threatened the normative values and beliefs of Puritan society. Punishment of alleged witches served to affirm the correctness of Puritan beliefs. Similar dynamics are evident in modern societies and affect retributive justice reactions. Consider the case studies described in section II.

II. Retributive Impulses and Infamous Crimes

R. v. Iutzi. In 1978, a two-year-old child was found dead in a rural county in Ontario (see Vidmar & Melnitzer, 1984). He had died of head injuries. The child's mother and father were both charged with second-degree murder, with each denying responsibility for the death and each accusing the other. Both parents had worked at a variety of menial jobs around the county, were frequent hitchhikers on rural roads, and were notorious for searching through trash heaps. A court order proscribed publication of any court proceedings, resulting in almost no mass media coverage of the event. Nevertheless, a survey of the county conducted on behalf of the defendants indicated that community gossip about the event was extensive and highly prejudicial to the accused. Community members discussed the case at home, with friends, and at work. The survey revealed that there was a clear sense of community shame and consternation that such a thing could happen in their community. The survey questions elicited comments like the following: "That happens in big cities [like Toronto or Detroit], not nice places like here"; and "It's a terrible shame on all of us." The survey also revealed strong beliefs that even if the mother had not killed the child herself, she should be held responsible and punished because "a mother is responsible for her child." Subsequently, some prospective jurors questioned in court not only revealed strong beliefs that one or both defendants were guilty, but also reinforced the survey findings that most members of the community believed that the killing had brought shame to the community.

The Mount Cashel cases. In 1989, a number of members and former members of the Congregation of Christian Brothers of Ireland, a Catholic religious order, were charged with sexually and physically abusing young boys who were under their care in the Mt. Cashel Orphanage in St. John's, Newfoundland, Canada, during the 1970s (see Ogloff & Vidmar, 1994). The allegations did not come to light until some of the victims were in their twenties. The government of Newfoundland set up a Royal Commission of Inquiry to ascertain if earlier reports of the abuse had been covered up by church authorities and government officials. The hearings were televised across Canada and shocked the nation when victims testified about the sexual abuse that took place in the orphanage. The former inhabitants of the orphanage described in graphic detail sexual acts perpetrated on them by various Christian Brothers (see Ogloff & Vidmar, 1994, for examples). The effects were most profound in St. John's itself, a community of approximately 160,000 persons, which is steeped in fishing and seafaring tradition and is often described as a small town wedded to continuity rather than to change. It is important for present purposes to indicate that the sense of historical continuity also involves uneasy currents of differences between Catholics and Protestants over religion and political and social influence. These divisions go back generations and remain deep, even in contemporary Newfoundland society.[1]

Not surprisingly, the uncovering of the Mt. Cashel events had profound effects on the St. John's community, causing extensive community discussion and numerous articles and letters to the editor in local papers (Vidmar, 1991). For instance, one newspaper article referred to "this blight on the social consciousness of Newfoundlanders." Another compared the Mt. Cashel events to Buchenwald and went on to state: "[T]he vast majority of us rejoice that justice has been done, and we

[1] Although a novel, Wayne Johnston's engrossing book *The Divine Ryans* (1990/1999) and the movie of the same title provide context for these sentiments and divisions in Newfoundland. In several interviews that I conducted in St. John's during August 2000 I learned that the repercussions from the Mt. Cashel cases continue to affect the community. The religious divisions remain, with Catholics still on the defensive. Although perpetrators were sentenced to prison, further criminal proceedings have continued sporadically. Most of the victims have not received promised financial compensation, and retributive feelings in the community remain high.

thirst for justice for those victims of the sadists and perverts who have allegedly desecrated the halls of Mt. Cashel with unspeakable acts of cruelty and licentiousness." Another described the need to purge and cleanse the community, another asserted a "moral chanchre eating away at the fabric of Newfoundland society," and another referred to "a collective moral collapse, a corruption of community." A survey of the community and interviews with St. Johns inhabitants in June 1991 uncovered high degrees of community discussion and gossip about the events and a desire to have the accused severely punished (Vidmar, 1991). However, the very strongest reactions came from Catholics rather than from Protestants. The perceived betrayal by their priests and the Christian Brothers ate at the very core of their faith and destroyed their private and public sense of religious and moral superiority over the Protestants.

Kidnaping and death on the shores of Lake Huron. In January 1988, Julie Bowers, a resident of Kincardine, Ontario, parked her car in front of a downtown doughnut shop and left her sleeping eleven-month-old boy in her unlocked car. When she came out a short time later, the child was missing. Frantic, she called the police and stated that her son had been kidnaped.[2] Local police in the town of 6,000 persons on the shores of Lake Huron contacted provincial police, and a provincewide search for the kidnapper was undertaken. A day later, the child was found in a snow-covered field outside of Kincardine, dead of hypothermia. After further police investigation, Bowers was charged with murder. Much was written about the case in the local and national papers, and much gossip occurred within Kincardine and surrounding communities. Much of it concerned the reputation of small-town Kincardine in the eyes of the world. Some examples are as follows: "This is perfect fodder for the rumor mill . . . and there are ugly rumors"; "almost everybody has prejudged the case"; "We're being belted left, right and center [by the media attention] – you'd think we were a big city or something." Strikingly, both the rumor mill and the local newspaper accounts continuously emphasized that while Julie Bowers's husband and family

[2] This summary is based upon unpublished data that was tendered in testimony in the Supreme Court of Ontario (Trial Division) in January 1989 on behalf of a defense motion to have the Bowers trial moved from Kincardine to Toronto, and on an unpublished student paper written by Liane Taylor in April 1990.

were lifelong residents of Kincardine, Julie was an outsider to the community: for example, "Mr. Bowers is a lifelong resident of Kincardine ... while Julie emigrated from England ten years ago."

The Violation of Community Values

In the three Canadian cases described here, it is important to observe that all of them involved homogeneous and relatively crime-free communities that were shocked by crimes that threatened perceived unique values of those communities. While Canadians outside those jurisdictions also exhibited punitive attitudes toward the alleged perpetrators, the responses in the local communities were exacerbated by the challenge to community values. Like the French towns observed by Durkheim, the Polish peasant societies described by Thomas and Znanecki (1902), and Erikson's Puritan communities, the reactions involved gossip and rumor that included attempts to achieve consensus about local values and to assert their legitimacy.

Although there is not space in this chapter to provide details, it is important to note that although the primary data in these cases were derived from randomly selected individuals responding to surveys, the questions assessed, with both closed- and open-ended items, the degree to which the respondents had discussed the case with others. Respondents' verbatim comments produced additional evidence, and in some cases the survey data were supplemented by in-depth interviews with members of the community and by newspaper accounts. The data strongly indicated that the attitudes were not developed in isolation, but rather through a process of social interaction.

These are not unique cases. Edward Bronson (1989) documented the effects of rumor and gossip involving a brutal interracial killing in a small Florida town. As one prospective juror in that community testified, "It was impossible to stop and have coffee in this county for three or four weeks without hearing about [the case]."

Similar reactions occur in more urban settings. The bombing of the Murrah Federal Building in Oklahoma in April 1995 with the loss of so many lives also caused discussion, rumor, and gossip throughout the United States (see Studebaker et al., 2000). It, too, threatened values and evoked calls for the death penalty as punishment. Importantly, citizens of Oklahoma City, where the bombing occurred, were stronger in their reactions and calls for justice than were members of other Oklahoma communities. Indeed, after reviewing testimony and survey data, Judge Matsch of the U.S. District Court concluded that "the entire state had become a unified community, sharing the emotional trauma of those who had become directly victimized" (*U.S. v. Mc Veigh*, 1997).[3] Denver, Colorado, further removed from the death, destruction, and personal knowledge of the victims, had the lowest level of reaction of the cities studied. These case studies strongly suggest that the more criminal events threaten group or community values, the stronger will be the punitive reactions and attempts to achieve consensus to reaffirm those values. The dynamics of this process are consistent with those analyzed in Allport and Postman's (1947) classic text, *The Psychology of Rumor*, and in Smelser's (1963) classic text, *Theory of Collective Behavior*.

Tyler and Boeckman (1997) explored the issue of moral factors in a different way in their examination of public support for California's "Three Strikes Law." In 1994, California voters passed a ballot initiative that mandated a life sentence for any person convicted of three felonies. The law, which is highly punitive in its intent and effect, is consistent with other punitive trends in American society (see, e.g., Ellsworth and Gross). Tyler and Boeckman conducted a survey involving a random sample of adults in northern California to test three hypotheses about bases of support for the three strikes law. The survey assessed crime-related concerns, concerns about social conditions, and social values. From these data two main concepts were compared: an instrumental judgment that the world is dangerous, and noninstrumental judgments.[4] These latter judgments involve beliefs that rule breaking is an affront to social and moral values and norms. Although the instrumental and symbolic expressions of attitudes were positively correlated, support for the three strikes initiative and expressions of general punitiveness were best predicted by concerns that the contemporary world lacks moral cohesion. Indeed, persons holding strong concerns about moral cohesion were willing to abandon procedural protections for persons charged with criminal offenses.

[3] In the decision to move the trial from Oklahoma (*U.S. v. McVeigh*, 1996) the court reviewed many sources of evidence and concluded that Oklahomans were "united as a family," that there was "extraordinary provocation of their emotions of anger and vengeance," that there was "a prevailing belief that some action must be taken to make things right again," and that the common reference in articulating these feelings was "'seeing that justice is done.'"

[4] Tyler and Boeckman use the term "relational" for these noninstrumental concerns.

Outsiders as Explanations of Deviance

An interesting facet of the Bowers "kidnaping" case involved many comments that Julie Bowers was not part of the community, that she was an outsider. The newspaper accounts and informal gossip continually stressed her English background, implicitly suggesting that a community insider would not have been capable of the act of leaving one's child to die in the woods. These expressions can be interpreted as attempts to explain why community norms were valid, that only an outsider would be likely to violate them. In the Iutzi case, the parents were notorious outsiders, social outcasts, long before their child was found dead. The mother was widely known for having mental problems and the father for excessive drinking and engaging in altercations. Thus, even though they were members of the community in one sense, they were clearly viewed as deviants.

Rene Girard's (1986, pp. 12–14) literary analysis of the scapegoating of individuals and of ethnic, religious, and racial groups from the time of the Black Death in the fourteenth century to the present day led him to conclude that persecutions by mobs generally occur in times of crisis, with an extreme loss of social order. There is an increased reciprocity of negative exchanges, a common reaction of ignoring any internal divisions in the community, and an assumption that there is a unitary view about internal normative states as contrasted with the outsiders, who are blamed for the conditions affecting the community.

Apostates and Retributive Justice

The deviant acts of the Christian Brothers posed a different problem than the Bowers and Iutzi cases. The Brothers had been viewed as leading members of the Newfoundland community, particularly among Catholics. Thus, for Catholics the crimes were a form of apostasy that threatened cherished beliefs about the Catholic subcommunity and increased judgments of their heinousness. Their reactions, relative to reactions of Protestants, were much more strident. Indeed, all of the quotations reported in my summary of the Mt. Cashel cases – the need to "cleanse the community," the "moral chanchre," the "collective moral collapse," and the "corruption of community" – are quotations from Catholic writers.

Lessons can also be learned from the death sentence imposed on author Salman Rushdie for publication of his novel *The Satanic Verses*.

(Pipes, 1990, 1998). Although there are complicated political issues entwined in the Rushdie matter, a basic element is the fact that fundamentalist Muslims are very sensitive about disparagement of their religion in Western media and tend to view fictional works in a singularly literal way. They view the power, wealth, and secularism of the West as threatening and as antithetical to their religious beliefs. The particular hatred toward Rushdie among fundamentalists can be ascribed to the fact that Rushdie "is, or was born, a Muslim; by rights he should protect the reputation of the Prophet Muhammad, not mock it" (Pipes, 1990, p. 14). Moreover, the fact that Rushdie lives in England and writes in the West "suggests that Rushdie has in some way joined the Christian world, that his allegiances have changed" (Pipes, 1990, p. 14). Rushdie may have further exacerbated hatred toward him by a statement in 1990 affirming his own Islamic faith but subsequently retracting the statement and referring to his enemies as "dinosaurs [who] represent absolutely nothing" (Pipes, 1998).

In short, social harm to the community is far worse when the deviant acts are committed by those who are in-group members than when they are committed by outsiders. The acts are viewed not only as a violation of rules, but also as an explicit rejection of the norms and values by one who is required by group membership to adhere to them. Thus, the acts are far more threatening to the members of the community who subscribe to the values. The reaction is further exacerbated when the acts come to the attention of outsider groups that are viewed as competing with the in-group, because the deviance lowers the in-group values relative to those of the out-group. Pipes (1990) suggested that if Rushdie had written his work from within the heartland of Islam and exclusively for a Muslim audience, the reaction against him might have been less extreme.

Excuses and Other Mitigating Conditions

Research into the social psychology of justice has centered on the effects of excuses and justifications, simultaneously drawing parallels to legal excuses and other mitigating factors in criminal responsibility (see, e.g., Darley & Zana, 1982; Heider, 1956; Schultz & Darley, 1991). The studies of individual reactions to hypothetical vignettes, most often involving college students as subjects, generally show that excuses and justifications mitigate retributive punitive reactions (see Vidmar, 2000a, for a partial review). In field studies these findings are not always supported.

In *R. v. Theberge* (1994), a thirty-seven-year-old male stalked, stabbed, and killed the teenage daughter of a local doctor in a northern Ontario community.[5] Notwithstanding the facts that until shortly before the crime the accused had been a responsible worker and family man with no prior criminal record, that he immediately ran to the police station to euphorically confess his crime, and that later evidence indicated that he suffered from a large brain tumor, many members of the community refused to consider any exculpatory evidence and insisted on severe punishment. Indeed, a survey of the community taken approximately four years after the killing found that 52% of the respondents would consider a trial verdict by judge and jury of not guilty by reason of insanity to be either unacceptable or very unacceptable. To be sure, some of those respondents were concerned about having the accused back in the community, but many expressed the reasoning that Theberge had to be held responsible and punished.

In *R. v. McGregor* (1991), the estranged husband of a Canadian government lawyer killed his wife in downtown Ottawa using a crossbow.[6] The killing occurred on the anniversary of the 1989 "Montreal massacre" in which fourteen female engineering students were killed by a lone gunman. Survey research in the Ottawa community a year later found that most respondents reported that they had discussed the McGregor case with family members, neighbors, or coworkers. Much like the *Theberge* case, 59% of respondents reported that they would consider a trial verdict by a judge and jury of not guilty by reason of insanity to be unacceptable or very unacceptable.

The insanity defense is a special case,[7] but the findings from these studies also raise important questions about the robustness of effects of other justifications and excuses when they are interpreted in the context of community sentiments about infamous acts. McGraw (1991) has provided a useful classification of excuses and justifications.

[5] This summary of the Theberge case is based on an unpublished affidavit dated May 20, 1994, that was tendered in a change of venue hearing in the Ontario Court of Justice (General Division) (North East Region).

[6] This summary is based on an affidavit submitted to the Ontario Court of Justice (Ottawa Region) in December 1992 with respect to a defense motion to have the accused tried by a judge alone, rather than by judge and jury.

[7] In considering the implications of the findings of these two studies, it must be noted that 17% of respondents in the McGregor case and 13% of respondents in the Theberge case stated that they would never accept an insanity defense in any case. Some of the reasons given involved utilitarian concerns that the defendant would be released and could kill again, but the predominant reason involved explanations that mental illness was no excuse to escape retributive punishment.

Excuses entail offering reasons involving past or present mitigating circumstances, horizontal or vertical diffusion of responsibility, and pleas of ignorance. Justifications involve explanations that the acts need to be seen in the context of past or present benefits that accrue from their results, comparisons to past acts or acts of others, comparisons to hypothetical situations, rules of fairness, and acts of conscience. Hamilton and Sanders (1992) explored some of these factors in their study of role responsibility in samples of Japanese and American respondents. They found that blame attribution is contingent on at least two factors, namely, what the person did and what the person was obliged to do.

Gibson and Gouws (1999) utilized these insights in a study of reactions to South Africa's Truth and Reconciliation Commission. During the years of apartheid, members of the government security forces and members of the forces struggling against apartheid committed many atrocities against the other side and against innocent civilians, sometimes on the barest of suspicions. In 1998, the Promotion of National Unity and Reconciliation Act, intended to heal the wounds of that era, provided for amnesty of persons of either side who confessed their deeds. In anticipation of the adoption of that act, Gibson and Gouws conducted a panel survey involving South Africans of all races in 1996 and 1997. They presented respondents with vignettes of a person who confessed to nefarious acts. Half of the respondents were told that the person was an agent of the South African Security Forces, and half were told that he was a member of the military wing of the African National Congress. Other factors were manipulated within each of these conditions: whether the person was a leader or a follower, whether the deaths caused by the person were those of combatants or of persons not involved in the struggle, and whether the perpetrator acted out of hatred toward the racial group or out of ideological motives. Respondents in the survey were asked to make judgments about the blameworthiness of the perpetrator and whether he should be forgiven or punished. Racial differences among respondents were complex, but Gibson and Gouws concluded that race affected the perceptions of the blameworthiness, with whites more forgiving of a government perpetrator and blacks more forgiving of an ANC perpetrator, albeit the processes by means of which the two groups ascribed blame did not substantially differ. Respondents who ascribed greater blame to the perpetrator were more likely to state that he should be punished rather than forgiven. Leaders were judged more responsible for their deeds than followers. However, one of the most interesting findings was that an excuse of noble motives (acting out of ideology rather than from racial hatred) did little to exonerate the violent acts. Finally, whether the victims of the acts were innocent civilians or combatants made little difference in judgments of blame or desire to punish. For our present purposes, the most important finding involves the racial differences between respondents, because it demonstrates that group membership mediates retributive responses.

The racial effects in the Gibson and Gouws study have a rough parallel to differences between African Americans and whites in their reactions to the O. J. Simpson case, which involved the brutal slaying of Simpson's wife and her friend Ron Goldman. In this instance, however, the pattern between whites and blacks was reversed. A survey by Graham, Weiner, and Zucker (1997) during the week following Simpson's arrest found that whites were more likely than African Americans to infer that Simpson was responsible for the crime, to feel more anger, and to believe that he should be punished in order to extract retribution, as well as to deter others. These racial differences in perceptions of the Simpson case were enhanced after Simpson's acquittal, indeed causing more than one commentator to conclude that "the trial clearly demonstrated how ethnicity trumps both gender and class in terms of group solidarity" (Cerroni-Long, 1996; and, generally, Barak, 1996; Linedecker, 1995).

Effects of Apologies and Remorse on Retributive Sentiments

Similar to studies of excuses and justifications, there is a body of social psychological literature that has examined the effects of apologies and expressions of remorse by rule violators on punitive attitudes (see Vidmar, 2000a, for a review). For instance, Robinson and Darley (1995) presented respondents with a set of scenarios involving a locksmith who considered stealing a set of coins or actually completed the theft. In some conditions, the locksmith was remorseful or attempted to return the coins. In these remorse conditions, respondents tended to report that he should not be held liable or, if liable, should not be punished. Kleinke, Wallis, and Stalder (1992) conducted an experiment that found that a rapist's expression of remorse lessened recommended prison sentences. However, a study by Taylor and Kleinke (1992) found that while expressions of remorse affected judgments about a drunk driver who caused a death, remorse had no effect on recommended sanctions. In an experiment involving a drunk driving death,

Robinson, Smith-Lovin, and Tsoudis (1994), however, found that expressions of remorse, as reflected in the culprit's nonverbal behavior during a confession, resulted in lesser sentences. The remorse affected respondents' perceptions of the offender's social identity.

Because of other factors, including the extreme emotions aroused in the Rushdie controversy, it is questionable whether Salman Rushdie would have placated his fundamentalist critics if he had offered a sincere and complete apology (see Pipes, 1990, 1998), but the fact that it was considered suggests the importance of apologies for the community that is offended by the rule violation. Apologies serve the dual purpose of helping to integrate the offender back into the group and helping to reaffirm the moral basis of the rule that was violated. Kai Erikson's (1966) research on Puritan society with regard to the witchcraft trials[8] is strongly supportive of Durkheim's thesis that deviance helps to define the boundaries of society and supplies a focus for group feeling. Throughout a period of social upheaval in which these events occurred, the trials of heretics and witches continually focused on confessions. Erikson observed that, strikingly,

> none of the executed witches had confessed and none of the many confessors had been executed. Far from establishing guilt, a well-phrased and tearfully delivered confession was clearly the best guarantee against hanging. (1966, p. 152)

Although there were other forces in play, it is apparent that confessions supported the validity of the Puritan's religious and other worldviews and thus reduced the tendency to levy the most harsh punishment.

The effects of confessions and remorse can be examined in a modern context with respect to jury verdicts for life imprisonment rather than capital punishment. Sundby (1998) studied thirty-seven sentencing hearings and conducted interviews with jurors who had participated in them. In nineteen cases the defendant received a death sentence, in seventeen the defendant received a life sentence without parole, and one case involved a jury that was split on the appropriate penalty. The main purpose of the research was to examine the effects of juror perceptions of remorse in sentencing decisions. While remorse can affect utilitarian considerations about potential dangerousness, the inter-

[8] Erikson also explored an arcane doctrinal controversy between factions of the Puritans and an invasion of Quakers into their communities that preceded the witchcraft trials and probably contributed to the social uncertainty.

views reflect a sense of anger about lack of remorse that strongly suggests retributive purposes of punishment. The interviews were with individual jurors, but unlike the subjects in many studies of punishment attitudes the jurors had deliberated as a group, and although they were charged with working within legal guidelines, their discussions reflected and considered community values. Sundby's research uncovered the fact that jurors closely scrutinize defendants' demeanor and behavior throughout the trial, and that these impressions play a significant part in their verdict on life or death. Strikingly, jurors reported that in almost all of the cases, both those resulting in a death verdict and those resulting in a life sentence verdict, defendants exhibited a lack of emotion during the trial. These included even the times when the prosecutor introduced horrific evidence depicting the crimes. The perceived attitudes of nonchalance, or even boredom, provoked astonishment and anger in the jurors. However, a distinguishing characteristic between death and life verdicts was arrogance and attitudes of defiance in the death sentence defendants: for example, "We saw no remorse – almost a cocky attitude." "The defendant acted as though the entire trial was a farce. It seemed as if he resented the fact that he had to be put through the process, as if we were inconveniencing him." (Sundby, 1998, pp. 1564–65) As one juror stated, the jury did not expect the defendant to beg for his life, but if he had indicated sorrow for what he had done the decision might have been for a life sentence. Another factor was denial or admission of responsibility for the killing. Verdicts for life sentences occurred in two cases in which the defendant admitted the killing and expressed regret in both substance and manner. In most of the remaining life cases, the jurors could not reach a consensus on the issue of remorse.

Remorse, whether in Puritan Salem or in modern-day murder trials, appears to serve the function of reaffirming moral values held by members of the community.

Failures to Punish

There is another issue about the social functions of retribution raised by the Julie Bowers case. What if the punishment is viewed as insufficient for the crime, or there is no punishment at all? Bowers's trial was moved from Kincardine to Toronto, and she was found not guilty.[9] The

[9] See note 1 for the source of this discussion.

trial produced evidence that was exculpatory of her. (There were indications that a relative may have taken the baby to teach Bowers a lesson about leaving children in cars, then panicked and left the baby in the woods when the police were called.) Nevertheless, many members of the Kincardine community remained convinced of her guilt and felt that a great injustice had occurred. There was even concern for her safety when she eventually returned to the community and to her husband.

In another case, *R. v. Reynolds* (see Vidmar, 2000b), a young woman was charged with stabbing her seven-year-old daughter eighty-four times in September 1997. She denied the killing, and there was opposing evidence that the daughter may have actually been killed by a pit bull.[10] Although community gossip was high at the time that the mother was charged, on the one-year anniversary of the child's death the local newspaper printed a memorial poem written by the mother that aroused such intense anger in some segments of the local community that a confidential memorandum by the police expressed concerns for Reynolds's physical safety. A survey of the community almost three years after the child's death (in June 2000) found many respondents remained frustrated and hostile because Reynolds still had not been punished for her alleged guilt.

In the Oklahoma bombing case, the retributive feelings among families of victims and persons with no familial connections to the victims are so great that even though co-conspirator Terry Nichols was sentenced to life imprisonment, prosecutors in the state of Oklahoma, responding to community pressure, moved for a separate trial that could result in a death penalty for Nichols (Rovella, 1998, 1999, 2000).

Similar social psychological dynamics appear to be behind the victim's rights movement in the United States and in other Western democracies (Fletcher, 1995; Mosteller, 1997; Sarat, 1997). The formal legal process in most countries has long preempted victims from participating in the prosecution of criminals. The process of punishment is seen as the duty of the state. However, the victim's rights movement is an attempt to move victims of crime back into an active role in the criminal trial by allowing victim impact statements during the trial. Much of the rhetoric in favor of the movement involves strong themes of retribution (see especially Sarat, 1997). The movement has some

[10] The trial was delayed for a number of legal reasons and eventually the charges against Reynolds were dropped (Appleby, 2001).

broad social and political support and has gained a foothold in case law that allows victim impact statements during the trial process. While reliable empirical research on the bases of community support for the movement is lacking, it is likely that the explanations for it reside in attitudes similar to those explored by Tyler and Boeckman (1997) regarding California's "Three Strikes Law," namely, affronts to moral values.

It is worth noting that Spanish law allows victims of crimes or their survivors to hire lawyers and prosecute cases as third parties in criminal trial proceedings, and something roughly similar is also built into recent Russian laws (Thaman, 2000). An interesting question is whether these procedures ameliorate victims' feelings that retributive justice is ignored by the legal process.[11] A related question is whether victim impact statements are a way of giving voice to retributive sentiments that reduce aggression and feelings of delegitimation of the legal process, or, as suggested by Sarat (1997), whether they instead have the potential to further inflame and create retributive behaviors by personalizing the legal process.

Similar issues arise with respect to proposals for "shaming penalties" as an alternative punishment for certain crimes (Brathwaite, 1989; see also Rosen, 1993; Will, 1996). Shaming penalties were common in colonial times (Rosen, 1993). The basic theory behind the contemporary proposals is to focus on developing the morality of the offender, eliminating the dysfunctional consequences of incarcerating legal offenders and allowing them to be integrated back into the community. Some judges have tried this form of punishment. In North Carolina, a judge sentenced a twenty-seven-year-old woman whose drunk driving accident resulted in a death to three years probation (Rochman, 1999). As part of the sentence the driver was required for the first year to carry a sign stating "I am a convicted drunk driver and as a result I took a life" in front of the courthouse one day each month. A newspaper photograph shows members of the victim's family watching the offender as she carried the sign. The family members expressed satisfaction with the penalty, stating that probation was insufficient. Shaming penalties have also been utilized in aboriginal communities, with some claimed success in reintegrating the offender and placating the victims.

[11] I am not unmindful that this question is relevant to the extensive literature on psychological catharsis (Feshback, 1984; Scheff & Bushell, 1984), but I do not have space to explore it in this chapter.

(Griffiths & Hamilton, 1996; Stuart, 1996). Shaming is part of traditional aboriginal culture, but there is evidence indicating that even in these societies shaming may be deemed insufficient for certain crimes and certain offenders because of the community's need for greater retribution. Thus, questions arise about the effectiveness of shaming as a substitute for other punishments intended to satisfy retributive needs, particularly when there are few cultural supports for it (Rosen, 1993).

III. Concluding Comments

Field studies of criminal cases provide evidence that retributive responses to criminal events are socially derived, or at least are mediated by social interaction. They also provide evidence that crimes have group as well as individual consequences, consistent with the theorizing of sociologists.

The experimental and field research of Nisbett and Cohen (1996) on the culture of honor is, I believe, directly relevant to the phenomenon of retributive justice (Vidmar, 2000a), because studies in that program of research directly examine cultural differences in behavioral reactions to violations of social norms. The research of Felson (1978; Felson & Tedeschi, 1995) and others (e.g., Bond & Kwok, 1991) examining reactions to insults involving group membership and group cohesion variables and the effects of cultural differences also provides insights about retributive responses. Research on group identity theory (e.g., Abrams & Hogg, 1990; Marques, 1990; Tajfel, 1978) may also provide insights into retributive justice. However, even in this research the emphasis has been on individual cognitive responses. Not only has the role of emotions been largely ignored, almost no research on retribution has focused on groups as a dependent variable. During the middle of the twentieth century, Kurt Lewin, Leon Festinger, Stanley Schachter, and many others had a genuine interest in group phenomena (see Cartwright & Zander, 1960). It seems clear that concepts like group cohesion and social comparison processes are very important in understanding how people respond to real-world violations of norms and values. Studies of retributive justice need to focus on these phenomena.

In my earlier chapter reviewing the dynamics of retributive justice (Vidmar, 2000a), I have argued that much more research needs to be addressed to retributive responses in noncriminal settings. In this call I have only echoed insights from Hans Kelsen (1943), Fritz Heider

(1958), and Hogan and Emler (1981). Retributive justice reactions occur in formal and informal settings as diverse as the nuclear family and large corporate organizations. In short, retributive justice is relevant to all aspects of human life. And the basic dynamics of retributive responses appear to be generally similar across all domains.

There are some methodological advantages to studying retribution in noncriminal settings. It is much easier to devise experiments to test the relationship between variables. As an example, it is most appropriate to conclude a chapter in a book honoring Mel Lerner by using one of his studies as an illustration.

Meindl and Lerner (1983) conducted an experiment in which a confederate engaged in an unprovoked verbal assault denigrating the intelligence and personal integrity of a student subject, the subject's assigned partner (whom the subject had not met and would not physically meet), or a third party. Subsequently, the subjects were provided the opportunity to punish the social norm violator, although at a cost of lost earnings to themselves. In the condition involving attacks against a third party, subjects avoided contact with the verbal abuser. If they were targets of the assault themselves, subjects were more likely to punish the offender, but the strongest punishment responses occurred when the partner had been the target of the attack. Meindl and Lerner explained these data by reference to the fact that the experiment made salient group norms requiring people to protect other group members. Meindl and Lerner's experiment can clearly be interpreted as a study of retributive justice, and, indeed, Lerner (1987) subsequently has done so.

I am tempted to devise here and now a thought experiment on how the Meindl and Lerner methodology could be adapted to look at group variables, in order to follow my own advice about thinking about group variables more broadly conceived. But that is for another day. The main goal of this chapter (see also Vidmar, 2000a) has been to provoke thought about the narrowness of focus that characterizes much of the experimental research on retribution. That narrowness includes a focus on individuals without considering group dynamics. It also includes a focus on cognitive elements to the exclusion of affective elements in retributive dynamics, particularly those aroused and reinforced through social interaction. And the narrowness also includes a focus on the antecedents of retributive impulses without consideration of the consequences after those impulses are aroused. Finally, most of the material reviewed in this chapter involves field studies and correlational research. The materials are a rich source of hypotheses, but lack the ability to rule out alternative explanations for observed phenomena. There is a great need for controlled experiments that can clarify cause-and-effect relationships in the dynamics of retributive justice.

REFERENCES

Abrams, Dominic, & Hogg, Michael (Eds.) (1990). *Social identity theory: Constructive and critical advances*. New York: Springer-Verlag.

Allport, Gordon, & Postman, Leo (1947). *The psychology of rumor*. New York: Holt.

Appleby, Timothy (2001). Mother cleared in killing of girl, 7. *Toronto Globe and Mail*, January 26, p. A1.

Barak, Greg (Ed.) (1996). *Representing O.J.: Murder, criminal justice and mass culture*. Guilderland, NY: Harrow and Heston.

Bond, Michael, & Kwok, Venus Chung (1991). Resistance to group or personal insults in an ingroup or outgroup context. *International Journal of Psychology, 26*, 83–94.

Braithwaite, John (1989). *Crime, shame and reintegration*. Cambridge: Cambridge University Press.

Bronson, Edward (1989). *The effectiveness of voir dire in discovering prejudice in high publicity cases*. Chico, CA: California State University, College of Behavioral and Social Sciences.

Cartwright, D., & Zander, A. (Eds.). (1960). *Group dynamics: Research and theory*. New York: Harper and Row.

Cerroni-Long, E. L. (1996). Ethnic expressive style and American public opinion: The O. J. Simpson case. In Greg Barak (Ed.), *Representing O.J.: Murder, criminal justice and mass culture* (pp. 34–47). Guilderland, NY: Harrow and Heston.

Darley, John, & Zanna, Mark (1982). Making moral judgments. *American Scientist, 70*, 515–521.

Durkheim, Emile (1967). *The division of labor in society* (George Simpson, Trans.). Glencoe, IL: The Free Press.

Ellsworth, Phoebe, & Gross, Samuel (1994). Hardening of the attitudes: Americans' views on the death penalty. *Journal of Social Issues, 50*, 19–52.

Erikson, Kai (1966). *Wayward Puritans: A study in the sociology of deviance*. New York: Wiley.

Felson, Richard, & Tedeschi, James (1995). *A social interactionist approach to violence: Cross-cultural applications*. In Barry Ruback & Neil Weiner (Eds.), *Interpersonal violent behaviors: Social and cultural aspects*. New York: Springer.

Feshback, Seymour (1984). The catharsis hypothesis, aggressive drive and the reduction of aggression. *Aggressive Behavior, 10*, 91–101.

Fletcher, George (1995). *With justice for some: Victim's rights in criminal trials*. Reading, MA: Addison-Wesley.

Garfinkel, Harold (1956). Conditions of successful degradation ceremonies. *American Journal of Sociology, 61,* 420–424.

Gibson, James, & Gouws, Amanda (1999). Truth and reconciliation in South Africa: Attributions of blame and the struggle over Apartheid. *American Political Science Review, 93,* 501–517.

Girard, Rene (1986). *The scapegoat.* London: The Athlone Press.

Graham, Sandra, Weiner, Bernard, & Zucker, Gail (1997). An attributional analysis of punishment goals and public reactions to O. J. Simpson. *Personality and Social Psychology Bulletin, 23,* 331–346.

Griffiths, Curt, & Hamilton, Roy (1996). *Sanctioning and healing: Restorative justice In Canadian aboriginal communities.* In Burt Galaway & Joe Hudson (Eds.), *Restorative justice: International perspectives* (pp. 175–191). Monsey, NY: Criminal Justice Press.

Hamilton, V. Lee, & Sanders, Joseph (1992). *Everyday justice: Responsibility and the individual in Japan and the United States.* New Haven, CT: Yale University Press.

Heider, Fritz (1958). *The psychology of interpersonal relations.* New York: Wiley.

Johnston, Wayne (1990/1999). *The divine Ryans.* New York: Broadway Books.

Kelsen, Hans (1943). *Society and nature.* Chicago: University of Chicago Press.

Kleinke, Chris, Wallis, Robert, & Stalder, Kevin (1992). Evaluations of a rapist as a function of expressed intent and remorse. *Journal of Social Psychology, 132,* 525–537.

Lerner, Melvin (1977). The justice motive: Some hypotheses as to its origins and forms. *Journal of Personality, 45,* 1–52.

(1981). *The justice motive in human relations: Some thoughts on what we know and what we need to know about justice.* In Melvin Lerner & Sally Lerner (Eds.), *The justice motive in social behavior* (pp. 11–38). New York: Plenum.

(1987). Integrating societal and psychological rules of entitlement: The basic task of each social actor and fundamental problem for the social sciences. *Social Justice Research, 1,* 107–125.

Linedecker, C. (1995). *O.J. A to Z: The complete handbook to the trial of the century.* New York: St. Martins Griffin.

McGraw, Kathleen (1991). Managing blame: An experimental test of the effects of political accounts. *American Political Science Review, 85,* 1133–1157.

Marques, Jose (1990). *The black-sheep effect: Out-group homogeneity in social comparison settings.* In Dominic Abrams & Michael Hogg (Eds.), *Social Identity Theory: Constructive and Critical Advances* (pp. 131–151). New York: Springer-Verlag.

Mead, George (1918). The psychology of punitive justice. *American Journal of Sociology, 23,* 577–602.

Meindl, James, & Lerner, Melvin (1983). The heroic motive: Some experimental demonstrations. *Journal of Experimental Social Psychology, 19,* 1–20.

Mosteller, Robert (1997). Victims' rights and the United States Constitution: An effort to recast the battle in criminal litigation. *Georgetown Law Review, 85,* 1691–1715.

Ogloff, James, & Vidmar, Neil (1994). The impact of pretrial publicity on jurors. *Law and Human Behavior, 18,* 507–525.

Pipes, Daniel (1990). *The Rushdie affair*. New York: Birch Lane Press Books.
(1998). Salman Rushdie's delusions and ours. *Commentary, 106*, 51–53.

Robinson, Dawn, Smith-Lovin, Lynn, & Tsoudis, Olga (1994). Heinous crime or unfortunate accident? The effects of remorse on responses to mock criminal confessions. *Social Forces, 73*, 175–190.

Robinson, Paul, & Darley, John (1995). *Justice, liability and blame: Community views of the criminal law*. Boulder, CO: Westview Press.

Rochman, Bonnie (1999). Sentenced to public shaming. Raleigh, North Carolina, *Raleigh News and Observer*, November 29, p. A1.

Rosen, Robert (1993). *Shaming penalties and social forgiveness deficit*. In F. Van Loon & K. Van Aeken (Eds.), *Sociology of Law, Social Problems and Legal Policy* (pp. 185–191). Amsterdam: Acco Leuven.

Rovella, David (1998). Making sure Terry Nichols is executed: A mixed verdict by federal jurors turns attention to planned state prosecutions. *The National Law Journal*, January 12, p. A6.
(1999). Nichols faces death a second time. *The National Law Journal*, May 24, p. A1.
(2000). It's Oklahoma's turn. *The National Law Journal*, July 31, p. A1.

Sarat, Austin (1997). Vengeance, victims, and the identities of law. *Social and Legal Studies, 6*, 163–189.

Scheff, Thomas, & Bushell, Don (1984). A theory of catharsis. *Journal of Research in Personality, 18*, 238–264.

Schultz, Thomas, & Darley, John (1991). *An information-processing model of retributive moral judgments based on "legal reasoning."* In William Kurtines & Jacob Gewirtz (Eds.), *Handbook of moral behavior and development* (Vol. 2, pp. 247–278). Hillsdale, NJ: Erlbaum.

Smelser, Neil (1963). *Theory of collective behavior*. Glencoe, IL: The Free Press.

Stuart, Barry (1996). *Circle sentencing: Turning swords into plowshares*. In Burt Galaway & Joe Hudson (Eds.), *Restorative justice: International perspectives* (pp. 193–206). Monsey, NY: Criminal Justice Press.

Studebaker, Chritina, Robbennolt, Jennifer, Pathak-Sharma, Maithilee, & Penrod, Steve (2000). Assessing pretrial publicity effects: Integrating content analytic results. *Law and Human Behavior, 24*, 317–336.

Sundby, Scott (1998). The capital jury and absolution: The intersection of trial strategy, remorse, and the death penalty. *Cornell Law Review, 83*, 1557–1598.

Thaman, Steven (1998). Europe's new jury systems: The cases of Spain and Russia, *Law and Contemporary Problems, 62*, 233–260.

Thomas, W. I., & Znaniecki, Florian (1943). *The Polish peasant in Europe and America, Vol. 2*. Chicago: University of Chicago Press.

Tyler, Tom, & Boeckman, Robert (1997). Three strikes and you are out, but why? The psychology of public support for punishing rule breakers. *Law & Society Review, 31*, 237–265.

U.S. v. McVeigh, 918 *Federal Supplement* 1467 (1996).

U.S. v. McVeigh, 955 *Federal Supplement* 1281 (1997).

Vidmar, Neil (1991). *Prejudicial pre-trial publicity in* R. v. Kenny. *Report and oral testimony*. Affidavit submitted to Supreme Court of Newfoundland, St. John's, Newfoundland, Canada.

(2001a). Retribution and revenge. In Joseph Sanders and V. Lee Hamilton (Eds.), *Handbook of Justice Research in Law* (pp. 31–63). New York: Plenum.

(2000b). *An assessment of public opinion in Frontenac County Ontario regarding* R. v. Louise Reynolds. Superior Court of Ontario, April 17, 2000.

Vidmar, Neil, & Melnitzer, Julius (1984). Juror prejudice: An empirical study of a challenge for cause. *Osgoode Hall Law School, 22*, 487–511.

Vidmar, Neil, & Miller, Dale (1980). Social psychological processes underlying attitudes toward legal punishment. *Law & Society Review, 14*, 565–602.

Will, George (1996). Restore the sting of shame. (Raleigh, North Carolina) *News and Observer*, February 1, p. 13A.

17. Just Punishments: Research on Retributional Justice

JOHN DARLEY

Famously, Lerner postulated that people have a belief in a just world. One expression of this belief is "what people get is what they deserve in life." I can still remember the excitement generated by his first set of experiments, which demonstrated that, if one saw a person getting a negative set of outcomes, one came to believe that there was something in the person's character or prior actions that in some sense caused the person to deserve those negative outcomes. To paraphrase, if bad things happened to a person, that person was somehow a bad person who deserved those outcomes. So the belief in a just world creates an inference warrant: if the world is such that people get what they deserve, then if they get a positive or a negative outcome, they must have deserved it.

In calling attention to justice and just worlds, Lerner called social psychology's attention to a large array of issues that had not received much attention in the psychology of the day. Many of those issues Lerner addressed in his own sustained and systematic research program; he encouraged the consideration of other issues in the justice arena by his equally sustained and generous efforts to create resources and publication outlets that would allow others to create theory and do research in the field as well. Lerner's leadership role is one for which we all can be grateful. I will express my gratitude to Professor Lerner in the typically constricted form of the social scientist, by describing some of the work I have been doing in the domain of retributive justice, one of a number of domains in the more general field of justice studies.

As this suggests, there are many domains in which justice is a central concept. That is, as we have increasingly attended to justice issues, we have discovered that there are a number of domains of human interaction about which we have a vocabulary of justice that we can deploy in each domain. Words such as "fair" and "moral" and "right" characterize discourse about justice; and words such as "unfair" and "immoral" and "wrong" are often the opening guns of justice talk. When we examine the domains in which such talk arises, I think we find a number of different spheres, linked together, yet with differing rule structures forming the systems we use to determine justice and injustice in the different areas.

Consider first the domain of "distributive justice." A person works hard and makes major contributions to a group product. What share of the profits does he deserve? Second, there is the domain of "retributive justice." A person deliberately inflicts terrible harm on another, or steals from another, or violates other criminal laws. What sort of punishment does he deserve? Another domain, close to but distinct from the retributive domain, involves a person needing to make good for the damages caused by his negligent actions. Here a person carelessly causes an accident that harms another. What sort of punishment does he deserve? Generally, he must give up resources to compensate the victim of his carelessness.[1]

That I could use the word "deserve" in all of the above cases, in the sense of moral deserts, documents the intuition that "justice" links all of these cases; however, it is important to notice that the rules we use to determine the answer to the question of what is deserved differ significantly in the three instances.

We can also ask "justice" questions about the fairness of the procedures used to determine the application of these substantive rule sets to the specific case at hand. Thus the existence of a new dimension of justice is signaled by the concept of "procedural justice." Procedural justice rules can be thought of as the rules we use to determine the application of the substantive rules that apply in the different domains of justice, and therefore as a separable segment of the rule set in each domain of justice. We have thus marked off three separable domains of justice, each with substantive and procedural rule sets.

The corner of the justice world in which I do research is the second domain, the set of substantive rules for punishing a person who

[1] Since the offender compensates the victim for the damages that his carelessness caused, it is tempting to call this category of justice "restorative justice." However, that term is used for a different conception of justice, in which the goal is to bring the offending person back into harmony with society, which may or may not be accomplished by payment for damages.

knowingly harms another. That is, the domain of justice that has concerned me for the last decade is the "retributive" one. A person knowingly harms another for no acceptable reason, and the harmed person and third-party onlookers judge that some punishment is in order for the actor. As others have remarked (Hogan & Emler, 1981; Vidmar & Miller, 1980), research on retributive justice, as compared to studies of distributive justice or procedural justice, has been scarce. Vidmar (this volume) comments that "new research on retribution is relatively sparse . . . the subject has received much less systematic attention by social scientists than it deserves."

So the research area is sparse, but not entirely empty. Some of the psychology and law researchers have been examining punishments for wrongdoing, and their work ought to be noted here. Lee Hamilton, often writing with Kelman (Kelman & Hamilton, 1989) or her collaborator Joseph Sanders, has done important work on how people think of sanctioning role superiors for the sins of their subordinates, and has then extended this to cross-cultural comparisons. Norman Finkel (1997) has systematically examined the punishment intuitions of ordinary people who might function as jurors and found them to make quite careful and subtle distinctions about issues that the legal system has difficulty dealing with. Peter Rossi and his associates (Rossi et al., 1974) have undertaken a major project for the National Institutes of Justice, comparing people's intuitions about the appropriate sentences for various crimes to the sentences proscribed by the federal sentencing commission. Still, one cannot deny the fact that, as compared to other domains of justice, much remains to be discovered about retributive justice; so I will turn to reporting on some work that I have done in the area.

Thinking about Retributive Justice

There is one characteristic of this retributive justice judgment, one marked for us by Heider (1957), that reveals a good deal about it. When an actor intentionally transgresses, that person "ought to" be punished. That is, that the transgressor should be punished is seen as objectively required; the interpersonal world has been put out of order, and it must be restored by punishment of the transgressor. As an indicator of this, noticed how puzzled a person is to be asked why the transgressor must be punished. The answer that will finally be given is that "the transgressor deserves the punishment."

That the person ought to be punished is not solely for the purpose of making the victim feel better, although it may do so. Even if the victim of the punishment, for some odd reason, does not call for punishment, we still think that punishment is appropriate. As this indicates, the punishment is seen as a societal requirement, not a personal one stemming from the victim. It is, on Heider's terms, an "ought force."

Of course, it is not possible to be too precise about this "ought force." As Vidmar (this volume) remarks, "[T]he psychological nature of 'oughtness' is typically a subjective phenomenon composed of an inchoate combination of cognitions and emotions whose separate elements cannot be isolated beyond words like 'justice' and 'injustice.'" Still, I would be surprised if the reader did not recognize the particular character of the force being described.

The Retributive Impulse Is Acquired Early

One partial explanation for why the impulse to punish seems impersonal and external may have to do with the remarkably early age at which moral thinking is acquired. Increasingly, psychologists who study moral development are converging on three as the age at which the first signs of the acquisition of moral impulses are shown. Some years ago, Ellen Klossen, Mark Zanna, and I demonstrated that children of five or six show quite sophisticated moral thinking patterns. First, children believe that transgressions require punishments; they assign punishments to various childish "crimes" at about the magnitudes that adults do. Second, they also understand the circumstances that reduce or negate the standard urge to punish.

The discovery that is important here centers around the concept of what are called "affirmative defenses." Ordinarily, when I intentionally harm another, I am at fault and deserve punishment; this is what we have called the "retributive impulse." However, it is possible that the social context surrounding the harming act is such as to reduce or even to eliminate the observer's judgment of the punishment deserved. This happens in two general ways. First, the circumstances may diminish the harmdoer's fault. For instance, if the act was in some way provoked by taunting or aggressive actions of the eventual victim, punishment is sometimes mitigated. Second, some contexts serve to make the harmdoer's act not just mitigated, but justified. Ordinarily, I must not kill you; but if you are attacking me with deadly force, and I cannot retreat, then braining you with the crowbar that I happen to have in my hand is justified. (The legal codes allow the self-defensive use of deadly force only when retreat is impossible, and the force is proportional to the attack. We have demonstrated that the rules that members of our culture hold are much less restrictive [Oleson and Darley, 1999].)

As we (Darley, Klosson, & Zanna, 1978) have shown, young children – kindergartners and first graders – can comprehend the information that creates excusing or justifying conditions for a harmdoing action, and when they perceive that those conditions are present, they reduce or eliminate the punishments they assign to the perpetrators of these actions to a degree not discriminably different than the punishment reductions given by adults. We have presented (Darley & Zanna, 1982) a sketch of how these excusing conditions, central to a theory of retributive punishment, are organized. Thomas Shultz and I (Darley & Shultz, 1990) have reviewed the literature on the acquisition of moral judgments and suggested that they are taught by the rule-enforcing practices of day care and early elementary school teachers; they are learned by children in social exchanges with peers that closely resemble court trials, with the authority mixing the roles of prosecutor and judge.

Moral principles, then, are learned young, and moral transgressions are associated with punishments at an early age. The two great psychologists who pioneered the study of moral judgments, Piaget and Kohlberg, tended to treat the development of moral reasoning as dependent on the development of general logical reasoning. More recently, psychologists have moved away from the program of a generalized development of reasoning systems that transcend domains in which the reasoning is displayed toward "domain-specific" learning of the rules of different physical and social arenas. Moral reasoning – justice thinking, for our present purposes – we would suggest is a domain with its own rules of reasoning, and it is one that is learned early. This may be why each of its tenets, particularly the obligation to have transgressors justly punished for their transgressions, seems such a natural and objective obligation, an obligation on the system rather than on specific players within it.

What Is the Essence of the Offense?

So at quite an early age, children learn that crimes require punishments. But what constitutes a "crime"? Legal philosophers have thought a great deal about this, without coming to any undisputed conclusions. Perhaps we can extract some clarity if we examine how ordinary people think about such questions. What exactly is it that a person does, or plans, that counts as a crime deserving punishment? One aspect of this question was called to my attention by Paul Robinson, an expert on criminal law, with whom I collaborate on retributive justice matters (Robinson & Darley, 1995). Begin by accepting the notion that a paradigmatically criminal action is one in which a person intentionally inflicts a harmful action, which he knows is morally wrong, on another. What is the essence of criminality here? When do we feel that the person's actions call forth the retributive justice motive, the impulse to punish that we have made so much of? In legal terms, the question concerns the core of the offense. On psychological terms, we ask about the essence of the thought, or behavior, or intention that calls forth the retributive motive in the observer.

The Subjectivist and Objectivist Stances

One place that we can look to for distinctions that might be useful is the legal code. Legal thinking gives us two answers to this question, and they are strikingly different ones. The "modernist" formulation one is called the subjectivist stance, and the older, more traditional one is called the objectivist stance. The difference between the two formulations is most vividly illustrated by their sharply competing definitions of when "attempt" is criminalized, when one has committed an "attempt" crime that deserves punishment. For the subjectivist formulation, one has committed an attempt offense when one has formed the "settled intent" to commit a crime. Interestingly, one of the arguments for the subjectivist stance was that it was the psychologically sophisticated one. Intent is what matters to the ordinary person, and so was considered the appropriate criterion to have instantiated in legal codes.

Since observers cannot read minds, the Model Penal Code (American Law Institute, 1962), which has adopted the subjectivist stance, uses the "substantial step" test. Once a person has taken some step that externalizes the internal settled intent, then an attempt crime has been committed. So, for a person who contemplates burglary, investigating the premises, or searching out a key that might unlock the premises, fits the subjectivist definition of attempted burglary, and the person does time in jail if caught doing these things. (Does time, that is, if caught in a state that has adopted this aspect of the Model Penal Code – not all have.)

How much time in jail? A lot. The Model Penal Code is remarkably thorough in its subjectivism. Since the essence of a crime is forming the settled intent to commit it, there is no important difference between an attempt and a completed crime. Therefore, the penalty for an attempted crime is simply set equal to the penalty for the completed crime.

The objectivist formulation, by contrast, centers its concerns on the actual occurrence of the harm. This standard holds that it is the bringing about of the harmful consequences of an act that is the core of criminal conduct, and liability for that harm is based on the attribution of responsibility for this harm to a given actor. The older common law tradition instantiated this position, and used the "dangerous proximity" test to determine attempt liability. This test is a mildly compromised version of what a strict occurrence of harm stance would demand. The strict occurrence of harm stance is the "no harm, no foul" rule of sports carried into everyday life. The logic that modifies it down to the dangerous proximity test is as follows. It would be ridiculous to maintain that a person who has taken so many steps toward the commission of a crime that he is on the verge of committing it has done nothing wrong. It would also be needlessly risky for innocent people. So the burglar, hiding for hours in a room with a cash safe in it, his burglar tools at the ready, has committed attempted robbery; we don't require that the police wait around until he has actually opened the safe and taken the cash for him to be guilty of an offense.

There are two points to note here. First, there is a large gap between the subjectivist and objectivist definitions of attempt. (In fact, several jurisdictions, unhappy with both formulations, have chosen to criminalize attempt somewhere between the extremes marked by the two competing formulations.) Second, true to the emphasis on objective harm, the older, common-law-influenced objectivist stance assigns a lower sentence to an attempt at the crime of X that it would give to a person carrying out the crime of X, which makes the gap between the two stances even wider (Darley, Sanderson, & LaMantia, 1996).

Subjectivist–Objectivist Studies

While I don't want to go into a great deal of descriptive detail here, I think the reader can see that the research designed to determine which of these two stances is found in the naïve psychology of ordinary people is not hard to carry out. One simply gives a respondent a number of short scenarios (randomly ordered, the respondent judges

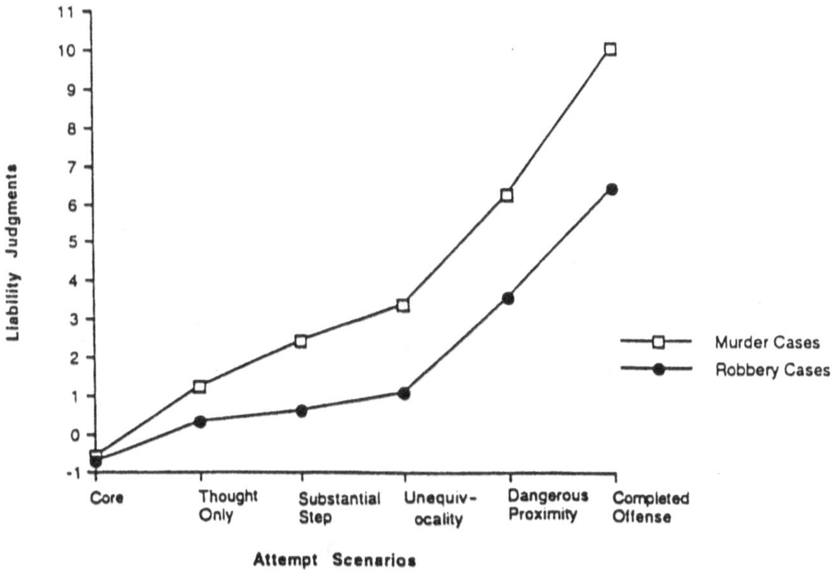

Figure 17.1. Liability judgments for attempt scenarios.

a sample or even all of the scenarios) and asks him or her to decide which represent criminal conduct and to assign penalties to those judged criminal. We have done such a study in the realm of attempt liability (Darley et al., 1996) Figure 17.1 shows a graph of the results. The scenarios are arrayed along the horizontal axis, and come closer to completion as we move to the right of the graph; the far right case is the completed offense. We tested two sets of scenarios: In one set the completed crime was murder; the other set of scenarios described a person taking more and more steps toward the completion of a robbery. As Figure 17.1 shows, the murder case shows a more steep rise in punishment assigned, but that is because it is a more serious crime. Figure 17.2 displays liability assigned at each attempt stage as a percentage of the liability assigned to the completed crime. There is a minor tendency to assign more severe punishments to intermediate levels of punishment for murder than for robbery, and this tendency is significant, but does not alter the general pattern of responses.

The "thought only" scenario is slightly misnamed; in it, the person decided to commit the offense. The next scenario involved the person taking what is called a "substantial step" toward the offense; it is at this point that the subjectivist stance assigns criminal liability, and does so

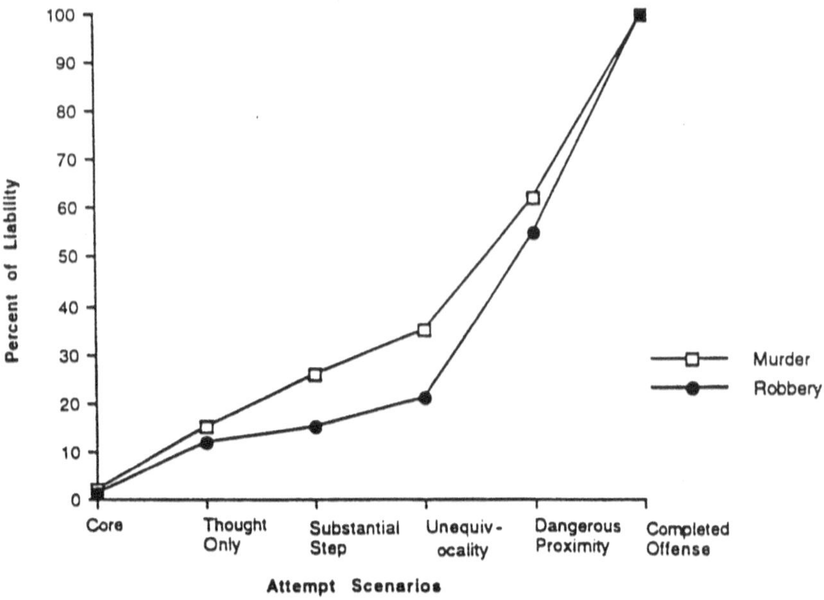

Figure 17.2. Percent liability of attempt scenarios.

with a severity equivalent to that assigned to the completed offense. Two steps later, we find the actor "in dangerous proximity" to completing the offense. It is at this stage that the objectivist stance criminalizes the offense, but still assigns it a penalty lower than that given to the completed offense.

Examining these results, we ask whether the subjective or objective formulation best fits our respondents' intuitions, and the answer is obvious. We see that the clear winner is the older, common law position that weights heavily the occurrence or near occurrence of the harm. The subjectivist stance would criminalize to the extent of the completed offense roughly at the scenario marked "substantial step." From then on, we would see a flat, high assignment of punishment equal to that given to the completed offense, rather than the gradually climbing assignments that the respondents give. Still, the subjectivists are not entirely wrong about people's thinking: Examining the left hand side of the graph, we notice that even the substantial step case generates a desire on the part of the modal respondent to punish the actor. That is, although people do not seem to think that forming a settled intent to commit a crime is everything, in the sense of calling for a punishment equivalent to that for the completed crime, neither do they think that it is nothing. This suggests a compromise formulation: People are subjectivist with respect to what the legal codes call the minimal requirements of action that generates liability. Externalizing a settled intent to commit a crime warrants punishment. However, people are objectivist with respect to the grading of the offense; the nearer to completing the crime the person comes, the higher the punishment he warrants.

In another study (Robinson & Darley, 1998), we had people respond to another set of scenarios that tested this complex formulation. In it, we examined several derivations from the objectivist stance that we thought would not correspond to our respondents' judgments. Three of the scenarios looked at closeness of harm; they varied in how close a murder came to completion, and in all three instances the actor came very close to committing the murder. We suspected that the respondents might see these cases as essentially similar and assign them the same punishments.

In one instance, a person whose father had been prosecuted and jailed for income tax evasion shoots and kills the prosecutor; in another case he shoots but misses; and in yet another case he is grabbed by a security guard as he takes aim.

Our expectations were wrong. Our respondents assigned a lower sentence to the security guard case than to the successful killing. Interestingly, the shoot-and-miss case was assigned an even lower sentence. The psychology that lies behind differentiating these two cases is not completely clear: Is it that people simply assign punishments according to how close the offense is to the prototype of the crime, or do they have some notion that even at the last moment, the offender who shot and missed had a sudden intrusion of nonmurderous intentions that conflicted with the murderous ones? While further research might clarify this, it is clear from this study and the attempt study that people care in their grading stance about nearness to completion even in the last stages of nearness to harm.

So far, the objectivist stance seems to be triumphing over the subjectivist one. But the scenario set in this study also included some cases that tested the further reaches of the objectivist stance, and enabled us to have another look at our suggestion that people were subjectivist with respect to minimal requirements for liability. The scenarios here are based on actual common law formulations in which the actor would not be found liable, and that now strike us as intuitively wrong. For instance, if you and I conspire to kill my rich uncle, and, unfortunately for my purposes, you are an undercover agent rather than a hit man, the common law holds that no conspiracy exists. Why? Because conspiracy requires real bilateral agreement between the two of us; there was no danger of harm unless the agreement was bilateral. Or if I purchase auto repair parts from an obviously illegal chop shop, but the chop shop is in fact a sting operation by the local police, who are selling legally obtained parts, I have committed no "receiving of stolen goods" offense even though I intended to do so, because the goods I received were not in fact stolen.

Those cases would be reacted to in one way if the respondent were objectivist with respect to minimum requirements, and in another way if he or she were subjectivist. Here we expected that respondents would not be objectivists with regard to minimal requirements for offenses. I, who commissioned the hit on my rich uncle, am guilty of conspiring, and I get a substantial penalty for doing so, even if I conspired with an undercover agent. I, who bought what I thought were stolen goods, am guilty of "receiving stolen goods," even if I purchased them from a sting operation.

And that is how the respondents judge these cases. Results showed that respondents thought that the actor should be punished for his offenses, and that they were genuine offenses, even though the punishments that they would assign were not as high as those they would assign to more prototypical instances of the offenses.

Conclusions on the Essence of the Crime

To summarize: Citizens are subjectivist with regard to minimal requirements for an offense – taking serious steps toward committing a crime deserves punishment. However, they are objectivist with regard to the punishment that is deserved by the offender – the nearer the actor is to completion of the offense, the more the punishment approaches the magnitude appropriate to an actor who had competed the offense.[2] They do not see the formation of the intent to commit a

[2] An interesting developmental issue arises here. How do parents punish children who intend to bring about harms, and how might this relate to the mixed subjectivist–objectivist stance displayed by most adults in our research? Some speculative remarks are possible, much in need of examination by research.

The task of the parent is likely to include educational goals, triggered into action more often than retributional ones. A parent who detects in a child the intention to harm another, a pet or a younger sibling, is in a complex position vis-à-vis proving that

crime as equal to the commission of that crime, the stance taken by the Model Penal Code.

We might pause here to reflect on what the consequences might be for a society in which the highly prestigious American Law Institute recommends the adoption of a subjectivist definition of the essence of a crime that markedly deviates from the intuitive definitions held by the citizens of that society. Elsewhere (Robinson & Darley, 1997) we have theorized about those consequences, consequences that we think are destructive to citizens' willingness to voluntarily abide by such laws. But here I want to make a different point: The response patterns of our respondents tell us something that is genuinely psychologically important about retributional justice. Taking steps toward the commission of an offense is reprehensible, and triggers the assignment of punishment – but not a punishment equivalent to the punishment given to the completed offense. The subjectivist stance, which holds that settled intent to commit an offense is the moral equivalent of completing the offense, on first examination seems a "psychological" one, one that elevates what really matters over the details of whether the crime actually came off successfully. But the data patterning reveals that people's true intuitions go elsewhere. This, I think, is an important discovery about the psychology of justice.

What Is the Motivation for Punishment?

These studies, and others we have done, tell us the patterning of the punishment assignments that citizens in our culture give to intentionally committed offenses. It then occurred to us to ask *why* it was that people assigned these punishments. What is the source of the intuition, that we all seem to hold, that transgressions require or deserve punishment?

the harm was actually intended and would be carried out. Also, the parent is not necessarily sure that the child was aware that the intended actions would have harmful effects. In these doubly ambiguous circumstances, the parent is likely to trade off punishing the child for educating the child regarding the hurtful consequences of the actions that the parent intuited, but could not prove, that the child intended. However, as the harm that the child intended becomes more and more clearly established by the child's taking a series of preparatory actions toward inflicting that harm, the parent's response is likely to include components of punishment as well as admonition. This would create a punishment gradient rather like the ones our subjects reported that they would apply.

An actor intentionally commits a serious harm. He assaults an older woman and takes her purse, or he robs the church poor box. We all would wish to inflict punishment on this actor, but *why* do we wish to do so? When a perpetrator is punished for committing a harm, what is the justification for that punishment in the mind of the punisher? There are some remarkably interesting legal policy issues that arise from this question (for a preliminary discussion of them, see Robinson & Darley, 1997), but in this forum, our attention is drawn to the fact that it is a question of considerable fundamental interest to those concerned with the psychology of justice.

There are, of course, a number of ways that persons commit offenses: the child who does not know that the act is an offense; the visitor from another culture who, following her culture's rules, commits what is an offense within the host culture; the accidental "killer" who sets in motion a chain of events that leads to the death of a person. However, we wanted to focus on what we take to be the prototype of an intentional harmful act, knowingly committed, by a knowledgeable member of the culture. We wanted, in other words, to ask why it was that we have the impulse to punish a person who has knowingly committed a "crime."

By now the reader will have realized that our strategy is to draw on philosophical and legal-philosophical sources for initial suggestions for answers. There is a long tradition of legal philosophy, going back to pre-Platonic era, that considers these sorts of questions and that supplies a starting point for our inquiry. The classic candidates for justifications for punishments are five: just deserts, rehabilitation, individual deterrence, deterrence of people in general, and incapacitation.

In the United States, there has been a rapid and dizzying process of transition among these motives as cultural justifications for criminal sentences. After a brief flirtation with rehabilitationist considerations, the process now seems to have settled on a mix of deterrence considerations, which warrant increases in punishments for any offense deemed to be on the rise, and a final resort to incapication considerations, requiring essentially lifelong prison sentences for those who commit an offense for a second or third time. (See Robinson & Darley, 1997, for a review of the transitions.)

Classically, since Bentham, Anglo-Saxon law has based punishments on a deterrence justification. For Bentham, it was obvious that "general prevention ought to be the chief end of punishment, as it is its real justification" (Bentham, 1962, p. 396). "If the apparent magnitude, or rather value of the pain be greater than the apparent magnitude or value of the pleasure or good he expects to be the consequence of the act, he will be absolutely prevented from performing it." The Model Penal Code, published by the influential American Bar Association in the 1960s, regards deterrance as the appropriate goal of punishment.

However, not all agree that deterrance is the obvious principle around which to build a penal system. Kant (1952, pp. 446–7) argued for a just deserts approach. "Punishment can never be administered merely as a means for promoting another good . . ." Punishment ought to be "pronounced over all criminals proportionate to their internal wickedness." Other societies, notably the current government of China, have espoused a rehabilitionist stance for many offenses, involving the reeducation of transgressors. (One notices that these "reeducational facilities" often are quite grim and involve beatings and other measures that seem to have more deterrence or deserts-based motives.)

But theory aside, and setting aside the vagaries of legislators' attempts to gain votes by being "tough on crime," why do ordinary people punish intentional transgressors? Are they seeking to deter, to incapicate, or to give a person what "he justly deserves?" We have begun a set of studies on this issue.

The first question we had to settle was how to extract people's beliefs. If one simply asks people whether they agree with these various motives for punishment, our experience is that they generally do agree with all of the motives. All of the motives sound socially desirable, and it is possible that people can think of instances in which they would sentence for each of those reasons. The fact of this general agreement is important, but it may reflect a conventional wisdom rather than what people would do when faced with specific cases of intentional transgression. Given this, we decided to present respondents with specific cases and to examine their motives for punishments. We used what is now called a "policy-capturing" approach to do this. We varied circumstances of the cases in ways that should affect punishment assignments, depending on the motive that the respondent held for assigning punishment.

A Study Pitting Just Deserts against Incapacitation

In the first study, we contrasted the incapacitation motive with the just deserts motive. Again, we will refer the reader elsewhere for details of the methodology (Darley, Carlsmith, & Robinson, 2000) and present just enough detail so that the reader can understand what was done, and what was found. We gave respondents a number of scenarios to react to, which they did by deciding whether the actor in the scenario was guilty of a crime and, if so, what liability (punishment) he deserved.

To develop the dimensions of variation chosen, we reasoned as follows: In a just deserts perspective, the seriousness of the harm committed is a major determinant of the sentence, assuming that the crime was intentionally committed. A number of studies have scaled the differential seriousness of various categories of crimes (Rossi et al., 1974; Warr, Meier, & Erickson, 1983) and demonstrated that a strong cultural consensus exists. Murder is a more serious offense than embezzlement, for instance; and, in general, crimes of violence against individuals are seen as the most serious crimes. As this suggests, the moral outrage the harmful act provokes determines the magnitude of the punishment assigned to it.

The incapacitation stance suggests that a wrongdoer's likelihood of committing future offenses should be the primary determinant of the assigned punishment. So we punish a person in the present to some extent based on our predictions of what he will do in the future. Punishment can be used for this purpose because in our culture punishment tends to be time in prison; while in prison, a person will not commit more crimes against the general populace. In the incapacitation stance, the respondent is trying to solve an attributional question: "Given what I can infer about the person, what is the likelihood that he will commit future harm?" Thus, information that allowed attribution of characteristics likely to predict repeat offending, such as a history of past offenses, would predict severity of punishment. Seriousness of the crime committed, aside from the attributional information that it provided, would be less important. From an incapacitation stance, a one-time offense that is very unlikely to be repeated would not provoke a severe punishment. More importantly, if the person is likely to repeat an offense, then a long time in prison is called for to prevent recidivism. Characteristics of the perpetrator rather than of the crime become the major determinant of the sentence.

Again, we did a scenario study. Respondents read and assigned sentences to many scenarios, with different levels of criminal seriousness crossed with no or several commissions of similar crimes in the past. The path analysis of the results is presented in Figure 17.3. As can be seen, the checks on the manipulations indicate that the manipulations

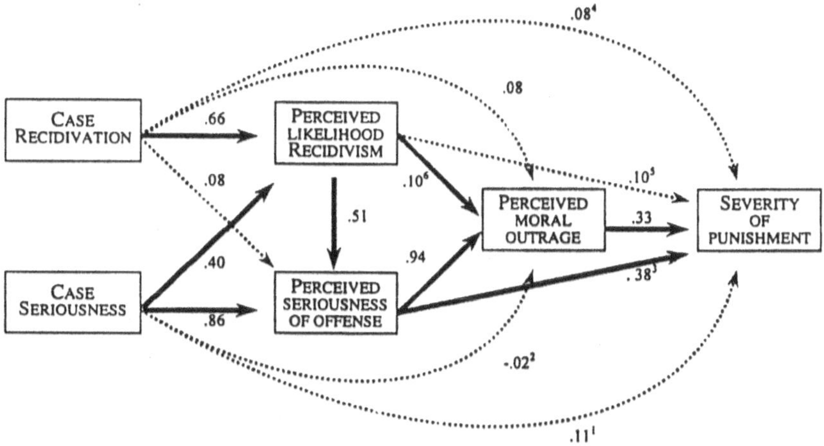

Figure 17.3. Regression path model predicting default sentence severity recommendations. Superscripts 1–6 represent mediated relationships, all others are zero-order correlations. All bold lines are significant, $p < .005$.

were successful. Respondents processed the information about criminal seriousness and likelihood of recidivism. But the perceived likelihood of recidivism did not much affect the sentence given; it did affect the degree to which the respondent was morally outraged by the crime, but it did not have a direct effect on the severity of punishment assigned. By contrast, the perceived seriousness of the offense strongly affected the degree to which the respondent was morally outraged by the crime, and both perceived seriousness and moral outrage directly affected the severity of punishment assigned.

We took this to be evidence that the just deserts–relevant variation was the one that caused sentences to vary, and we interpreted this as supporting the conclusion that people impose sentences largely from just deserts considerations rather than incapacitation ones. A second finding supported this conclusion. We had the respondents twice more assign sentences to all ten cases, once from a just deserts perspective and once from an incapication perspective. Their first, uninstructed sentencing pattern closely resembled the one they gave under the just deserts instructions, and did not much resemble the one they gave in response to the incapication instructions.

We wanted to test the limit of the triumph of just deserts over incapacitation, so we created one more case, in which we made it clear that an actor killed another person because the actor had a brain tumor. This case does not fit the prototype of an actor freely committing a known wrong; in a very important sense, the brain tumor was the cause of the murder, not the actor's will. (Pilot testing made clear that we needed to add quite a bit of detail validating the physical existence of the tumor and its role in causing the violence, to bring people to read the murder as purely tumor-caused, rather than as a causal mix of internal volition and the external force of the tumor.) In this case, 93% of the subjects decided against the standard just deserts punishment and assigned the person to a hospital-like facility where he would remain as long as the tumor made him dangerous.

Just Deserts Pitted against Deterrance

We have recently completed a second study (Carlsmith, Darley, & Robinson, 2000) pitting deterrance considerations against just deserts motives. To capture people's determinants of punishment severity, we asked respondents to evaluate harmdoing cases and to assign the severity of punishments that the cases called for. We manipulated the seriousness of the crime and its motive, as well as some "deterrent-relevant" characteristics of the offense, and measured the respondents' sentence assignments. Given the criticisms possible of within-subjects designs, we conducted this one as a between-subjects design.

To increase the generalizability of the results, we created three versions of the stimulus materials, specifically varying different versions of information relevant to just deserts and deterrance.

Results pooled across these variations showed that there was no main effect for deterrence, but that there was a large effect for deservingness. In the low punishment deservingness condition, the average punishment was 4.1 on a seven-point scale, whereas in the high punishment deservingness condition, the average was 5.4. These results suggest that in recommending sentences, people are highly sensitive to just deserts considerations and insensitive to deterrence considerations.

A just deserts motivation is presumed to be driven by concerns about the seriousness of the crime and the moral outrage it evokes. We performed a mediational analysis (Kenny, Kashy, & Bolger, 1998) to show that the effects of our deservingness manipulation operated through these psychological mediators. The critical step is to show that the direct effect between the independent variable and the dependent variable is zero after controlling for the effect of the mediator. The direct effect of deservingness on severity of punishment (.48) is reduced to

–.01 when perceived seriousness and moral outrage are controlled, establishing complete mediation. From all of this, we conclude that just deserts considerations dominate over deterrance considerations when one is sentencing a specific individual for a specifically described crime.

Conclusions

One way of describing what I have been doing is to say that I have been studying the psychology of punishment. As I have done more worth in this area, I have found it increasingly ironic that, for a field that includes thousands of studies of punishment within the operant conditioning framework, we have done so little on the psychology of the person delivering the punishment. What do we seek to do when we punish another? As my studies followed one another, I found that it was the later ones, those done when I increasingly realized how little we knew, that were the most basic or fundamental. Reversing my chronological path through the studies I have presented, here is how I would outline their findings.

We punish others who have committed prototypic "crimes" – intentional infliction of wrongful, immoral harms on others – because we wish to give the actor his justly deserved punishment for the wrongful action he took. While we may think that the magnitude of punishment we inflict might deter others from committing similar acts, and might even deter the offender in the future, that is not our core purpose in punishing. Our purpose is to inflict a punishment proportionate to the magnitude of the wrong the offender has committed.

This is sometimes called a retributionist stance, and some equate it with support for the death penalty, but this is not a necessary equation. A person can judge that the punishment for an offense should be proportional to the moral gravity of the offense, but not identical to it, and thus not require the death penalty even for one who has murdered another.

Committing the wrongful act matters, as opposed to just thinking about it. We understand that people have intentions, and we think forming a settled intent to wrongfully harm another deserves punishment, but much less punishment than we would inflict on a person who completed the wrongful act. We are surprisingly "objectivist" in our judgments here; even when someone shoots to kill, and a passing wind deflects the bullet, we do not sentence the shooter to the penalties we would give to a windless, and therefore successful, murderer.

Young children "get it" in the sense that they punish transgressions with penalties whose magnitudes are close in relative severity to adult punishments. Do they do so for reasons of just deserts? Could this connect to Piaget's old notion of immanent justice, in which the natural world magically acts to inflict punishments on rule transgressors? This would be an interesting discovery of a possible origin for the just deserts orientation, one that might explain the impersonal nature of Heider's postulated "ought force."

The chance to think about and do research on such issues, issues that Lerner invited us to reflect on, has given me great pleasure over the years.

REFERENCES

American Law Institute (1962). Draft of a Model Penal Code. Philadelphia: American Law Institute.

Bentham, J. (1962). Principles of penal law. In John Bowring (Ed.), *The Works of Jeremy Bentham* (p. 396). Edinburgh: W. Tait.

Carlsmith, K., Darley, J., & Robinson, P. (2000). Just deserts vs. deterrance as motives for the punishment of transgressors. Unpublished manuscript, Princeton University.

Darley, J. D., Carlsmith, K. M., & Robinson, P. H. (2000). Incapacitation and just deserts as motives for punishment. *Law and Human Behavior, 24*, 659–683.

Darley, J. M., Klosson, E. C., & Zanna, M. P. (1978). Intentions and their contexts in the moral judgments of children and adults. *Child Development, 49* (1), 66–74.

Darley, J. M., Sanderson, C. A., & LaMantia, P. S. (1996). Community standards for defining attempt: Inconsistencies with the Model Penal Code. *American Behavioral Scientist, 39* (4), 405–420.

Darley, J. M., & Shultz, T. R. (1990). Moral rules: Their content and acquisition. *Annual Review of Psychology, 41*, 525–556.

Darley, J. M., & Zanna, M. P. (1982). Making moral judgments. *American Scientist, 70* (5), 515–521.

Finkel, N. J. (1997). Commonsense justice, psychology, and the law: Prototypes that are common-senseful, and not. *Psychology, Public Policy, and Law, 3*, 461–489.

Kelman, H. C., & Hamilton, V. L. (1989). Crimes of obedience: Toward a social psychology of authority and responsibility. New Haven, CT: Yale University Press.

Heider, F. (1958). *The psychology of interpersonal relations*. New York: Wiley.

Hogan, R., & Emler, N. (1981). Retributive justice. In M. J. Lerner & S. Lerner (Eds.), *The justice motive in social behavior* (pp. 125–144). New York: Plenum.

Kant, I. (1952). *The science of right* (W. Hastie, Trans.). Reprinted in Robert Hutchins (Ed.), *Great books of the Western world*. Chicago: Encyclopedia Britannica in collaboration with the University of Chicago Press.

Kenny, D. A., Kashy, D. A., & Bolger, N. (1998). Data analysis in social psychology. In D. Gilbert, S. Fiske, & G. Lindzey (Eds.) 4th ed. New York: *Handbook of social psychology*, Oxford University Press.

Miller, D., & Vidmar, N. The social psychology of punishment reactions. In M. J. Lerner & S. Lerner (Eds.), *The justice motive in social behavior* (pp. 145–172). New York: Plenum.

Oleson, K. C., & Darley, J. M. (1999). Community perceptions of allowable counterforce in self-defense and defense of property. *Law and Human Behavior, 23* (6), 629–651.

Robinson, P. H., & Darley, J. M. (1995). *Justice, liability and blame: Community views and the criminal law*. Boulder, CO: Westview Press.

(1997). The utility of desert. *Northwestern University Law Review, 91*, 453–499.

(1998). Objective vs. subjectivist views of criminality: A study in the role of social science in criminal law theory. *Oxford Journal of Legal Studies, 18*, 409–447.

Rossi, P. H., Waite, E., Bose, C. E., & Berk, R. E. (1974). The seriousness of crimes: Normative structure and individual differences. *American Sociological Review, 39*, 224–237.

Warr, M., Meier, R. F., & Erickson, M. L. (1983). Norms, theories of punishment, and publicly preferred penalties for crimes. *Sociological Quarterly, 24*, 75–91.

18. Deservingness, Entitlement, and Reactions to Outcomes

N. T. FEATHER

When we say that a person is entitled to some outcome, do we also mean that the person deserves that outcome? Can deservingness (or desert and deservedness – to use equivalent terms) be distinguished from entitlement? Or do both terms carry the same meaning? My aim in this chapter is to consider these questions and to describe a study whose results imply that it is important to distinguish between deservingness and entitlement. I will argue that judgments of deservingness involve reference to a person's actions and that they usually relate to positive or negative outcomes that are contingent on a person's positively or negatively valued behavior. Judgments of entitlement are more externally based, and they depend upon a formal or informal set of rules, laws, principles, expectations, or social norms that refer to or imply a person's rights. First, however, it is necessary to clear some semantic and conceptual ground.

Some Background Literature

I have provided examples from social psychology and legal theory of the ways in which entitlement and deservingness have been used in the literature on social justice in my recent book, *Values, Achievement, and Justice: Studies in the Psychology of Deservingness* (Feather, 1999b), as well as a conceptual analysis of the two concepts. I present here a summary of some of the main contributions, focusing on how the concepts of entitlement and deservingness have been discussed and incorporated into theory and research about social justice issues.

The research in this chapter was supported by a grant from the Australian Research Council.

Subsequently, I will provide more detail about my own analysis of entitlement and deservingness. I begin with the important contributions made by Lerner (1980, 1987, 1998). Lerner (1987) considered the experience of entitlement to be:

> . . . the essential psychological ingredient of an entire family of human events associated with social justice: issues of equity, deserving, rights, fairness, and the justice of procedures, distribution, and retributive acts . . . The cognitive component of this generic event is the judgment, often tacit, that someone, or some category of people, is entitled to a particular set of outcomes by virtue of who they are or what they have done. The "entitled to" is experienced affectively and motivationally as an imperative, a sense of requiredness between the actor's perceived outcomes and the person's attributes or acts. (pp. 107–108)

In Lerner's analysis entitlement was therefore seen as a general class of events that includes deservingness as a specific instance.

Judgments concerning entitlement were assumed by Lerner to relate to information that comes from the social structure (e.g., normative prescriptions such as the norm of reciprocity, status and role-based expectations, social concepts and stereotypes) and also to general assumptions about social motivation, self-interest, and rational decision making. This information is processed and becomes incorporated into each person's psychological structure so that "people's conceptions of their world, what they are and others want or are entitled to, are to some extent fairly direct representations of that publicly available reality" (p. 109). That is not to say, however, that people always make their judgments in terms of that reality. Under conditions of high emotion and high personal engagement in a situation, people may use more primitive cognitive associations and scripts that they have acquired early in life and that continue to exert an influence at the preconscious level. They may then move from a conscious, rational consideration of events and make their judgments according to more simple beliefs that people live in a just world, and that good people deserve good outcomes and bad people deserve bad outcomes. Thus, while judgments of entitlement usually follow the consciously given prescriptions relating to norms, roles, and obligations, they may also be based upon more primitive and irrational constructions, especially in motivationally and emotionally charged situations where norms are violated and the person is threatened (Lerner, 1980, 1987, 1998).

Other social psychologists who assign entitlement and related concepts important roles in their discussions of social justice issues are

Mikula (1993), Major (1994), Skitka and Tetlock (1992), Deutsch (1985), and Crosby (1976, 1982), among others (see Feather, 1999b). Some of these theorists use the terms entitlement and deservingness interchangeably, and they relate beliefs about entitlement to theoretical frameworks that refer to social comparison processes and relative deprivation (e.g., Crosby, 1976; Major, 1994).

Legal theorists and social theorists provide careful analytic discussions of entitlement and deservingness (or desert), drawing distinctions between the two terms (e.g., Feinberg, 1970; Heath, 1976; von Hirsch, 1986). For example, Feinberg (1970) argued that there can be desert without entitlement, as, for example, when an unemployed person is perceived to deserve social benefits but is not entitled to them under the law, and entitlement without desert, as, for example, when an unemployed person is clearly entitled to social benefits under the law but is perceived not to deserve them. As another example, we may say that a politician is qualified or entitled to be elected to office by virtue of receiving a majority vote. Yet, for whatever reason, people may say that he or she did not deserve to be elected. This judgment of desert was assumed by Feinberg to depend upon some perceived characteristic of the person (e.g., the person's perceived integrity) or on some prior activity that the person has undertaken (e.g., performing "good" deeds rather than "bad" deeds). Thus, according to Feinberg (1970),

> "Deserve," "fitting," and "appropriate," on the one hand, and "right," "entitlement," and "rule" on the other, are terms from altogether different parts of our ethical vocabularies; they are related in such a way that there is no paradox in saying of a person that he deserves (it would be fitting for him to have) certain modes of treatment which, nevertheless, he cannot claim as his due. (p. 86)

Similar distinctions were made by Heath (1976) in his discussion of differences in the concepts of rights, deserts, and need. He proposed that these three concepts are often used "to refer to a general moral or normative entitlement, . . . as synonyms for 'ought' " (p. 137). However, we also use them to refer to different kinds of moral claim. Thus, an appeal to rights involves an appeal to some agreed-upon body of law or to formal or informal rules; an appeal to desert is "more a matter of giving people what their own personal behaviour or personal qualities merit" (p. 138); and an appeal to need relates to the personal qualities or situation of an individual but focuses on some lack or deprivation.

People can subscribe to all three principles without being inconsistent. Thus, a person may be seen as having a right to a particular outcome in terms of the rules, as deserving the outcome given his or her personal qualities and past actions, and as needing the outcome because being deprived of it would have important negative consequences. Often, however, there are trade-offs, given the fact that the three principles may come into conflict in particular situations. For example, there may be a judgment that a person deserved to lose his or her job because of dishonest conduct, but the knowledge that he or she has a large family to support may lead to a conflicting judgment that the person ought to be allowed to keep the job.

Distinguishing between Entitlement and Deservingness

It should be clear from the preceding discussion that there are conceptual grounds for distinguishing between entitlement and deservingness and that such a distinction has psychological meaning. I prefer to use the term entitlement in regard to those situations where a claim for some outcome can be justified by appeal to an agreed-upon set of rules, laws, principles, expectations, social norms, and obligations. This set of prescriptions may have legal or quasi-legal status; the rules of entitlement may be formally codified, or they may operate in an informal, tacit way and be derived, for example, from social comparison to similar others. Generally, these rules relate to a person's rights in a situation, and injustice occurs when these rights are violated. Thus, the victim of an industrial accident may be entitled to compensation according to the prescribed industrial law; a woman may be entitled to the same benefits as a man in the same occupation according to equal opportunity legislation; at a less formal level and following social comparison, a worker may feel entitled to the same rewards as similar others receive; and a child is believed to be entitled to the care and protection provided by its parents. Note that, in these examples, entitlement relates to positive treatments. In everyday language the term is not customarily used to refer to negative treatments. We do not say that a person is entitled to be treated in a negative way, although perhaps in a legal sense a criminal might be deemed to be entitled to punishment according to the criminal law.

It should be clear, therefore, that entitlement has an external referent, based on a framework of formal or informal rules and prescriptions that attach to groups and institutions within the social structure and to the norms and social roles associated with them. These legal and quasi-legal "rules of the game" serve the function of regulating and controlling social conduct, and they assist in the resolution of social conflicts.

In contrast to entitlement, I use the term deservingness (and its negative, undeservingness) to refer to judgments about outcomes that are associated with a person's actions. For example, a student who studied hard for an exam may be seen to deserve the high grade that he or she obtained; a criminal who is found guilty of harming another person may be seen to deserve the penalty that is imposed; a politician who is universally judged to be honest and caring may be seen to deserve to be reelected to office. In each of these examples, the actions and their contingent outcomes are positively or negatively valued. The outcome is seen as a fitting one, as something that ought to happen in this situation, given the action. A positive outcome follows a positive action, and a negative outcome follows a negative action.

In other cases an outcome may be perceived to be undeserved. For example, a student who studied hard may be seen not to deserve the low grade that he or she obtained; a dishonest politician may be seen not to deserve reelection to office. Again, the actions are either positively or negatively valued, but, in these examples, the positive or negative outcome is seen as out of harmony with the person's behavior, as something that ought not to happen in the situation. Either a negative outcome follows a positive action, or a positive outcome follows a negative action.

Thus, judgments of deservingness or undeservingness are made in situations where either positively or negatively valued outcomes follow either positively or negatively valued actions. The judgments presume a perceived contingency or link between a person's behavior and the outcomes that follow from that behavior. As I have stated previously (Feather, 1999b), "We do not use the language of deservingness to describe outcomes that are clearly independent of a person's actions and that are the result of causes that are beyond the person's control" (p. 25).

Note that judgments of deservingness or undeservingness may be made by a third party or outside observer who judges the outcome of another, or by a person reflecting on his or her own outcomes. They may be moderated by whether the other person who is being judged is liked or disliked by the person who is judging, is a member of the judge's in-group, or belongs to an outgroup.

Judgments of deservingness and undeservingness are also closely related to judgments of responsibility. However, judgments of deservingness and judgments of responsibility do not always run in parallel. It is generally the case that people tend to be seen as not deserving outcomes for which they are not responsible. Thus, a student whose illness led to a low grade on an exam would generally be judged not to be responsible for nor to deserve the low grade that he or she obtained. In fact, any judgment of deservingness or undeservingness in this situation may be seen as inappropriate. However, people can certainly be seen to deserve outcomes for which they are responsible. For example, an athlete who trained hard for a track event would be seen to be responsible for and to deserve winning a medal for his or her performance. But the relation between responsibility and deservingness can also go the other way. People can be seen not to deserve outcomes for which they are responsible. Thus, a shady business entrepreneur who engaged in dishonest practices would be seen not to deserve the considerable fortune that he or she has amassed, even though he or she was responsible for acquiring the fortune.

It should be clear, therefore, that judgments of deservingness and undeservingness concerning the outcomes of other or of self are made within a context that involves judgments of responsibility and positive or negative evaluations that relate to the actions that are performed, the outcomes that are seen to follow from or are contingent on the actions, and the person who performs the actions. These evaluations are themselves a function of different variables that include the judge's own values as an important influence (Feather, 1999a, 1999b). The judgments may also be moderated by information about in-group/out-group membership. The judgment that an outcome is deserved is more likely to occur when the knowledge structure of beliefs and evaluations is organized in a balanced or harmonious way, providing a minimum of tension.

Modelling Deservingness and Its Effects

I have incorporated these ideas into a structural model of deservingness that refers to a situation where person *p* is evaluating other *o*, the way o acted, and the contingent outcome that follows o's action, and where p also has information about o's responsibility for the action and information about group membership (Feather, 1999a, 1999b). The structures that I present in the deservingness model involve attitudinal and unit relations (Heider, 1958). I assume that judgments of deservingness will occur when these relations fit together in a balanced or consistent way, where balance is defined by using Heider's (1958) principle. But when relations are unbalanced, a person will be more likely to judge that the outcome is undeserved. The variables within this model clearly relate to deservingness rather than to entitlement, following the distinction made in the previous section.

Judgments of deservingness and undeservingness have important consequences, both affectively and behaviorally. People feel pleased when an outcome is seen to be deserved; they are displeased when an outcome is seen to be undeserved. These general positive or negative emotions may take more specific forms depending on context. We may feel sympathetic toward a person who suffers an undeserved negative outcome, or resentful toward a person who benefits from an undeserved positive outcome. We may seek more information, conduct an attributional search for causes, or engage in social protest when an outcome is perceived to be undeserved. We may behave in various positive ways when an outcome is seen to be deserved. For example, we may provide tangible rewards for a deserved achievement.

Many of the consequences of judgments of deservingness and undeservingness in specific situations remain to be investigated. I have studied some of these reactions in relation to a social-cognitive process model of how people react to penalties that are imposed for offenses, in relation to success and failure outcomes that occur in test situations, and also in relation to the wider context of becoming employed or remaining unemployed (Feather, 1992, 1996, 1998, 1999a, 1999b; Feather & Atchison, 1998; Feather & Dawson, 1998; Feather & Deverson, 2000; Feather & Oberdan, 2000).

Combining Deservingness and Entitlement

The distinction that I have made between entitlement and deservingness implies that in some situations these two principles may be compatible and that in other situations they may be in conflict. Logically, using a fourfold classification, people may be seen to deserve an outcome to which they are also entitled, not to deserve an outcome to which they are entitled, to deserve an outcome to which they are not entitled, and not to deserve an outcome to which they are not entitled. For example, a person may be perceived both to deserve a reward by virtue of his or her positive actions and also to be entitled to it because the reward was consistent with the rules. On the other hand, a person may be perceived to deserve negative treatment because of his or her negative actions but may also be perceived to be entitled to positive consideration because of the norms or rules that prevail in that particular social context.

We investigated compatibilities and conflicts between deservingness and entitlement in a recent study that used a hospital setting (Feather & Johnstone, 2001). In this study we investigated the reactions of nurses to hypothetical scenarios in which either a patient diagnosed as schizophrenic or a patient diagnosed as suffering from personality disorder behaved aggressively and damaged hospital property. The aggressive behavior was witnessed by a nurse in the scenario, who either responded in a positive manner (bandaging the patient's hand and listening to the patient's problems) or negatively (rebuking the patient and having the patient removed from the area where the offense was committed). We were interested in how the nurses, who were themselves employed in a psychiatric hospital, would respond both cognitively and affectively to the events and outcomes in these scenarios.

We predicted that the personality disorder patient in the scenario would elicit more negative reactions from the nurses when compared with the schizophrenic patient and that the personality disorder patient would be judged to be more responsible for the aggressive behavior. We also expected that the personality disorder patient's behavior would be perceived as more negative and serious. These predicted differences between the two types of patient are consistent with the clinical literature (e.g., Gallop, Lancee, & Garfinkel, 1989; Lewis & Appleby, 1988). Consistent with the deservingness model (Feather, 1999a, 1999b), these predicted differences imply that the personality disorder patient would be judged to be more deserving of a negative response to the offense and less deserving of a positive response when compared to the schizophrenic patient. They also imply that the nurses would tend to report more positive affect about the positive response that followed the aggressive episode and less positive affect about the negative response for the schizophrenic patient when compared to the personality disorder patient.

However, these differences would be moderated by beliefs and expectations about how the nurse in each scenario should behave in relation to a nurse's occupational role and the norms that attach to that role. These norms emphasize caring for patients and acting in positive ways in the interests of helping patients to recover. They do not condone acting negatively or punitively toward patients. Thus, the scenarios that we presented were also expected to elicit considerations of entitlement that relate to patients. We expected that the judges in our study, who were nurses themselves, would believe that patients are entitled to positive treatment, given the social norms that are inculcated in nurses' training and that are part of nurses' occupational role within a hospital setting. They would tend to view a negative response to patients who behaved aggressively as inappropriate and in conflict with their entitlement as patients. Hence, in the experimental condition where the nurse responded negatively, beliefs about entitlement would act against finding large differences in deservingness between the two types of patient (schizophrenic and personality disorder). The major differences in deservingness between the two types of patient were expected to be found in the experimental condition where the nurse responded positively in a manner that was consistent with social norms relating to entitlement.

The results of the study supported these predictions. Figure 18.1 shows that the nurses in our study judged both types of patient as deserving a positive response to the offense they committed rather than a negative response ($p < .001$). However, the interaction between type of patient and type of response was statistically significant ($p < .001$). The nurses judged the schizophrenic patient as deserving a positive response to the offense more than the personality disorder patient, and a negative response less. The difference between the two types of patient was larger for the positive treatment condition than for the negative treatment condition, and statistically significant only for the positive treatment condition (Tukey test, $p < .01$).

Similar findings were obtained for reported positive affect about the response to the offense made by the nurse in the scenarios. Positive affect was measured by combining ratings of annoyance, disappointment, and pleasure about the nurse's response, after reverse coding the annoyance and disappointment items. Figure 18.2 shows that the nurses in our study reported more positive affect when the nurse reacted positively than when the nurse's response was a negative one ($p < .001$). The interaction between type of patient and type of response was again statistically significant ($p < .001$). The nurses reported more positive affect when the schizophrenic patient was treated positively than when the personality disorder patient was treated positively (Tukey test, $p < .01$), and less positive affect when the schizophrenic patient received negative treatment than when the

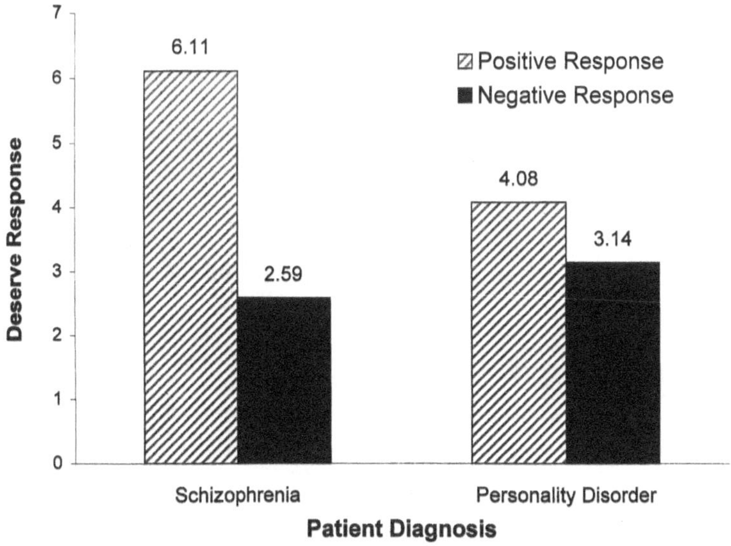

Figure 18.1. Differences in deserve outcome across experimental conditions.

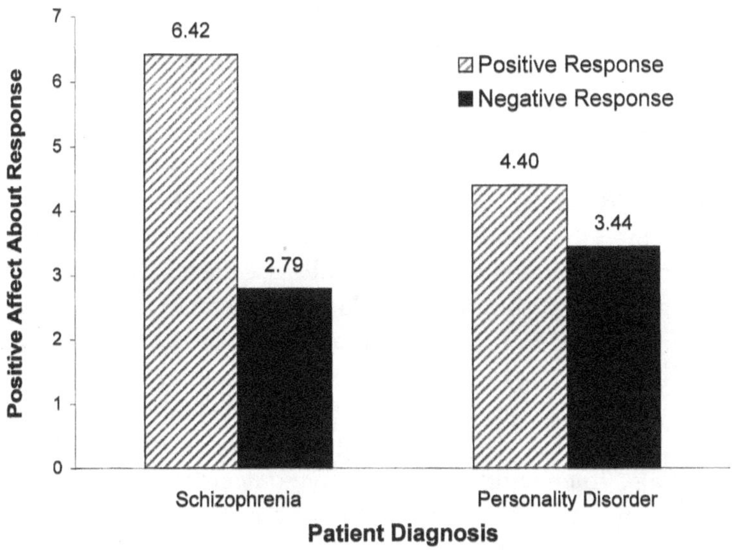

Figure 18.2. Differences in positive affect about outcome across experimental conditions.

personality disorder patient received negative treatment (Tukey test, $p < .05$); but, as predicted, the difference was larger for the positive treatment condition.

Further results from this study pertaining to the deservingness model and the social-cognitive process model of reactions to penalties (Feather, 1999a, 1999b) are reported in Feather and Johnstone (2001). Note that the results showed that the personality disorder patient was perceived to be more responsible for the aggressive behavior when compared to the schizophrenic patient, and also to have a more negative personality, to be more deceptive, more demanding, stronger, and less confused than the schizophrenic patient. These differences were in line with our predictions. Positive versus negative attitudes toward the offender and beliefs about degree of responsibility would also be expected to influence deservingness judgments, consistent with the deservingness model.

Further Elaboration

The study that I have described presented participants with situations where one could assume that there was a conflict between judgments of deservingness and beliefs about entitlement.

Figure 18.3 presents the different forms that compatibilities and conflicts between deservingness and entitlement can take. This figure is simplified to the extent that positive or negative deservingness judgments are related only to evaluated actions and their outcomes; other variables in the deservingness model are not included. It is also assumed in Figure 3 that beliefs about entitlement concern positive outcomes. As I proposed earlier, people generally use the term entitlement in relation to positive outcomes or rewards rather than to negative outcomes or punishments. In Figure 18.3 the positive or negative sign in parentheses after the deserve and entitlement variables refers to the outcome. For example, deserve (+) and entitlement (+) in cell 1 together refer to a situation where a person is judged to deserve a positive outcome and also to be entitled to a positive outcome in terms of the norms or rules appropriate to the situation; not deserve (–) and not entitled (+) in Cell 8 together refer to a situation where a person is judged not to deserve a negative outcome and not to be entitled to a positive outcome in terms of the norms or rules. Four of the cells in Figure 18.3 involve relations between deservingness and entitlement that are compatible. They are cells 1, 4, 6, and 7. The remaining four

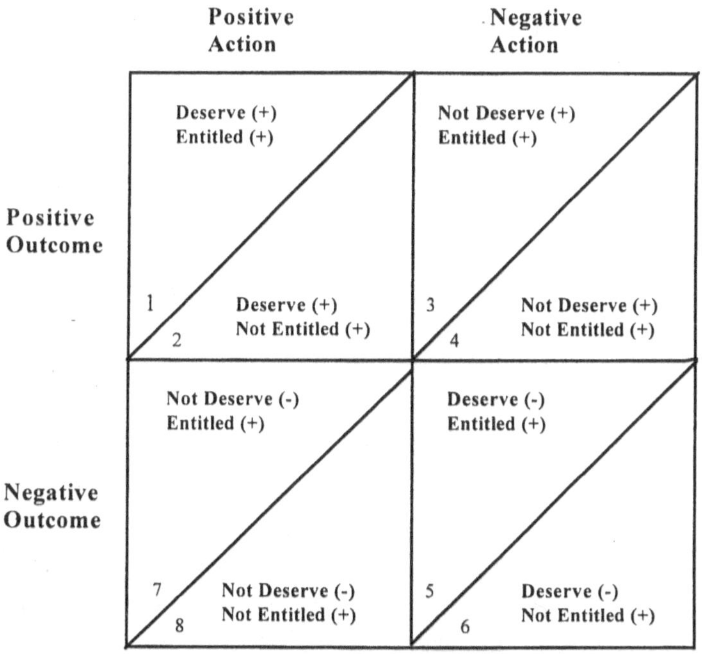

Figure 18.3. Different combinations of deservingness and positive entitlement.

cells involve incompatible or conflicting relations between deservingness and entitlement. They are cells 2, 3, 5, and 8.

The situations presented in the scenarios that we used in the study described in the previous section are presented in cell 3 and cell 5 in Figure 18.3. Cell 3 represents a situation where a person's negative action is followed by a positive outcome and where the person is also perceived to be entitled to the positive outcome in terms of the prevailing norms. This is the situation of the patient who behaved aggressively and damaged hospital property but who received a positive response from the nurse in the scenario. The deservingness model (Feather, 1999a, 1999b), using the balance principle, implies that the patient would be judged not to deserve the positive outcome that followed the negative action. But this judgment of undeservingness would come into conflict with the prevailing social norms concerning entitlement, and our results implied that these norms had an important effect on the judgments made by the nurses in our study. Thus, the schizophrenic and personality disorder patients were judged to deserve the positive outcome, the former more than the latter, and ratings of positive affect about the nurse's positive response were in the same direction.

The other conflict in our study is represented in cell 5 of Figure 18.3. Here the situation is one in which a person's negative action is followed by a negative outcome and where the person is again perceived to be entitled to a positive outcome in terms of the prevailing norms. This is the situation of the patient who behaved aggressively but who received a negative response from the nurse. In this case, the deservingness model (Feather, 1999a, 1999b) implies that the patient would be judged to deserve the negative outcome, because this outcome is consistent with the patient's negative action. But again, this judgment would come into conflict with the prevailing social norms concerning the patient's entitlement. These norms would oppose the negative treatment of patients, and they would block any overt expression by the nurses that the negative response to the patient's aggressive behavior by the nurse in the scenario was a deserved outcome. Privately, the nurses may have believed that each patient deserved some penalty or reprimand as a result of the aggressive behavior, the personality disorder patient more than the schizophrenic patient. But our results implied that the social norms associated with the culture of the hospital and the nurses' occupational role overrode any negative responses to the aggressive episode, attenuating differences in judgments of deservingness and ratings of positive affect for the two types of patient when the outcome was negative.

That is not to say, however, that variables assumed to influence deservingness judgments were not effective. The evidence showed that ratings of deservingness were associated in the expected direction with other variables that were measured in the study. For example, the personality disorder patient was viewed more negatively and was perceived to be more responsible for the aggressive episode when compared to the schizophrenic patient, and these differences were reflected in the deservingness judgments made by the nurses.

In summary, therefore, the results implied that the nurses' reactions were influenced by information about the aggressive event and its positive or negative outcome, and that their reactions were also related to knowledge structures in which social norms concerning perceived entitlement, beliefs about the defining characteristics of schizophrenic and personality disorder patients, and attitudes toward these patients were important components.

Finally, the different cells in Figure 18.3 suggest future avenues for research. For example, we could investigate situations where judgments of deservingness are compatible with beliefs about entitlement in contrast to situations where deservingness judgments are incompatible with entitlement beliefs. Separating deservingness from entitlement opens up the possibility of new types of investigation that focus on the relative importance of the effects of the structure of social norms, rules, and laws on judgments in specific situations when compared to the effects of the evaluative structure of a person's actions and outcomes in combination with the other variables that are part of the deservingness model. At a more general level, we could also examine shifts in the public's views of deservingness and entitlement across time and in the relative emphasis assigned to each by citizens both within and across societies. Social and economic change in some societies may lead to differences in emphasis, so that, for example, there may be either a general shift toward a shared belief that people are entitled to or have a right to positive benefits without having to work for them and without necessarily deserving them, or a general shift to the reverse belief that benefits should be provided only to those who work for them and deserve them because of their positive actions. There may also be similarities and differences across cultures in the emphasis given to deservingness relative to entitlement, and these similarities and differences may in turn reflect the operation of cultural values and other variables (e.g., Fiske et al., 1998).

It is evident, therefore, that the model that I have presented has both pragmatic and theoretical implications. It is heuristic in the sense that it implies new directions for research. It makes a useful theoretical contribution by distinguishing between judgments of deservingness that take account of positive or negative evaluations of a person's behavior and behavioral outcomes, and judgments of entitlement that relate more to rights that are prescribed by social norms, laws, rules, and other externally generated principles. My research program has been primarily concerned with judgments of deservingness. There is now a need also to investigate the antecedents and consequences of judgments of entitlement and to examine how the two types of judgments interact to influence the way people respond to outcomes relating to self and others.

REFERENCES

Crosby, F. (1976). A model of egoistical relative deprivation. *Psychological Review, 83*, 85–113.

(1982). *Relative deprivation and working women.* New York: Oxford University Press.

Deutsch, M. (1985). *Distributive justice: A social-psychological perspective.* New Haven, CT: Yale University Press.

Feather, N. T. (1992). An attributional and value analysis of deservingness in success and failure situations. *British Journal of Social Psychology, 31,* 125–145.

(1996). Reactions to penalties for an offense in relation to authoritarianism, values, perceived responsibility, perceived seriousness, and deservingness. *Journal of Personality and Social Psychology, 71,* 571–587.

(1998). Reactions to penalties committed by the police and public citizens: Testing a social-cognitive process model of retributive justice. *Journal of Personality and Social Psychology, 75,* 528–544.

(1999a). Judgments of deservingness: Studies in the psychology of justice and achievement. *Personality and Social Psychology Review, 3,* 86–107.

(1999b). *Values, achievement, and justice: Studies in the psychology of deservingness.* New York: Kluwer Academic/Plenum Press.

Feather, N. T., & Atchison, L. (1998). Reactions to an offence in relation to the status and perceived moral character of the offender. *Australian Journal of Psychology, 50,* 119–127.

Feather, N. T., & Dawson, S. (1998). Judging deservingness and affect in relation to another's employment or unemployment: A test of a justice model. *European Journal of Social Psychology, 28,* 361–381.

Feather, N. T., & Deverson, N. (2000). Reactions to a motor vehicle accident in relation to mitigating circumstances and the gender and moral worth of the driver. *Journal of Applied Social Psychology, 30,* 77–95.

Feather, N. T., & Johnstone, C. (2001). Social norms, entitlement, and deservingness: Differential reactions to the aggressive behavior of schizophrenic and personality disorder patients. *Personality and Social Psychology Bulletin, 27,* 755–767.

Feather, N. T., & Oberdan, D. (2000). Reactions to penalties for an offence in relation to ethnic identity, responsibility, and authoritarianism. *Australian Journal of Psychology, 52,* 9–16.

Feinberg, J. (1970). *Doing and deserving.* Princeton, NJ: Princeton University Press.

Fiske, A. P., Kitayama, S., Markus, H. M., & Nisbett, R. E. (1998). The cultural matrix of social psychology. In D. T. Gilbert, S. T. Fiske, & G. Lindzey (Eds.), *The handbook of social psychology,* New York: Oxford University Press. 4th ed. (Vol. 2, pp. 915–981).

Gallop, R., Lancee, W., & Garfinkel, P. (1989). How nursing staff respond to "Borderline Personality Disorder." *Hospital and Community Psychiatry, 40,* 815–819.

Heath, A. (1976). *Rational choice and social exchange.* Cambridge: Cambridge University Press.

Heider, F. (1958). *The psychology of interpersonal relations.* New York: Wiley.

Lerner, M. J. (1980). *The belief in a just world: A fundamental delusion.* New York: Plenum.

(1987). Integrating societal and psychological rules of entitlement: The basic task of each social actor and fundamental problem for the social sciences. *Social Justice Research, 1,* 107–125.

(1998). The two forms of belief in a just world: Some thoughts on why and how people care about justice. In L. Montada & M. J. Lerner (Eds.), *Responses to victimization and belief in a just world* (pp. 247–269). New York: Plenum.

Lewis, G., & Appleby, L. (1988). Personality disorder: The patients psychiatrists dislike. *British Journal of Psychiatry, 153,* 44–49.

Major, B. (1994). From social inequality to personal entitlement: The role of social comparisons, legitimacy appraisals, and group membership. In M. P. Zanna (Ed.), *Advances in experimental social psychology* (Vol. 26, pp. 293–355). New York: Academic Press.

Mikula, G. (1980). On the role of justice in allocation decisions. In G. Mikula (Ed.), *Justice and social interaction* (pp. 127–166). New York: Springer-Verlag.

Skitka, L. J., & Tetlock, P. E. (1992). Allocating scarce resources: A contingency model of distributive justice. *Journal of Experimental Social Psychology, 28,* 491–522.

von Hirsch, A. (1986). *Doing justice: The choice of punishments.* Boston: Northeastern University Press.

19. Just World Processes in Demonizing

JOHN H. ELLARD, CHRISTINA D. MILLER,
TERRI-LYNNE BAUMLE, AND
JAMES M. OLSON

There has been steady growth in recent years in psychologists' interest in phenomena that have long been the concern of moral philosophers, legal scholars, and theologians, including moral responsibility (e.g., Alicke, 2000; Weiner, 1995), moral emotions such as shame and guilt (e.g., Eisenberg, 2000; Tangney et al., 1996), moral hypocrisy (Batson et al., 1999), spirituality (e.g., Emmons, 1999), justice (e.g., Montada & Lerner, 1998; Tyler et al., 1997; Robinson & Darley, 1995), character and integrity (Sabini & Silver, 1998), destructive obedience (e.g., Blass, 1999; Darley, 1995; Kelman & Hamilton, 1989), forgiveness (e.g., Kelln & Ellard, 1998; McCullough, Worthington, & Rachal, 1997; Worthington, 1998), and evil (e.g., Baumeister, 1997; Darley, 1992; Staub, 1999). Our concern here is with evil and, more specifically, perceptions of evilness in the character of others. Against the background of ongoing discussions among social scientists about the meaningfulness of distinguishing evil acts from other acts, or even whether some people are truly "evil" (Baumeister, 1997; Berkowitz, 1999; Darley, 1992; Magid, 1988), we focus on the circumstances and individual propensities that give rise to character attributions of evilness – a process we call *demonizing*. Consistent with previous analyses by John Darley (1992) and more recently Roy Baumeister (1997) and Leonard Berkowitz (1999), our approach assumes that perceptions of evilness in the character of perpetrators is in some measure "in the eye of the beholder," reflecting the perceiver's cognitive and motivational processes.

Understanding the tendency for people to attribute harmful acts to the perpetrator's evil character is important for a number of reasons. Demonizing has the potential to interfere with perceivers' ability and inclination to consider more complex but well-documented situationist understandings of the factors that lead people to inflict horrific harm on others (Baumeister, 1997; Miller, Gordon, & Buddie, 1999; Zimbardo, 1995). The actions of a demonized perpetrator are unlikely to be understood in more situational terms insofar as initial characterological attributions for harmful behavior tend to be undercorrected by situational information (Miller et al., 1974), particularly when the behavior is morally reprehensible (Reeder & Brewer, 1979). While demonizing may be satisfying, it is seldom edifying.

At the same time, demonizing results in a preoccupation with making the perpetrator suffer (Baumeister, 1997; White, 1995), particularly if demonizing dehumanizes perpetrators (Bandura, Underwood, & Fromson, 1975; Opotow, 1990). The focus on punishing in turn draws attention away from other potentially effective courses of corrective action (Drabeck & Quarantelli, 1964).

Probing everyday understandings of evil also provides insight into the nature of evil behavior. Analyses of the origins of evil acts identify the vilification and dehumanization of others as one of the enabling conditions for evil (Bandura; 1999; Baumeister, 1997; Kelman, 1973; Staub, 1999). This gives rise to the *paradox of demonizing* – that those given to perceiving evil in others may be at increased risk for committing evil themselves.

Finally, understanding the dynamics of demonizing can expand our understanding of basic person perception processes and stereotyping. Understanding demonizing may shed more light on why some stereotypes have recurrent universal themes and content and why some stereotypes more than others are imbued with passionate contempt (cf. Jones, 1990, p. 107).

Why Do People Demonize?

Available evidence suggests that demonizing is a multidetermined phenomenon with both cognitive and motivational underpinnings. The cognitive component of demonizing considered in the research reported here postulates an *evilness schema*, comprised of an integrated set of evilness character stereotypes (Simms & Ellard, 2000), stereotypical behaviors and motivations (Baumeister, 1997; Darley, 1992), and images (Baumeister, 1997; Ivie, 1980; Keen, 1986). We hypothesize that harmful acts that activate the evilness schema facilitate character attributions of evilness to the perpetrator of the harm. Evilness schema activation is assumed, in most instances, to reflect the presence of *evilness cues*. The studies we report focus on the evilness cueing potential of particular sadistic behaviors that result in perceivers' categorizing the inflicted harm as evil, which in turn results in correspondent inferences of evilness (Darley, 1992). We also incorporate cues intended to activate the evilness schema by raising questions about the comprehensibility and rationality of the perpetrator's motivation (Darley, 1992).

A number of motivational processes could plausibly contribute to demonizing. In some instances, it may be a variant of scapegoating, by means of which perceivers seek to reduce their anxieties, frustrations, and guilt by putting all of the blame on an identifiable perpetrator (Drabeck & Quarantelli, 1964, 1969). The desire to fix blame exclusively on the perpetrator gains plausibility if he or she is cast as the sort of malevolent person capable of such harm. A terror management theory analysis of transgression suggests the possibility that demonizing may help perceivers to manage the death anxiety that malevolent deeds arouse by threatening universal moral principles (Rosenblatt et al., 1989). For some, demonizing may reflect defensive projection processes (Newman, Duff, & Baumeister, 1997), which might arise in situations where perceivers find vicarious pleasure in the malfeasance of others (cf. Baumeister & Campbell, 1999) or harbor unconscious wishes to destroy or annihilate others (Becker, 1975; Freud, 1930). Perceivers may also favour demonizing because alternative ways of making sense of the harm may imply condoning it (Miller et al., 1999). Demonizing others may also be an effective means of maintaining a positive self-image (Baumeister, 1997).

We were particularly interested in the possibility, suggested by John Darley (1992), that demonizing may help people to maintain their just world beliefs. The just world hypothesis holds that people need to believe that they live in a world where people get what they deserve and deserve what they get (Lerner, 1980). Just world research has shown that people will react to evidence that the world is unjust, either behaviorally or cognitively, in a manner that allows them to maintain their belief. For instance, victim blaming preserves the belief in a just world because in a truly just world, only deserving victims suffer – there are no innocent victims.

The idea that demonizing may have the same protective function for just world beliefs as victim blaming seems paradoxical and counterintuitive. After all, if evil behavior is threatening, isn't demonizing just the opposite of what people should do to protect their belief in a just world? Why would people want to populate their just world with evil people?

Darley's hypothesis becomes more compelling and less paradoxical when the alternative to demonizing is considered. If evil persons are not the source of evil, then the more disturbing possibility must be entertained that evil might be a relatively diffuse and commonplace phenomenon that normal people can get caught up in. The alternative, as Darley (1992) points out, also makes evil less recognizable. If you believe that evil is the product of evil character, your world can be orderly and fair as long as the evil people are not around. It is much less easy to feel sanguine about the essential justness of one's world if basically good people can be the authors of evilness, because evil could presumably then be perpetrated by almost anyone at any time and in any situation where the conditions are right.

Demonizing probably also trades on people's hunches about the base rates for evil characters in the population. The notion that only evil and hopefully rare people do evil things is again less threatening to the belief that the world is a just place than the alternative. In that sense, evildoers become the rare exceptions that prove the rule that the world is in fact a just place.

Finally, personifying evil behavior may also sustain people's just world beliefs by making evil seem more controllable. Once the forces of evil have been located in individuals, there are steps that can be taken to contain them, to manage the threat.

Study I: Evilness Cues and Individual Differences in Just World Beliefs

The research strategy for the first investigation was to determine whether or not priming of the evilness schema would affect observers' tendency to demonize a perpetrator, in this case a kidnapper. By incorporating a measure of individual differences in the strength of participants' just world beliefs, we also endeavored to determine whether or not just world concerns motivate demonizing.

Participants in the study were asked to review materials from an ostensibly real kidnapping case in which details about the motives and behavior of the kidnapper were varied so that features hypothesized to reflect the evilness schema were either present or absent. The materials included a police "incident report," "witness report," "rap sheet," transcript of a police interview with the kidnapper, and a "victim impact statement." In one condition, representing the *bad* scenario, the perpetrator kidnapped a young woman for money with the intent of returning her unharmed. In the *evil* scenario, the kidnapper's motivation was more complex and obscure. The money was less important than "having people scramble for me." He kidnapped her because he "felt like it" and because the victim was pretty and "she looked like she would be fun." Information in a statement ostensibly provided by the victim also included references to him laughing and enjoying her suffering that were absent in the bad condition. Participants also reviewed information allegedly provided by the victim's psychotherapist, documenting the continuing negative psychological effects the kidnapping was having for her. Before reviewing the case materials, participants completed a measure of their just world beliefs (Lipkus, 1991).[1]

The dependent variables included ratings of both the kidnapper and the victim on seven-point bipolar trait adjective rating scales, a total of fourteen different ratings. The bipolar character ratings included separate target items assessing badness (bad – not bad) and evilness (evil – not evil). These two items were analyzed separately, and the remaining twelve (e.g., likable – unlikable, warm – cold, sincere – insincere) were combined into a composite character evaluation index.

We expected the presence of evilness cues associated with the kidnapper's actions in the evil condition to prime the evilness schema, resulting in more negative kidnapper evaluations overall and more extreme ratings of evilness in the evil than in the bad condition. Our analysis of just world dynamics and demonizing led us to expect positive correlations between the individual difference measure of beliefs in a just world and negative evaluations of the kidnapper, with the strongest relation being on the demonizing (evil) measure.

The research design allowed us to explore possible interactions between just world beliefs and the bad/evil manipulation. For instance, if the evil manipulation is itself threatening to just world beliefs, an ordinal interaction seemed plausible, with the strongest relation between individual differences in just world beliefs and demonizing appearing in the evil condition. Our expectations for interaction effects were nonetheless provisional in the absence of a clear sense of the just world impact of the evil/bad manipulation.

[1] Each study in this chapter was part of a larger investigation of dimensions of demonizing. For the sake of brevity, only those measures relevant to the hypotheses reported here are discussed.

In hierarchical regression analyses incorporating the bad/evil manipulation, just world individual difference scores, and the interaction between the manipulation and just world scores as predictors, findings for the manipulation of evilness indicated that participants rated the kidnapper as more bad ($p < .05$) and evil ($p < .10$) in the evil than in the bad condition, but the effect did not approach significance on the composite character evaluation index. The expected tendency for just world beliefs to be positively related to kidnapper demonizing was apparent on the bad ($p < .05$) and evil ($p < .05$) items, but again no significant effect appeared on the composite index. Although the interaction between the evilness manipulation and individual differences in just world beliefs was not significant, we note that the correlation between the just world measure and ratings of kidnapper evilness was stronger and marginally significant in the evil condition ($r = .35$, $p = .05$) but not significant in the bad condition ($r = .27$, ns.). None of the correlations within the bad or evil conditions between just world beliefs and the bad item or the character evaluation measures were significant. A parallel set of regression analyses was conducted on the comparable ratings of the victim's character evaluation, badness, and evilness. These analyses revealed no reliable effects.

These findings indicate that perceivers are indeed responsive to evilness cues associated with harmful acts in determining the evilness of the perpetrator. The pattern of findings involving the individual difference measure of just world beliefs also suggests that at least one motivational process involved in demonizing is the need to believe in a just world. That the hypothesized relations were limited to the bad and evil measures and did not appear on other evaluative attributes assessed by the general character index (such as likable – unlikable and warm – cold) further suggests that evilness is a distinguishable attribute and exists, as Darley (1992) puts it, as an "enduring kernel" that may be present in a perpetrator but need not be apparent on other trait dimensions. The fact that the strongest relation between individual differences in just world beliefs and judgments of the kidnapper occurred on the measure of perceived evilness in the evil condition is also consistent with a just world analysis of demonizing.

A replication and extension of Study I added a manipulation designed to either threaten or affirm participants' just world beliefs before they considered the kidnapping scenario. This follow-up study replicated the original finding: demonizing ratings were highest in the presence of evilness cues. In this study, the individual difference measure of just world beliefs interacted with both the just world and evilness cues manipulations, and, importantly, this interaction was only observed on the measure of perpetrator evilness. Space limitations preclude detailed discussion of the findings, but the original pattern of a positive relation between just world beliefs and demonizing was replicated in the aftermath of a manipulation designed to threaten just world beliefs, but only when the kidnapping scenario included evilness cues.

Study II: Evilness Cues, Perpetrator Remorse, and Individual Differences in Just World Beliefs

In a second study, we again investigated the impact of evilness cues on attributions of evil, as well as the predictive role of individual differences in the belief in a just world. We moved away, however, from the kidnapping scenario to examine demonizing in a different setting. Specifically, participants read an alleged newspaper report about a man who broke into a house at 2 A.M., was discovered by the homeowner, and shot the owner twice. Different versions of the newspaper article were created to vary evilness cues. We independently manipulated the presence/absence of two evilness cues, one that was also manipulated in Study I and one that was not. The repeated cue was the nature of the perpetrator's motives. Half of the participants learned in the alleged article that the man broke into the house because he needed money (rational motive), and the other half learned that he broke into the house "just for the thrill of it" (bizarre motive). The latter condition was expected to activate the evilness schema. The novel cue in this study was the remorsefulness of the perpetrator. Half of the participants learned that the individual "was sorry for what he did and wanted to apologize to the homeowner," and the other half learned that he "was not sorry for what he did and would never apologize to the homeowner." We expected that the expression of remorse would neutralize attributions of evil, whereas denying any remorse would activate the evilness schema. Remorse implies that a perpetrator empathizes with the victim and recognizes the wrongfulness of his or her act – two things that are not generally expected of evil people. An unrepentant perpetrator, by contrast, confirms suspicions that he or she lacks feelings, thereby implying a hostile, evil nature.

Before reading the focal newspaper article, participants completed Rubin and Peplau's (1975) scale measuring just world beliefs. After reading the article, participants evaluated the perpetrator on an overall good-to-evil scale ranging from 1 (very good person) to 3 (good person) to 5 (neither good nor bad person) to 7 (bad person) to 9 (evil person). Participants also rated the perpetrator on thirteen additional dimensions, including four key ones: evil, bad, immoral, and moral. Participants were also asked to suggest how long a jail sentence the perpetrator should receive.

The six principal dependent measures (overall good–evil rating, evil, bad, immoral, moral, length of sentence) were submitted to hierarchical multiple regressions, with motive and remorse effect-coded and just world beliefs treated as a continuous variable. The manipulation of motive affected three measures: evil rating, bad rating, and length of sentence. Perpetrators who committed the crime for a thrill were rated as significantly more evil and bad and were given longer sentences than perpetrators who committed the crime for money. Thus, motive again seemed to serve as an evilness cue in this study. The manipulation of remorse also affected participants' perceptions of the perpetrator, affecting two key dependent measures: the overall good–evil rating and the bad rating. As expected, perpetrators who denied any remorse were rated as more evil and bad than perpetrators who expressed remorse. Thus, at least in the context used in this study, lack of remorse seemed to be an evilness cue.

The main effect for beliefs in a just world was significant on the overall good–evil rating and on the moral rating, such that stronger beliefs in a just world were associated with higher ratings of evil ($r = .30$, $p < .01$) and lower ratings of morality ($r = -.23$, $p < .02$). The most interesting findings were significant interactions between the manipulation of remorse and just world beliefs, which occurred on three measures: the ratings of evil, bad, and moral. In each case, the correlation between beliefs in a just world and demonizing was significant in the presence of the evilness cue (the no remorse condition) but not significant in the absence of the evilness cue (the remorse condition). Specifically, in the no remorse condition, stronger beliefs in a just world were associated with higher ratings of evil ($r = .31$, $p < .05$), higher ratings of badness ($r = .33$, $p < .05$), and lower ratings of morality ($r = -.52$, $p < .001$), whereas in the remorse condition, these relations disappeared (all $r < .02$). Beliefs in a just world did not interact reliably with the manipulation of motive on any of the dependent measures, nor was the three-way interaction reliable on any of the measures.

Thus, Study II confirmed the findings in the first study that strong beliefs in a just world were associated with demonizing and that this relation was most robust when evilness cues were present. It appears that strong believers in a just world perceive evil in others in order to protect their beliefs, at least in part. Demonizing thus serves a defensive function for these individuals. Of course, attributions of evil are more likely to be made by all perceivers when evilness cues (e.g., lack of remorse) are present, presumably because the evilness schema is activated. Like many other social psychological phenomena, therefore, demonizing represents an integration of cognitive and motivational processes.

Conclusions

The findings from our studies confirm that, at least in the context of criminal acts of deviance, demonizing the criminal is most apparent in the presence of evilness cues, presumably through the activation of an evilness schema. That demonizing may also have a motivational basis in people's justice concerns was also apparent in the tendency for people scoring high on measures of just world beliefs to demonize, particularly in the presence of evilness cues. That the relationship was strongest in the presence of evilness cues suggests that the effect of evilness cues may, in part, be motivational insofar as the cues may add to the just world threat of the transgression.

As initial investigations into the psychology of demonizing, these studies of course raise as many questions as they answer. We will focus here on the just world theory aspects of the research. A fundamental issue about the justice imperative in demonizing is whether demonizing is a justification for or antecedent to retribution. Do people's concerns about justice lead them to demonize harmdoers because demonizing makes it easier to justify carrying out acts of retribution (see Darley, this volume), or does demonizing arise directly from just world concerns in the same way that victim derogation does? The issue is made more complex by the observation that at least one reason why just world concerns produce a desire to personify evil is because such personification makes evil visible and controllable. But how might we distinguish the desire to "manage" evil from the desire to punish it? However daunting the empirical challenge of distinguishing the two possibilities, attempts should be made, given the centrality of the issue for a justice motive analysis of demonizing.

There are also extensions of the justice analysis of demonizing to other evilness phenomena. If personification of evil assuages justice anxiety, the notion of people being "possessed" by demonic forces beyond their control should be particularly threatening, because the forces of evil are simultaneously manifest but also beyond control but for the mysterious prospect of exorcism (which, by corollary, strong believers in a just world should be more inclined to believe in). At the same time, we need to know more about why acts of contrition and remorse appear to extinguish the justice imperative in demonizing. Is the effect one of reducing anxieties about repeated transgressions, or is it the assumption that a contrite transgressor is communicating his or her essential commitment to a just world?

More work also needs to be done to clarify the relation between aspects of the evilness schema and justice concerns. We speculate that the elements of evilness cues that arouse justice concerns as opposed to, for instance, concerns about the mental stability of the perpetrator are the ones most likely to distinguish attributions of "evil" from attributions of "crazy." For instance, evidence of sadistic pleasure may be particularly potent for demonizing attributions (as opposed to, for instance, inflicting harm without "rational" basis) precisely because of the clear incremental injustice implied: not only is the victim suffering, but the perpetrator is extracting gains from the suffering in a most egregious way; the more the victim suffers, the more the perpetrator benefits. It is hard to imagine a situation where the forces of injustice conspire more completely to challenge any sense of the world as a just place. Studies employing more refined manipulations of evilness cues reflecting these conceptual distinctions will be able to establish more definitively the link between the justice concerns of the perceiver and the features of harmful acts that give rise to the demonizing of harmdoers.

Finally, the link between demonizing and justice concerns offers a perspective on the unease many experience with situationist or other "banality of evil" analyses of some of the more horrific episodes in human history, including the Holocaust (Berkowitz, 1999; Darley, 1995; Miller et al., 1999). Although the unease is partly based on specific quarrels with the relevance and usefulness of available social science wisdom to adequately explain some of the more egregious and horrific aspects of these historical episodes, we wonder to what extent the horrors and accompanying sense of injustice and moral outrage are so great in these situations as to virtually require the invocation of evilness as a necessary part of the story. All explanations other than evil are, in a sense, just world threatening, because they locate the origins of such terrifying events in the mundane dynamics of social life and personal pathology. We are thus led to wonder whether objections to situationist or psychopathological accounts of horrific deeds have less to do with their somehow condoning the perpetrators (Miller et al., 1999) or excusing them (Baumeister, 1997; Staub, 1989) than with a deeply rooted sense that any notion of the world as a just place is meaningless if we accept that such atrocities are mere eruptions of excess in the normal dynamics of human experience. Consider the reflections of Hitler biographer and physician Redlich (1999), who probably more than any other has exhaustively probed the physical and psychological details of Hitler's life in search of a diagnosis to explain the horrors he perpetrated, in the closing paragraph of the epilogue to his book:

> At this point my wife interrupted my speech and asked, "Was he mentally ill?" "Yes, he was, in a way," I replied. "And what was the diagnosis?" she wanted to know. I mumbled something like political paranoia. For a while she sat quietly and thoughtfully, then said, "Er war ein schlechter Mensch" – he was an evil person. (p. 341)

While the good doctor gave the last word to his wife, the implication is clear – no logical or rational account adequately captures the malevolence of someone like Hitler. The paradox arising from our view of demonizing is that analyses such as Dr. Redlich's create the illusion that rational explanations are inadequate because those explanations threaten perceptions of a just world more than the simpler demonizing alternative.

REFERENCES

Alicke, M. D. (2000). Culpable control and the psychology of blame. *Psychological Bulletin, 126*, 556–574.

Bandura, A. (1999). Moral disengagement in the perpetration of inhumanities. *Personality and Social Psychology Review, 3*, 193–209.

Bandura, A., Underwood, B., & Fromson, M. E. (1975). Disinhibition of aggression through diffusion of responsibility and dehumanization of victims. *Journal of Research in Personality, 9*, 253–269.

Batson, C. D., Thompson, E. R., Seuferling, G., Whitney, H., & Strongman, J. A. (1999). Moral hypocrisy: Appearing moral to oneself without being so. *Journal of Personality & Social Psychology, 77*, 525–537.

Baumeister, R. F. (1997). *Evil: Inside human cruelty and violence.* New York: W. H. Freeman.

Baumeister, R. F., & Campbell, W. K. (1999). The intrinsic appeal of evil: Sadism, sensational thrills, and threatened egotism. *Personality and Social Psychology Review, 3*, 210–221.

Becker, E. (1975). *Escape from evil.* New York: The Free Press.

Berkowitz, L. (1999). Evil is more than banal: Situationism and the concept of evil. *Personality and Social Psychology Review, 3,* 246–253.

Blass, T. (1999). The Milgram paradigm after 35 years: Some things we now know about obedience to authority. *Journal of Applied Social Psychology, 29,* 955–978.

Darley, J. M. (1992). Social organization for the production of evil. *Psychological Inquiry, 3,* 199–218.

(1995). Constructive and destructive obedience: A taxonomy of principal-agent relationships. *Journal of Social Issues, 51,* 125–154.

Drabeck, T. E., & Quarantelli, E. L. (1964). Scapegoats, villains, and disasters. *Trans-Action, 2,* 12–17.

(1969). Blame in disaster: Another look, another viewpoint. In D. G. Dean (Ed.), *Dynamic social psychology* (pp. 604–615). New York: Random House.

Eisenberg, N. (2000). Emotion, regulation, and moral development. *Annual Review of Psychology, 51,* 665–697.

Emmons, R. A. (1999). *The psychology of ultimate concerns: Motivation and spirituality in personality.* New York: Guilford.

Freud, S. (1930). *Civilization and its discontents.* London: Hogarth.

Gilbert, D. T. (1998). Ordinary personology. In D. T. Gilbert, S. T. Fiske, & G. Lindzey (Eds.), *The handbook of social psychology,* 4th ed. (Vol. 2, pp. 89–141). New York: McGraw-Hill.

Ivie, R. L. (1980). Images of savagery in American justifications for war. *Communication Monographs, 47,* 270–294.

Jones, E. E. (1990). *Interpersonal perception.* New York: W. H. Freeman.

Keen, S. (1986). *Faces of the enemy: Reflections of the hostile imagination.* New York: Harper and Row.

Kelman, H. C. (1973). Violence without moral restraint: Reflections on the dehumanization of victims and victimizers. *Journal of Social Issues, 29,* 25–61.

Kelman, H. C., & Hamilton, V. L. (1989). *Crimes of obedience: Toward a social psychology of authority and responsibility.* New Haven, CT: Yale University Press.

Kelln, B. R. C., & Ellard, J. H. (1998). An equity theory analysis of the impact of forgiveness and retribution on transgressor compliance. *Personality and Social Psychology Bulletin, 25,* 864–872.

Lerner, M. J. (1980). *The belief in a just world: A fundamental delusion.* New York: Plenum.

Lipkus, I. (1991). The construction and validation of a global belief in a just world scale and exploratory factor analysis of the multidimensional belief in a just world. *Personality and Individual Differences, 12,* 1171–1178.

Magid, B. (1988). The evil self. *Dynamic Psychotherapy, 6,* 99–113.

McCullough, M. E., Worthington, E. L., & Rachal, K. C. (1997). Interpersonal forgiving in close relationships. *Journal of Personality and Social Psychology, 73,* 321–336.

Miller, A. G., Gillen, B., Schlenker, C., & Radlove, S. (1974). The prediction and perception of obedience to authority. *Journal of Personality, 42,* 23–42.

Miller, A. G., Gordon, A. K., & Buddie, A. M. (1999). Accounting for evil and cruelty: Is to explain to condone? *Personality and Social Psychology Review, 3,* 254–268.

Montada, L., & Lerner, M. J. (Eds.). (1998). *Responses to victimizations and belief in a just world.* New York: Plenum.

Newman, L. S., Duff, K. J., & Baumeister, R. F. (1997). A new look at defensive projection: Thought suppression, accessibility, and biased person perception. *Journal of Personality and Social Psychology, 72,* 980–1001.

Opotow, S. (1990). Moral exclusion and injustice: An introduction. *Journal of Social Issues, 46,* 1–20.

Redlich, F. (1999). *Hitler: Diagnosis of a destructive prophet.* New York: Oxford University Press.

Reeder, G., & Brewer, M. B. (1979). A schematic model of dispositional attribution in interpersonal perception. *Psychological Review, 86,* 61–79.

Robinson, P. H., & Darley, J. M. (1995). *Justice, liability, and blame: Community views and the criminal law.* Boulder, CO: Westview Press.

Rosenblatt, A., Greenberg, J., Solomon, S., Pyszczynski, T., & Lyon, D. (1989). Evidence for terror management theory: I. The effects of mortality salience on reactions to those who violate or uphold cultural values. *Journal of Personality and Social Psychology, 57,* 681–690.

Rubin, Z., & Peplau, L. A. (1975). Who believes in a just world? *Journal of Social Issues, 31,* 65–89.

Sabini, J., & Silver, M. (1998). *Emotion, character, and responsibility.* New York: Oxford University Press.

Simms, C. D., & Ellard, J. H. (1999). Demonizing and stereotypes of evilness. Poster session presented at the annual meeting of the Canadian Psychological Assocation, Ottawa, Ontario.

(2000). Just world beliefs and evil and bad stereotypes. Poster session presented at the annual meeting of the Canadian Psychological Assocation, Ottawa, Ontario.

Staub, E. (1989). *The roots of evil: The origins of genocide and other group violence.* New York: Cambridge University Press.

(1999). The roots of evil: Social conditions, culture, personality, and basic human needs. *Personality and Social Psychology Review, 3,* 179–192.

Tangney, J. P., Miller, R. S., Flicer, L., & Barlow, D. H. (1996). Are shame, guilt, and embarrassment distinct emotions? *Journal of Personality and Social Psychology, 75,* 1256–1269.

Tyler, T. R., Boeckmann, R. J., Smith, H. J., & Huo, Y. J. (1997). *Social justice in a diverse society.* Boulder, CO: Wesview Press.

Weiner, B. (1995). *Judgments of responsibility: A foundation for a theory of social conduct.* New York: Guilford.

White, Ralph K. (1995). When does intervention make sense? *Peace & Conflict: Journal of Peace Psychology, 1,* 85–95.

Worthington, E. L., Jr. (Ed.) (1998). *Dimensions of forgiveness: Psychological research and theological perspectives.* Philadelphia: Templeton Foundation Press.

Zimbardo, P. G. (1995). The psychology of evil: A situationist perspective on recruiting good people to engage in anti-social acts. *Research in Social Psychology, 11,* 125–133.

JUSTICE AND REACTION TO ONE'S OWN FATE

20. Belief in a Just World as a Personal Resource in School

CLAUDIA DALBERT AND JÜRGEN MAES

Students often complain about being treated unfairly in school. Some argue that they deserve another grade. Others feel that they have been punished unfairly while other pupils who behaved more inappropriately were reproved less. If students are asked to describe a good teacher, fairness is usually one of the top three characteristics (see Hofer, Pekrun, & Zielinski, 1986). Furthermore, Gage and Berliner (1996) claim that unfair grades significantly decrease students' achievements. Thus, for those who deal with everyday classroom problems, dealing with unfairness and the consequences of unfairness is a central issue. Nevertheless, there are few examples of justice psychology being applied in the school context. This is a great pity. Justice psychology and, in particular, justice motive theory could significantly enhance our knowledge of justice concerns in school.

Melvin Lerner was the first to describe the justice motive theory. He proposed (1965, 1970; Lerner & Simmons, 1966) that people have the need to believe in a just world in which all people, including themselves, get what they deserve and deserve what they get. This belief in a just world (BJW) provides individuals with the confidence that they will be treated fairly by others and that they will not become victims of unforeseeable misfortune. Additionally, it provides a conceptual framework that helps to interpret the events of one's personal life in a meaningful way. And this confidence, security, and meaning serve important adaptive functions. Therefore, people are motivated to defend their BJW when it is threatened by the confrontation with unfairness. Hence, the BJW indicates the strength of a justice motive. In order to substantiate the just world, individuals high in BJW are motivated to behave fairly and feel good when doing so, and they feel less worthy when engaging in motive-incongruent behavior (e.g., Dalbert, 1999).

After more than thirty years of just world research, a great deal is known about the effects of the belief in a just world: These effects range from helping behavior and attempts to restore or establish justice to degrading and blaming innocent victims (see Dalbert, 1996; Maes, 1998). Researchers, especially those using self-report measures, have portrayed belief in a just world as an antisocial trait associated with the devaluation and derogation of innocent victims, and with conservatism and authoritarianism (Furnham & Procter, 1989). As more and more studies confirmed these correlation patterns, the adaptive functions of just world beliefs became increasingly obscured. Only in the last few years have studies been published (e.g., Dalbert, 1996; Hafer & Correy, 1999; Tomaka & Blascovich, 1994) that illuminate the belief in a just world as a personal resource that helps individuals by protecting their mental health, providing a buffer against stress, enabling investment in long-term goals, and motivating achievement behavior. Until now, however, BJW has not be regarded as a personal resource in school.

From justice motive theory, several hypotheses can be derived for explaining achievement and well-being in school. Justice motive theory states that the BJW enhances feelings of security. If an individual satisfies the criteria for being "good" and behaves fairly, the person is protected from injustice and will get what she or he deserves. Thus, subjects high in BJW should feel confident that their efforts will be rewarded, which will better enable them to adapt to day-to-day stress. Furthermore, subjects high in BJW should trust that they will confront only fair achievement tasks, that is, tasks that can be dealt with successfully. As a consequence, they should gain better results. Tomaka and Blascovich (1994) presented their subjects with two laboratory tasks and found the predicted BJW effects. On both tasks, subjects high in BJW scored higher than subjects low in BJW. Pupils high in BJW thus should score higher on achievement tasks.

The amount of negative emotion someone has to handle when facing a potentially stressful situation, as well as the kind of coping someone may choose, depends on the primary appraisal of the stressful event. Subjects who appraise the event as a challenge, in contrast to those who appraise the event as a threat, are likely to feel less distressed and to cope more adaptively (Lazarus, 1991; Lazarus & Folkman, 1984). Individuals who maintain a high BJW have a host of strategies at their disposal that help them to cope with potentially stressful (unjust) events. Depending on the situation that they are facing, high BJW subjects can choose various coping strategies, such as restoring justice in reality or psychologically, or minimizing the unfairness. For these subjects, potentially stressful events are appraised in a way that makes them appear to be a challenge rather than a threat.

These considerations lead to the prediction that individuals high in BJW should perform better when facing an achievement situation. Individuals who maintain a strong BJW should feel less threatened and more challenged by the achievement request, and, in particular, they should reveal less negative emotion in the achievement situation. In Tomaka and Blascovich's study (1994), for example, subjects who maintained a high BJW showed a significantly lower degree of threat appraisal on both experimental tasks. In general, they rated the tasks as more of a challenge than a threat (i.e., they perceived the threat to lie within their perceived ability to cope). By contrast, subjects low in BJW felt threatened by the tasks (i.e., they perceived the threat to exceed their perceived ability to cope). After completing the tasks, and consistent with their appraisals, subjects high in BJW reported experiencing less stress than subjects low in BJW. The autonomic reactivity of the subjects was also in line with their self-reports. Furthermore, BJW was shown to provide a buffer against feelings of anger (Dalbert, 1997). In general, BJW has been shown to be positively correlated with well-being (Dalbert, 1998; Lipkus, Dalbert, & Siegler, 1996). In achievement contexts, this should result in BJW reducing feelings of threat, stress, and anger and enhancing well-being.

Individuals high in BJW are motivated to defend their BJW when confronted with unfairness. This is not only true for observers of an unfairness (for a review, see Lerner & Miller, 1978), but also for persons facing an unfairness by themselves (Bulman & Wortman, 1977; Comer & Laird, 1975). Dalbert (1996), for example, found that subjects high in BJW evaluated their fate as less unfair than did individuals low in BJW; and this was true for samples as different as unemployed blue-collar workers and mothers of a disabled child. Lipkus and Siegler (1993) found that old and middle-aged adults high in BJW described themselves less as victims of several discriminations than did adults low in BJW. Hafer and Correy (1999) found that high BJW subjects in a student sample were more likely to make internal attributions and less likely to make external attributions for their negative outcomes, leading to reduced feelings of unfairness, which, in turn, led to less negative emotion. Bierhoff (1998) reported an experiment on achievement motivation in an economic context that further underlined the importance of fairness cognitions. Subjects were presented with a scenario of an interaction between employee and boss. Individuals low in anger and high in perceived fairness revealed a higher achievement motivation. Taken collectively, this research indicates that BJW increases perceived fairness, a positive emotional state, and higher achievement motivation.

Hafer and Correy's (1999) study also found that BJW leads to internal attributions. Internal attributions are especially important about achievement behavior. An internal attribution enables the successful achiever to feel proud about his or her achievement and to feel confident that he or she will be equally successful in the future (Heckhausen, 1989; Rheinberg, 1993). For the unsuccessful achiever, an attribution to unstable causes, like chance or effort, increases optimism about a better achievement in the future, and an internal attribution on unstable causes provides him or her with knowledge of how to positively influence future achievements. Thus, BJW's effect on internal attributions may mediate its positive effect on achievement and well-being. Nevertheless, the results about the relationship between BJW and internal attributions remain mixed (for a review, see Dalbert, 1996). There is evidence that BJW may increase internal attributions; but when these attributions are unrealistic, they can prove to be maladaptive rather than adaptive (e.g., Dalbert, 1996; Dalbert & Warndorf, 1995). It is important to note, however, that these studies were not conducted in a school setting.

Based on previous research, we expected BJW to work as a personal resource. Specifically, we expected it to enhance school achievement, promote the perception of a fair school climate (= perceived fairness of own teachers), increase internal attributions, and reduce distress in school. Because individuals high in BJW should expect the achievement demands to be within their perceived ability to cope and expect to be fairly rewarded for their efforts, various predictions could be made: (a) they should perform better in school; (b) they should reveal less overall distress in school; and (c) they should show better overall well-being. Furthermore, to the extent the relationship between BJW, school grades, and well-being is mediated by perceived fairness, we can expect that (d) students high in BJW should feel treated more fairly by their teachers (fair school climate) than students low in BJW and, as a consequence, experience less distress. Furthermore, (e) subjects high in BJW should be more likely to attribute their achievement results internally, to their own effort and abilities, which should result in heightened feelings of fairness and reduced negative feelings. Finally, in line with coping research (e.g., Lazarus, 1991; Lazarus & Folkman, 1984), we expected that level of personal resource (BJW) and perceived fairness (fair school climate) should be more important in predicting school stress than school grades per se. These hypotheses were tested in two large questionnaire studies.

Study 1: BJW in School: A Path Model

The first study was conducted in Germany with 1,537 pupils from modern secondary schools (*Realschule*). Students attend this type of school beginning with the fifth grade up to the tenth grade. After finishing the school, most students apply for vocational training in the area of white-collar work. A smaller group of students will continue their school training for three more years at a university-bound school (*Gymnasium*). Students were sampled from all grade levels, with the fifth grade somewhat underrepresented (6.3% of the sample compared to 16.1% to 21.4% for the other grade levels), both male (48.5%) and female (51.5%). Students' ages ranged from ten to eighteen years.

Measures. BJW. Recent studies have distinguished between personal and general BJW and find that the former is more important in predicting distress, well-being, and behavior in line with the justice motive (Dalbert, 1999; Lipkus, Dalbert, & Siegler, 1996). As a consequence, BJW was measured with the Personal Belief in a Just World Scale (Dalbert, 1999), consisting of seven items that measure the conviction that, overall, events in one's life are fair (Alpha = .79).

Achievement. As a measure for school achievement, pupils were asked for their grades in their three main courses on the last midterm report. For all students, the three courses were mathematics, native language (= German), and main foreign language (= English). School grades could vary from 1 (very good) to 6 (unsatisfactory); thus, a low number indicated high achievement. The three grades were averaged to construct a general achievement indicator (Alpha = .63).

Fairness. Fairness perception was measured with four items. Pupils were asked to rate each of the three grades as very fair (6) to very unfair (1). Additionally, pupils rated their teachers' behavior toward them as very fair (6) to very unfair (1). These four fairness ratings were averaged to depict overall perceived fairness (Alpha = .62).

Stress. Perceived stress in school was assessed by two items asking whether pupils like to go to school (reverse coded) and whether the

Table 20.1. Means, standard deviations, and correlations of personal BJW and school variables (N ≥ 1515 pupils)

Variable	*M*	*SD*	Personal BJW	Grades	Perceived Fairness
Personal BJW	4.20	.86			
Grades	3.29	.72	−.14***		
Perceived fairness	4.52	.93	.33***	−.43***	
Distress	3.42	1.10	−.33***	.18***	−.26***

*** $p < .001$.

pupils experience their school days as stressful. Both ratings ($r = .54$) were averaged to measure distress. Distress could vary between 1 and 6, with 6 indicating strong distress.

Results. All variables were significantly correlated in the expected direction (see Table 20.1). To further clarify the relationships between personal BJW, school grades, perceived fairness, and distress, a path analysis was performed by stepwise multiple regressions ($p < .01$), with gender and class level always entered first and the BJW and school variables entered second. Class level and gender were depicted by dummy variables, with 1 meaning female or being a member of the specific class level. In the first multiple regression, personal BJW was regressed on gender and class level. In a second multiple regression, grades were regressed on personal BJW, gender, and class level. In the third analysis, perceived fairness was regressed on grades, personal BJW, gender, and class level. In the final analysis, distress was regressed on all of the aforementioned variables. Moreover, it was tested whether the observed relationships among the four variables (personal BJW, grades, perceived fairness, distress) were equally true for all class levels. The accepted models ($p < .01$) are depicted in Table 20.2.

BJW. Personal BJW did not vary between boys and girls, but was lower for the older pupils. To assess this age trend, the marginally significant effect of tenth grade was also included in the regression equations. Pupils in grades eight, nine, and ten did less strongly endorse the personal BJW than did pupils in grades five, six, and seven.

Grades. School grades varied between boys and girls; between grades five, nine, and ten compared to grades seven, eight, and nine;

Table 20.2. A path model for personal BJW, school variables, class level, and gender (accepted models)

Predictor	R	ΔR^2	b	beta	T	p
Personal BJW: F (3,1541) = 13,241; $p < .001$						
Eighth grade	.11	.01***	–.34	–.15	–5.664	<.001
Ninth grade	.15	.01***	–.25	–.12	–4.385	<.001
Tenth grade	.16	.003*	–.13	–.06	–2.038	.042
Constant			4.33			
Grades: F (5,1493) = 19,236; $p < .001$						
Gender	.13	.02***	–.19	–.13	–5.138	<.001
Fifth grade	.16	.01***	–.34	–.12	–4.467	<.001
Tenth grade	.18	.01***	–.22	–.11	–4.353	<.001
Ninth grade	.20	.006**	–.16	–.09	–3.562	<.001
Personal BJW	.25	.02***	–.12	–.14	–5.685	<.001
Constant			3.98			
Perceived fairness: F (3,1494) = 185,091; $p < .001$						
Gender	.11	.01***	.12	.06	2.876	.004
Grades	.44	.18***	–.49	–.38	–17.069	<.001
Personal BJW	.52	.08***	.31	.29	12.863	<.001
Constant			4.79			
Distress: F (6,1483) = 47,321; $p < .001$						
Sixth grade	.11	.01***	–.30	–.10	–4.271	<.001
Gender	.14	.01***	–.17	–.08	–3.106	.002
Fifth grade	.17	.01***	–.31	–.07	–2.788	.005
Personal BJW	.37	.10***	–.35	–.27	–10.522	<.001
Perceived fairness	.39	.02***	–.15	–.13	–4.575	<.001
Grades	.40	.01**	.12	.08	2.907	.004
Constant			5.33			

*** $p < .001$; ** $p < .01$; * $p < .05$.

and school grades were positively correlated with personal BJW. Girls got better grades than boys. Pupils got better grades at the beginning (fifth grade) and at the end of their school careers (grades nine and ten) than in between (grades six, seven, and eight). Moreover, pupils strong in personal BJW received better grades than pupils low in BJW.

Fairness. Perceived fairness varied between boys and girls, and it was positively correlated with school grades and personal BJW. Specifically, girls perceived their teachers as more fair than did boys. In addition, pupils with good grades and strong in personal BJW perceived their teachers as more fair than pupils with poor grades and low in personal BJW. School grades more strongly affected perceived fairness (beta = –.38) than personal BJW (beta = .29). Notice, however, that three of the four fairness items asked especially about the fairness of the grades.

Distress. Distress varied between boys and girls, between grades five and six compared to grades seven, eight, nine, and ten, and was significantly correlated with grades, perceived fairness, and personal BJW. Girls and pupils at the beginning of their school careers (grades five and six) felt less distressed than boys and pupils in the higher grades. Furthermore, pupils high in personal BJW and high in perceived fairness revealed less distress than pupils low in BJW and low in perceived fairness. Finally, pupils with poor grades reported more distress than pupils with better grades. As expected, the personal BJW's effect on distress was greatest (beta = –.27), and the effect of perceived fairness on distress (beta = –.13) was greater than the effect of grades on distress (beta = .08).

Summary. Overall, the results are very much in line with the hypotheses. Personal BJW significantly predicted school grades, perceived fairness, and distress. The more the pupils endorsed the belief that, overall, events in their lives were just, (a) the greater their achievement, (b) the more they felt they were treated fairly by their teachers, and (c) the less they felt distressed by their school visits. Moreover, (d) the personal BJW, a stable person disposition, could be distinguished from school-specific fairness perceptions. Perceived fairness was affected by personal BJW as well as by school grades. In addition, personal BJW as well as perceived fairness explained distress. Thus, personal BJW can be seen as a coping resource that enhanced achievement and reduced unfairness perceptions. Both better grades and reduced feelings of unfairness appear to mediate the BJW's adaptive effect on distress. Furthermore, coping resources (e.g., personal BJW) and the coping product (e.g., perceived fairness) had a greater effect on distress than the event (e.g., grades) itself. In sum, this study's results demonstrated that BJW is an important personal resource in school, enhancing school achievement, promoting the perception of a fair school climate, and reducing distress in school. In particular, the results underline the notion that stress in school seems to be more strongly derived from fairness conflicts than from achievement problems.

Study 2: BJW in School: Subjective Well-being and Achievement

The second study was carried out within the framework of a school model test in the state of Rhineland-Palatinate, Germany. During the 1990s there was an ongoing discussion in Germany about the length of the German schooling period. After four years of elementary schooling, German pupils can attend any of three different school forms, from which the grammar school leads to matriculation in nine more years. It was argued that compared to other European countries, German pupils are too old when they enter the university and that twelve instead of thirteen years of schooling should be enough. In our school model test, a subgroup of pupils regarded by their teachers as particularly gifted and productive were given the opportunity to reach matriculation in twelve years. Between the fifth and the tenth grade, they were taught in special test classes that resulted in their saving one school year (i.e., completing in five years what took other students six years). From the eleventh to the thirteenth school year, they were reunited with their peers and received the standard education (for a more detailed description of the design, see Kaiser et al., 1994). A large questionnaire study was conducted involving 1,070 pupils from five different test schools.

Data were gathered from summer 1992 to the end of 1993. Subjects were students from the fifth to the twelfth grade level. Fifty percent were from regular classes; 18.2% were from test classes; 25% were from the upper-class levels; 7.3% were from so-called normal classes (class levels in which no separation into test and regular classes was accomplished). Forty-nine percent were boys, 50% girls; students' ages ranged from ten to twenty-one.

BJW. BJW was not measured with a general scale but with school-specific instruments (Maes, 1996). The items express the general expectation of meeting justice or injustice in school, of being punished or rewarded fairly, and of getting deserved results. This study went beyond Study 1 to include measures of achievement motivation and attributions of success and failure. This addition permits us to test whether there exists a positive relationship between school-specific BJW and achievement attributions or achievement motivation. Furthermore, an extensive set of mental health dimensions were integrated, which allows us to replicate and extend the hypothesis of a positive relationship between school-specific BJW and mental health.

Table 20.3. Mean differences in BJS and BUS for regular classes and test classes (N ≥ 1030 pupils)

Variable	Group	*M*	*SD*	t
BJS	Regular class	2.80	.93	−3.18**
	Test class	3.03	.83	
	Former regular class	2.24	.85	−3.04**
	Former test class	2.63	.74	
BUS	Regular class	2.69	.99	4.13**
	Test class	2.35	.92	
	Former regular class	2.76	.93	4.07**
	Former test class	2.27	.75	

** $p < .01$.

Finally, data were gathered in another school type, which allows us to test whether the hypothesized relationships are true for different school types.

School-specific belief in justice was measured twofold. Belief in a just school (BJS) was measured using a five-item scale (Alpha = .72; e.g., "All in all, life is very just in school"), and belief in an unjust school scale (BUS) consisted of seven items (Alpha = .80; e.g., "School life is full of injustices"). It is common for factor analysis to yield two factors for justice and injustice items (Maes, 1994; Dalbert et al., 2001). Scales run from 0 (do not agree) to 5 (agree totally).

We expected pupils in test classes to differ in BJS and BUS compared to their companions in regular classes. The reason for this is that students in the test classes were selected on the basis of their teachers' judgments of their high motivation and ability. High BJS (or low BUS) may be seen as a resource providing good learning conditions and enabling achievement. Nevertheless, good results and learning experiences may in turn promote BJS. Actually, BJS was significantly higher in test compared to regular classes (see Table 20.3). The same was true for those members of higher grade levels (eleven and twelve) who had been in test classes earlier in their school careers. By contrast, BUS was significantly higher in regular classes and among those who had never been members of test classes. However, the overall correlational patterns for BJS or BUS with attributions, achievement motivation, and mental health did not differ between (former) regular class and (former) test class members. Hence, the results were collapsed across the two groups.

Attributions. The perceived causes of success and failure have a decisive influence on achievement behavior. In particular, BJW should promote achievement by promoting internal attributions. Attributions of success and failure were measured with a sixty-five-item questionnaire. Nine scales emerged from the factor analysis (all: Alpha >.70). Results could be attributed to *external causes*, such as (1) chance, (2) class climate (e.g., support and understanding in the class), and (3) the teachers (their competence and efforts), as well as to *internal variable causes*, such as (4) one's own effort, (5) doing homework with care and diligence, and (6) the use of learning strategies (knowing how to memorize things, how to read effectively), and (7) blandishment (flattering teachers, making oneself popular with teachers), and also to *internal stable causes*, such as (8) native ability and (9) assertiveness (asserting oneself against teachers, against companions). BJS was most consistently correlated with attributions to internal variable causes, with the exception of the school-inappropriate strategy of blandishment, which was highly correlated with BUS. BUS most consistently related to external explanations and attributions to internal, but stable, causes. Overall, pupils high in BJS were most likely to explain their own success and failure in school by their own efforts, their homework, and

Table 20.4. Correlations of BJS and BUS with school variables (N ≥ 1000 pupils)

Variables	BJS	BUS	Variables	BJS	BUS
Attributions for success and failure:			*Symptom check list:*		
Chance	–.18**	.30**	Pressure to achieve	–.22**	.17**
Class climate	.12**	.11**	Test anxiety	–.17**	.10**
Teachers	–.23**	.39**	Aversion against school	–.32**	.22**
Own efforts	.21**	.04	Vegetative dystonia	–.16**	.06
Working at home	.26**	.02	Shyness	–.13**	.04
Learning strategies	.15**	–.01	Introversion	–.19**	.15**
Blandishment	–.24**	.41**	Amount of quarrels	–.10**	.08**
Native ability	–.01	.16**	Depressive mood	–.18**	.07
Assertiveness	–.03	.24**	Assertiveness	.14**	–.04
Achievement motivation:			*Contentment with*		
Pride in achievement	.37**	–.01	Own achievement	.34**	–.25**
Confidence in success	.28**	–.10**	School experiences	.34**	–.22**
Moderate aspiration level	.31**	–.02	Own life	.22**	–.07
Fear of failure	–.10**	.27**			
Low aspiration level	–.02	.16**			
High aspiration level	.13**	.16**			

** $p < .01$.

the applied learning strategies, whereas pupils high in BUS tended to explain their school achievements by external forces such as chance, class climate, and their teachers, by their own blandishment, or by innate ability and assertiveness.

Achievement motivation. Research on achievement motivation (Heckhausen, 1989) has consistently shown that pride in one's own achievements and confidence in future success foster investments in future achievement, while achievement anxiety and fear of failure often undermine achievement. It has also been shown that a moderate aspiration level is most conducive to successful task-related behavior, with a low aspiration level producing diminished effort and a high aspiration level producing conflicts. BJW fosters (1) the appraisal of stressful events as challenging, (2) the presumption that one is being treated fairly, and (3) the attribution to internal unstable causes. Thus, BJW, and in particular BJS, should be positively correlated with favorable achievement conditions (pride, confidence, medium aspiration level) and BUS with unfavorable ones (fear, high or low aspiration level). Scales for measuring these variables emerged from the factor analysis of a thirty-two-item-questionnaire (all: Alpha >.70). As expected, pupils high in BJS revealed more pride in their own achievements (e.g., "I am proud on my achievements in school"), more confidence in success ("I am confident that my next class test will be good"), and a moderate aspiration level ("I try to get results a little bit better than the last ones"), while pupils high in BUS showed more fear of failure ("I am always afraid of worse results") and low aspiration level ("I am satisfied if I don't have to stay down a year"). On the other hand, a high aspiration level ("I want to be the best") correlated with both BJS and BUS.

Well-being. In this study, school-specific well-being was assessed along with more general well-being indicators. Nine well-being dimensions were derived from a seventy-item symptom checklist (Maes, 1996; all: Alpha >.68) that asked individuals to indicate the extent to which they were experiencing various physical symptoms and feelings. BJS was more consistently related to these symptoms than was BUS. BJS went along with lower feelings of pressure to achieve (fear that others expect too much), less test anxiety, less aversion to school (reluctance to go to school, dislike of classes), less vegetative dystonia (e.g., headache, stomachache, dizziness), less shyness (feeling shy, lonely, inhibited), less introversion (ruminating, desire to be alone), fewer quarrels outside school (with parents, friends, siblings), and fewer depressive moods (feeling blue, sad), but was associated with high assertiveness (feeling self-confident, complacent). While the symptom checklist was used to measure current distress and strain, a life contentment questionnaire was used to measure overall well-being. Only the 250 pupils of higher grade levels (eleven and twelve) were asked to assess all their experiences in school. Three aspects could be differentiated: contentment with their achievements (their performance, their grades), contentment with their school (school climate, climate in their age group), and contentment with their own life (whole life, relations to friends, leisure time). BJS correlated positively with all three aspects, while BUS correlated negatively with contentment with one's own achievements and the school experiences. Here, a priori analyses revealed the only significant difference in correlations between the members of former test or regular classes, respectively. The positive correlation between contentment with one's own life was found among members of the former test classes (r = .65), but not among members of former regular classes (r = .09).

Discussion

Both studies reported here support the relevance of justice motive theory to school-related processes. In particular, the results indicated the following. (a) Personal belief in a just world (BJW) or school-specific justice belief (BJS) were demonstrated to promote pupils' school-specific as well as overall well-being. Students with a high belief in justice felt less distressed in school, felt less pressed toward achievement, revealed less test anxiety and less aversion to school, and were more satisfied with their achievements and school experiences. Moreover, pupils with high justice beliefs revealed fewer physical symptoms, were less shy and introverted, felt less depressed, suffered fewer quarrels outside school, and felt more self-confident. (b) BJW was positively correlated with the pupils' achievement results; pupils high in BJW had better grades in their three main courses. (c) The better their grades were, the less distressed the pupils felt in school. (d) However, it was shown that this direct effect of grades on distress was accompanied by even stronger effects of perceived fairness and BJW on distress. This latter result supports the notion that BJW and school- or class-specific fairness perceptions work differently. BJW can be seen as coping resource, and fairness ratings can be interpreted as coping products. BJW's effect on well-being was only partly mediated by the subjects' fairness perceptions. Most importantly, BJW, as compared to the fairness perceptions and the grades, revealed the strongest effect on distress. The second study's results shed further light on the mediating processes. (e) The belief in a just school (BJS) seems to promote internal variable attributions that are known to promote fairness perceptions (e.g., Hafer & Correy, 1999) and future achievement (e.g., Heckhausen, 1989). (f) Furthermore, an adaptive level of achievement motivation was more common among pupils high in BJS.

Several shortcomings of the reported studies should kept in mind when interpreting the results. Both studies were cross-sectional and correlational in nature. Therefore, no causal relationships were tested. In particular, it may be questioned whether BJW enhances achievement and well-being, or whether good achievement products and well-being influence beliefs in justice. Nevertheless, there is some evidence from outside school research that supports the hypothesis that BJW is a cause and not a consequence of well-being (Dalbert, 1998, 1999) and achievement (e.g., Tomaka & Blascovich, 1994). Longitudinal studies are needed to more clearly differentiate between predictor and dependent variables. Such research would allow us to interpret the assumed path model as a causal one. In addition, in both studies recently developed (personal BJW, see Dalbert, 1999) or concurrently developed (BJS, BUS) scales were used to assess the subjects' belief in justice. Preliminary evidence on the concurrent and construct validity of personal BJW and its stability across experimental conditions was provided by Dalbert (1999). However, since the BJS and BUS differed among pupils with different school backgrounds (regular compared to test classes), scale stability and overall validity need further study.

To our knowledge, these two studies were the first to apply justice motive theory to a school setting. The results suggest that this first attempt was successful. In line with justice motive theory as introduced by Melvin Lerner (e.g., 1965, 1970; Lerner & Simmons, 1966), BJW serves as personal resource in school. The belief in a just world provided the pupils with trust in being treated fairly by their teachers; it endowed the pupils with a schema that enabled them to interpret the school events in their life in a meaningful way; and it enhanced their tendency to make variable internal attributions of their achievements. As a consequence, BJW strengthened achievement behavior and promoted school-specific and overall well-being. Additional research is needed to further validate the belief in a just world consequences in school. A suitable basis for such studies is the proposed path model. BJW promotes achievement motivation, achievement behavior, and internal variable attributions of one's own success or failure; it leads to the perception of a fair class climate and supports pupils' well-being in and outside school. As a consequence, achievement behavior can be seen as directly and indirectly mediated by the achievement motive – affected, in turn, by students' BJW. This is even more true for students' well-being. The students' school-specific well-being and their general well-being were most strongly and directly affected by their BJW. Besides this direct effect, BJW's adaptive effect on well-being can be seen as mediated by the achievement results, the internal variable attributions, and a fair class climate.

REFERENCES

Bierhoff, H. W. (1998). Ärger, Aggression und Gerechtigkeit: Moralische Empörung und antisoziales Verhalten [Anger, aggression, and justice: Moral indignation and antisocial behavior]. In H. W. Bierhoff & U. Wagner (Eds.), *Aggression und Gewalt: Phänomene, Ursachen und Interventionen* [Aggression and violence: phenomenon, causes, and interventions] (pp. 26–47). Stuttgart: Kohlhammer.

Bulman, R. J., & Wortman, C. B. (1977). Attributions of blame and coping in the "real world": Severe accident victims react to their lot. *Journal of Personality and Social Psychology, 35*, 351–363.

Comer, R., & Laird, J. D. (1975). Choosing to suffer as a consequence of expecting to suffer: Why do people do it? *Journal of Personality and Social Psychology, 32*, 92–101.

Dalbert, C. (1996). *Über den Umgang mit Ungerechtigkeit. Eine psychologische Analyse* [Dealing with injustice: A psychological analysis]. Bern: Huber.

(1997). *The belief in a just world: Personal disposition or situational construction, illusory conviction or reality description?* Paper presented at the Sixth Biennial Meeting of the International Network for Social Justice Research, Potsdam, Germany.

(1998). Belief in a just world, well-being, and coping with an unjust fate. In L. Montada & M. J. Lerner (Eds.), *Responses to victimization and belief in a just world* (pp. 87–105). New York: Plenum.

(1999). The world is more just for me than generally: About the Personal Belief in a Just World Scale's validity. *Social Justice Research, 12*, 79–98.

Dalbert, C., Lipkus, I. M., Sallay, H., & Goch, I. (2001). A just and an unjust world: Structure and validity of different world beliefs. *Personality and Individual Differences, 30*, 561–577.

Dalbert, C., & Warndorf, P. K. (1995). Informationsverarbeitung und depressive Symptome bei Müttern behinderter Kinder: Die Bedeutung von

Ungewißheitstoleranz, Selbstzuschreibungen und Heilungsprognosen [Information processing and depressive symptoms of mothers of a disabled child: The role of uncertainty tolerance, self-attribution, and healing prognoses]. *Zeitschrift für Klinische Psychologie, 24,* 328–336.

Furnham, A., & Procter, E. (1989). Belief in a just world: Review and critique of the individual difference literature. *British Journal of Social Psychology, 28,* 365–384.

Gage, N. L., & Berliner, D. C. (1996). *Pädagogische Psychologie* [Educational psychology]. Weinheim: Psychologie Verlags Union.

Hafer, C. L., & Correy, B. L. (1999). Mediators of the relation of beliefs in a just world and emotional responses to negative outcomes. *Social Justice Research, 12,* 189–204.

Heckhausen, H. (1989). *Motivation und Handeln* [Motivation and action]. Berlin: Springer.

Hofer, M., Pekrun, R., & Zielinski, W. (1986). Die Psychologie des Lerners [The psychology of the Learner]. In B. Weidenmann, A. Krapp, M. Hofer, G. L. Huber, & H. Mandl (Eds.), *Pädagogische Psychologie* [Educational psychology] (pp. 219–275). Weinheim: Psychologie Verlags Union.

Kaiser, A., Lüken, A., Maes, J., & Winkels, R. (1994). Schulzeitverkürzung – Auf der Suche nach dem bildungspolitischen Kompromiß [On shortening the school period – Searching for a compromise in educational politics]. *Grundlagen der Weiterbildung. Zeitschrift für Weiterbildung und Bildungspolitik im In- und Ausland, 5,* 219–223.

Lazarus, R. S. (1991). *Emotion and adaptation.* New York: Oxford University Press.

Lazarus, R. S., & Folkman, S. (1984). *Stress, appraisal and coping.* New York. Springer.

Lerner, M. J. (1965). Evaluation of performance as a function of performer's reward and attractiveness. *Journal of Personality and Social Psychology, 1,* 355–360.

(1970). The desire for justice and reactions to victims. In J. Macaulay & L. Berkowitz (Eds.), *Altruism and helping behavior* (pp. 205–229). New York: Academic Press.

Lerner, M. J., & Miller, D. T. (1978). Just world research and the attribution process: Looking back and ahead. *Psychological Bulletin, 85,* 1030–1051.

Lerner, M. J., & Simmons, C. H. (1966). The observer's reaction to the "innocent victim": Compassion or rejection? *Journal of Personality and Social Psychology, 4,* 203–210.

Lipkus, I. M., Dalbert, C., & Siegler, I. C. (1996). The importance of distinguishing the belief in a just world for self versus others. *Personality and Social Psychology Bulletin, 22,* 666–677.

Lipkus, I. M., & Siegler, I. C. (1993). The belief in a just world and perceptions of discrimination. *Journal of Psychology, 127,* 465–474.

Maes, J. (1994). Blaming the victim – belief in control or belief in justice? *Social Justice Research, 7,* 69–90.

(1996). FEES – Die Fragebögen zur Erfassung der Einstellung zum Schulversuch [The questionnaires for the assessment of altitudes toward the school experiments]. In Ministerium für Bildung, Wissenschaft und Weiterbildung Rheinland-Pfalz (Hrsg.), *Entwicklung und Erprobung von Modellen der Begabtenförderung am Gymnasium mit Verkürzung der Schulzeit. Abschlußbericht* [Development and testing of different models for nurturing the gifted in grammar schools with a shortened school period. Final results] [= Schulversuche und Bildungsforschung, 80] (pp. 34–51). Mainz: Hase & Koehler.

(1998). Eight stages in the development of research on the construct of belief in a just world? In L. Montada & M. J. Lerner (Eds.), *Responses to victimization and belief in a just world* (pp. 163–185). New York: Plenum.

Rheinberg, F. (1993). *Motivation* [Motivation]. Stuttgart: Kohlhammer.

Tomaka, J., & Blascovich, J. (1994). Effects of justice beliefs on cognitive, psychological, and behavioral responses to potential stress. *Journal of Personality and Social Psychology, 67*, 732–740.

21. Awakening to Discrimination

FAYE J. CROSBY AND STACY A. ROPP

Melvin Lerner's concept of the justice motive has made a major contribution to social psychology. His observations – supported by a raft of elegant experiments – about how people like to think that they are just and like to imagine that they live in a just world have profoundly influenced the shape of social psychology in America. Among the many psychologists to follow the path laid down by Lerner is the first author of this piece, Faye Crosby.

Our chapter contains three parts. In the first, we review briefly Mel Lerner's ground-breaking scholarship on "the fundamental delusion," the need to believe that one's world is fair. The second part of the chapter explores one elaboration of the phenomenon: the denial of personal discrimination. In the second part, we see that people (or at least people in our culture) defend more against recognizing injustices to the individual than against recognizing injustices to groups. People may be particularly resistant to seeing the self as the victim of an injustice. In the final section of the chapter, we peek at preliminary findings of an ethno-methodological study of women who have awakened to discrimination and are now seeking legal means to reestablish justice in their worlds. Throughout the chapter, we see that as the focus of attention (on the self, on another, or on groups) changes, so do the ways that individuals make decisions about justice.

Believing in a Just World

How do people decide who deserves punishment for a crime or who deserves public assistance? How is it that progressive liberals regularly turn a blind eye to the suffering of a needy beggar? What accounts for the fact that people can sometimes be compassionate and sometimes show a stony heart? It was to solve puzzles such as these that Melvin Lerner began his ground-breaking studies in the mid 1960s. Over the next decade and a half, Lerner published almost twenty articles in psychological journals, which he then synthesized in his great book, *The Belief in a Just World* (Lerner, 1980).

Lerner's views have gained wide currency. Today, social psychologists take as a given that in any justice decision people rely on the belief that the world is a just place. We all know that for the person on the street, and even for ourselves, living in a just world means that good people are rewarded while bad people are punished. If you work hard and are good to the people around you, then you will succeed in life, professionally and personally. If you are lazy and mean, then you will fail. People who have "bad" things occur to them in their lives must also be "bad." They must have done something to deserve the negative outcomes they receive. To preserve the illusion of justice, we convince ourselves, for example, that the person who requires public assistance or the woman who has been sexually harassed are "worse" people than those who are more fortunate. In the laboratory, this has been shown when participants devalue an "innocent" victim (i.e., Lerner & Simmons, 1966). Seeing victims in this light insures us that we (the good people) will not suffer the fate of them (the bad people).

Lerner (1980) has outlined the tactics people use to defend their just world beliefs. These tactics include two types of psychological defenses. The first is denial-withdrawal. In this case, individuals do not put themselves in situations where they see unjust events. If they see an unjust event, they withdraw. The second psychological defense is reinterpretation of the event. There are three different reinterpretations that can take place: reinterpretation of the outcome, of the cause, or of the character of the victim. Reinterpreting the outcome could mean rationalizing that the suffering was not that severe or that the suffering was character-building. Reinterpreting the cause could mean rationalizing that the suffering was in some way caused by the victim. Reinterpreting the character of the victim could mean rationalizing that the victim's fate was not unjust.

Mel Lerner did not just philosophize about the fundamental delusion. He systematically demonstrated each aspect of his theory through carefully controlled laboratory studies. Typical was the early experiment with Simmons. Participants in Lerner and Simmons's (1966) experiment watched a woman receive electric shocks. Half of the subjects were led to believe that the woman had chosen her own fate, and half thought she had no choice. Cross-cutting the presumed choice manipulation was another manipulation, by which half of the subjects were able to intervene while the other half were not. When they were able to intervene and stop the shocks, subjects rated the woman in a more positive fashion than when they were unable to intervene. The harshest ratings were given to the woman who putatively had chosen her own negative fate.

Looking back at Lerner's just world experiments two or three decades later, we are able to see not only that they are brilliant, but also that they take a certain perspective. American psychology in the 1960s, 1970s, and 1980s was intensively individualistic (Sampson, 1977), and Mel Lerner was no more able to escape his time and place than we are today. Virtually all of the research on the just world dealt with how people make justice decisions about individuals (usually other than the self), and none concerned the ways in which people make justice decisions about groups. In Lerner's (1980) book, *The Belief in a Just World,* over forty experiments are described in detail, and only one experiment (Miller, 1977) questions how people react to misfortunes that befall groups or categories of people. Lerner and other researchers seemed to assume that people would react to information about groups in the same way that they react to information about individuals. The question arose: Do they? Do people have the same resistance to acknowledging injustice at the group level as they do at the individual level?

Denying Personal Discrimination

It was in part to extend Lerner's just world theory and in part to test empirically several models of relative deprivation theory that the first author of this chapter conducted in 1979 an elaborate survey of employed men, employed women, and housewives living in Newton, Massachusetts (Crosby, 1982, 1984). Following the advice of Thomas Pettigrew, Crosby distinguished between egoistical (personal) deprivation and fraternal (group) deprivation. The distinction meant that she ended up assessing separately how people react to individual instances of sex discrimination and how people react to sex discrimination in general.

Much to Crosby's surprise, she discovered different patterns for judgments about groups than for judgments about the self. As a group, the employed women in the survey were objectively the victims of sex discrimination. They earned significantly less money than the employed men, although the two groups were exactly comparable in levels of education, occupational prestige, training, age, and avowed commitment to their jobs. Subjectively, most of the women showed no awareness of discrimination. On the whole, the women reported being as satisfied with their jobs and their pay as the men were.

In minimizing their own suffering, the Newton women were acting as one would expect on the basis of Lerner's theories and in line with prior studies of self-blame. Rubin and Peplau (1973) had shown that immediately after hearing the results of a draft lottery that indicated that they would soon be drafted, men both devalued themselves and had lower self-esteem. Comer and Laird (1975) had tested self-blame experimentally by telling half of their subjects that they would be required to eat a worm. Those who believed they were about to taste a worm adjusted their thinking by devaluing themselves or increasing the value of the "bad" outcome. Bulman and Wortman (1977) had demonstrated that people who were paralyzed in accidents adjusted best after the accident if they blamed themselves and were happiest if they were still strong believers in a just world.

Where the Newton results were unexpected was in the employed women's acknowledgment of the general problem of sex discrimination. All three groups in the survey (employed men, employed women, and housewives) were aware of, and aggrieved about, gender inequities. The employed women, furthermore, were significantly more aware and significantly more upset than either the employed men or the housewives. While denying that they themselves faced the problems that in fact they faced, the Newton women forcefully acknowledged that sex discrimination was a serious issue for women.

What accounted for the discontinuity between justice judgments concerning the self and justice judgments concerning women in general? Crosby speculated that two factors were at play: cognition and emotion. Cognitively, it seemed likely to Crosby that group comparisons allow for more certain inferences than do comparisons between individuals. But cognitive factors alone did not constitute the entire explanation. "[I]t may be emotionally aversive to see anyone, including oneself, as a victim," Crosby opined, " because such a vision challenges a person's ability to believe in a just world" (Crosby, Cordova, & Jaskar, 1993, p. 100). To underscore the likely emotional component to processes she had uncovered, Crosby labeled the Newton phenomenon as "the denial of personal discrimination," which she saw as part of the larger phenomenon "the denial of personal disadvantage."

Soon after completing the Newton study, Crosby and her students conduced a set of follow-up studies to test whether the phenomenon she discovered would be replicated among other populations (Crosby et al., 1989). One group whom Crosby and associates (1989) queried were (nonstudent) lesbians living in Northampton, Massachusetts, contacted through snowball sampling procedures. In an initial study, the lesbians reported that they thought they personally faced virtually no discrimination in terms of salaries, job opportunities, housing, or general treatment. The same sample did, however, think that lesbians in the United States generally faced rather severe discriminatory barriers in terms of salaries, job opportunities, housing, and general treatment.

In response to Crosby's glee that the phenomenon found in Newton had been replicated, the student collaborators on the project replied: "But wait! These data only prove what we already know: Northampton is a great place for gay women to live." To rule out the possibility that the women in the first sample were simply making veridical judgments about their own privilege relative to lesbians living elsewhere in the United States, Crosby and colleagues interviewed a second sample of professional women living in Northampton, each of whom also self-identified as a lesbian. Women in the second sample were asked about their own lives, the lives of other lesbians in Northampton, and the lives of lesbians in the United States generally. Contrary to the expectations of the students and consistent with the pattern found in Newton, the second sample showed an awareness of discrimination against lesbians throughout the United States and in their own town but showed no appreciation of being at any personal disadvantage (Crosby et al., 1989).

Crosby is not the only investigator to have found that people are generally much more aware of discrimination against their group than of discrimination against themselves. In the United States, Canada, and Europe, numerous investigators (e.g., Hafer & Olson, 1993; Postmes et al., 1999; Ruggiero, Taylor, & Lydon, 1997; Taylor et al., 1990) have corroborated and replicated the basic paradigm. Samples have included college students, working women, and immigrant populations. In recognition of the fact that people may be exaggerating the degree of group disadvantage as well as minimizing the degree of personal disadvantage, the phenomenon has been relabelled "the personal-group discrimination discrepancy" (Taylor et al., 1990; Taylor, Wright, & Porter, 1994).

Researchers have not simply replicated the findings of Newton. They have also expanded our understanding of *why* people claim less injustice for the self than for the group to which the self belongs. We see three ways in which research has advanced our understanding of the dynamics of personal denial.

One important observation that deepens the understanding of the dynamics of the phenomenon was made by Don Taylor and his colleagues. It is this: The discrepancy between personal dissatisfaction and group dissatisfaction is sometimes due to an exaggeration of group suffering as well as to the minimization of personal suffering observed by Crosby (see Taylor et al., 1990; Taylor, Wright, & Porter, 1994). Stereotypes about prejudice and discrimination could lead people to assume that certain groups (e.g., women) are the victims of discrimination. These stereotypes, in turn, lead to an exaggeration of the perception of group-level discrimination.

Another advance has been the documentation of how cognition may account for the Newton phenomenon. In a series of experiments, subjects were given materials about how rewards were distributed in organizations and asked to judge the fairness of the distribution. Systematic unfairnesses were built into the materials, so that, for example, workers at Plant A were paid more than workers at Plant B; women were paid more than comparable men; men were paid more than comparable women. When subjects were given the information case by case, they were generally unable to perceive the unfairnesses; but when they were given the exact same information in aggregate form, they did detect the injustices. Emotional investment in the matters under review, furthermore, did not influence people's judgments. Noting that the case-by-case format is the analog of decisions about individuals, including the self, and that the aggregated format is the analog of decisions about groups, Crosby and her colleagues concluded from their series of experiments that the Newton phenomenon could be accounted for in part, or even wholly, by factors in human information processing (for a review, see Clayton & Crosby, 1992).

Finally, researchers have begun to look at the conditions under which victims of discrimination are able to perceive their own disadvantaged status. Three factors have been shown to be important in recognizing discrimination: attributional ambiguity, belief in a just world, and the availability of social support. Starting with Crocker and Major's ambiguity work (Crocker & Major, 1989; Major & Crocker, 1993) on how members of a disadvantaged group (e.g., black college students) can use discrimination as a self-protective explanation for their own poor performance on tasks, several researchers have thought it likely that attributional ambiguity might also influence how members of disadvantaged groups explain the poor rewards they receive from others. Attributing a poor reward to discrimination allows members of disadvantaged groups to retain their individual self-esteem on a given task, while concluding that their actions were met with discrimination.

Believing in a just world has been found to affect a woman's willingness to recognize, and to act against, discrimination. Lipkus and Siegler (1993) found that individuals with strong just world beliefs reported less personal discrimination in their lives than individuals with weak just world beliefs. Hafer and Olson (1989) showed that strong believers in a just world were more likely to think personal deprivation (in an experimental setting) was fair, compared to weak believers in a just world. Hafer and Olson (1993) also surveyed working women, who were objectively in a disadvantaged position in comparison to working men. Strong believers in a just world were less likely to be upset that their group was disadvantaged. Further, women with stronger just world beliefs were less likely to act out against unfairness in their job, both personally and collectively, than women with weaker just world beliefs. Theoretically, "strong believers in a just world would be less likely to engage in behavioral attempts to change their negative outcomes than would weak believers" (Olson & Hafer, 1998).

Social support has been found to be important by Ruggiero, Taylor, and Lydon (1997). In a condition of 50% probability of discrimination (four of eight male judges), women were told that they had failed a test of future career success, then given information about the availability of social support. In a control condition of no informational or emotional support available, women were more likely to attribute their failure to their performance, rather than to discrimination. When one form of social support was available (either emotional or informational), women were equally likely to attribute their failure to discrimination or to performance. However, when both informational and emotional support were available to the participants, women more likely to attribute their failure to discrimination, rather than to performance.

How important is social support when one moves from the controlled and contrived laboratory to the world outside it? We have begun to address this and other questions in a preliminary survey of women who have brought sex discrimination suits against their employers.

The Awakening

Given how difficult it is for people to recognize individual cases of discrimination, even when they belong to disadvantaged groups, one may wonder how the pattern is ever broken. As a preamble to a full-blown study of how one awakens to discrimination, we have contacted one group of aggrieved individuals: faculty women at Stanford University who, individually and collectively, have brought complaints against the university for sex discrimination. In a set of individual interviews and focus group interviews, we have sifted through the variables to see which seem most important. We have looked for evidence on the importance of social support, and also for evidence of three factors about which Crosby (1982) had speculated when she first discovered the denial of personal discrmination: politeness, readiness for action, and vividness.

On the basis of dozens of hours of materials from twelve Stanford women, it is clear that social support plays a critical role in fighting injustice. The influence of social support in the Stanford women's fight for justice has been evident to us throughout our study. We had first come to learn of the women through a network of contacts, some of whom were employed at Catalyst, an organization that works to promote gender equity in corporate America. In all of the newspaper accounts and personal testimonies, the women consistently acknowledged and thanked each other. In the focus group meetings, each woman spoke of how difficult it would have been to continue the battle had it not been for the support of the other victims and for the support of their families and friends. Whether reliance on a support group enabled the initial liberation from denial – as opposed to the continued struggle for justice – is, however, hard to say. It is certain that at least one of the women, Linda Mabry, J.D., came to an awareness of personal discrimination well before she had the feeling that anyone outside her immediate family would lend support.

What about politeness? Crosby (1982) had speculated that perhaps the employed women in her Newton study were simply too polite to mention that sex discrimination might be part of their lives. This speculation leads to the testable hypothesis that people who are unconcerned with the social niceties will be more willing to recognize discrimination than are people who are concerned with the social niceties. We found no evidence to substantiate Crosby's speculation. To be sure, a complaint of discrimination hardly qualifies as an expression of polite sentiment. Yet, a desire to be polite does not appear to have motivated denial any more than a desire to be impolite motivated recognition. All of the women in our Stanford sample were well versed in the social amenities. They had to be – just by virtue of having made their way into the rarefied atmosphere of a major university. Some of the women were willing to use coarse language, but most were not. One of the women came from a more rough-and-tumble background than the others; and two came from extremely dignified and protected backgrounds. All in all, we found that neither the desire to be respected nor the desire to be respectful played much of a role in the denial of personal discrimination or in the end of denial.

Crosby had also speculated that people deny their own victimization until they are ready to take corrective action. Here the evidence gave some, but not total, validation. Clearly, all the women we interviewed had decided to take corrective action, or they would not have been in our sample. But while some began to take action immediately after coming to recognize discrimination, others waited for a long period of time. Indeed, two of the women with whom we spoke waited over a year before they decided to take any kind of action. Mature adults with many responsibilities are capable of saying, in effect, "I would like to fight this unfairness that I see affecting me, but I cannot afford to risk my livelihood or the harmony of my family life."

Finally, to explain the denial of personal discrimination, Crosby had speculated that people deny the personal relevance of discrimination unless they can identify the perpetrator of it. When groups are disadvantaged, society can be blamed; but each individual victim seems to call for an individual villain. This speculation leads to the testable hypothesis that people are more likely to recognize themselves as the victims of discrimination when they can identify someone who perpetuates the discrimination than when they must identify structural causes for the discrimination. A corollary hypothesis is that people need something perceptible, such as a dramatic or critical incident, if they are to recognize personal disadvantage. The slow accretion of subtle injustices probably accounts for the greatest portion of the gap between advantaged and disadvantaged, but it most likely does not account for anyone's recognition of that gap.

Clear and unequivocal support was found for the importance of a vivid precipitant to awareness and the existence of clear villains. In every single case, there was a critical incident or set of events so dramatic that they could not be ignored. For one woman, awareness of discrimination came when she found out that a man had been named to head an initiative that she had started. For another, awareness began when she was stripped of lab space. Yet another discovered that she had been explicitly excluded from a governing committee. In every story, one could identify individuals who perpetuated the injustices against the various women.

Not atypical is the story of Colleen Crangle, who had been working as a medical researcher at Stanford. Dr. Crangle had come from South Africa to obtain her Ph.D. at Stanford and, after spending some years raising small children, had returned to the university to work. At the time that we met her, she had brought an individual lawsuit against Stanford and was one of the women who had joined the complaint against Stanford filed with the U.S. Department of Labor (Workman, 1999). Crangle opened a lecture to a class at the University of California by saying:

> Let me start by telling you of a day at Stanford University in the School of Medicine that changed my life and led me to this point where I am prepared to talk publicly about one of the most painful periods of my life.
>
> On this day, a male colleague unexpectedly walked into my office and said he was there to tell me about some restrictions that were going to be placed on me. I was in the middle of writing research proposals to fund my continued appointment as a Senior Research Scientist in the Section on Medical Informatics. (Medical Informatics is an interdisciplinary field concerned with the theory and application of information science in medicine. It used to be called "medical computer science.") My colleague began to lay out the restrictions: I could not write any proposals that brought in large amounts of money or supported any research associates. For me to do so would be "like the tail wagging the dog," he said. He outlined that I could write proposals only in certain areas. He acknowledged that he saw me as a threat to him, and he claimed he had the right to place these restrictions on me.

Dr. Crangle outlined to the class how the "astonishing conversation" led to increasing problems and brought her, finally, to the conclusion that legal measures had to be taken. As the only female senior research scientist in her group (and indeed, the only female scientist at any level), she suspected sex discrimination. She pointed out to the chief of her section that

> it was inconceivable to me that the conversations we had been having would have taken place had I been a man and my colleague a woman. I said I thought the day had long gone when a woman would be asked to curtail her activities to avoid threatening a male colleague. I said that I wanted to work in an environment where excellence and hard work were rewarded, not squelched because they appeared to pose a threat to a male colleague.

Dr. Crangle judged that "[f]rom that moment on, the environment became somewhat hostile, even in comparison to what it had been." But she also pointed out how she came to reassess previous incidents, seeing only in hindsight the level of pervasive ambient sexism. At the beginning of her battle, said Crangle, "I found myself waking in the night thinking: 'this cannot be happening. This is Stanford, the famous institution I came to this country to attend. This is Stanford, the institution that seeks knowledge and truth.'"

Denise Johnson, M.D., spoke eloquently of the sex and race discrimination that had been a constant part of her early life. Responding to e-mailed questions after a focus group session, Dr. Johnson wrote:

> How did I recognize discrimination?
>
> 1. My mother and her family were perceived as Caucasian. My brother was thought to be Caucasian. I directly experienced the rejection of other Caucasians when I approached my family in the company of Caucasians. These episodes occurred during my early childhood 4–6.
>
> 2. My father was an officer in the Army. During his officer training school, we were housed with majority, Caucasian families. Whenever I went to shopping malls or just walking, teams of teen boys would spit on me, called me "nigger" and followed me with the threat of "hurting" or raping me. I was a young lady, 12 or 13 at the time. It was so frightening, because I was by myself and so many Caucasian adults passed me by and never said anything to the teens who taunted me. I was completely frightened. However, I refused to run, cry or talk to them. I felt completely alone and knew that no one would help.
>
> 3. I had been ranked number one in high school for four years, had the second highest grade point average in the Chicago area, including suburbs, and had been accepted to a competitive Six Year Medical School program at Northwestern. My counselor told me that I should turn down the offer, because as a Black woman, I would never fit in that environment. Also, I probably would just get married and never finish medical school. This counselor also encouraged other Black students to turn down earned academic scholarships. That is when I realized the sickness of racism.
>
> There are so many examples.

Despite a lifetime of discrimination, Dr. Johnson thought that the elite atmosphere of Stanford would spell an end to base racial and gender discrimination. Asked if she had been surprised when she recognized the sex and race discrimination against her at Stanford, Dr. Johnson replied, "Oh, yes! Cruelty is always a surprise! It took some dramatic incidents for me to open my eyes."

Nor do the Stanford women in our pilot study seem to be different from women elsewhere. While they were awakening to discrimination on the West Coast, women at MIT were undergoing similar processes on the East Coast. At the very moment the Stanford women were encountering massive resistance and retaliation from Stanford administration, a panel of tenured women scientists at MIT were asking for and winning relief from persistent inequities there. Feminists around the country paid attention. When one of the MIT women, Dr. Nancy Hopkins, gave a talk at UCLA, Professor Barbara Lawrence of UCLA's Anderson School of Management sent out an e-mail description to colleagues throughout the nation. Wrote Lawrence:

> Nancy Hopkins gave a talk at UCLA about her MIT experiences. She is extremely articulate, and, though she would probably deny it, she's also funny. There were several important "take-aways" for me that I hadn't gotten previously . . .
>
> 1) The problems each woman faculty member experienced individually could all be explained away. It was only in the aggregate, when the committee interviewed the fifteen women in sequence, that a convincing pattern of discrimination was observed.
>
> 2) One pattern was a difference in the perceptions of junior and senior women. Junior women didn't see themselves as experiencing much discrimination. They perceived senior women as experiencing discrimination because "things were different" when those senior women were younger. Junior women felt that "that won't happen to me because things have changed." The senior women reported feeling the same way as the junior women when they were younger. After becoming senior and working through years of "pinpricks," a circuit finally blew and they re-interpreted their experiences.

What caused 'the circuit to blow' for most of the women? Some dramatic incident or some particularly vivid comparison. Drip by drip, the tub of discrimination fills; but no one notices until one day it overflows.

Making a Difference

When Mel Lerner and his associates documented the human need to believe in justice, they made an enormous contribution to psychology and its understanding of justice motives. Subsequent research in our lab and elsewhere has shown that people are no more ready to see themselves as the victims of discrimination than as the perpetrators of it. As long as we stay at the level of the individual, it seems to be extremely hard for us to acknowledge the existence of unfairness.

Why is it important to recognize discrimination when faced with it? Recognizing discrimination is an important step in taking action against that discrimination (Taylor & McKirnan, 1984). Foster and Matheson (1999) found that women who reported small discrepancies between personal and group discrimination were more likely to take collective action than women who reported larger discrepancies. Further, when women are encouraged to blame the situation on society they are less likely to accept the situation than those women who are encouraged to blame themselves (Foster, Matheson, & Poole, 1994).

If it is difficult for most people to recognize personal injustices, it is also difficult for some people to ignore the injustices once they have registered. The greater the force, the greater the counterforce. That is why the small band of Stanford women keep fighting against the giant institution that employed them and that does not hesitate to try to crush them. Loath to perceive injustice, Colleen Crangle had tried to ignore the sex discrimination in her environment. When it became impossible to keep her blinders on, Crangle sought to banish discrimination from view through a harsh, courageous struggle. In April 1999, Dr. Crangle told students at the University of California:

> As powerful as Stanford is, I will not be bullied by it. I have filed a suit in Federal court. That was one year ago. The events I described to you began one year prior to that time, and the date set for my trial is one year from now. By the time of my trial, three years of my life will have been taken up with this battle, and it may not end there.
>
> I could have been spending this time continuing my research into innovative ways of giving breast-cancer patients access to medical information. I could have been serving as a resource for other women at Stanford struggling to make it in a predominately and historically male environment. I could have, and would have, been achieving great things in my own career. But I could not walk away from these events. Standing up against Stanford is the most difficult thing I have done in my life. But I will see the battle through, and I believe it will make a difference.

Indeed, her battle did make a difference. In March 2000, a jury found that Stanford University had discriminated against Colleen Crangle.

One may be heartened to know that the court awarded Crangle the largest settlement allowed by law. The legal finding should prove influential in the multiwoman complaint lodged against Stanford with the Department of Labor, where one of the world's most prestigious universities could be at risk of losing some of its $500 million in annual federal funding.

REFERENCES

Bulman, R. J., & Wortman, C. B. (1977). Attributions of blame and coping in the "real world": Severe accident victims react to their lot. *Journal of Personality and Social Psychology, 35,* 351–363.

Clayton, S. D., & Crosby, F. J. (1992). *Justice, gender, and affirmative action.* Ann Arbor: University of Michigan Press.

Comer, R., & Laird, J. D. (1975). Choosing to suffer as a consequence of expecting to suffer: Why do people do it? *Journal of Personality and Social Psychology, 32,* 92–101.

Crocker, J., & Major, B. (1989). Social stigma and self-esteem: The self-protective properties of stigma. *Psychological Review, 96,* 608–630.

Crosby, F. J. (1982). *Relative deprivation and the working woman.* New York: Oxford University Press.

(1984). The denial of personal discrimination. *American Behavioral Scientist, 27,* 371–386.

Crosby, F. J., Cordova, D., & Jaskar, K. (1993). On the failure to see oneself as disadvantaged: Cognitive and emotional components. In M. A. Hogg & D. Abrams (Eds.), *Group motivation: Social psychological perspectives* (pp. 87–104). New York: Harvester Wheatsheaf.

Crosby, F. J., Pufall, A., Snyder, R. C., O'Connell, M. O., & Whalen, P. (1989). The denial of personal disadvantage among you, me, and all the other Ostriches. In M. Crawford & M. Gentry (Eds.), *Gender and thought: Psychological perspectives* (pp. 79–99). New York: Springer-Verlag.

Foster, M. D., & Matheson, K. (1999). Perceiving and responding to the personal/group discrimination discrepancy. *Personality and Social Psychology Bulletin, 25,* 1319–1329.

Foster, M. D., Matheson, K., & Poole, M. (1994). Responding to sexual discrimination: The effects of societal versus self-blame. *Journal of Social Psychology, 134,* 743–754.

Hafer, C. L, & Olson, J. M. (1989). Beliefs in a just world and reactions to personal deprivation. *Journal of Personality, 57,* 799–823.

(1993). Beliefs in a just world, discontent and assertive actions by working women. *Personality and Social Psychology Bulletin, 19,* 30–38.

Lerner, M. J. (1980). *The belief in a just world: A fundamental delusion.* New York: Plenum.

Lerner, M. J., & Simmons, C. H. (1966). The observer's reaction to the "innocent victim": Compassion or rejection? *Journal of Personality and Social Psychology, 4,* 203–210.

Lipkus, I. M., & Siegler, I. C. (1993). The belief in a just world and perceptions of discrimination. *Journal of Psychology, 127*, 465–474.

Major, B., & Crocker, J. (1993). Social stigma: The consequences of attributional ambiguity. In D. M. Mackie & D. L. Hamilton (Eds.), *Affect, cognition, and stereotyping: Interactive processes in group perception* (pp. 345–370). San Diego, CA: Academic Press.

Miller, D. T. (1977). Altruism and threat to a belief in a just world. *Journal of Experimental Social Psychology, 13*, 113–126.

Olson, J. M., & Hafer, C. L. (1998). Affect, motivation, and cognition in relative deprivation research. In R. M. Sorrentino & E. T. Higgins (Eds.), *Handbook of motivation and cognition: The interpersonal context* (Vol. 3, pp. 85–117). New York: Gilford.

Postmes, T., Branscombe, N. R., Spears, R., & Young, H. (1999). Comparative processes in personal and group judgments: Resolving the discrepancy. *Journal of Personality and Social Psychology, 76*, 320–338.

Rubin, Z., & Peplau, A. (1973). Belief in a just world and reaction to another's lot: A study of participants in the National Draft Lottery. *Journal of Social Issues, 29*, 73–93.

Ruggiero, K. M., Taylor, D. M., & Lydon, J. E. (1997). How disadvantaged group members cope with discrimination when they perceive social support is available. *Journal of Applied Social Psychology, 27*, 1581–1600.

Sampson, E. E. (1977). Psychology and the American ideal. *Journal of Personality and Social Psychology, 35*, 767–782.

Taylor, D. M., & McKirnan, D. J. (1984). A five stage model of intergroup relations. *British Journal of Social Psychology, 23*, 291–300.

Taylor, D. M., Wright, S. C., Moghaddam, F. M., & Lalonde, R. N. (1990). The personal/group discrimination discrepancy: Perceiving my group, but not myself, to be a target for discrimination. *Personality and Social Psychology Bulletin, 16*, 254–262.

Taylor, D. M., Wright, S. C., & Porter, L. E. (1994). Dimensions of perceived discrimination: The personal/group discrmination discrepancy. In M. P. Zanna & J. M. Olson (Eds.), *The psychology of prejudice* (Vol. 7, pp. 233–255). Hillsdale, NJ: Erlbaum.

Workman, B. (1999). Shadow on diversity at Stanford. *San Francisco Chronicle*, February 15, pp. A13, A16.

22. Deservingness and Perceptions of Procedural Justice in Citizen Encounters with the Police

JASON SUNSHINE AND LARRY HEUER

Distributive justice theories (e.g., relative deprivation, equity, justice motive theory) have consistently postulated that disputants' satisfaction with the outcomes of social conflicts is influenced by the extent to which allocations are consistent with salient standards of deservingness or entitlement. So, for example, relative deprivation theorists (e.g., Crosby, 1976; Davis, 1959; Gurr, 1970; Runciman, 1966) have shown that feelings of indignation or outrage stemming from deprivation are moderated by notions of entitlement. They have revealed that judgments about what individuals feel they deserve are based on comparisons with what others within their group or within a similar context have received rather than on absolute outcomes. This theory explains why those in an objectively positive situation can evaluate their situation negatively, and why those in a seemingly poor situation can view their situation optimistically. Crosby's (1982) study of working women identified two preconditions essential for relative deprivation – lesser outcomes than one wants, and lesser outcomes than one deserves.

Similarly, equity theorists (Adams, 1965; Homans, 1961; Walster, Berscheid, & Walster, 1976) assume that an individual's sense of equity acts as a powerful norm influencing social behavior. This norm is comprised of the belief that outcomes, both positive and negative, should be proportional to one's contribution and involvement within the group. When an inequitable distribution of outcomes is perceived, it is argued that individuals will experience "inequity distress." It is theorized that the dissonance this perception creates will motivate the individual to restore equity. Adams (1963) has asserted that even individuals profiting from inequity would feel "inequity distress" and attempt to restore equity. Thus, individuals experience dissonance both when they get more as well as when they get less than they perceive they deserve.

Although distributive justice theories have consistently included notions of deservingness in their models, none have located it as centrally as Mel Lerner's justice motive theory (Lerner, 1977, 1987). So, for example, while equity theory includes justice as one of various motives that influence people's satisfaction with the outcomes of social conflicts, justice motive theory (JMT) assumes a "preeminent guiding principle or motive in the commitment to deserving which serves to organize most goal-seeking behavior" (Lerner, 1977, p. 23). Subsequently, Lerner (1987) asserted that "the experience of entitlement is the essential psychological ingredient of an entire family of human events associated with social justice" (pp. 107–108).

According to JMT, the justice motive is not merely a consequence of enlightened self-interest, as assumed by equity theorists (e.g., Walster et al., 1976; Walster, Walster, & Berscheid, 1978). Rather, notions of entitlement are shaped by unconscious processes occurring in the early stages of cognitive development. One consequence of the centrality of deservingness in JMT is that violated *entitlements* are explicitly identified as the essential ingredient that distinguishes injustices from simple disappointments or frustrations – it is *injustices* that lead to anger and outrage (Lerner, 1987). Thus, while equity theory points to a variety of motives (including self-interest as well as justice) to explain individuals' reactions to inequity, JMT emphasizes the preeminence of the commitment to deserving.

However, despite the centrality of deservingness in theories of distributive justice, theories of procedural justice are largely silent about its role in perceptions of fairness and satisfaction. So, for example, in their seminal theory of procedural justice, Thibaut and Walker (1975, 1978) asserted that variations in the degree of control over conflict resolution procedures impact perceptions of fairness. According to this theory, procedures will be perceived as fair to the extent that they promote fair outcomes. Thus, control over the presentation of evidence (process control or "voice") and control over the final decision (decision control) are predicted to be important to disputants because they are expected to influence decisions; in other words, they are important for instrumental reasons. Because of the underlying assumption of self-interested individuals present in Thibaut and Walker's theory (an assumption this theory shares with equity theory), Lind and Tyler (1988) have referred to it as a self-interest model. While an abundance of research has been overwhelmingly supportive of their prediction that process and decision control are crucial determinants of procedural fairness (e.g., Folger, 1977; Kanfer et al., 1987; LaTour, 1978; Lind et al., 1980; Lind, Lissak, & Conlon, 1983; Tyler, Rasinski, & Spodick, 1985), the theory is largely silent about the role of entitlement in the control–fairness relationships except as it is involved in equity theory. So, for example, virtually none of the research testing the control model has examined situational variables that might be expected to affect disputants' judgments that they are entitled to process or decision control (see Brockner et al., 1998, for a notable exception).

Recently, responding in part to findings inconsistent with the self-interest model of procedural justice, Lind and Tyler (1988; Tyler, 1994; Tyler & Lind, 1992) have proposed a group value theory of procedural justice. The group value model emphasizes individuals' concern about their relationships with social groups and the authorities representing those groups. It assumes that group identification and group membership is psychologically rewarding, and that individuals are motivated to establish and maintain group bonds. According to this theory, when individuals are focused on their long-term relationships with groups, they evaluate the fairness of procedures according to a different set of criteria than the control variables proposed by Thibaut and Walker. Lind and Tyler proposed that under such circumstances procedures are evaluated according to three criteria: the trustworthiness of the authorities enacting the procedures; the neutrality of those authorities; and information emanating from the procedure about the individual's standing in the group. Numerous studies provide indirect support for Lind and Tyler's suggestion that individuals are sensitive to issues such as polite and respectful treatment (e.g., Bies & Moag, 1986; Bies & Shapiro, 1987; Tyler & Bies, 1990; Tyler & Folger, 1980) and information about their standing in the group (Huo et al., 1996; MacCoun et al., 1988; Tyler & DeGoey, 1995). Additional research (e.g., Tyler, 1989, 1994) is directly and strongly supportive of Lind and Tyler's (1992; Tyler, 1989) claim that trust, neutrality, and standing are strongly linked to procedural justice judgments, and that these relational concerns explain considerable variation in justice perceptions that is not explained by the control variables or self-interest motives specified by Thibaut and Walker's (1975, 1978) model. It is clear from such research that individuals evaluate the fairness of their treatment on more dimensions than simply their opportunity for control.

However, like the self-interest model of procedural justice, the group value model does not explicitly address the role of entitlement for the effect of trust, neutrality, and standing on procedural fairness. So, for example, the group value model asserts that respectful treatment, because of the positive message it communicates about an individual's within-group standing, enhances procedural fairness.

We suspect that the relationship between respectful treatment and procedural fairness is more complex. Our reasoning here borrows heavily from the distributive justice theories reviewed here – just as distributions are perceived as fair and satisfactory according to the extent that they are consistent with people's notions of entitlement, we hypothesize that procedural fairness judgments are a function of the fit between people's beliefs that they deserve respect and their beliefs that they have received it (see Heuer et al., 1999, for a more thorough explication of theoretical considerations consistent with our reasoning about why people might feel entitled to respectful treatment).

Preliminary Research

The moderating effect of deservingness on the relationship between respect and perceptions of fair procedure has been previously examined by Heuer and colleagues (1999). Drawing upon Feather's (1992) matching hypothesis, which states that positive outcomes are perceived as fair when they follow positively valued acts, as are negative outcomes when followed by negatively valued acts, Heuer and his associates proposed that the same pattern of matches would exist between the valence of a person's attributes (such as, but not limited to, within-group status) and the manner in which individuals are treated by others. A similar view was put forth by Pepitone and L'Armand (1996), who proposed that a state of justice is perceived when the valence of the person observed has the same sign as the valence of the outcome experienced by that person. In other words, good things are perceived to happen to those with positive attributes and bad things to those with negative attributes. In the Pepitone and L'Armand study, matches between attributes and outcomes were perceived as significantly more fair than mismatches.

In the Heuer and colleagues (1999) inquiry, the deservedness hypothesis was strongly supported in three studies. Studies 1 and 2 used vignettes to test the hypothesis that the relation between respectful treatment and procedural fairness is qualified by the positive or negative value of the treatment recipient's behaviors. In Study 1, participants read and responded to a vignette describing a manager's treatment of an employee. The vignettes varied according to the manipulations of the value of the employee's behavior, the level of responsibility attributed to that behavior, and whether or not the employee was treated respectfully by the manager. Results supported the matching hypothesis: Participants rated procedures as more fair when positively valued behaviors were matched with respectful treatment and when negatively valued behaviors were matched with disrespectful treatment. Moreover, as predicted, the value of behavior by respectful treatment interaction was further qualified by attributions about the protagonist's' responsibility for his behavior: The two-way interaction between respect and fairness was strongest when the protagonist was responsible for his positively or negatively valued behavior. One finding in this study that is especially supportive of the deservingness view is that respondents rated disrespectful treatment as more fair than respectful treatment of individuals who were responsible for performing negatively valued behaviors – a reversal of the typically reported relation between respect and fairness. This reversal is not predicted by either the instrumental or group value models of procedural justice, but it is consistent with the deservingness model being advanced here.

Study 2 was conducted in part to address the possibility that the results of Study 1 are limited to observations of the way others are treated. In this study, undergraduate participants imagined themselves in an encounter with a professor in whose class they were enrolled. Across the eight versions of the vignette, the student performed either positively or negatively valued classroom behaviors for reasons attributed to internal controllable causes or to external uncontrollable ones. Afterward, the student met with the professor, who treated the student respectfully or disrespectfully. The results of this study again supported the derservingness hypothesis, showing that respect was most fair when individuals were responsible for positively valued classroom behaviors, but least fair when individuals were responsible for negatively valued classroom behaviors. This study also included a measure of the respondent's belief that they deserved the treatment that they received. This additional measure permitted a test of the expectation that beliefs about deservingness mediate the relation between respect and fairness. The mediation hypothesis was supported: Path analyses showed that fairness was most affected by respondents' perception that they had received the treatment they deserved; furthermore, the direct effects of respect and the two-way interaction between respect and entitlement on fairness were mediated by participants' report that they had received the treatment they deserved.

Study 3 surveyed several hundred New Yorkers about a recent encounter with another individual and included questions about how respectfully they had been treated by the other individual and how fair they thought their treatment by the other individual had been. Additional measures included items from the Coopersmith Self-Esteem Inventory (Coopersmith, 1981). These data enabled a test of the deservingness hypothesis in a field setting, as well as an extension of our reasoning to another variable that might qualify the relation between respect and fairness. In this study, we predicted that high self-esteem individuals would be more likely than low self-esteem individuals to evaluate the fairness of their treatment according to the relational concerns described by Tyler and Lind. (This hypothesis follows from Feather's matching hypothesis, with the assumption that high self-esteem is equivalent to a positive appraisal of one's self value.) This interaction hypothesis was strongly supported: The effect of respect on fairness was considerable for individuals high in self-esteem but negligible for those low in self-esteem.

While all three of these studies supported our predictions, the present research improves upon this work in several ways. First, two of our earlier studies tested our hypothesis by having the participants read imaginary vignettes. The third studied actual encounters, but not necessarily encounters between a subordinate and an authority, as has typically been the case in previous tests of the group value theory. (Participants in our previous field survey were asked to think of an encounter with another individual, with no mention of whether the other individual had more or less decision authority than they did.) Thus, it is conceivable that the previous findings are at least partly an artifact of the type of encounter examined. The present study examines the perceptions of civilians in a recent encounter with a police officer.

In addition, while our previous studies tested the deservingness hypothesis by looking for matches between respect and either the value of one's behavior or self-esteem, the present study looks for matches between civilians' perception of their standing in a valued social group and their perception of the police officer's judgment of their intragroup standing. Thus, the present study addresses the concern with intragroup standing specified by Lind and Tyler's (1988) group value theory.

Finally, the present study extends the test of the matching hypothesis to look for the match between perceptions of the treatment deserved and the treatment received on several dimensions in addition to within-group standing. Thus, civilian respondents in this study are asked to report what manner of treatment they feel entitled to and what manner of treatment they received from the police officer that would reflect the officer's views of the value of their behavior, their self-esteem, and the value of their group. While our earlier (Heuer et al., 1999) research found support for the matching hypothesis on the dimensions of the value of one's behavior and self-esteem, this study is the first to test the matching hypothesis on the dimension of one's perception of the standing of one's group vis-à-vis other groups (as opposed to the intra-group perceptions addressed by the group value theory). Arguably, most of our civilian respondents will perceive police officers as out-group members, and will be sensitive to what the police officer's behavior indicates about his or her impressions of the civilian's salient social group.

Method

Participants

Respondents were 354 males, 110 females, and 52 individuals who left the gender question unanswered, yielding a sample size of 516. The respondents ranged in age from fourteen to eighty-three ($M = 30.6$). The ethnic breakdown of the sample was as follows: 291 Caucasians, 75 African-Americans, 30 Hispanics, 55 indicating "other," and 63 individuals who left this question unanswered.

Procedure

In order to test the moderating effect of deservingness across multiple motivations on the relationship between respect and perceptions of fair procedure, civilians were approached in various locations throughout New York City and invited to participate in a study of police–civilian encounters. Approximately half (52%) of the respondents had received a summons from a police officer to appear in misdemeanor court. These respondents were approached while they waited for their cases to be called. Those who agreed to participate were asked to think about the encounter with a police officer that resulted in their summons. The remaining respondents (48%) were approached outside coffee shops in New York City. These respondents were asked to think about a recent encounter with a New York City police officer. All participants were offered a token of appreciation for completing the survey, with a value of approximately $1.50.

All respondents were asked to provide a brief description of their encounter with a New York City police officer and to answer a series of 158 questions in reference to that encounter. Respondents were also asked to identify a social group that they belonged to and valued greatly, in order to enable them to respond to questions about what they thought the police officer ought to think about their group as well as what they thought the officer actually did think about their group. Except for demographic measures about themselves and the police officer, all questions employed Likert-type scales designed to tap the relevant constructs, such as treatment deserved and treatment received (multiple items were used to measure each of these constructs), on each of the dimensions of group value/intragroup standing, intergroup standing, value of behavior (VOB), and social self-esteem (SSE).

The moderation hypothesis (that matches between "received" and "deserved" will be perceived as fairer than mismatches) was tested by looking for interactions between the treatment deserved (respectful–disrespectful) and the treatment received on each of these four dimensions. In particular, we expect that individuals will think treatment is more fair not simply because police officers' treatment suggests that the police officer thinks highly of their standing in their social group, or the standing of their group vis-à-vis other groups, or their behaviors, or their value as individuals. Rather, we expect that such positive views will be related to fairness judgments to the extent that the officer's treatment suggests an evaluation on each of these dimensions that matches our respondents' notions that they are entitled to have others think favorably of their within-group standing, their intergroup standing, their behaviors, or their value as individuals.

Measures

Multiple items were employed to measure each of the constructs of treatment received (questions asking respondents about the treatment received) and each entitlement judgment (questions asking respondents about the treatment they felt they deserved) corresponding with that attribute.

Separate principal component analyses were performed on the items tapping each of the four entitlement constructs and each of the four treatment constructs. The resulting component scores were then used as an index for the construct. Indices were created in this way in order to maximize the relevant proportion of variance examined, thereby increasing measurement accuracy.[1] These constructs were measured as follows:[2] intragroup standing received (four items, e.g., 9 = "I was treated like a high-status member of the community"; these questions yielded a single component accounting for 75.5% of the variance); intragroup standing deserved (four items, e.g., 9 = "I deserved to be treated like a high-status member of the community"; these items yielded a single component accounting for 66% of the variance); intergroup standing received (three items, e.g., 9 = "The police officer seemed to have a favorable view of my group"; these items yielded a single component accounting for 75.6% of the variance); intergroup standing deserved (three items, yielding a single component accounting for 76% of the variance); social self-esteem received (two items, e.g., 9 = "The police officer thought I'm popular with persons my own age"; these items were taken from the Coopersmith Self-Esteem Inventory [Coopersmith, 1987] and yielded a single component accounting for 68% of the variance); social self-esteem deserved (two items, yielding a single component accounting for 87% of the variance); VOB received (three items, e.g., 9 = "The police officer thought highly of my behavior"; these items yielded a single component accounting for 79% of the variance); VOB deserved (three items, yielding a single component accounting for 79% of the variance). Procedural fairness judgments were measured with four questions (e.g., 9 = "The police officer treated me in a fair and reasonable way") yielding a single component accounting for 75% of the variance.

Interaction terms were created by multiplying each received index with its corresponding deserved index. Thus, high scores on the interaction variable indicate matches, and low scores indicate

[1] All correlations between the unit-weighted composite measures and the respective principal component were >.9 ($p < .001$). The coefficient alpha for the items on every construct employed exceeded .7.

[2] Since each deserved–received pair employed highly similar items, we report the received items for the first dimension only. The wording of all items employed for each of the constructs employed in this study is available from the second author upon request.

mismatches, between perceptions of treatment deserved and treatment received.

Results

In order to test the matching hypothesis, a principal components regression analysis was performed (Belsley, 1991; Daling & Tamura, 1970; Farrar & Glauber, 1967; Greenberg, 1975; Kendall, 1957; Massy, 1965; Sclove, 1968; Urban & Von Hippel, 1988). The PC regression procedure was appropriate for our data because the standard regression procedure yielded unstable beta weights. (This was caused by the fairly high correlations among the constructs tapping the civilians' perception that the police officer's treatment reflected positive assessments of the their intragroup standing and their intergroup standing [$r = .75$, $p < .001$].) PC regression avoids the collinearity problem by taking advantage of the orthogonal structure of a principal component matrix. Standard regression is performed on a subset of uncorrelated component scores constructed through a principal components analysis of the independent variables desired for use as predictors. The beta weights obtained for each component are then multiplied by the corresponding factor loadings for each variable within each component and summed across components. The result is a standardized regression beta weight for each original independent variable that is analogous to the standardized beta weights obtained from traditional regression procedures.

In the present analysis, principal components analysis on the four "treatment deserved" variables, the four "treatment received" variables, and the four hypothesized deserved × received interactions variables yielded three factors accounting for 60% of the variance. The four "received" variables loaded on the first component, the four "deserved" variables loaded on the second, and the four interaction terms loaded on the third component. The dependent measure of procedural fairness was then regressed on the three principal components.

In block one, the first and second components (those upon which the main effects of "treatment deserved" and "treatment received" loaded in the PC analysis) were entered. This block accounted for a significant portion of the variance in the dependent variable, $F(2, 513) = 157.16$, $p < .001$, $R^2 = .38$. Table 22.1 reports the beta weights for the original eight main effects (the products of the betas in the PC regression

Table 22.1. Beta weights obtained from principal component regression of perception of fairness on received, deserved, and received × deserved variables

Main Effects	β
Received intragroup	0.57
Deserve intragroup	–0.19
Received intergroup	0.52
Deserve intergroup	–0.13
Received VOB	0.50
Deserve VOB	–0.03
Received SSE	0.43
Deserve SSE	–0.16
Interaction Terms	**β**
Deserve × received intragroup	0.28
Deserve × received intergroup	0.26
Deserve × received VOB	0.24
Deserve × received SSE	0.06

and the factor loadings of the eight original main effects on their respective components in the PC analysis). As seen in Table 22.1, each of the four "treatment deserved" effects are negative, indicating that procedures are generally considered less fair with increases in civilians' notions of entitlement. Alternatively, each of the "treatment received" effects are positive, indicating that procedures are considered more fair with increases in the favorability of the treatment received. In other words, for example, as the police officer's behavior was interpreted as indicating a favorable view of the civilians' standing within their group, the civilians report that they were treated more fairly. This is sensible, and is supportive of the group value theory's claim that procedural fairness is enhanced as a result of the view that others view us as members of high standing in our valued social groups.

The second block added the hypothesized interaction terms to the equation, and constitutes the test of our matching hypothesis. This block added significantly to the proportion of variance accounted for by the equation, R^2 change = .05, $F(1, 512) = 128.0$, $p < .001$. The beta weights obtained for the original variables are presented in Table 22.1. Note that, as hypothesized, the coefficients for each of the four

Table 22.2. Standardized coefficients for treatment received at high and low levels of treatment deserved

	Deservedness	
Treatment	Low	High
Received intragroup	0.29	0.85
Received intergroup	0.26	0.78
Received VOB	0.26	0.74
Received SSE	0.37	0.49

interaction terms are positive, and at least three (intragroup, intergroup, and VOB) are of a substantial magnitude. In other words, for at least these three dimensions, procedural fairness is greater when there is a match between the treatment deserved and the treatment received. Unfortunately, at present there is no procedure available to determine the statistical significance of each beta weight for the original variables.

Solving for the effect of "treatment received" at both high (one standard deviation above the mean) and low (one standard deviation below the mean) levels of "treatment deserved" (see Cohen & Cohen, 1975) is one way of understanding the implications of these interactions. Table 22.2 shows the values of treatment received at high versus low levels of entitlement on each of the four dimensions examined in this study. As predicted by the matching hypothesis, for the dimensions of intragroup standing, intergroup standing, and VOB, it is clear that favorable treatment has a considerably greater positive effect on procedural fairness when civilians' notions of entitlement are high. Although the magnitude of the effect for self-esteem is smaller, it too is positive, and consistent with our prediction.

Discussion

We began our inquiry with the observation that distributive justice theories have consistently noted the importance of deservingness for people's judgments that the outcomes they received are fair and satisfactory. These theories are distinguished from straightforward hedonic theories by virtue of their assumption that fairness and satisfaction derive from obtaining what one is entitled to rather than simply what one desires. On the other hand, procedural justice theories, such as

Thibaut and Walker's (1975, 1978) theory, interactional justice theories (e.g., Bies, 1987; Bies & Moag, 1986; Bies & Shapiro, 1987, 1988; Bies, Shapiro, & Cummings, 1988; Cropanzano & Folger, 1989; Folger & Bies, 1989; Tyler & Folger, 1980), and group value theory (Lind & Tyler, 1988; Tyler, 1989; Tyler & Lind, 1992) have not obviously included the same assumption. So, for example, we suggested that while group value theory offers a compelling link between respectful treatment and procedural satisfaction or preference, the link between respect and justice judgments is less clearly specified.

Based upon arguments about the centrality of entitlement for distributive justice judgments advanced most clearly by Lerner (1977, 1980, 1987) and supported in numerous studies by Lerner and his colleagues (e.g., Braband & Lerner, 1975; Lerner, Miller, & Holmes, 1977; Simmons & Lerner, 1968), we argued that notions of entitlement can be expected to play a similar role in affecting the relation between how people are treated and their reports that they have been treated in a fair and satisfying manner. Thus, for example, we proposed that people will evaluate the way others treat them as fair not simply because it implies that others think highly of their standing in social groups, but rather because the treatment they receive matches their judgments about what they are entitled to have others believe about their standing in social groups.

In order to test this matching hypothesis, we surveyed civilians about a recent encounter with a New York City police officer. We first asked them questions pertaining to their beliefs about whether they deserved to have the police officer think highly of (a) their standing in their community, (b) the standing of their self-identified social group vis-à-vis other social groups, (c) the value of the behavior that led up to their encounter with the police officer, and (d) their individual social worth. In addition, we asked them about their perception that the police officer's behavior communicated that the officer actually did think highly of their standing in their community, the standing of their self-identified social group vis-à-vis other social groups, the value of the behavior that led up to their encounter with the police officer, and their individual social worth. We predicted that civilians' procedural fairness judgments would be influenced not simply by how favorably the officer treated them, but rather by the match between their notions of entitlement and the officer's treatment.

Overall, this hypothesis was strongly supported. While the regression analyses revealed a substantial main effect of being treated in a respectful manner, the magnitude of this effect was considerably qualified by the civilians' notions of the kind of treatment they were entitled to. On each of the dimensions measured – intragroup standing, intergroup standing, value of behavior, and self-esteem, favorable treatment had a greater positive effect on procedural fairness when civilians' notions of entitlement were high than when they were low.

This finding adds to the evidence from three earlier studies that were similarly supportive of the deservingness hypothesis for procedural justice (Heuer et al., 1999). However, this study extends that work in some important ways. First, two of our earlier studies were experiments that varied respectful treatment and value of behavior in an orthogonal design, and showed that respectful treatment was considered more fair when it followed positively valued acts. The present study produces a similar result regarding the match between positively valued behaviors and respectful treatment in a field survey of civilians recounting their recent encounters with police officers. Thus, the present findings converge with our earlier ones, while employing a different method and different measures, and do so in a manner that strengthens our claims to external validity while sacrificing a bit in terms of internal validity.

The present findings also extend the deservingness argument, and the theoretical reasoning about the relationship between respect and procedural fairness, by looking at the effect of respect on other motives in addition to the group value motive (the belief that we are members in good standing of our valued social groups). Thus, the present findings suggest that respect is also valued for its implications for what others' behavior communicates about their view of the standing of our group, the value of our behaviors, and our value as social beings. The main effects of "treatment received" on each of the dimensions of intergroup standing, value of behavior, and self-esteem point to the variety of messages communicated by respectful treatment; and the evidence for matches resulting from the positive interactions between each of these and the "treatment deserved" measures provides still further evidence for the deservingness argument in procedural justice.

A final comment is in order regarding the positive main effects for each of the measures of "treatment received" in this study – an effect that is qualified by deservingness perceptions, but not eliminated even when entitlement is low. In its strongest form, the deservingness argument suggests that fairness should result exclusively from the fit between what is deserved and what is received, rather than from any direct effect of what is received. We think several explanations for the main effects observed in our study effect are possible. First, equity theorists suggest that fairness is likely to result from satisfaction of a variety of motives, including hedonic ones, as well as the justice motive. So, for example, Adams (1965) suggests that the threshold for inequity distress is higher when the inequity works to our advantage rather than to our disadvantage. One possibility is that a similar process affects the relationship between positive treatment and procedural justice.

Alternatively, we think that two other processes – ones that are consistent with the deservingness argument advanced here – are likely. One is suggested most clearly by Major (1994), who summarizes theoretical and empirical evidence (e.g., Berger et al., 1972; Deutsch, 1985; Heider, 1958; Homans, 1961) indicating that people tend to legitimate the status quo, whether it is advantageous or disadvantageous to the self. As Major points out, this legitimating effect can work in two ways – people can come to view both their overly favorable and their overly unfavorable outcomes as deserved. So, for example, Major suggests that this legitimating effect is part of the reason that women who are clearly disadvantaged relative to men fail to perceive their relative deprivation as unfair.

In a similar vein, Lerner's just world hypothesis (e.g., Lerner 1975; Lerner & Miller, 1978; Lerner et al., 1976) argues that the motivation to believe in a just world can lead people to infer that those who are advantaged must be more deserving. Just as we think that the deservingness argument extends to procedural justice, we suspect that such reasoning about legitimating processes is likely to affect peoples' beliefs about the nature of their treatment. Such processes are capable of explaining the positive main effects of favorable treatment observed in our data, independent of the matching effect observed in the interactions. If such a legitimating process is operating among the civilians who participated in our study, we would expect a main effect of respect on fairness as was obtained, since the legitimating process is a different one than would be captured by our rather specific measures of entitlement. In other words, the legitimating process would led civilians to conclude that they deserve the respect that they received, but not because of their notions of entitlement stemming from any of the four motives examined in our study. Importantly, however, our argument is that even these main effects would be expected to diminish if the appropriate psychological mediator were included in our model. One possibility would be to include a general measure, such as "I was treated the way I deserved to be treated." This argument is supported by the inclusion of such a measure in the Heuer and colleagues (1999) study, which significantly mediated the main effect of respect. While there was still a significant main effect of respect in that study, even with the mediator included, its magnitude was smaller than any of the main effects for favorable treatment obtained in the present study.

A final possibility is that the civilians in our study believed they were entitled to respect because of considerations related to additional specific motives not included in our model. We do not claim to have included an exhaustive list of the motives that might be gratified by respectful treatment. Among the most likely additional possibilities are that the civilians are motivated to obtain favorable and fair outcomes. Respect might be viewed as an indication that such outcomes are more likely. If so, we would expect the main effect of respect shown in our model to be further reduced if we incorporated matches between the way the civilians were treated and the type of outcomes they felt they deserved.

Overall, we think these findings considerably strengthen our claim that procedural justice researchers should integrate notions of entitlement into their procedural justice models. At the same time, we think the findings underscore the importance of Lerner's early claims about the centrality of entitlement to justice judgments. Our findings merely apply Lerner's insights about entitlement to the domain of procedural justice.

Acknowledgments

The research reported in this chapter was funded by a grant to the second author from the National Science Foundation (SBR-9710946).

We wish to thank Steven Penrod for his comments on earlier versions of this manuscript and Mel Lerner for his thoughtful feedback throughout our efforts to develop the line of reasoning presented here.

REFERENCES

Adams, J. S. (1963). Toward an understanding of inequity. *Journal of Abnormal and Social Psychology, 67*, 422–436.

(1965). Inequity in social exchange. In L. Berkowitz (Ed.), *Advances in experimental social psychology*, (Vol. 2, pp. 267–299). New York: Academic Press.

Berger, J., Zelditch, M., Jr., Anderson, B., & Cohen, B. P. (1972). Structural aspects of distributive justice: A status value formulation. In J. Berger, M. Zelditch, Jr., & B. Anderson (Eds.), *Sociological theories in progress* (Vol. 2, pp. 119–146). Boston: Houghton Mifflin.

Bies, R. J. (1987). The predicament of injustice: The management of moral outrage. In L. L. Cummings & B. M. Staw (Eds.), *Research in organizational behavior* (Vol. 9, pp. 289–319). Greenwich, CT: JAI Press.

Bies, R. J., & Moag, J. S. (1986). Interactional justice: Communication criteria of fairness. In R. J. Lewicki, B. H. Sheppard, & M. H. Bazerman (Eds.), *Research on negotiations in organizations* (pp. 43–55). Greenwich, CT: JAI Press.

Bies, R. J., & Shapiro, D. L. (1987). Interactional fairness judgments: The influence of causal accounts. *Social Justice Research, 1*, 199–218.

(1988). Voice and justification: their influence on procedural fairness judgments. *Academy of Management Journal, 31*, 676–685.

Belsley, D. A. (1991). *Conditioning diagnostics: Collinearity and weak data in regression.* New York: Wiley.

Braband, J., & Lerner, M. J. (1975) "A little time and effort" . . . Who deserves what from whom? *Personality and Social Psychology Bulletin, 1*, 177–180.

Brockner, J., Heuer, L., Siegel, P., Wiesenfeld, B., Martin, C., Grover, S., Reed, T., & Bjorgvinsson, S. (1998). The moderating effect of self-esteem in reaction to voice: Converging evidence from four studies. *Journal of Personality and Social Psychology, 75*, 394–407.

Coopersmith, S. (1981). *Self-esteem inventories.* Palo Alto: Consulting Psychologists Press.

Cropanzano, R., & Folger, R. (1989). Referent cognitions and task decision autonomy: Beyond equity theory. *Journal of Applied Psychology, 74*, 293–299.

Crosby, F. (1976). A model of egoistical relative deprivation. *Psychological Review, 83*, 85–113.

(1982). *Relative deprivation and working women.* New York: Oxford.

Daling, J. R., & Tamura, H. (1970). Use of orthogonal factors for selection of variables in a regression equation – an illustration. *Applied Statistics, 19* (3), 260–268.

Davis, J. (1959). A formal interpretation of the theory of relative deprivation. *Sociometry, 22*, 280–296.

Deutsch, M. (1985). *Distributive justice: A social-psychological perspective.* New Haven, CT: Yale University Press.

Farrar, D. E., & Glauber R. R. (1967). Multicollinearity in regression analysis: The problem revisited. *The Review of Economics and Statistics, 49* (1), 92–107.

Feather, N. T. (1992). An attributional and value analysis of deservingness in success and failure situations. *British Journal of Social Psychology, 31*, 125–145.

Folger, R. (1977). Distributive and procedural justice: Combined impact of "voice" and improvement on experienced inequity. *Journal of Personality and Social Psychology, 35*, 108–119.

Folger, R., & Bies, R. J. (1989). Managerial responsibilities and procedural justice. *Employee Responsibilities and Rights Journal, 2*, 79–90.

Greenberg, E. (1975). Minimum variance properties of principal component regression. *Journal of the American Statistical Association, 70* (349), 194–197.

Heider, F. (1958). *The psychology of interpersonal relations.* New York: Wiley.

Heuer, L., Blumenthal, E., Douglas, A., & Weinblatt, T. (1999). A deservingness approach to respect as a relationally based fairness judgment. *PSPB, 25* (10), 1279–1292.

Gurr, T. R. (1970). *Why men rebel.* Princeton: Princeton University Press.

Homans, G. C., (1974). *Social behavior: Its elementary forms.* New York: Harcourt, Brace, and World.

Huo, Y. J., Smith, H. J., Tyler, T. R., & Lind, E. A. (1996). Superordinate identification, subgroup identification, and justice concerns: Is separatism the problem; is assimilation the answer? *Psychological Science, 7*, 40–45.

Kanfer, R., Sawyer, J., Earley, P. C., & Lind, E. A. (1987). Participation in task evaluation procedures: The effects of influential opinion expression and knowledge of evaluative criteria on attitudes and performance. *Social Justice Research, 1*, 235–249.

Kendall, M. G. (1957). A course in multivariate analysis. London: Charles Griffin and Company.

LaTour, S. (1978). Determinants of participant and observer satisfaction with adversary and inquisitorial modes of adjudication. *Journal of Personality and Social Psychology, 36*, 1531–1545.

Lerner, M. (1977). The justice motive: Some hypotheses on its origins and forms. *Journal of Personality, 45*, 1–52.

(1980). *The belief in a just world: A fundamental delusion.* New York: Plenum.

(1987). Integrating societal and psychological rules of entitlement: The basic task of each social actor and fundamental problem for the social sciences. *Social Justice Research, 1*, 107–125.

Lerner, M., Miller, D. T., & Holmes, J. G. (1976). Deserving and the emergence of forms of justice. In L. Berkowitz (Ed.), *Advances in experimental social psychology* (Vol. 3, pp. 133–162). New York: Academic Press.

Lind, E. A., Kurtz, S., Musante, L., Walker, L., & Thibaut, J. W. (1980). Procedure and outcome effects on reactions to adjudicated resolution of conflicts of interest. *Journal of Personality and Social Psychology, 39*, 643–653.

Lind, E. A., Lissak, R. I., & Conlon, E. E. (1983). Decision control and process control effects on procedural fairness judgments. *Journal of Applied Social Psychology, 13*, 338–350.

Lind, E. A., & Tyler, T. R. (1988). The social psychology of procedural justice. New York: Plenum.

MacCoun, R. J., Lind, E. A., Hensler, D. R., Bryant, D. L., & Ebener, P. A. (1988). Alternative adjudication: An evaluation of the New Jersey automobile arbitration program. Santa Monica, CA: Institute for Civil Justice, RAND Corporation.

Massy, W. F. (1965). Principal components regression in exploritory statistical research. *Journal of the American Statistical Association, 60* (309), 234–256.

Pepitone, A., & L'Armand, K. (1996). The justice and injustice of life events. *European Journal of Social Psychology, 26* (4), 581–597.

Runciman, W. G. (1966). Relative deprivation and social justice: A study of attitudes to social inequality in twentieth-century England. Berkeley: University of California Press.

Sclove, S. L. (1968). Improved estimators for coefficients in linear regression. *Journal of the American Statistical Association, 63* (322), 596–606.

Simmons, C. H., & Lerner, M. J. (1968) Altruism as a search for justice. *Journal of Personality and Social Psychology, 9*, 216–225.

Thibaut, J., & Walker, L. (1975). *Procedural justice: A psychological analysis.* Hillsdale, NJ: Erlbaum.

(1978). A theory of procedure. *California Law Review, 66*, 541–566.

Tyler, T. R. (1987). Conditions leading to value expressive effects in judgments of procedural justice: A test of four models. *Journal of Personality and Social Psychology, 52*, 333–344.

(1989). The psychology of procedural justice: A test of the group-value model. *Journal of Personality and Social Psychology, 57*, 830–838.

(1994). Psychological models of the justice motive: Antecedents of distributive and procedural justice. *Journal of Personality and Social Psychology, 67* (5), 850–863.

Tyler, T. R., & Bies, R. J. (1990). Beyond formal procedures: The interpersonal context of procedural justice. In J. S. Carroll (Ed.), *Applied social psychology in business settings* (pp. 77–98). Hillside, NJ: Erlbaum.

Tyler, T. R., & Degoey, P. (1995). Collective restraint in social dilemmas: Procedural justice and social identification effects on support for authorities. *Journal of Personality and Social Psychology, 69*, 482–497.

Tyler, T. R., & Folger, R. (1980). Distributional and procedural aspects of satisfaction with citizen-police encounters. *Basic and Applied Social Psychology, 1*, 281–292.

Tyler, T. R., & Lind, E. A. (1992). A relational model of authority in groups. In M. Zanna (Ed.), *Advances in experimental social psychology* (Vol. 25, pp. 115–191). New York: Academic Press.

Tyler, T. R., Rasinski, K., & Spodick, N. (1985). Influence of voice on satisfaction with leaders: Exploring the meaning of process control. *Journal of Personality and Social Psychology, 48*, 72–81.

Urban, G. L., & Von Hippel, E. (1988). Lead user analysis for the development of new industrial products. *Management Science, 34* (5), 569–82.

Walster, E., Berscheid, E., & Walster, G. W. (1976). New directions in equity research. In L. Berkowitz (Ed.), *Advances in experimental social psychology* (Vol. 9, pp. 1–42). New York: Academic Press.

Walster, E., Walster, G. W., & Berscheid, E. (1978). *Equity: Theory and research.* Boston: Allyn and Bacon.

23. Fairness Judgments as Cognitions

E. ALLAN LIND

Thirty years ago, at the beginning of the Thibaut and Walker project on procedural justice, the psychology of justice was a relatively cognitive undertaking. The two most prominent and active justice literatures at that time were those based on Adams's (1965) equity theory, an analysis of feelings of deservingness that was strongly grounded in Festinger's theories of cognitive dissonance and social comparison, and Lerner's just world hypothesis (Lerner, 1971, 1980; Lerner & Miller, 1978), an analysis of impression formation and judgment that had links both to cognitive balance ideas and to attribution theory. In both lines of work, unfairness and injustice were viewed as cognitive manifestations of an incongruence between ideal and experienced states of being, and the fundamental psychological processes employed to explain fairness judgment processes involved mental efforts to remedy or explain away the inconsistency. Thus, in Adams's analysis of equity judgments, people were seen as gathering information about the relative contributions and outcomes of others, and they were then seen as changing their attitudes and behavior in such a way as to make their perceptions of their own contributions and outcomes congruent with those of others. In Lerner's just world work, people were seen as struggling to reconcile the misfortunes of others with their own belief in a just world, and this reconciliation induced a derogation-of-victim effect, so that the victim's fate could be seen as deserved. In both instances, there was a fairly fine-grained analysis of the cognitive dynamics underlying the justice effects in question.

The Movement Away from Cognitive Analyses of Fairness Judgments

From about the time of the Thibaut and Walker project, in the early 1970s, until rather recently, the tone and focus of the psychological investigation of justice changed. In both the study of distributive fairness and the emerging and then developing study of procedural fairness, attention moved away from the thought processes of the person judging fairness to a more descriptive concern with reactions to outcomes or to structural and relational features of the environment. For example, the intellectual heirs of Adams's equity research became interested in how people attempted to be fair in allocations, and the focus changed from the beliefs of recipients about whether they had received a fair share – an analysis of the cognitive dynamics of those beliefs – to a description of how allocators attempted to give a fair share to someone else (see, e.g., Cook & Hegtvedt, 1983; Deutsch, 1985; Major & Deaux, 1981; Leventhal, 1976; Mikula, 1974; Walster, Berscheid, & Walster, 1973). Distributive fairness became an issue of competing norms, not of inconsistent cognitions.

In procedural fairness research, the dual focus of the Thibaut and Walker work, which looked both for practical procedures for doing justice and for the psychological reasons that people might have for viewing one procedure as fairer than another, was largely abandoned in favor of investigation of which procedures instill feelings of fairness. As procedural justice work began to grow in volume, the key research topics had to do with the perceived fairness of adversary versus nonadversary hearing procedures (e.g., LaTour, 1978; Lind et al., 1978; Sheppard, 1985) or with the relative importance of decision and process control in procedural fairness judgments (e.g., Houlden et al., 1978; Lind, Lissak, & Conlon, 1983). Once these questions were settled, we procedural justice researchers tended to focus on examining procedural fairness judgments versus outcomes as determinants of obedience and acceptance of authority (e.g., Lind, Kanfer, & Earley, 1990; Tyler, 1990; Tyler & Mitchell, 1994; Tyler, Rasinski, & McGraw, 1986; see generally Tyler & Lind, 1992) or other attitudes and behaviors (e.g., Lind, MacCoun et al., 1990; Konovsky & Cropanzano, 1991; Moorman, 1991; see generally Folger & Greenberg, 1985; Lind & Tyler, 1988; Tyler et al., 1997). While these later investigations could have taken on a cognitive tone, we tended to shy away from the fundamental psychology of why procedural fairness matters in favor of documentation of correlations between fairness judgments and politically or legally relevant behaviors and attitudes.

Of course, since most of the researchers working on questions of procedural and distributive fairness were social psychologists, the change was not absolute. There was still occasional speculation about the cognitive dynamics of fairness judgments. Good examples are Folger's work on referent cognition theory (1986) and Messick's work on self-protective and self-serving biases in fairness judgments (e.g., Messick et al., 1985; Messick & Sentis, 1979). But, on the whole, the period of the late 1970s, the 1980s, and the early 1990s saw a noticeable absence of either theory or research on the cognitive dynamics involved in fairness judgments.

This is not to say that these decades were unproductive; but the major advances were descriptions of phenomena, not real psychological explanations of these phenomena. Using procedural justice research as an example, the major empirical discoveries were (1) that the key component of adversary disputing procedures that makes participants see these procedures as fairer than nonadversary procedures is that adversary procedures offer greater control over the process, (2) that the decisions rendered by fair procedures are themselves seen as fairer (the "fair process" effect, Folger, 1977), (3) that, compared to outcome evaluations or expectations, procedural fairness judgments account for as much or more of the variance in obedience to law, acceptance of decisions and policies, and commitment to groups and organizations, (4) that nuances of quality of treatment – things like dignity and politeness – exert remarkably strong effects on procedural fairness judgments, and (5) that it is not uncommon for procedural justice effects to be stronger when outcomes are negative than when they are positive. With the possible exception of the last of these advances, however, we procedural justice researchers have not probed much into the psychological "why" of the phenomenon. Thus, as we investigated various explanations for the adversary effect, we paid more attention to the opportunity to present arguments than to felt control as an explanatory variable. We never really explained why procedural fairness judgments should "bleed over" into distributive fairness judgments in the fair process effect. In trying to explain the extraordinary potency of procedural fairness judgments, we noted that fair procedures are seen as allowing people to express their values and that they might give reassurance of the perceiver's standing with important groups or institutions, but we never explained why these features of fair procedure might be linked to the particular attitudes and behaviors that procedural fairness affects. Most distressing of all, we never explained why people should show such strong reactions to fairness judgments. We noted that quality of treatment antecedents of procedural fairness judgments seem to be related to the relationship between the perceiver and whoever is enacting the high- or low-quality treatment, but we never explained why fairness should be so closely tried to reactions to and behavior in the relationship in question.

Thus, while there have been substantial advances in the empirical literature on fairness judgments, and reasonable advances in descriptive theoretical accounts about how and when fairness judgments have the effects that they have, there have been only sporadic advances in the underlying psychological theory of fairness judgments. Recently, however, a number of justice scholars have begun to think about the cognitive dynamics of fairness judgments. I describe here some of the elements of my own attempt at this sort of analysis.

Fairness Heuristic Theory

Fairness heuristic theory (see Lind, 2001, for a full presentation of the theory) began as my attempt to see if our understanding of fairness judgment processes could be pushed ahead by recognizing that fairness judgments were not just aspects of interpersonal process, but were also cognitions. Two questions motivated the theory: (1) Why, after all is said and done, should it be *fairness judgments* that have such profound effects on things like acceptance of decisions or willingness to follow laws? (2) If we think of fairness judgments as cognitions, with whatever psychological function is implied by the answer to the preceding question, what can we expect with respect to the cognitive dynamics of the fairness judgment process? In other words, from a cognitive perspective, why do people pay so much attention to fairness, and how do they form and modify fairness judgments?

Thinking back on the literature on fairness judgments, it seemed to me that the substantial effects of – and the great attention apparently paid to – fairness judgments might derive from the usefulness of fair treatment as an indicator of inclusion and security vis-à-vis another person, group, organization, or institution. It seemed to me reasonable to suppose that people use their judgment of the overall fairness of their treatment as gauge of sorts, to which they refer as needed to decide how much of their time, resources, and identity to invest in the relationship in question. If one thinks that one is in general being fairly treated, then, I suggest, one is willing to abandon a self-oriented analysis of the rewards and costs of particular actions in favor of a more relationship-oriented analysis of the consequences of actions or policies. This, in turn, would produce the acceptance of authority effects that have been observed to be so closely linked to justice judgment. For example, if I feel fairly treated by my employer, I am more likely to invest my time and my identity in my organization; I am more likely to accept organizational policies and hierarchy; and I will evaluate organizational actions more in terms of whether they seem good for the organization than in terms of whether they are good for me individually. On the other hand, if I feel unfairly treated, I will give my time and effort to the organization only if it is clearly in my individual interest to do so; I will focus my social identity on other aspects of my life; and I will accept organizational policy and supervisory requests only if the benefits of complying or the costs of disobedience are clear, probable, and substantial. People use fairness as an indicator of security in their personal, political, and organizational lives.

In sum, fairness judgments seem to be acting as a heuristic to guide decisions and actions in either an egoistic, self-interest-focused direction or in a group-oriented, socially focused direction. I have argued (Lind, 1995, 2001) that it is reasonable for people to need a heuristic to direct them in this way, because of the massive cognitive effort that would be involved in constantly updating one's impression of one's standing vis-à-vis others, or of analyzing event by event and investment by investment the likelihood of exploitation, so that one could decide whether to be individually or socially oriented. It is much more efficient to have some guiding principle or rule of thumb that allows one to make these decisions quickly and easily (if not always absolutely accurately) and then to get on with life.

But, to return to one of the two central questions, why fairness judgments? Why should fairness be the heuristic judgment that changes people from self-interested actors into socially oriented, "good," cooperative social actors? Part of the answer, I have argued, is that fairness is not *the* heuristic judgment, it is one of several heuristics that people use in this fashion. But fairness is a heuristic that is applicable across a variety of relationship types and that is therefore useful in a number of important social contexts. Other heuristics may hold sway in special relationships: In a close family relationship – in a parent's consideration of how much he or she will sacrifice for an infant child, for example

– relational identity may be the operative heuristic for decisions about self-sacrifice or personal investment; for an ideologue confronting a political choice, the party's philosophy may be the touchstone for any decision. But for most interpersonal, organizational, and institutional relationships, fairness is the most useful, and the most widely used, heuristic.

Still, why fairness? The answer, I believe, has to do with the capacity of fairness to address two of the most fundamental threats that arise in a wide variety of social, organizational, and institutional relationships. These two threats are the threat of exploitation and the threat of rejection. Fairness – and by this I mean perceived fairness – touches on both issues. We know from a variety of sources (see Lind & Tyler, 1988; Tyler et al., 1997, for reviews) that feelings of unfair treatment tend to derive from experiences that suggest one of two things: exploitation or exclusion. Of course, we have known from the time that Adams did his original work on equity theory that fairness judgments are closely tied to feelings that one has been exploited. The connection with exclusion came later; but as Tyler and I have noted in our review of the procedural justice literature (Lind & Tyler, 1988, Chapter 10), the accumulated research in that area points rather convincingly to the conclusion that fairness judgments are sensitive to nuances of treatment that suggest, or deny, inclusion in the group, organization, or institution in question.

The argument, then, is that when one is fairly treated, concerns about exploitation or exclusion are put to rest, and one feels free to engage the relationship in a more open, less defensive fashion. There is a cognitive story to be developed and tested about how people use fairness judgments as heuristics, but to date there has been little research on that topic. The cognitive features of the analysis that have been more fully explored, and for which there is much more research support, have to do with what using fairness as a heuristic might suggest about how fairness judgments are generated and modified. It is to that story that I now turn.

If we assume for the moment that fairness heuristics are used as I have just suggested, then we can look for a cognitive dynamic that would support the heuristic function of fairness judgments, and this exploration of how fairness *ought to* work should give us some interesting ways to test the theory. If fairness judgments serve as heuristics for social choices, for example, it would make sense for the judgments to be formed rapidly at the outset of a relationship, even if this quick formation involved some shortcuts in the derivation of the fairness judgment. Rapid construction of an overall impression of fair treatment would be needed to allow the person in question to have the heuristic ready to guide early choices about how much to invest his or her identity and personal resources in the relationship. In addition, once constructed, the fairness judgment would be of greatest use if it were relatively stable, so we might expect that fairness judgments would not be reprocessed and reevaluated very often. If the judgment were constantly being reprocessed, with new data constantly being sought, analyzed, and incorporated into a revised judgment, it would have little value as a heuristic. It would be much more useful, in terms of cognitive efficiency, if the fairness judgment were instead stored away and used to make decisions, and only reevaluated when there was some sign of rather fundamental change in the relationship.

These ideas lead to two sets of predictions about the psychology of fairness. First, because the processing and reevaluation of fairness judgments is seen as episodic, rather than continuous, the impact of fairness-relevant information on fairness judgments will depend on whether the person is in what might be termed "judgmental mode" or "use mode" with respect to the heuristic. Judgmental mode refers to a cognitive state where information relevant to the question of whether one it being treated fairly is being processed and fairness judgments are being generated or revised. Use mode refers to a cognitive state in which fairness judgments are being used to decide on actions and to form attitudes about social relationships; but in use mode, new fairness information tends to be evaluated in terms of existing fairness judgment rather than the other way around. At the beginning of relationships or at times of salient change in the nature of the relationship, when judgmental mode is in play, whatever fairness-relevant information is at hand will be seized upon and incorporated into an overall judgment of fairness. At other times, fairness-relevant information is much more likely to be assimilated to the preexisting judgment than to be used to change that judgment much, and new fairness questions will be answered by reference to the existing basic fairness judgment. This last point suggests that, during use mode, fairness experiences that were used to derive the basic fairness judgment will appear to drive judgments on fairness dimensions about which one did not have much "data" during the judgmental mode. Each of these predictions, which we have termed the "episodic" and "substitution" predictions, respectively, have been tested, and each has received some research support.

The idea that people construct overall fairness judgments rapidly at the outset of a relationship, then store and use the judgments without much reevaluation, suggests that fairness judgments may often show a primacy effect. When people in a work situation encounter a new boss, for example, the theory predicts that they will go into judgmental mode; and whatever fairness-relevant information is encountered early in the interaction should exert much more influence on their ultimate fairness judgments than would the same information if encountered later. The logic of the episodic effect – that is, that the distinction between what I am terming "judgmental mode" and what I am terming "use mode" will be stronger the more likely it is that identity and investment decisions must be made – suggests further that this primacy effect should be more apparent when the person in question feels a stronger relationship with the organization or work unit. In a recent experiment, Laura Kray, Leigh Thompson, and I (Lind, Kray, & Thompson, in press) looked for and found just such a pattern of effects.

We told undergraduate subjects that they would be doing three businesslike tasks (budget reconciliation, scheduling, etc.) while working at a computer station that would freeze up from time to time during each task. (The subjects had no trouble believing that this was a good simulation of working conditions in many business settings!) The subjects were told that they could tell their supervisor (supposedly another undergraduate subject, but actually an experimental confederate) about their "down time," and that the supervisor could take such problems into account in awarding bonus points that would buy lottery tickets for a prize to be awarded after the experiment. The subjects were told, however, that it was in the final analysis up to the supervisor whether or not to consider their messages about computer problems. Before the work trials began, the subjects either did or did not participate in a group-identification enhancing exercise with the other subjects in their experimental session. The group-identification manipulation was modeled on one used by Kramer, Pommerenke, and Newton (1993): Participants in the high-identification condition held a discussion prior to the work session to name their work group and to develop a slogan for it, and they wore an identifying badge with the name they chose.

We manipulated the timing of a fairness-relevant experience: the denial of voice by the supervisor. The supervisor refused, with a rather rude message, to consider the subject's down-time message on one of the three tasks periods in the experiment. We manipulated whether this

Table 23.1. Primacy effects in fairness judgments

Group Identification	Unfair Experience on First Task	Unfair Experience on Second Task	Unfair Experience on Third Task
High	−1.14	−.51	.37
Low	−.58	−.83	−.24

Note: Values are mean ratings on a seven-point scale, from −3 = "very unfair" to +3 = "very fair."

refusal occurred on the first, second, or third task. (On the other two tasks the supervisor accepted and appeared ready to consider the subject's message.) We predicted, using the logic outlined above, that ratings of the fairness of the supervisor would be most negative if the denial of voice occurred on the first task, less negative if the denial of voice occurred on the second task, and least negative if the denial of voice occurred on the third trial. We predicted further that this primacy effect would be most evident in the condition where the subjects had experienced the group-identification enhancing exercise.

Table 23.1 shows the fairness ratings for each of the conditions just described – the values are average ratings on a +3 to −3 scale calling for ratings of the fairness of the supervisor. (The values are all close to the midpoint, as we expected in light of the fact that all subjects received a mixture of fair and unfair treatment experiences. Apparently the primacy effect does not overwhelm all other fairness judgment processes.) An ANOVA bore out the pattern seen in the table: There was a significant interaction between unfairness timing and group identification. Within the high group-identification condition there was a significant primacy effect, within the low identification condition there was not.

In the context of the argument I am advancing here, the point of these findings is not that the study produced findings that are favorable to fairness heuristic theory, but rather that an analysis of the cognitive dynamics of fairness judgments yielded some novel, testable hypotheses, and that the analysis bore fruit in the demonstration of a hitherto undocumented fairness effect. The study admittedly leaves unanswered some interesting theoretical issues. For example, was the primacy effect due to higher attention to fairness issues early in the experiment, or was it due to a tendency to assimilate later information to existing fairness judgments once they were formed? I suspect that both processes are at work – both are congruent with the theory – but further research is needed to confirm this. What is clear, however, is that predictable and interesting cognitive processes are at work here.

Note, too, that the effect thus demonstrated is not of value just for the abstract testing of some academic theory. The existence of a primacy effect on fairness judgments in the presence of group identification has some real implications for how – or, more properly, when – one might most successfully instill feelings of fairness in relationships, organizations, and institutions. Another study shows that primacy may not always be the operative effect. Instead, the key question might be whether something has happened recently to put the perceiver back into judgmental mode. Early in employment (or in other relationship types), primacy may be the rule; but later events can stimulate a reevaluation of fairness of treatment, leading to recency effects.

The study in question, a field study of the perceptions and behavior of laid-off and fired workers (Lind et al., 2000), showed that the episodic processing of fairness information is not limited to the beginning of relationships. In the Lind and colleagues study, we predicted, because it is certainly a time of significant change in the relationship, that fairness experiences encountered in the last days of a worker's employment would figure more prominently than all preceding fairness experiences in shaping the worker's attitude toward his or her former employer and the worker's propensity to sue. We found that this was indeed the case. Fairness-related aspects of treatment at termination – things like whether the worker felt he or she had been treated with dignity and whether the employer was thought to have given an honest explanation of the reason for the termination – were far and away the strongest predictor of post-termination retributive thoughts and behaviors.

I noted earlier that another implication of the hypothesis that fairness cognitions are rapidly formed estimates of overall safety in relationships is that people might substitute one type of fairness for another as they move from the generation of a heuristic judgment to "use mode," where there is an attempt reconcile that judgment across the various dimensions of fairness. Kees van den Bos and his colleagues (Van den Bos, Vermunt, & Wilke, 1997; Van den Bos et al., 1997; Van den Bos et al., 1998) have conducted a series of studies on this "substitution" effect, with results that show just the sort of effects predicted by the theory. In essence, the Van den Bos studies show that people substitute procedural fairness judgments for distributive fairness judgments when, but only when, they lack enough social or personal information to infer directly how fair the outcomes they encounter are. In all of these studies, outcome information preceded process information; but without social or personal information to turn outcome information into *fairness* information, the development of the heuristic judgment must wait. Once the procedural fairness information is encountered and a heuristic fairness judgment is formed, the theory would argue, the outcome information is interpreted in terms of this new judgment.

These studies show that process sometimes has substantial effects on distributive fairness judgments and sometimes does not. The key determinants of whether process experiences affect outcome fairness judgments are whether the person has little personal experience of the outcome in question and whether there is comparison information of the sort identified by equity theory. When direct experience or comparison information is present, procedural fairness experiences exert little influence on distributive fairness judgments; when direct experience and comparison information is lacking, procedural fairness experiences exert strong effects on distributive fairness judgments. The substitution process is limited to an effect of one type of fairness for another. Another finding of the Van den Bos studies is that, as the theory would predict, fairness judgments are not substituted for nonfairness dimensions of outcome evaluations, such as satisfaction, for example.

These effects are congruent with predictions from fairness heuristic theory, but again, my point here is not so much that they are in line with any particular theory. What is important for the current line of argument is that studies like those described here show how the interpretation of outcomes or processes as fair or unfair can be profoundly influenced by whether the person in question has already formed an impression of overall fairness. Thus, the substitutability effect can offer a cognitive explanation of the general observation that procedural fairness has greater impact on the attitudes and behaviors that are affected by fairness judgments. If we assume, as seems reasonable, that procedural information is most often encountered before outcome information is encountered, then procedures and impressions of their justice will be more likely to contribute to the initial development of the overall, heuristic fairness judgment. Later outcome information will be interpreted in light of this preexisting judgment and will most likely be assimilated to it, and it follows that the process information will have the most impact. We can look for this effect to be reversed when outcome information is encountered before process information; and in fact this reversal has been demonstrated empirically (Daly & Tripp, 1996).

It is interesting to speculate about how these sorts of processes might play out against some of the classic justice judgment phenomena. For example, might Lerner's just world effects have been early demonstrations of the same basic phenomena that Van den Bos and his colleagues have shown in more recent studies? In many of the just world studies, the only fairness-relevant information held at the time the participants were asked to make judgments about the target was their overall belief that the world is just. In this context, the theory would predict that they would substitute their overall just world belief for the then-unavailable fairness evaluation of the bad outcome experienced by the target person. Could one find circumstances that turn around that effect, so that the fundamental justice of the context is evaluated in terms of the ill or good fate of those in it, just as Daly and Tripp turned the classic "fair process" effect into a "fair outcome" effect by changing the common sequencing of information? Suppose, for example, that the participants had more acquaintance with the target or the process by which the outcome was generated. In this situation, overall just world beliefs might have much less impact, and these more direct sources of information might determine whether the bad outcome was seen to be deserved.

A thought experiment might illustrate the point I am trying to make here. Suppose we are concerned with how people evaluate coworkers who lose their jobs. Suppose further that the job termination occurs either in the standard operation of a stable firm with generally good employee relations or in the context of a merger or acquisition. Fairness heuristic theory would predict that in the stable-company scenario, the classic "blaming the victim" effect would be evident, because people would be interpreting the termination in terms of their underlying perception that the firm treats its employees fairly. On the other hand, in the merger scenario, fairness heuristic theory might predict that the real and symbolic changes in the nature of the employment relationship, changes made salient by the merger, would push the workers into judgmental mode, and the poor outcomes would not be blamed on the terminated employees but would rather be attributed to the merged company.

Conclusions

I have used my own theory to illustrate the sorts of insights and novel perspectives that can be had from more cognitive analyses of fairness judgment processes. As I noted earlier in this chapter, mine is not the only recent attempt to push theory in this direction. Folger and Cropanzano (1998) advance what they term "fairness theory," which seeks to explain justice effects in terms of attribution-based cognitive accounts of injurious actions. When there are not convincing other reasons for injuries, they suggest, procedures, outcomes, and social processes are seen as unfair. In yet another effort, Brockner (2000) looks at the interplay of procedural fairness judgments and self-esteem processes as he attempts to explain when people will accept negative outcomes and, more importantly, the negative self-evaluations that come with them, and when they will devalue the process in an effort to maintain self-esteem. Both of these theories use quite different cognitive explanations of justice judgment phenomena than does fairness heuristic theory, but all three theories share an approach that seeks to understand how various fairness and fairness-related cognitions play off against each other. In this respect, all three theories represent a return to the sort of analysis that drew Adams's and Lerner's attention to fairness. Perhaps by coming back to these quintessentially psychological "takes" on fairness, informed this time by a much richer empirical literature than was available to Adams or Lerner in their early work, we can advance our understanding of this fascinating topic. Certainly we have good reason to do so, since whatever the nature of the accompanying theory, we now know a good bit more about just how important fairness judgments are.

REFERENCES

Adams, J. S. (1965). Inequity in social exchange. In L. Berkowitz (Ed.), *Advances in experimental social psychology* (Vol. 2, pp. 267–299). New York: Academic Press.

Brockner, J. (2000). High procedural fairness may reduce or heighten the influence of outcome favorability: Towards a reconciliation. Unpublished manuscript, Columbia University.

Cook, K., & Hegtvedt, K. (1983). Distributive justice, equity, and equality. *Annual Review of Sociology, 9,* 217–241.

Deutsch, M. (1985). *Distributive justice.* New Haven, CT: Yale University Press.

Folger, R. (1977). Distributive and procedural justice: Combined impact of "voice" and improvement of experienced inequity. *Journal of Personality and Social Psychology, 35,* 108–119.

Folger, R. (1986). Rethinking equity theory: A referent cognitions model. In H. W. Beirhoff, R. L. Cohen, & J. Greenberg (Eds.), *Justice in social relations* (pp. 145–162). New York: Plenum.

Folger, R., & Cropanzano, R. (1998). *Organizational justice and human resource management.* Beverly Hills, CA: Sage.

Folger, R., & Greenberg, J. (1985). Procedural justice: An interpretative analysis of personnel systems. In K. Roland & G. Ferris (Eds.), *Research in personnel and human resource management* (Vol. 3, pp. 141–183). Greenwich, CT: JAI.

Houlden, P., LaTour, S., Walker, L., & Thibaut, J. (1978). Preferences for modes of dispute resolution as a function of process and decision control. *Journal of Experimental Social Psychology, 14,* 13–30.

Konovsky, M. A., & Cropanzano, R. (1991). Perceived fairness of employee drug testing as a predictor of employee attitudes and job performance. *Journal of Applied Psychology, 76,* 698–707.

Kramer, R. M., Pommerenke, P., & Newton, E. (1993). The social context of negotiation: Effects of social identity and interpersonal accountability on negotiator decision making. *Journal of Conflict Resolution, 37,* 633–654.

LaTour, S. (1978). Determinants of participant and observer satisfaction with adversary and inquisitorial modes of adjudication. *Journal of Personality and Social Psychology, 36,* 1531–1545.

Lerner, M. J. (1971). Justified self-interest and the responsibility for suffering: A replication and extension. *Journal of Human Relations, 19,* 550–559.

(1980). *The belief in a just world.* New York: Plenum.

Lerner, M. J., & Miller, D. T. (1978). Just world research and the attribution process: Looking back and ahead. *Psychological Bulletin, 85,* 1031–1051.

Leventhal, G. S. (1976). The distribution of rewards and resources in groups and organizations. *Advances in Experimental Social Psychology, 9,* 91–131.

Lind, E. A. (1995). *Social conflict and social justice: Some lessons from the social psychology of justice.* Leiden, Netherlands: Leiden University Press.

(2001). Fairness heuristic theory: Justice judgments as pivotal cognitions in organizational relations. In J. Greenberg & R. Cropanzano (Eds.), *Advances in organizational behavior* (pp. 56–89). San Francisco, CA: New Lexington Press.

Lind, E. A., Erickson, B. E., Friedland, N., & Dickenberger, M. (1978). Reactions to procedural models for adjudicative conflict resolution: A cross-national study. *Journal of Conflict Resolution, 22,* 318–341.

Lind, E. A., Greenberg, J., Scott, K. S., & Welchans, T. D. (2000). The winding road from employee to complainant: Situational and psychological determinants of wrongful termination lawsuits. *Administrative Science Quarterly, 45,* 557–590.

Lind, E. A., Kanfer, R., & Earley, P. C. (1990). Voice, control, and procedural justice: Instrumental and noninstrumental concerns in fairness judgments. *Journal of Personality and Social Psychology, 59*, 952–959.

Lind, E. A., Kray, L. J., & Thompson, L. (in press). Primacy effects in justice judgments: Testing predictions from fairness heuristic theory. *Organizational Behavior and Human Decision Processes.*

Lind, E. A., Lissak, R. I., & Conlon, D. E. (1983). Decision control and process control effects on procedural fairness judgments. *Journal of Applied Social Psychology, 4*, 338–350.

Lind, E. A., MacCoun, R. J., Ebener, P. A., Felstiner, W. L. F., Hensler, D. R., Resnik, J., & Tyler, T. R. (1990). In the eye of the beholder: Tort litigants' evaluations of their experiences in the civil justice system. *Law & Society Review, 24*, 953–996.

Lind, E. A., & Tyler, T. R. (1988). *The social psychology of procedural justice.* New York: Plenum.

Major, B., & Deaux, K. (1981). Individual differences in equity behavior. In J. Greenberg & R. L. Cohen (Eds.), *Equity and justice in social behavior* (pp. 43–76). New York: Academic Press.

Messick, D. M., Bloom, S., Boldizar, J. P., & Samuelson, C. D. (1985). Why we are fairer than others. *Journal of Experimental Social Psychology, 21*, 480–500.

Messick, D. M., & Sentis, K. P. (1979). Fairness and preference. *Journal of Experimental Social Psychology, 15*, 418–434.

Mikula, G. (1974). Nationality, performance, and sex as determinants of reward allocation. *Journal of Personality and Social Psychology, 29*, 435–440.

Moorman, R. H. (1991) The relationship between organizational justice and organizational citizenship behaviors: Do fairness perceptions influence employee citizenship? *Journal of Applied Psychology, 76*, 845–855.

Sheppard, B. H. (1985). Justice is no simple matter: Case for elaborating our model of procedural fairness. *Journal of Personality and Social Psychology, 49*, 953–962.

Thibaut, J., & Walker, L. (1975). *Procedural justice: A psychological analysis.* Hillsdale, NJ: Erlbaum.

(1978). A theory of procedure. *California Law Review, 66*, 541–566.

Tyler, T. R. (1990). *Why people obey the law.* New Haven, CT: Yale University Press.

Tyler, T. R., Boeckman, R. J., Smith, H. J., & Huo, Y. J. (1997). *Social justice in a diverse society.* Boulder, CO: Westview Press.

Tyler, T. R., & Lind, E. A. (1992). A relational model of authority in groups. In M. Zanna (Ed.), *Advances in experimental social psychology* (Vol. 25, pp. 115–192). New York: Academic Press.

Tyler, T. R., & Mitchell, G. (1994). Legitimacy and the empowerment of discretionary legal authority. *Duke Law Journal, 43*, 703–815.

Tyler, T. R., Rasinski, K., & McGraw, K. (1985). The influence of perceived injustice on support for legal authority. *Journal of Applied Social Psychology, 15*, 700–725.

Van den Bos, K., Lind, E. A., Vermunt, R., & Wilke, H. A. M. (1997). How do I judge my outcome when I do not know the outcome of others? The psychology of the fair process effect. *Journal of Personality and Social Psychology, 72,* 1034–1046.

Van den Bos, K., Vermunt, R., & Wilke, H. A. M. (1997). Procedural and distributive justice: What is fair depends more on what comes first than on what comes next. *Journal of Personality and Social Psychology, 77,* 95–104.

Van den Bos, K., Wilke, H. A. M., Lind, E. A., & Vermunt, R. (1998). Evaluating outcomes by means of the fair process effect: Evidence for different processes in fairness and satisfaction judgments. *Journal of Personality and Social Psychology, 74,* 1493–1503.

Walster, E., Berscheid, E., & Walster, G. W. (1973). New directions in equity research. *Journal of Personality and Social Psychology, 25,* 151–176.

Name Index

Abrams, D., 308
Abramson, L. Y., 156, 157, 158
Ackerman, P., 234
Adams, J. S., 43, 229, 397, 411, 416, 417, 428
Aderman, D., 128, 143, 241
Ajzen, I., 141
Aldeguer, C. M. R., 238
Alicke, M. D., 350
Allegro, J., 163
Allport, G. W., 123, 298
American Law Institute, 319, 325
Anderson, B., 411
Appleby, L., 341
Appleby, T., 306*n*10
Aristotle, 72
Arps, K., 227, 233
Asche, S., 13
Atchison, L., 340

Baeyer, C., 156
Bandura, A., 99, 177–8, 272, 351
Barak, G., 303
Barlow, D. H., 350
Baron, J., 98
Baron, L., 56
Baron, R. A., 172
Baron, R. M., 198
Barrientos, S., 228, 234
Bar-Tal, D., 261
Batson, C. D., 5, 98, 99, 101, 175, 226, 228, 231, 232–3, 234–5, 236–7, 238, 239, 246, 272, 273, 350
Batson, J. G., 228, 234, 238
Bauermann, M., 51
Baumeister, R. F., 176, 350–1, 352, 360
Bayly, M. J., 228, 234
Bazerman, M. H., 229
Beaman, A. L., 227, 233
Beaton, A. M., 206, 209
Becker, E., 352
Bednar, L. L., 234, 238
Belsley, D. A., 406
Bem, D. J., 152
Bentham, J., 326
Berger, J., 411
Berk, R. E., 328
Berkowitz, L., 192–3, 196, 199, 261, 350, 359
Berliner, D. C., 365
Berscheid, E., 43, 63, 123, 175, 176, 180, 397, 398, 417
Bierhoff, H.-W., 6, 193, 195, 197, 200
Bies, R. J., 162, 171–2, 173, 174, 176, 177, 178, 179, 180, 182, 184, 367, 399, 409
Birch, K., 234
Bird, C., 112
Bjorgvinsson, S., 399
Blader, S., 6
Blasi, A., 272, 284
Blaskovich, J., 123, 366, 367, 378
Blass, T., 350
Bless, E., 175
Bless, H., 243
Block, C. J., 204
Block, J., 55, 123
Block, J. H., 123
Bloom, S., 200, 418
Blumenthal, E., 400–2, 403, 410, 412
Bobo, L., 206
Bobocel, D. R., 6, 206*n*1, 208, 209, 210, 211, 213, 214, 215, 216, 219, 230
Bodenhausen, G. V., 243
Boeckmann, R. J., 43, 226, 227, 231, 298, 307, 350, 417, 421
Bogaert, A. F., 123
Boldizar, J. P., 200, 418
Bolger, N., 330
Bond, M. H., 308
Boom, E., 154

Bose, C. E., 328
Braband, J., 12, 409
Bradley, B. P., 112
Braithwaite, J., 307
Brandt, J. R., 228, 234
Brannick, M. T., 206
Branscombe, N., 386
Braudel, F., 69
Brehm, S. S., 128, 143, 241
Brewer, M. B., 351
Brickman, P., 217*n*2
Brockner, J., 47, 56, 64, 184, 242, 399, 428
Brodsky, C. M., 155, 161
Bronson, E., 297
Brown, J. D., 156–7, 189
Brown, R., 206, 209
Brown, S. L., 227, 234
Brummett, B. H., 238
Bryant, D. L., 399
Buckley, T., 234
Buddie, A. M., 350–1, 352, 359, 360
Bulman, R. J., 123, 367, 385
Bunge, M., 51
Burroughs, T., 123
Bushell, D., 307*n*11
Buttram, R. T., 217

Cameron, K. S., 184
Campbell, W. K., 352
Cantril, H., 85
Carlo, G., 233
Carlsmith, K. M., 327–8, 330
Cartwright, D., 308
Cerroni-Long, E. L., 303
Chandler, M., 28
Chapman, M., 103
Chaves, W., 206
Chen, E. S., 229–30, 232
Chiriboga, D., 27
Chirot, D., 81
Chrisjohn, R. D., 119
Churchill, W. S., 170
Cialdini, R. B., 227, 233, 234
Clark, R. D. III., 258
Clayton, S. D., 387
Cody, M. J., 174
Cohen, B. P., 411
Cohen, D., 308
Cohen, R. L., 56, 230
Coke, J. S., 233
Comer, R., 367, 385
Committee for the Compilation of Materials, 276
Conlon, D. E., 417
Conlon, E. E., 399
Conrad, M. A., 206
Conway, M., 215
Cook, K., 417
Cook, R. E., 156
Cooper, R., 184
Coopersmith, S., 402, 405
Cordova, D., 385
Correia, I., 34
Correy, B. L., 366, 367, 368, 378, 386, 388
Cottrell, L., 13, 14
Crangle, C., 391–2, 394
Crocker, J., 387
Cropanzano, R., 207, 409, 428
Crosby, F. J., 8, 204, 213, 217, 336, 382, 384, 385–6, 387, 389, 390, 397
Cummings, L. L., 182

DaGloria, J., 34
Dalbert, C., 8, 34, 54, 123, 130, 132, 136, 191, 195–6, 199, 200–1, 365, 366, 367, 368, 369, 374, 378
Daling, J. R., 406
Daniels, L. R., 192–3, 196, 199
Darley, J. M., 7, 99, 100, 192, 227, 255, 300, 303, 317, 318, 319, 320, 321, 323, 325, 326, 327–8, 330, 350, 351–2, 353, 355, 358, 359
Davey, L. M., 206*n*1, 208, 209, 216, 219, 230
Davis, J., 397
Davis, K. E., 175
Dawson, S., 340
Deaux, K., 417
Deci, E. L., 99
DeConchy, P., 33
Defense Monitor, The, 271
Degoey, P., 44, 399
den Hartigh, E., 158–9
Denning, D. L., 206
de Rivera, J. H., 7, 55, 272, 285
Deutsch, M., 13, 56, 206, 217, 230, 263, 265, 336, 411, 417
Deverson, N., 340
Dickenberger, M., 417
Diekmann, K. A., 229
Dietz-Uhler, B. L., 206
Dinnerstein, J. L., 98
Dion, K. K., 127–8
Dion, K. L., 127–8
Doise, W., 32
Dollard, J., 52
Doob, L. W., 52
Douglas, A., 400–2, 403, 410, 412
Dovidio, J. F., 206, 258
Drabeck, T. E., 351, 352
Drout, C., 206
Duerr, H. P., 71
Duff, K. J., 352
Duncan, B., 234

Dunn, J., 100
Dunnette, M. D., 229
Durkheim, E., 79, 84, 85, 291, 293–4, 297, 304

Earley, P. C., 399, 417
Early, S., 175, 272
Ebener, P. A., 399, 417
Eco, U., 71
Edelstein, W., 55
Einarsen, S., 156, 161
Eisenberg, N., 232–3, 235, 262–3, 350
Eisenhardt, K. M., 172, 184
Elias, N., 67, 68, 69–71
Ellard, J. H., 8, 350, 351
Ellsworth, P., 298
Emler, N., 35, 308–9, 316
Emmons, R. A., 350
Epstein, S., 58, 93, 243
Erickson, B. E., 417
Erickson, M. L., 328
Erikson, K., 291, 294, 297, 304
Evers, G., 151, 154

Fabes, R. A., 233
Farrar, D. E., 406
Feather, N. T., 7, 334, 336, 338, 339, 340, 341, 344, 345, 346, 400, 402
Feinberg, J., 336
Felson, R., 308
Felstiner, W. L. F., 417
Fernandez-Dols, J.-M., 4–5, 34, 85–6, 87–8
Feshback, S., 307*n*11
Festinger, L., 100, 308
Filipp, S., 32
Finkel, N. J., 316
Finklestein, M. A., 233
Finlay, K., 124
Fishbein, M., 141, 285
Fishkin, J., 55
Fiske, A. P., 347
Fiske, S. T., 273–4
Fletcher, G., 175, 306
Flicer, L., 350
Folger, R., 6, 52, 162, 173, 179, 180–1, 183, 184, 207, 217, 398, 399, 409, 418, 428
Folkman, S., 366, 369
Forgas, J. P., 242–3
Forsyth, D. R., 152
Fox, D. C., 273–4
Freedman, J. L., 100, 175
Freeman, S. J., 184
Freud, S., 11, 70, 352
Friedland, N., 417
Frieze, I. H., 156
Fromson, M. E., 351
Fry, W. R., 162

Fultz, J., 227, 233, 235, 272
Funder, D. C., 123
Furby, L., 64, 65–6
Furda, J., 160, 161
Furnham, A., 35, 132, 191, 366

Gaertner, S. L., 206, 258
Gage, N. L., 365
Galinsky, A. D., 242
Gallop, R., 341
Garfinkel, H., 291
Garfinkel, P., 341
Gaskell, G., 80
Gavanski, I., 175
Gergen, K. J., 152
Gerstmann, E., 55, 272
Gewirtz, J. L., 99
Gibson, J., 302–3
Gignac, M., 28, 29
Gilligan, C., 102
Girard, R., 293, 299
Glasl, F., 53
Glass, D., 175
Glauber, R. R., 406
Glew, D. J., 149
Glover, J., 81
Goch, I., 374
Goffman, E., 171, 173
Goldberg, J. H., 83, 91, 93, 94, 111, 241
Gonzales, M. H., 174, 176–7, 179, 181, 182
Goode, E., 217*n*2
Gordon, A. K., 350–1, 352, 359, 360
Gorsuch, R. L., 284
Goudsblom, J., 67
Gouws, A., 302–3
Graham, S., 303
Gramzow, R., 175
Green, D. P., 51
Greenberg, E., 406
Greenberg, J., 172, 178, 182, 229, 240, 352, 425
Griffin, R. W., 149
Griffit, C. A., 234, 238
Griffiths, C., 307–8
Gross, S., 298
Grover, S., 399
Gunter, B., 132
Gurr, T. R., 397

Haan, N., 55
Hafer, C. L., 5, 112, 114, 119, 121, 123, 124, 191, 201, 366, 367, 368, 378, 386, 388
Hagendoorn, L., 208
Haidt, J., 58, 93
Halberstadt, L. J., 158
Hamilton, R., 307–8

Hamilton, V. L., 177, 230, 239, 302, 316, 350
Hardin, R., 44, 53
Hardin, T. S., 157
Harmon-Jones, E., 234, 238
Harrell, K. L., 228, 234
Harrison, D. A., 206
Haugen, J. A., 174, 176, 177, 181, 182
Hay, D., 103
Heath, A., 336
Heatherton, T. F., 176
Heckhausen, H., 156, 368, 376, 378
Hegtvedt, K., 417
Heider, F., 99, 128, 292–3, 300, 308–9, 316, 340, 411
Heilman, M. E., 204
Hensler, D. R., 399, 417
Heuer, L., 8, 47, 399, 400–2, 403, 410, 412
Highberger, L., 234, 237, 238
Himmelweit, H. T., 80
Hobbes, T., 43–4, 101
Hodder, S. L., 112
Hodgins, H. S., 173, 174, 176–7, 179, 181
Hofer, M., 365
Hoffman, M. L., 232, 233, 234, 235, 237, 240, 242, 243, 244, 260
Hogan, R., 308–9, 316
Hogg, M., 308
Holmes, J. G., 16, 57, 91, 92, 123, 127, 153, 409, 411
Holmvall, C. M., 216
Homans, G. C., 20, 43, 397, 411
Hopkins, N., 393
Hostein, C., 93
Houlihan, D., 227, 233
Hub, E., 93
Hubert, A., 151, 160–1
Huo, Y. J., 43, 226, 227, 230, 231, 350, 399, 417, 421

Imhoff, H. J., 234, 238
Isen, A., 235
Ivie, R. L., 351

Jaccard, J. J., 284
Jahoda, M., 13
Jaskar, K., 385
Jesuinho, J., 34
Johnson, D., 392
Johnston, W., 295*n*1
Johnstone, C., 341, 344
Joiner, T. E., Jr., 157
Joly, S., 206, 209
Jones, E. E., 152, 175, 351
Jorgenson, D. O., 229
Jose, P. E., 190
Jost, J. T., 229
Jucker, J. V., 172, 184

Kagan, J., 103
Kaiser, A., 373
Kampf, H. C., 98
Kanfer, R., 399, 417
Kant, I., 96, 327
Karuza, J., 162
Kashy, D. A., 330
Katz, L. B., 128, 143, 241
Kay, A. F., 271
Keen, S., 351
Kelley, H. H., 123
Kelln, B. R. C., 350
Kelman, H. C., 177, 230, 239, 316, 350, 351
Kelson, H., 308
Kendall, M. G., 406
Keniston, K., 55
Kenny, D. A., 198, 330
Kitayama, S., 347
Klein, R., 195, 197
Klein, T. R., 234, 237, 238, 239
Kleinke, C., 303
Kleinpenning, G., 208
Kliemt, H., 51, 52
Klossen, E. C., 317, 318
Kluegal, J. R., 206
Knorz, C., 150
Kobrynowicz, D., 98
Kohlberg, L., 91, 261, 267, 318
Kohn, A., 235, 244
Konovsky, M. A., 173, 184, 417
Korzeniowski, K., 251
Koumarelas, M., 121
Kramer, R. M., 423
Kramp, P., 195, 197
Kravitz, D. A., 206
Kray, L. J., 423
Krebs, D. L., 233, 261
Krettenauer, T., 55
Kulla, M., 150
Kunda, Z., 100
Kurtines, W. M., 99
Kurtz, S., 399
Kwok, V. C., 308

Laird, J. D., 367, 385
Lalonde, R. N., 386, 387
LaMantia, P. S., 320, 321
Lamb, S., 103
Lambert, A. J., 123
Lancee, W., 341
Landes, D. S., 69, 76
Lane, R. E., 44
L'Armand, K., 400
Latane, B., 192, 227, 255

LaTour, S., 399, 417
Lawrence, B., 393
Lazarus, R. S., 366, 369
Lea, J. A., 208
Leiberson, S., 53
Lepper, M. R., 100
Lerner, M. J., 3–4, 5, 12, 16, 17, 19, 21–2, 23, 27, 29, 33, 41, 45, 49, 56, 57–8, 63, 64, 65–6, 80–1, 83, 89, 91–5, 99, 103, 104, 109, 110, 111, 112, 113, 116, 122, 123–4, 127, 128–9, 131, 143–4, 150, 153, 162, 163, 164, 168, 169, 170–1, 183, 189, 190, 191, 192, 204, 205, 206, 217, 221, 226, 229, 231, 241, 245–6, 251, 268, 271, 292, 309, 314, 332, 335, 350, 352, 365, 367, 378, 382, 383, 384, 393, 398, 409, 411, 412, 416, 427, 428
Le Roy Ladurie, E., 73, 75
Leventhal, G. S., 13, 47, 162, 206, 417
Levine, E. L., 206
Levinger, G., 123
Lewicki, R. J., 162
Lewin, K., 3, 308
Lewis, B. P., 227, 234
Lewis, G., 341
Lewis, H., 175–6, 178
Leymann, H., 150, 155–6
Lickona, T., 189–90
Liebestand, E., 173, 174, 181
Lifton, R. J., 56
Lincoln, A., 123
Lind, E. A., 9, 44, 46, 162, 163, 207, 398, 399, 402–3, 409, 417, 419, 420, 421, 423, 425–6
Lindsay, R. C. L., 208
Linedecker, C., 303
Lipkus, I. M., 191, 200, 354, 367, 369, 374
Lipson, A., 93
Lissak, R. I., 399, 417
London, P., 265
Long, G., 12
Louis, W. R., 386
Lucardie, E., 158–9
Luce, C., 227, 234
Lucus, J., 204
Luken, A., 373
Lutchins, A. S., 80
Lutchins, E. H., 80
Lydon, J. E., 386, 388

MacCoun, R. J., 86, 399, 417
MacGregor-Morris, R., 112
MacLeod, C., 111
MacLeod, C. M., 112
Maes, J., 8, 34, 123, 132, 134, 190, 200, 366, 373, 374, 376
Magid, B., 350
Magnusson, J., 234, 244
Maisels, L., 55, 272
Major, B., 52, 57, 336, 387, 417
Manning, D. J., 174, 176, 177, 181, 182
Marks, M. L., 172
Markus, H. R., 260, 347
Marques, J., 308
Martin, C., 184, 399
Martin, J., 57
Massey, W. F., 406
Mathews, A. M., 111, 112
Mayer, J., 232
McConahay, J. B., 209
McCullough, M. E., 350
McDavis, K., 233
McGraw, K. M., 272, 301–2, 417
McKinnon, C., 55
McKirnan, D. J., 394
McLaughlin, M. L., 174
McMullen, S., 123
McNeely, B. L., 238–9
Mead, G. H., 14, 101, 291
Medinnus, G. R., 190
Meglino, B. M., 238–9
Meier, R. F., 328
Meindl, J., 29, 309
Meissner, A., 136
Melnitzer, J., 294
Merton, R. K., 251
Messick, D. M., 200, 238, 418
Metalsky, G. I., 157, 158
Meyer, W., 156
Mikula, G., 191, 229, 336, 417
Milgram, S., 177
Miller, A. G., 350–1, 352, 359, 360
Miller, D. T., 16, 57, 63, 91, 92, 109, 123, 127, 128–9, 130, 131, 153, 191, 194, 201, 204, 251, 261, 268, 293, 316, 367, 384, 409, 411, 416
Miller, N., 52
Miller, P. A., 233
Miller, R. S., 350
Minton, J. W., 162
Mishra, A. K., 184
Mitchell, G., 417
Mitchener, E. C., 234, 238
Moag, J. S., 162, 174, 399, 409
Mogg, K., 112
Moghaddam, F. M., 231, 386, 387
Mohiyeddini, C., 130–1
Montada, L., 4, 32, 34, 44, 49, 50, 54, 56, 57, 63, 123, 127, 128, 130–1, 132, 134, 135, 136, 146, 191, 195, 199, 200–1, 229, 237–8, 272, 350
Moore, B., Jr., 68, 71
Moorman, R. H., 417
Moscovici, S., 79

Moser, G., 33
Moskowitz, G. D., 242
Mosteller, R., 306
Mowrer, O. H., 52
Munn, P., 100
Murray, A., 57
Murrell, A. J., 206
Musante, L., 399

Nacoste, R. W., 206
Nagata, D. K., 230
Neidenthal, P. M., 175
Neisser, U., 152
Neuberg, S. L., 227, 234
Newcomb, T. M., 20
Newman, L. S., 352
Newton, E., 423
Nguyen, T., 123
Niedl, K., 156
Nisbett, R. E., 152, 308, 347
Nosworthy, G. J., 208

Oberdan, D., 340
Oceja, L. V., 85, 87–8
O'Connell, M. O., 386
Ogloff, J., 295
O'Hair, H., 174
O'Leary-Kelly, A. M., 149
Oleson, K. C., 318
Oliner, P., 253, 265–6
Oliner, S. P., 253, 257–8, 265–6
Olson, J. M., 191, 201, 386, 388
Opotow, S., 56, 230, 242, 351
O'Quin, K., 235
Oresick, R. J., 272, 284
Ortberg, J., 284
Oskam, M., 161

Pacini, R., 243
Pagès, R., 33
Paoli, P., 149
Parry, J. H., 81
Parsons, P., 69
Pastore, N., 52
Peckrun, R., 365
Peekna, H. M., 228, 234
Pennebaker, J. W., 184
Penner, L., 233
Pepitone, A., 400
Peplau, L. A., 92, 114, 130, 154, 158–9, 190–1, 199, 356, 385
Perry, R. P., 234, 244
Piaget, J., 101, 153, 189, 190, 193, 318, 332
Piliavin, I. M., 227
Piliavin, J. A., 227, 242, 258
Pipes, D., 299–300, 304

Platt, J., 123
Plug, K., 154
Polycappou, M. P., 234, 238
Pomazal, R. J., 284
Pommerenke, P., 423
Porter, L. E., 387
Postman, L., 298
Postmes, T., 386
Pratto, F., 206
Pritchard, D., 229
Procter, E., 191, 366
Pufall, A., 386
Pugh, S. D., 6
Putnam, R. D., 88–9
Pyszczynski, T., 352

Quarantelli, E. L., 351, 352

R. v. Iutzi, 294
R. v. McGregor, 301
R. v. Reynolds, 306
R. v. Theberge, 301
Rachal, K. C., 350
Radke-Yarrow, M., 103
Ramb, B.-T., 50
Rand, A., 96
Rasinski, K., 399, 417
Ratner, R. K., 63
Rawls, J., 43–4, 50, 91, 217, 244
Redlich, F., 360
Reed, T., 399
Reeder, G. D., 351
Reichle, B., 5–6, 34, 54, 123, 127, 132, 133, 134, 135, 136
Reid, D. G., 27
Reis, H. T., 284
Resnik, J., 417
Reykowski, J., 7, 260, 261, 262, 273
Rheinberg, F., 368
Rheingold, H., 103
Robinson, D., 304–5
Robinson, P. H., 303, 319, 323, 325, 326, 327–8, 330, 350
Rochman, B., 307
Rodin, J., 227
Rodriguez-Mosquera, P., 85
Ropp, S., 8
Rosen, R., 307, 308
Rosenberg, M., 159
Rosenblatt, A., 352
Rosenfield, D., 152
Ross, L., 229
Rossi, P. H., 316, 328
Rousseau, D. M., 172
Rovella, D., 306
Rubin, Z., 92, 114, 130, 154, 158–9, 190–1, 199, 356, 385

Ruggiero, K. M., 386, 388, 389
Runciman, W. G., 397
Rushdie, S., 299–300
Rushton, J. P., 119
Russell, C. J., 206
Ryan, W., 128

Sabini, J., 350
Salancik, G. R., 215
Sallay, H., 374
Salvarani, G., 175, 272
Sampson, E. E., 384
Samuels, S. M., 229
Samuelson, C. D., 200, 418
Sanders, J., 302
Sanderson, C. A., 320, 321
Sarat, A., 306, 307
Sawyer, J., 399
Schachter, S., 308
Schaller, M., 227, 233
Scheff, T., 307*n*11
Schlenker, B. R., 152
Schmitt, M., 5–6, 34, 54, 56, 128, 130, 131, 132–3, 136, 146, 190, 191, 195, 199, 200–1
Schneider, A., 54, 123, 127, 132, 133, 134, 135, 136, 229, 237–8, 272
Schoenrode, P., 272
Schofield, J. W., 273–4
Schrag, P. G., 275
Schul, Y., 217*n*2
Schultz, T. R., 100, 300, 318
Schwartz, S., 100
Schwartz, S. H., 255, 257, 272, 284
Schwartz, W., 173, 174, 181
Schwarz, N., 215, 243
Schweder, R. A., 58, 93
Sclove, S. L., 406
Scotson, J. L., 67, 68
Scott, K. S., 425
Sears, R. R., 52
Sedlak, A. J., 100
Seligman, M. E. P., 156
Semmel, A., 156
Sentis, K. P., 418
Seuferling, G., 101, 273, 350
Shapiro, D. L., 182, 399, 409
Shapiro, I., 51
Shaw, L. L., 237, 238, 239
Shea, C. L., 233
Shell, R., 233
Sheppard, B. H., 162, 417
Sidanius, J., 206
Siegle, P., 399
Siegler, I. C., 191, 200, 367, 369
Silver, M., 350
Silverman, R. A., 53
Simmons, C. H., 91, 123, 129, 131, 153, 168, 192, 231, 365, 378, 383, 409
Simms, C. D., 351
Simons, C., 242
Skarlicki, D., 179, 180–1, 183
Skitka, L. J., 336
Slingsby, J. K., 228, 234
Smelser, N., 298
Smith, E. R., 206
Smith, H. J., 43, 44, 226–7, 231, 350, 399, 417, 421
Smith, M. B., 55
Smith-Lovin, L., 304–5
Snyder, M. L., 152
Snyder, R. C., 386
Solomon, S., 352
Somers, D. G., 27, 31, 32
Son Hing, L. S., 206*n*1, 208, 209, 211, 213, 214, 215, 216, 219, 230
Spaans, E., 64
Spears, R., 386
Speer, A. L., 233
Spodick, N., 399
Sprengelmeyer, P., 228, 234
Stalder, K., 303
Stanley, D. J., 208, 209, 230
Staub, E., 99, 255, 350, 351, 360
Steensma, H., 6, 151, 154, 158–9, 160, 161, 163
Stephan, W. G., 152
Steven, W. G., 124
Steyer, R., 132, 133
Stiensmeijer-Pelster, J., 157
Stillwell, A. M., 176
Strongman, J. A., 101, 273, 350
Stuart, B., 307–8
Studebaker, C., 297
Sundby, S., 304–5
Sunshine, J., 8
Sutton, R., 172, 184
Switzer, G., 233

Tajfel, H., 68, 152, 253, 308
Tamura, J., 406
Tangney, J. P., 175, 178, 350
Taylor, C., 303
Taylor, D. M., 231, 386, 387, 388, 389, 394
Taylor, L., 296–7
Taylor, S. E., 156–7, 189
Teasdale, J. D., 156
Tec, N., 265
Tedeschi, J., 308
Tessler, R. C., 284
Tetlock, P. E., 336
Thaman, S., 307
Thibaut, J. W., 44, 45, 46, 47, 123, 162, 217, 398, 399, 408–9, 416, 417

Thomas, W. I., 291, 294, 297
Thompson, E. R., 101, 273, 350
Thompson, L., 423
Tierney, M., 27
Tietzel, M., 50
Todd, R. M., 228, 234, 238
Todorov, T., 99
Tolstoy, L., 96
Tomaka, J., 123, 366, 367, 378
Tornblom, K., 33, 46
Tougas, F., 206, 209
Troyer, D., 233
Tsoudis, O., 304–5
Turk, C. L., 239
Turner, J., 68, 253
Turner, M. E., 206
Tyler, T. R., 6, 43, 44, 46, 162, 163, 226–7, 229–30, 231, 232, 238, 241, 272, 298, 307, 350, 398, 399, 402–3, 409, 417, 421

Underwood, B., 351
Urban, G. L., 406
U. S. v. McVeigh, 298

Valla, G., 34
Van den Bos, K., 44, 425–6
Vanderplas, M., 235
VanDeVeer, C., 204
van Dijke, R., 157
van Duijn, S., 151
Vermunt, R., 4, 44, 46, 64, 161, 163, 425–6
Vidmar, N., **7**, 291, 292, 293, 294, 295, 296, 300, 303, 306, 308, 309, 316, 317
von Hippel, E., 406
Von Hirsch, A., 336

Wagner, E., 103
Wagner, P. E., 175
Waite, E., 328
Walker, L., 44, 45, 46, 47, 162, 217, 398, 399, 408–9, 416, 417
Wallington, S. A., 175
Wallis, R., 303
Walster, E., 13, 43, 45, 63, 123, 175, 176, 180, 397, 398, 417
Walster, G. W., 43, 63, 175, 176, 180, 397, 398, 417
Walton, M. D., 100
Warndorf, P. K., 368
Warr, M., 328
Weber, M., 79, 84, 85
Weeks, J. L., 234
Weinblatt, T., 400–2, 403, 410, 412
Weiner, B., 156, 192, 234, 243–4, 303, 350
Welchans, T. D., 425
Werthmiller, T., 121
West, M., 103
Whalen, P., 386
White, R. K., 351
Whitehead, L. A., 56, 162
Whitney, H., 101, 273, 350
Wiesenfeld, B. M., 64, 399
Wiggins, G., 102
Wilke, H. A. M., 44, 46, 425–6
Will, G., 307
Williams, J. M. G., 111
Williams, R., 112
Wilson, A. D., 98
Winkels, R., 373
Working in the 1990s, 172
Workman, B., 391
Worthington, E. L., Jr., 350
Wortman, C. B., 123, 367, 385
Wright, S. C., 386, 387

Young, H., 386

Zahn-Waxler, C., 103
Zajonc, R. B., 260
Zanna, M. P., 206*n*1, 208, 209, 211, 213, 214, 215, 216, 219, 230, 300, 317, 318
Zander, A., 308
Zapf, D., 150, 156
Zdaniuk, A., 216
Zelditch, M., Jr., 411
Zielinski, W., 365
Zimbardo, P. G., 351
Znaniecki, F., 291, 294, 297
Zorge, F., 64
Zucker, G., 303
Zuckerman, M., 284

Subject Index

achievement
  motivation, 376, 378–9
  in school, 368–71, 377, 379
action-outcome model, 66, 72, 76, 77
actor-observer effect, 152, 154
affirmative action, 205–7
  equal treatment policy, 210
  global concept of, 211
  preferential treatment policy, 209, 215
  tie-break policy, 210
allocentric motives, 259–60, 266, 268, 272
Altruistic Personality Project, 253
anger, 54, 272, 273, 281, 282–4, 286, 292, 298n3, 305, 306, 367–8
apartheid, 302–3
attributional style, 156, 368, 375, 378–9
authoritarianism, 191
automatic reactions, 19, 22
axiological motives, 261–3, 267, 268, 272
  example of, 264

belief in a just world (*see also* justice motive)
  correlated with social responsibility, 196–7
  function of, 110, 116–22
  general and personal, 200, 369
  individual differences in, 114, 116, 130–1, 153, 190–1, 366–7
  overview of theory, 64, 91, 127, 153, 189, 365, 383
  as a personal resource, 368–9, 372
  as a positive illusion, 123
  stability of, 135–7, 140, 153, 378
  threat to, 110–16, 123–4, 153, 355
belief in a just world, restoration of
  action strategies, 127, 128–9, 132, 136, 140–1
  cognitive strategies, 127–8, 130, 132, 136, 140–1
  compensation, 191–2
  self-efficacy and, 130

Churchill effect, 170
crime, 318–19

demonizing, 350–1
  paradox of, 351
  functions of, 351–3, 358
deservingness, 338–40, 400–3, 408
  and entitlement, 397–8
discrimination (*see also* prejudice)
  belief in a just world and, 388
  denial of, 384–7, 389–90
  perception of, 387, 389–91
  social support and, 388–9
  workplace, 213–16, 241, 385

egoistic motive, *see* self-interest
empathy, 128, 143–5, 175, 178, 259–60, 268, 280
  altruistic personality and, 233
  definition of, 226, 232
  justice and, 235–43
  limitations on, 234–5
  prosocial actions and, 228, 232–46
  self interest and, 233–4
entitlement, 408, 409–10
  and deservingness, 334, 336, 340, 397–8
  definition of, 335, 337
equity, 12–13, 43, 45, 175, 397–8, 411, 416
ethical motive, 80–1
  consequences of, 81–3
evil, 350, 353
  evilness schema, 351–2, 353, 354, 356, 358
  possession, 358–9
exchange fiction, 57–8
excuses, 176–7

fairness heuristic theory
  episodic effect, 423–5
  explanation of, 419–21
  judgmental and use modes, 422
  substitution effect, 425–7
fear, 54
free-riding dilemma, 58
functional illusions, 31–2
fundamental attribution error, 171
fundamental delusion (*see also* belief in a just world), 92, 382, 383

guilt, 54, 56, 84, 175–6, 261

harmdoers
  ability to repair relationship, 181
  excuses, 176–7
  face threat, 179
  motivation to maintain relationship, 181
  refusals, 177
  retaliation distress, 180–1
Hiroshima bombing, 276, 281

identity templates (*see also* unit templates; non-unit templates), 14, 15, 292
in-group and out-group, 19, 252, 264–5, 267, 292, 299, 300, 403
injustice
  in a conflict, 53
  emotional responses to, 54–6, 171, 229
  prosocial behavior and, 238
  as a threat, 112–16, 122
injustice stress theory, 163
Inquisition, the, 73–6
intuitive jurist assumption, 177

justice
  construction of, 56–7
  efficacy and, 271
  and empathy, 235–40, 243–5
  as an end or a means, 48–9
  immanent and ultimate, 190, 200, 251, 332
  life satisfaction and, 64, 191, 377
  micro- and macrojustice, 217n2
  as a normative standard, 41, 45, 47
  standards of, 42
justice, distributive, 315, 397–8, 408, 417
  merit principle of, 206, 207–8, 210, 213–15, 217–19, 220
justice, interactional, 162, 172–3
justice motive (*see also* belief in a just world), 204
  evidence for, 52–3
  explanation for, 92–3
  implicit and explicit, 93–4
  as primary, 41, 49, 94
  prosocial behavior and, 227–8, 231–2
justice, neglecting, 48–9
justice, procedural, 44, 162–3, 216, 315, 398–9, 417–18
  consistency principle of, 206, 209, 211, 217–19, 220
  group value theory of, 46, 163, 399–400, 410
  and self-interest, 229
justice, retributive, 113–14, 241, 291, 315–16
  affirmative defences, 317
  effect of excuses, 300–3
  effect of remorse, 303–5
  group norms and, 293–4, 299, 308–9
  six-stage model of, 292–3
just world belief, *see* belief in a just world
Just World Scale (Rubin & Peplau, 1975), 114, 130, 154, 158–9, 191, 199, 356

learned helplessness, 156
locus of control, 191
long-term planning, 116–22
  through just means, 119–21

managerial distancing, 174
mitigation-aggravation continuum, 174
moral development, 261, 262, 267, 317, 318
moral exclusion, 230
moral hypocrisy, 98, 100–1, 350
moral integrity, 98–9
moral motivation, 91, 95, 97
  as emergent, 101–2
  motivation not to be immoral, 98
  as received, 99–100
  relative weakness of, 99
  ultimate vs. instrumental distinction, 97
moral order, 84, 251–2
moral orientation, 193
moral principles, 95–6, 262, 318, 352
moral realism, 189–90

non-unit templates, 15
  changing from identity to non-unit, 25–6
normative imperative, 84–5
  when frustrated, 88
normocentric motives, 260–1, 268, 272

pain (*see also* suffering), 27–8
personal contract, 11–12, 65, 92, 153, 189, 190
personal responsibility, 272–3, 275, 280, 339, 344

perverse norms, 35, 86, 87
  consequences of, 86
  empirical support for, 87–8
  and Prohibition, 86
positive illusions, 123, 156–7, 189
prejudice (*see also* discrimination), 206–8
  ethnocentrism, 252
  as a predictor of attitudes, 208, 211–12
  racism, 208, 209
  sexism, 209, 386
prosocial behavior, 128, 143, 226–7
  motivations for, 227–8, 259–62
  nuclear weapons and, 271, 275–6, 286
  toward Jews, in World War II, 239, 253–68
prosocial goal, 255, 257
Protestant ethic, the, 65–6
psychodynamic theory, 70
psychological defences, 383
punishment
  capital, 293, 297, 304, 331
  failure to punish, 305–8
  justifications for, 326–31
  objectivist stance, 320
  subjectivist stance, 319–20, 325

rational choice hypothesis, 43–4, 55
  criticisms of, 51–2
refusals, 177
relative deprivation, 10, 52, 55, 134, 137–9, 397
  egotistical and fraternal, 384–5

self-esteem, 44, 47, 157, 159–60, 164, 171, 191, 200, 254, 402, 408
self-interest, 12, 23, 43, 45, 48, 50–1, 58, 63, 227, 228, 398
Self-Report Delinquency Scale, 119
self-serving bias, 152, 154, 157, 231, 241
shame, 175–6, 178, 261, 294–5
shaming penalties, 307
social exchange theory, *see* equity
social figurations, 67–8, 71–2
social responsibility, 189, 192, 196–200
  attributional principles, 192
  as a norm, 192
  personal obligation, 192–3
  similarities to just world hypothesis, 193
societal context, 67
societal norms, 13, 20–2, 44, 190, 192, 260–1, 267, 293–4
  legitimate norms, 84
stress, 366–7, 369–70
Stroop task, modified, 111
  reactions to threat-related words, 111–16
suffering (*see also* pain), 28, 80
symbolic interaction, 14

terror management theory, 352

unemployment, 30–2, 135–6, 144–5, 172, 183–4
unit templates, 14, 15

victims
  belief in a just world and, 157, 159
  blaming of, 57, 80, 92, 109, 117–18, 153–4, 157, 352, 427
  derogation of, 109, 114–16, 117–18, 120, 122, 128, 129, 140, 153, 168, 177–8, 192, 231, 314, 383, 416
  disassociating from, 109–10, 115, 118, 120, 169, 176, 177
  identification with, 128, 169, 241–2
  self-esteem, 157, 159–60
Vietnam War, 55, 230, 239
Vietnam War draft lottery, 92, 385
violence in the workplace
  causes of, 151
  costs of, 149–50
  European statistics, 149
  external aggression, 150, 152–5
  internal aggression, 150, 155–62
  prevention of, 152, 164
  workers and supervisors, 154, 155, 160–2

well-being, 64, 191, 376–7

For EU product safety concerns, contact us at Calle de José Abascal, 56–1°, 28003 Madrid, Spain or eugpsr@cambridge.org.

www.ingramcontent.com/pod-product-compliance
Lightning Source LLC
LaVergne TN
LVHW090258210926
848480LV00001B/61
9780521087933